Your Lie in April

*I met the girl
under full-bloomed cherry blossoms,
and my fate has begun to change.*

5

Naoshi Arakawa

✲ STORY & CHARACTERS ✲

When his mother died in the autumn of his 12th year, piano prodigy Kōsei Arima lost his ability to play. Without a purpose, his days lost all color and continued on in a drab monotone. But in the spring when he was 14, his encounter with the exceptionally quirky violinist Kaori Miyazono started to change his fate.

Kaori had advanced to the second round of the Tōwa Music Competition when she ordered Kōsei to provide her piano accompaniment. Although Kōsei's trauma kept him from hearing the music when wrapped up in a performance, once he overcame that barrier, the audience's thunderous applause awaited him.

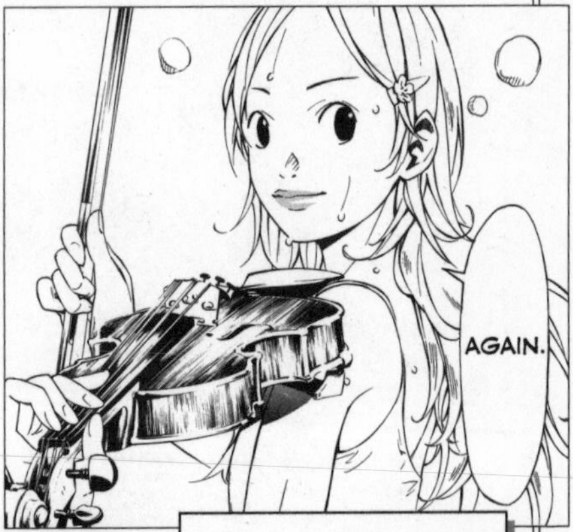
AGAIN.

✲ Kaori Miyazono

A violinist who is overwhelmingly unique. She forces Kōsei to enter the Maihō Music Competition as his gift to her to celebrate her discharge from the hospital.

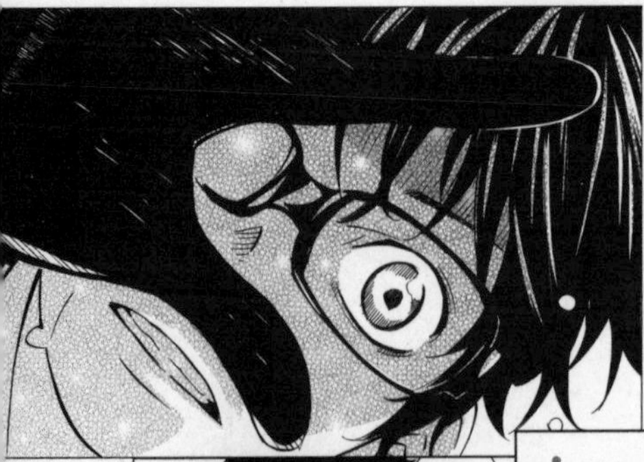

✲ Kōsei Arima

An ex-piano prodigy who lost his ability to play when his mother died. Meeting Kaori gives him the motivation he needs to devote himself to the world of music once more.

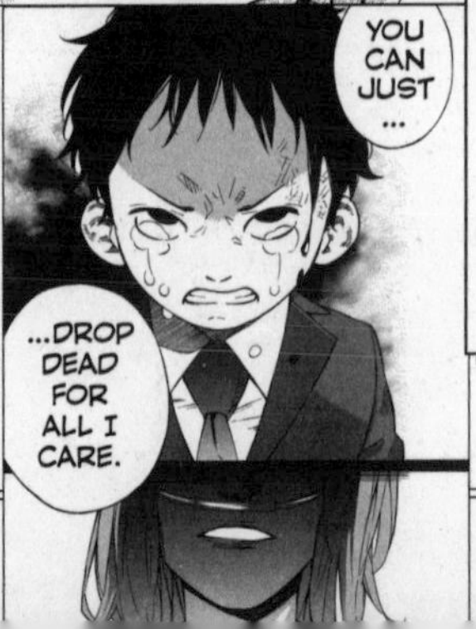
YOU CAN JUST ...
...DROP DEAD FOR ALL I CARE.

DON'T MISS THE MOST ACCLAIMED ACTION MANGA OF 2013!

"Gripping doesn't begin to describe Vinland Saga. 5 stars."
—ICv2

"Deeply engrossing… If you have any interest at all in Vikings, the Medieval period, or pirates, this is not a series you want to miss."
—Anime News Network

"The art is gorgeous, a combination of beautiful cartooning and realistic backgrounds. Yukimura is also a master of pacing, both in frenetic battle scenes and charged emotional moments."
—Faith Erin Hicks, *Friends With Boys*

"For those who love Berserk, you'll love this too… Worth the long wait."
—A Case Suitable for Treatment

"It will be impossible to stop watching this story unfold."
—Japan Media Arts Awards jury

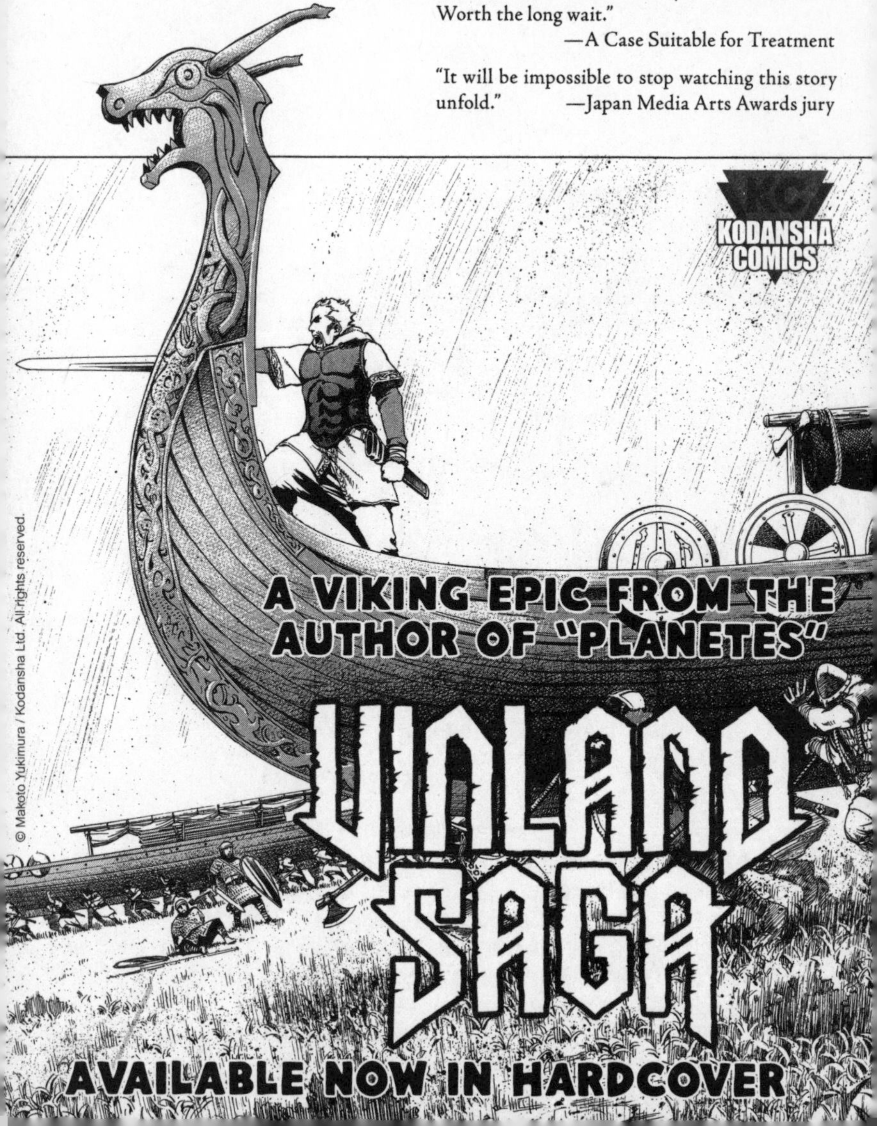
KODANSHA COMICS
A VIKING EPIC FROM THE AUTHOR OF "PLANETES"
VINLAND SAGA
AVAILABLE NOW IN HARDCOVER
© Makoto Yukimura / Kodansha Ltd. All rights reserved.

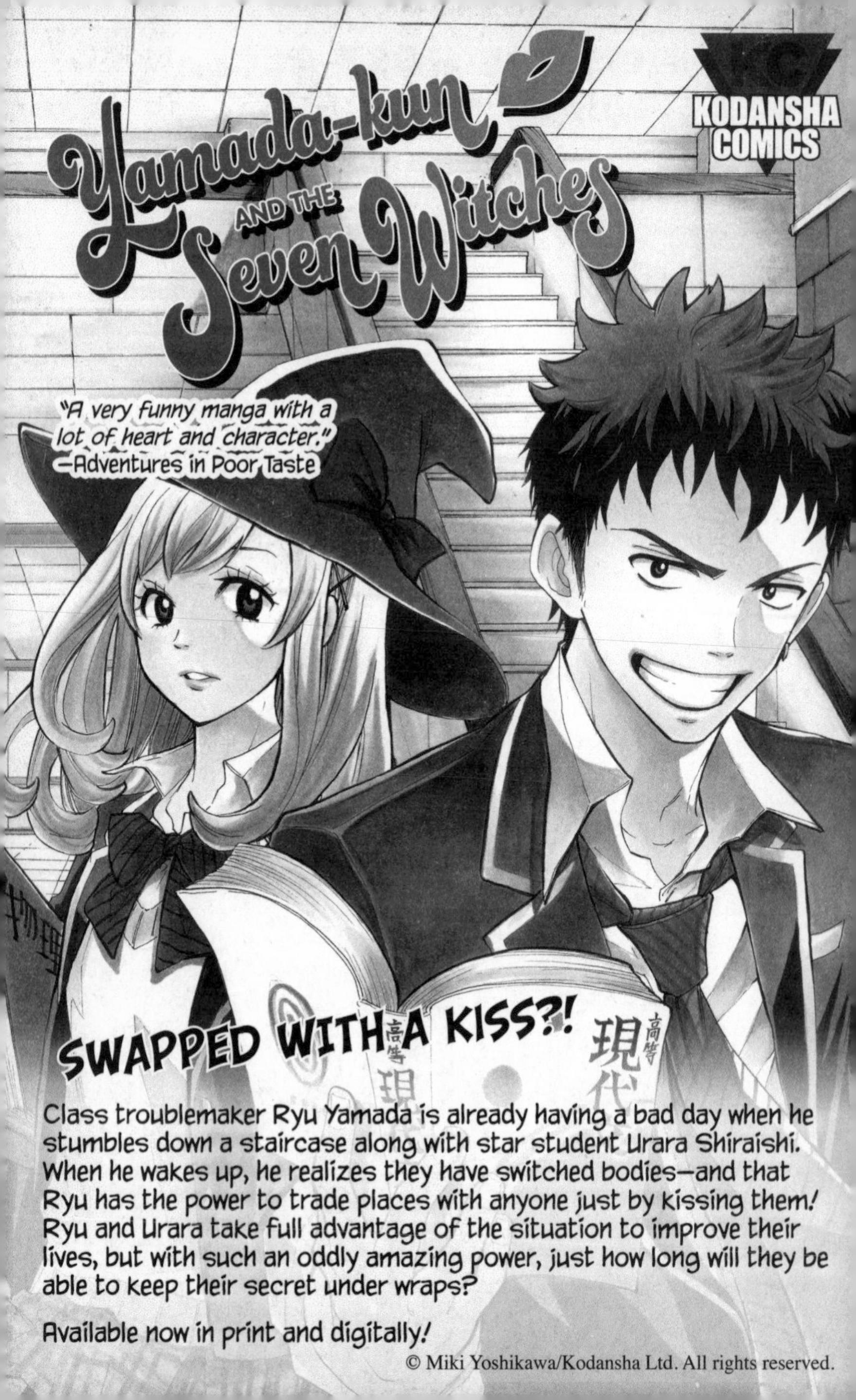
KODANSHA COMICS
Yamada-kun AND THE Seven Witches
"A very funny manga with a lot of heart and character." —Adventures in Poor Taste
SWAPPED WITH A KISS?!
Class troublemaker Ryu Yamada is already having a bad day when he stumbles down a staircase along with star student Urara Shiraishi. When he wakes up, he realizes they have switched bodies—and that Ryu has the power to trade places with anyone just by kissing them! Ryu and Urara take full advantage of the situation to improve their lives, but with such an oddly amazing power, just how long will they be able to keep their secret under wraps?
Available now in print and digitally!

Fairy Tail takes place in a world filled with magic. 17-year-old Lucy is a wizard-in-training who wants to join a magic guild so that she can become a full-fledged wizard. She dreams of joining the most famous guild, known as Fairy Tail. One day she meets Natsu, a boy raised by a dragon which vanished when he was young. Natsu has devoted his life to finding his dragon father. When Natsu helps Lucy out of a tricky situation, she discovers that he is a member of Fairy Tail, and our heroes' adventure together begins.

FAIRY TAIL

MASTER'S EDITION

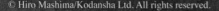

a Silent Voice

KODANSHA
COMICS

"The word heartwarming was made for manga like this."
–Manga Book-shelf

"A harsh and biting social commentary... delivers in its depth of character and emotional strength." -Comics Bulletin

"A very powerful story about being different and the consequences of childhood bullying... Read it."
–Anime News Network

Shoya is a bully. When Shoko, a girl who can't hear, enters his elementary school class, she becomes their favorite target, and Shoya and his friends goad each other into devising new tortures for her. But the children's cruelty goes too far. Shoko is forced to leave the school, and Shoya ends up shouldering all the blame. Six years later, the two meet again. Can Shoya make up for his past mistakes, or is it too late?

Available now in print and digitally!

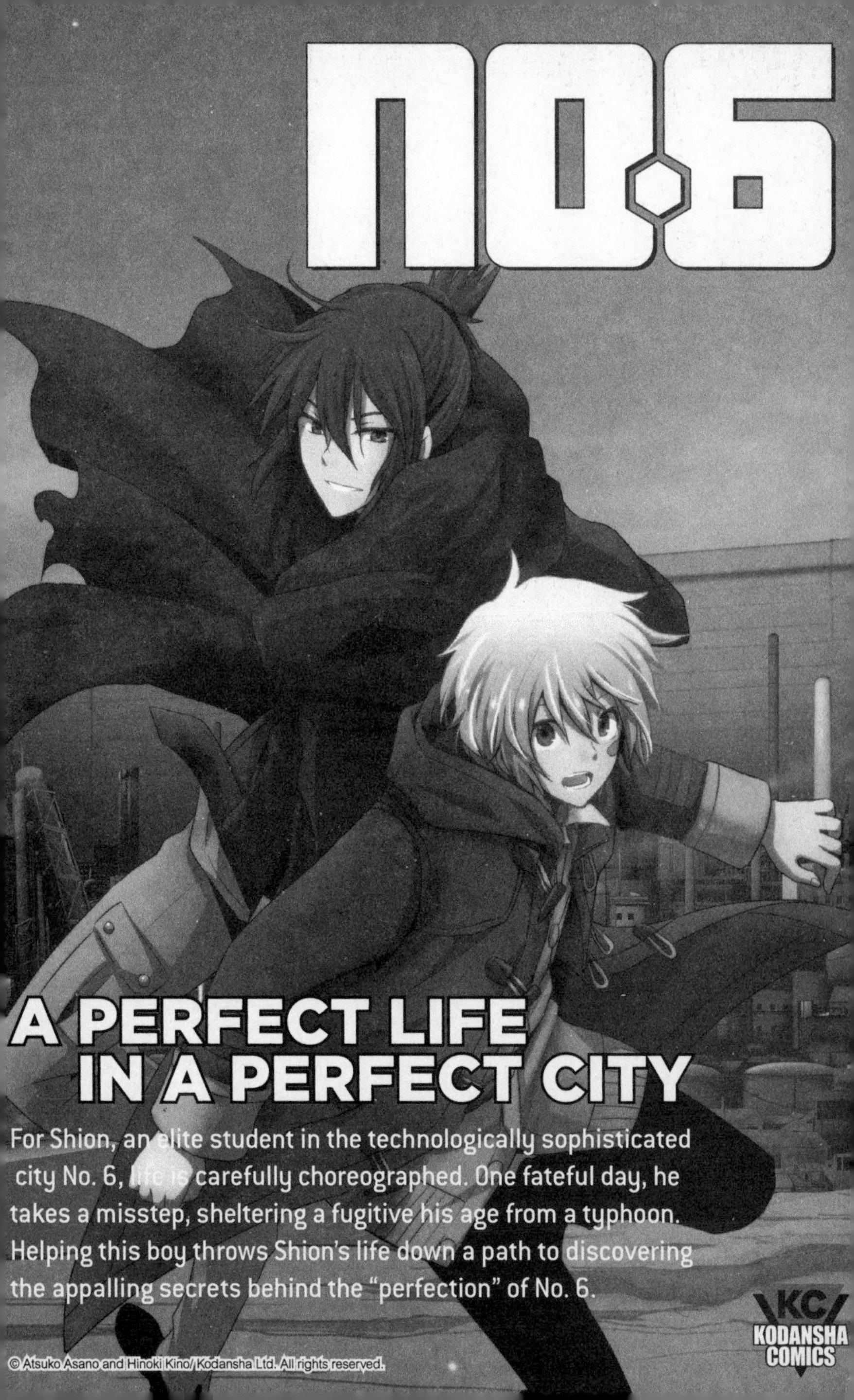
NO.6
A PERFECT LIFE IN A PERFECT CITY
For Shion, an elite student in the technologically sophisticated city No. 6, life is carefully choreographed. One fateful day, he takes a misstep, sheltering a fugitive his age from a typhoon. Helping this boy throws Shion's life down a path to discovering the appalling secrets behind the "perfection" of No. 6.
KC
KODANSHA COMICS
© Atsuko Asano and Hinoki Kino/ Kodansha Ltd. All rights reserved.

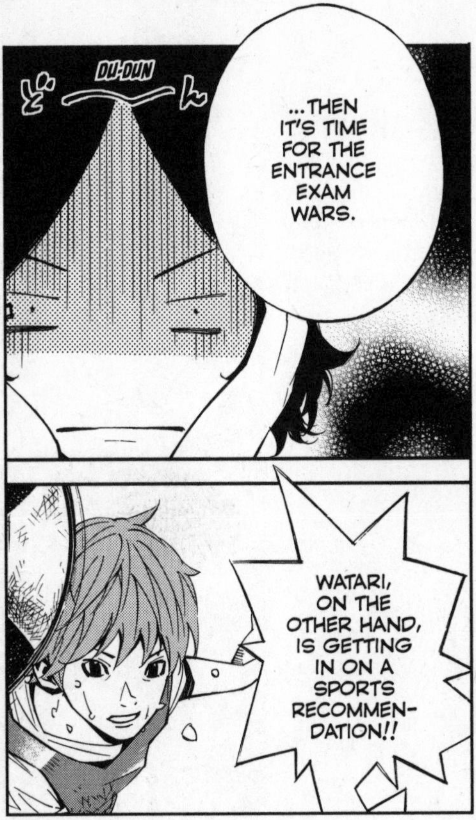
DU-DUN
...THEN IT'S TIME FOR THE ENTRANCE EXAM WARS.
WATARI, ON THE OTHER HAND, IS GETTING IN ON A SPORTS RECOMMEN-DATION!!

Entrance exams and sports recommendations,

page 164

In Japan, kids don't just go to the school they live closest to. They have a choice of what school they want to attend, and if they're accepted, they're in. The most common way to get accepted is to pass the school's entrance exam, so many middle school third-year students spend all their extra time studying to get into the school or their (or their parents') choice. In Watari's case, he managed to get recommended to a school due to his excellent soccer abilities.

Super Robots,
page 126

In the Japanese, Takeshi uses the term *Chōgōkin*. *Chōgōkin* is written in Japanese with the characters for "super" and "alloy." It is the name of a fictional metal from Go Nagai's famous super robot manga, *Mazinger Z*. In the 1970s, a line of metal robots and character toys were released under the same name to great success. People use the term *Chōgōkin* to refer to these toys.

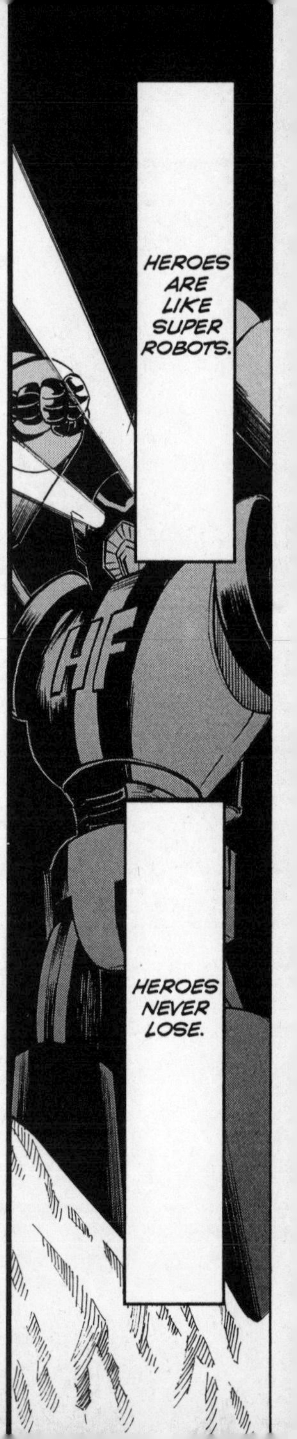
HEROES ARE LIKE SUPER ROBOTS.
HEROES NEVER LOSE.

Translation Notes

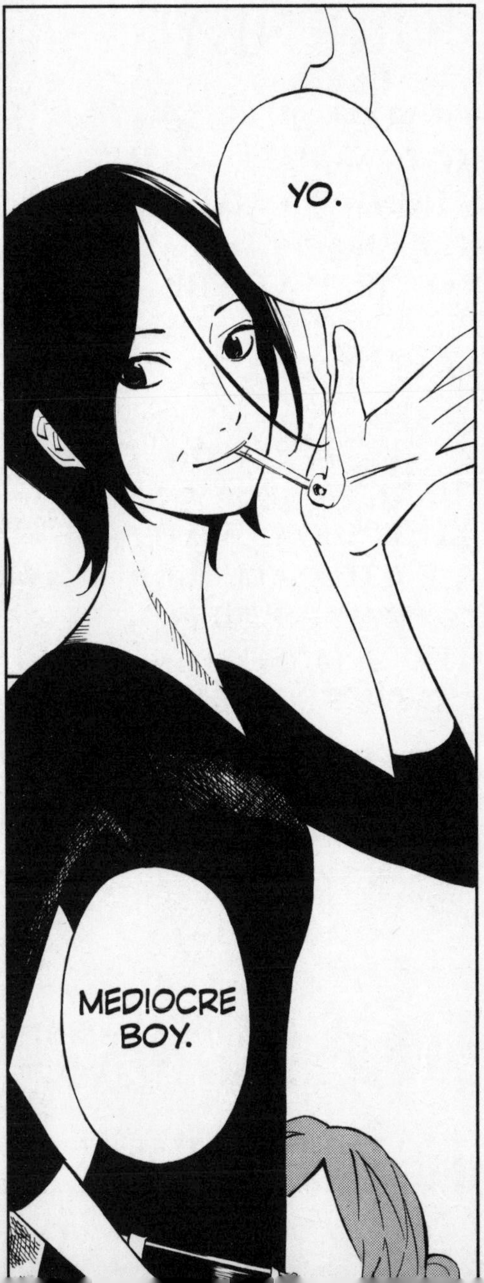
YO.
MEDIOCRE BOY.

Mediocre Boy,
page 95

Hiroko Seto's nickname for Kōsei is *bonsai*, which literally means "average talent," as opposed to what most people call him: *tensai*, the Japanese word for "genius" or "prodigy," which literally means "heavenly talent."

IT WAS THE START OF A NEW JOURNEY.

A SINGLE INVITATION ARRIVED
FROM TŌWA HALL—
AN INVITATION FOR KAORI AND
KŌSEI TO PERFORM IN THE GALA
CONCERT. THE TWO BEGIN
PRACTICING FOR THEIR RETURN
AS THE ULTIMATE DUO.

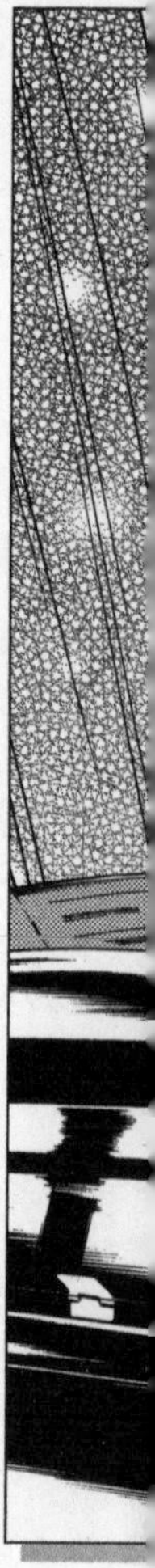

HOWEVER, FOR
UNKNOWN REASONS,
KŌSEI SHOWS A HALF-
HEARTED ATTITUDE
TOWARD THEIR
PERFORMANCE PIECE,
"LOVE'S SORROW"…

Your Lie in April Naoshi Arakawa

VOL. 6 COMING FEBRUARY 2016!

I met the girl under full-bloomed cherry blossoms, and my fate has begun to change.

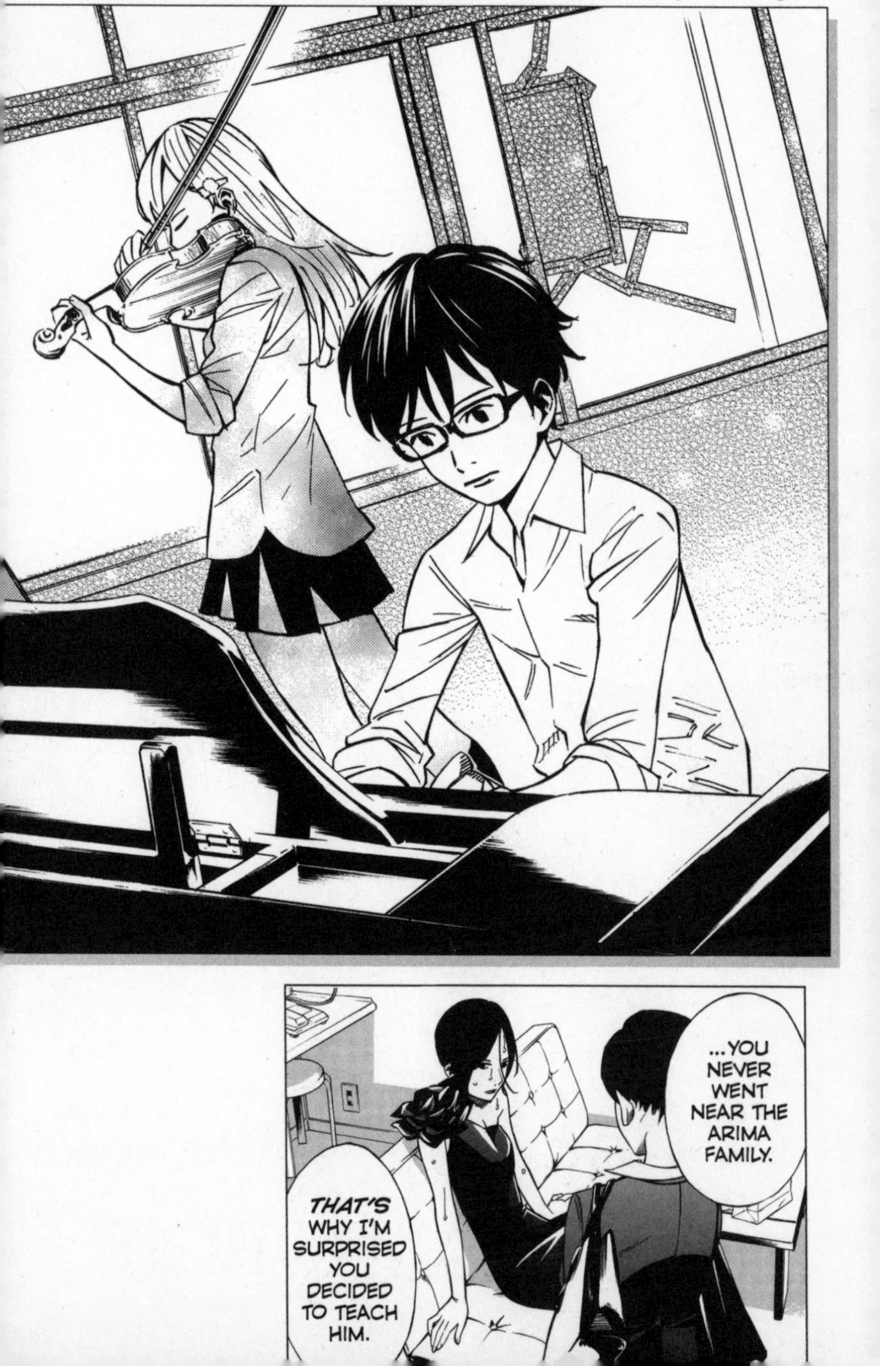
...YOU NEVER WENT NEAR THE ARIMA FAMILY.
THAT'S WHY I'M SURPRISED YOU DECIDED TO TEACH HIM.

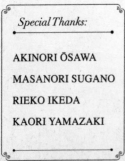

Special Thanks:

AKINORI ŌSAWA

MASANORI SUGANO

RIEKO IKEDA

KAORI YAMAZAKI

"YOU KNOW, I'M NOT ALWAYS GOING TO BE AROUND TO HELP YOU."

-CHARLIE BROWN

Peanuts, May 25, 1994
Created by Charles M. Schulz

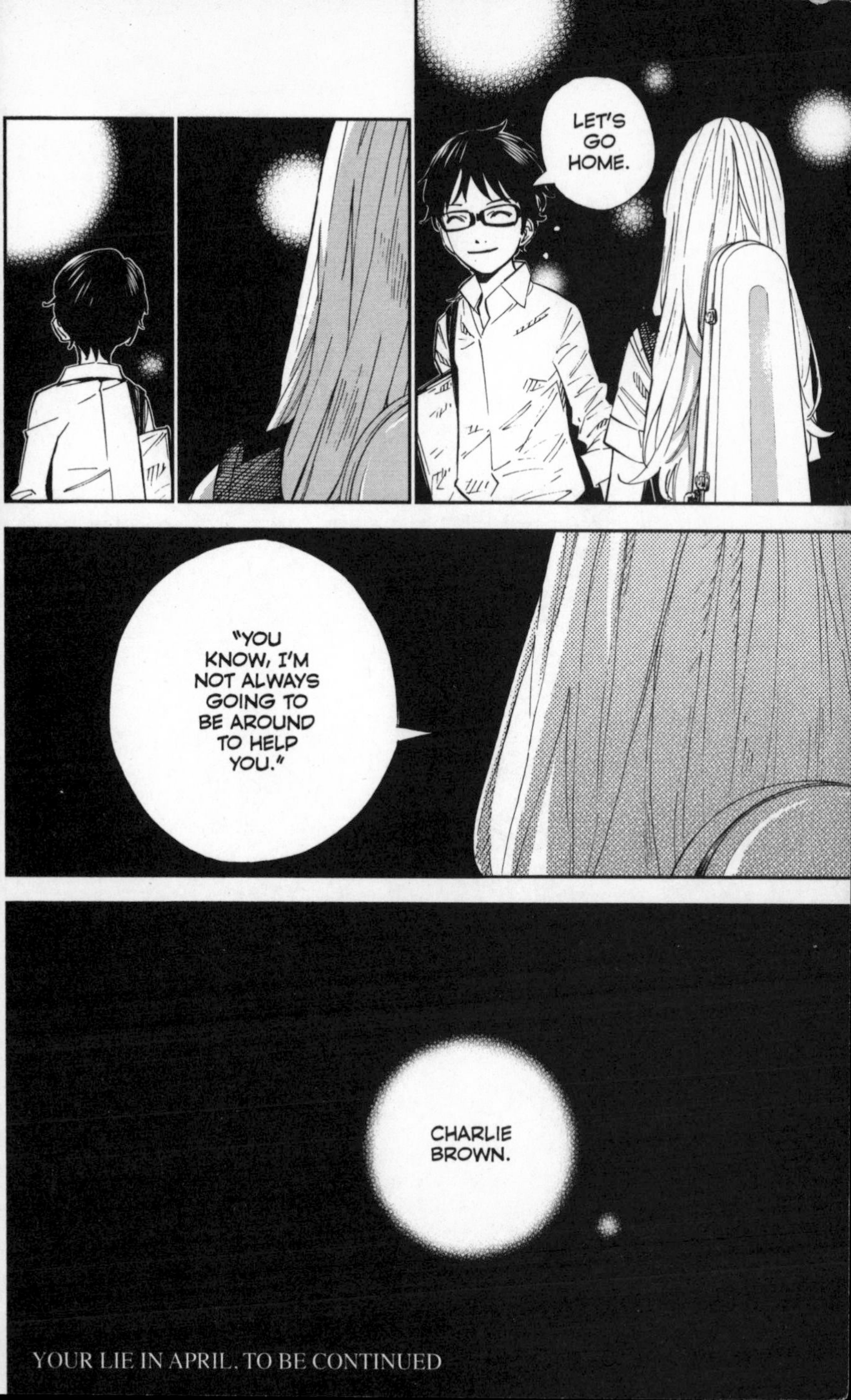
LET'S GO HOME.
"YOU KNOW, I'M NOT ALWAYS GOING TO BE AROUND TO HELP YOU."
CHARLIE BROWN.
YOUR LIE IN APRIL, TO BE CONTINUED

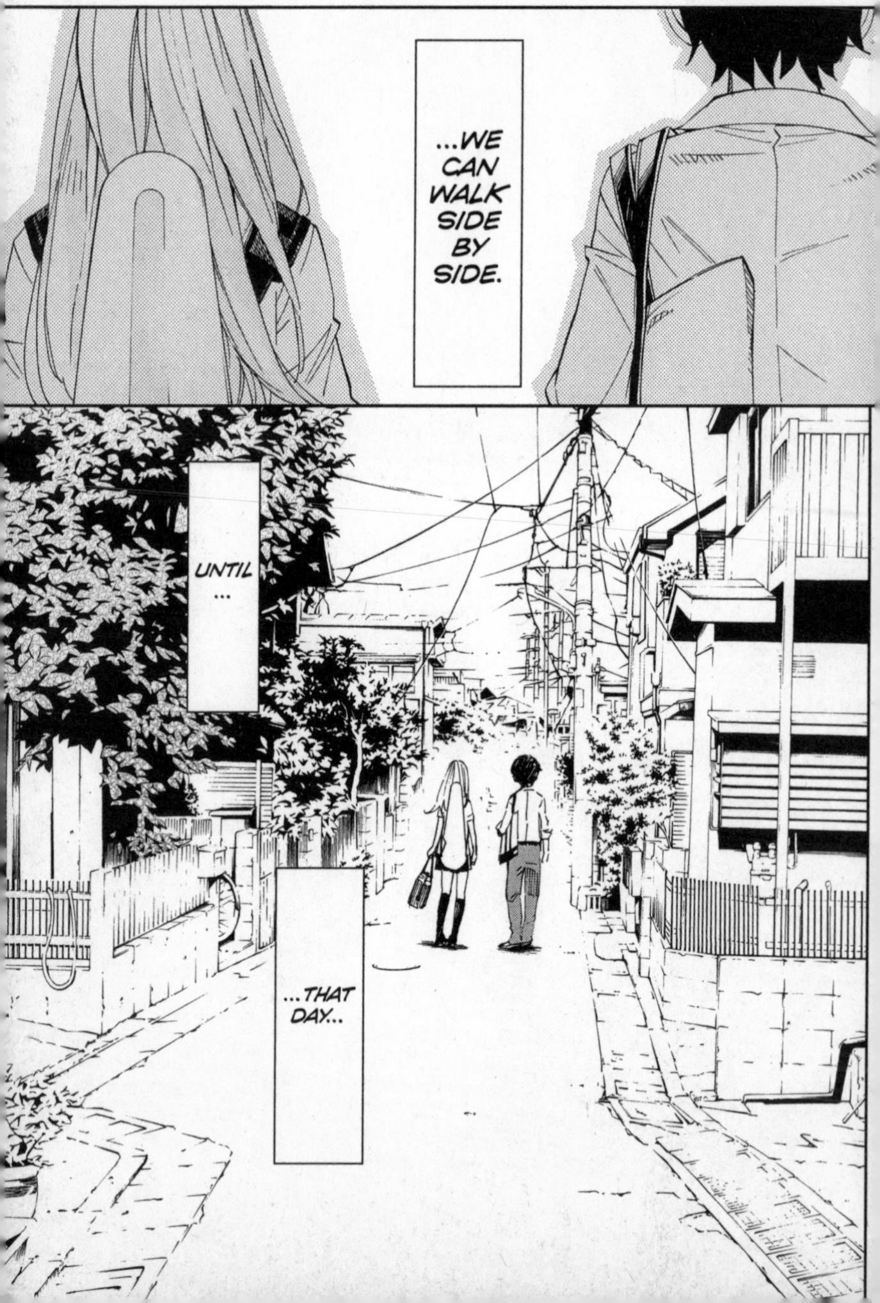
...WE CAN WALK SIDE BY SIDE.
UNTIL ...
...THAT DAY...

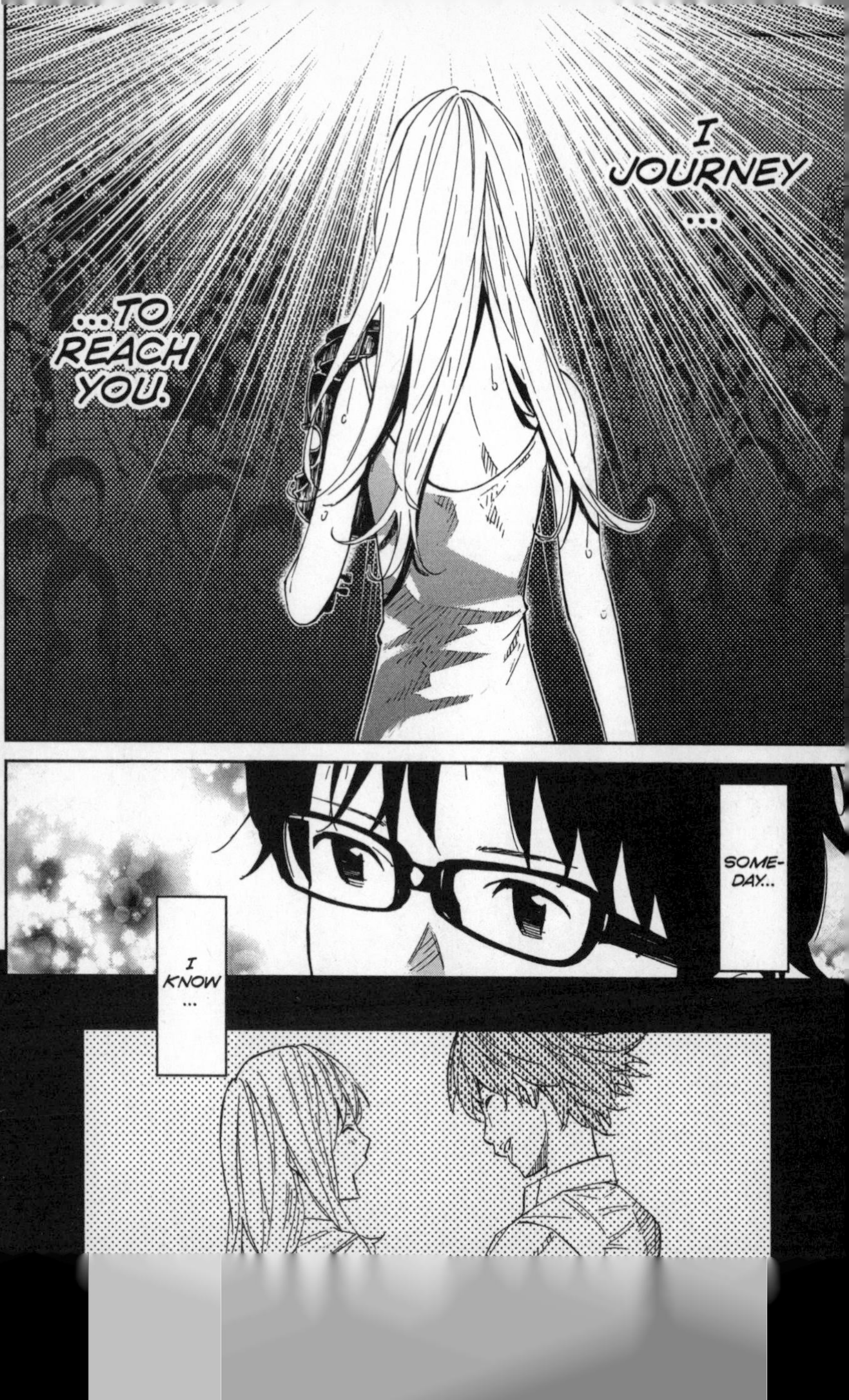
I JOURNEY ...
...TO REACH YOU.
SOME-DAY...
I KNOW ...

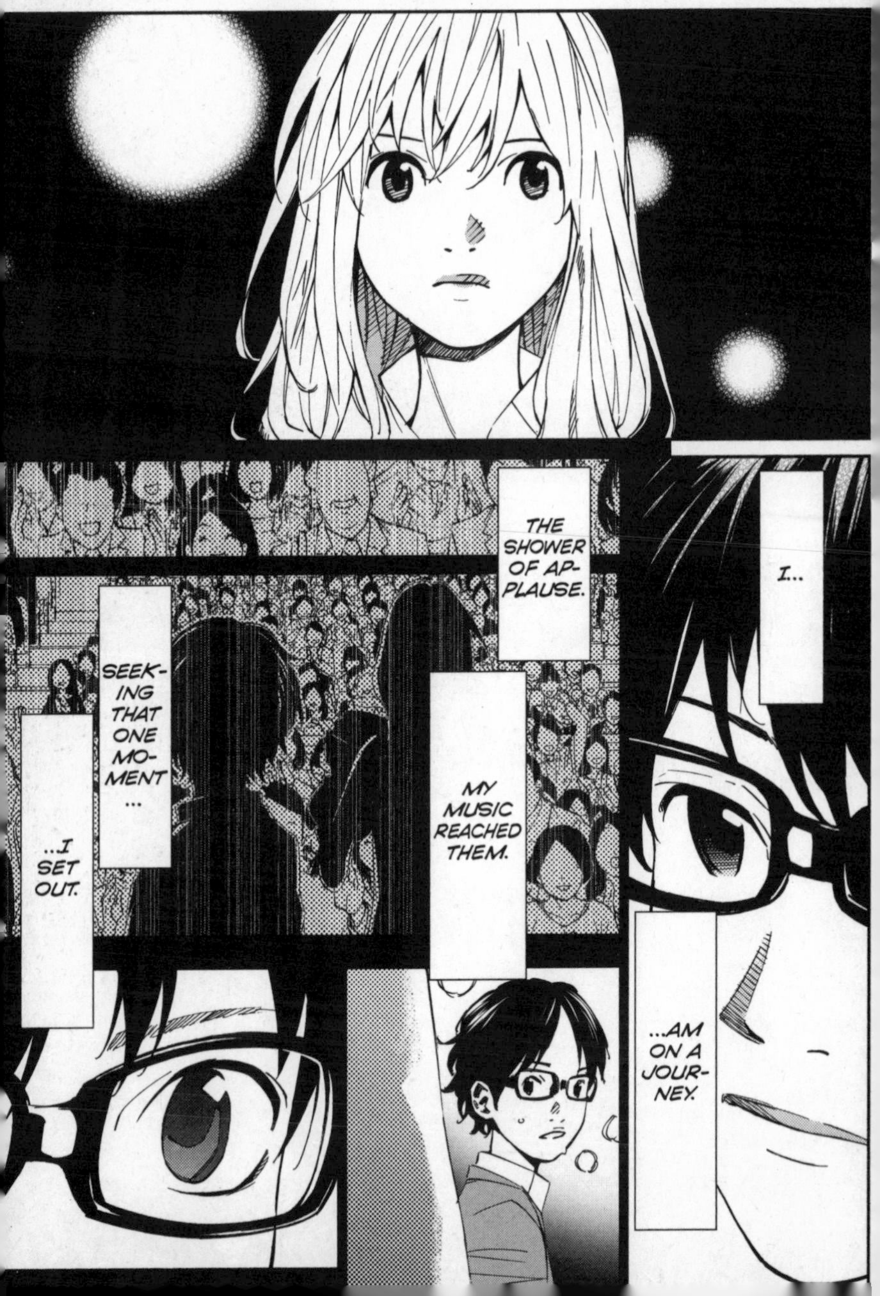
I...
...AM ON A JOURNEY.
THE SHOWER OF AP-PLAUSE.
MY MUSIC REACHED THEM.
SEEK-ING THAT ONE MO-MENT ...
...I SET OUT.

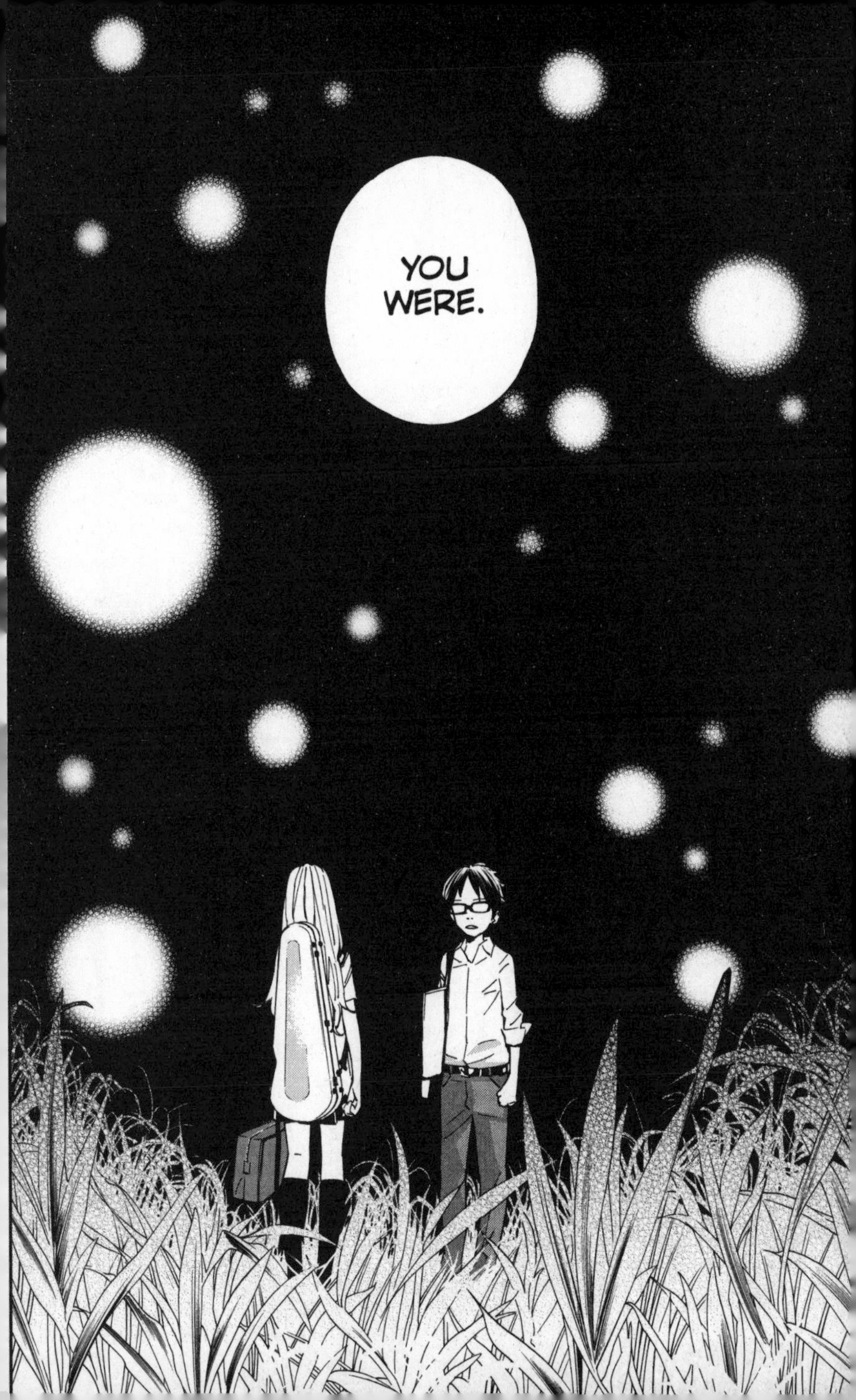
YOU WERE.

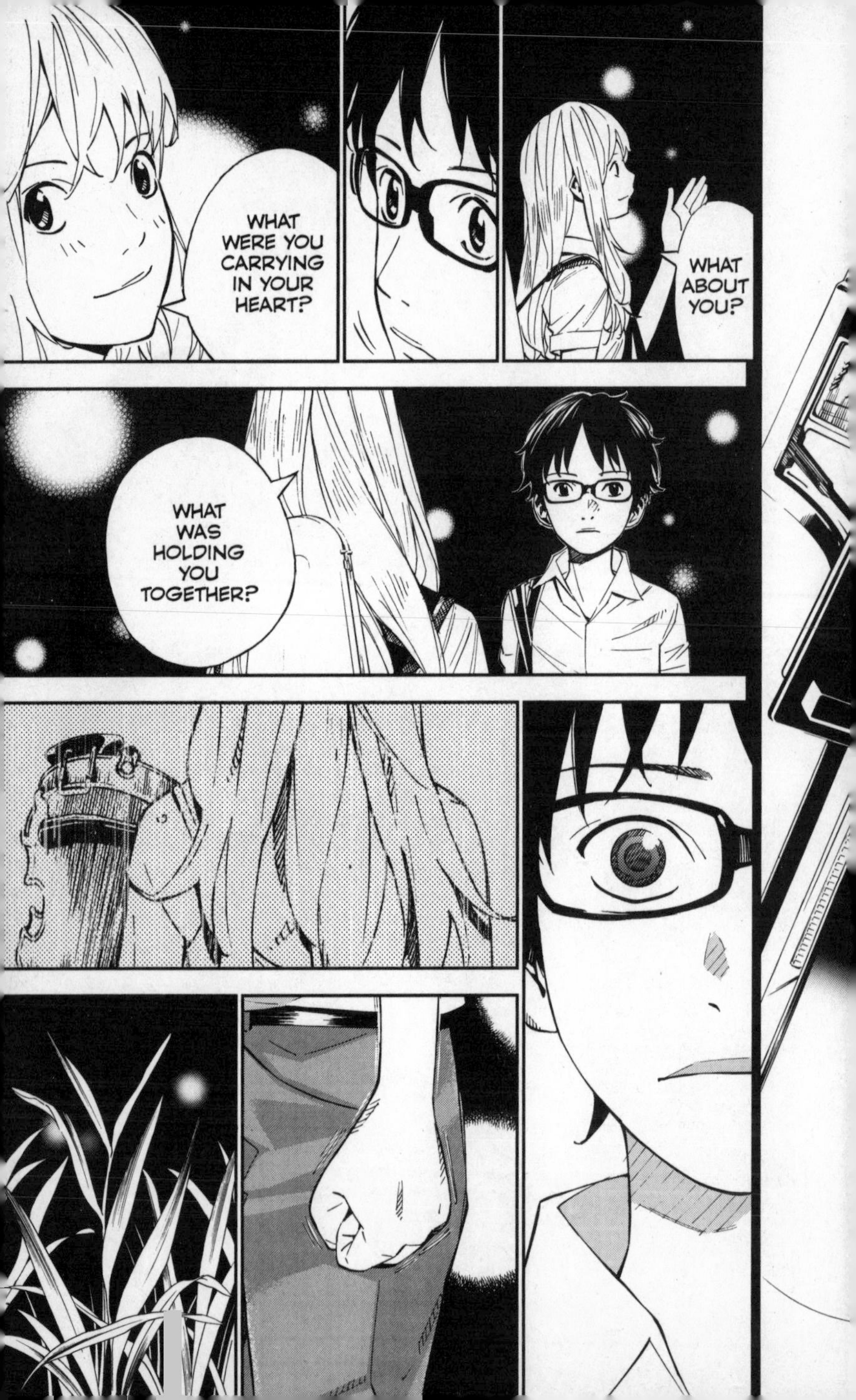
WHAT ABOUT YOU?
WHAT WERE YOU CARRYING IN YOUR HEART?
WHAT WAS HOLDING YOU TOGETHER?

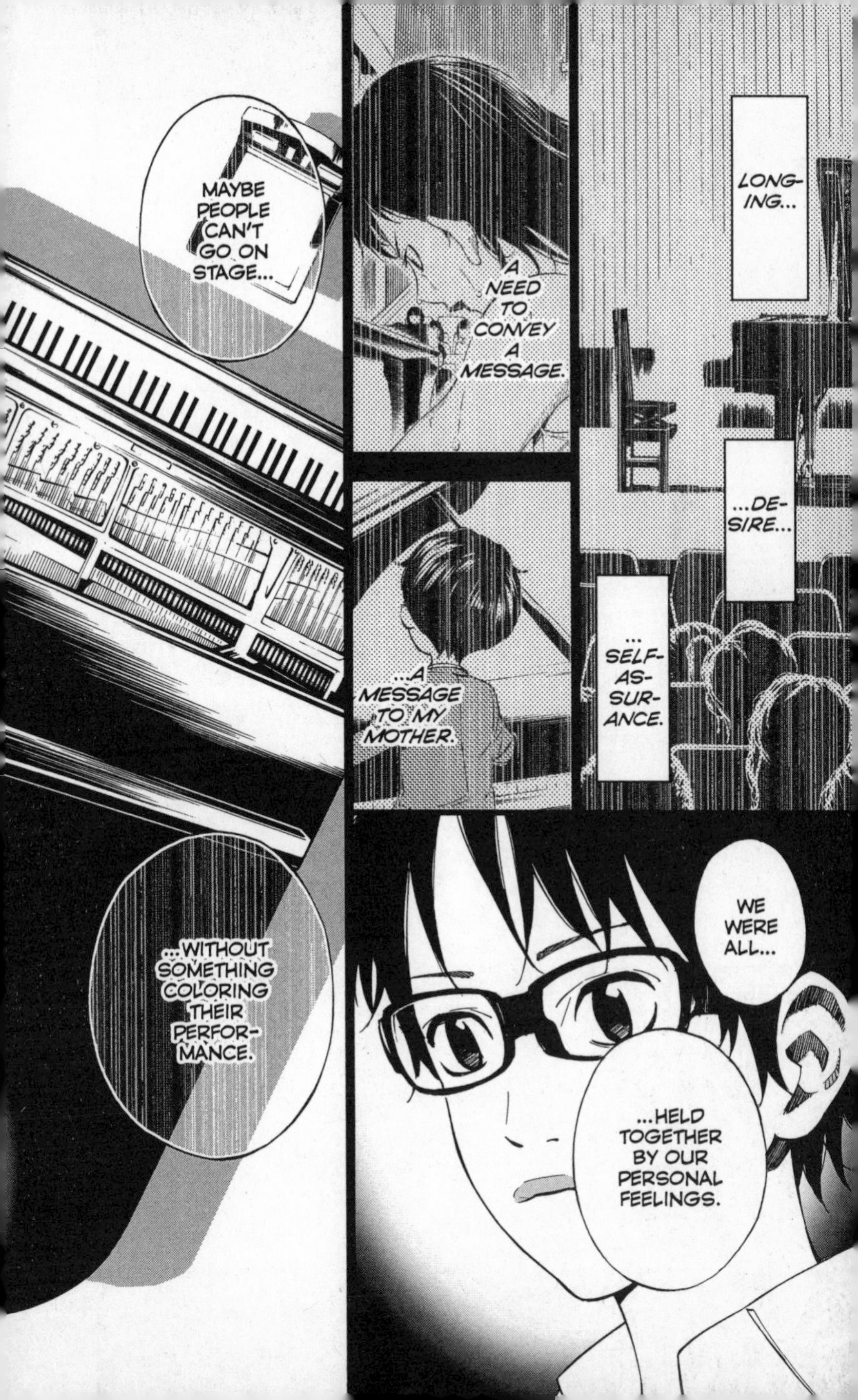
LONG-ING...
...DE-SIRE...
...SELF-AS-SUR-ANCE.
A NEED TO CONVEY A MESSAGE.
...A MESSAGE TO MY MOTHER.
WE WERE ALL...
...HELD TOGETHER BY OUR PERSONAL FEELINGS.
MAYBE PEOPLE CAN'T GO ON STAGE...
...WITHOUT SOMETHING COLORING THEIR PERFOR-MANCE.

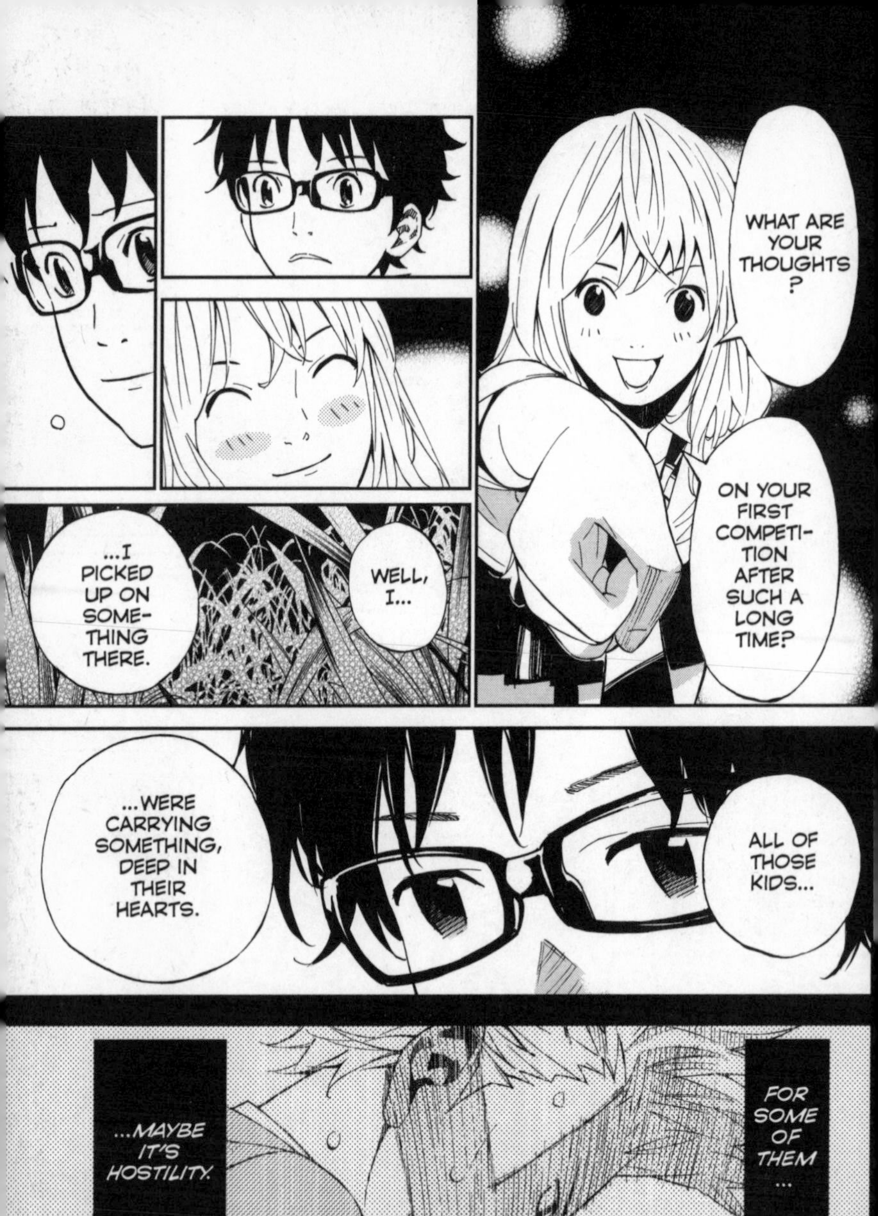
WHAT ARE YOUR THOUGHTS?
ON YOUR FIRST COMPETITION AFTER SUCH A LONG TIME?
WELL, I...
...I PICKED UP ON SOMETHING THERE.
ALL OF THOSE KIDS...
...WERE CARRYING SOMETHING, DEEP IN THEIR HEARTS.
FOR SOME OF THEM...
...MAYBE IT'S HOSTILITY.

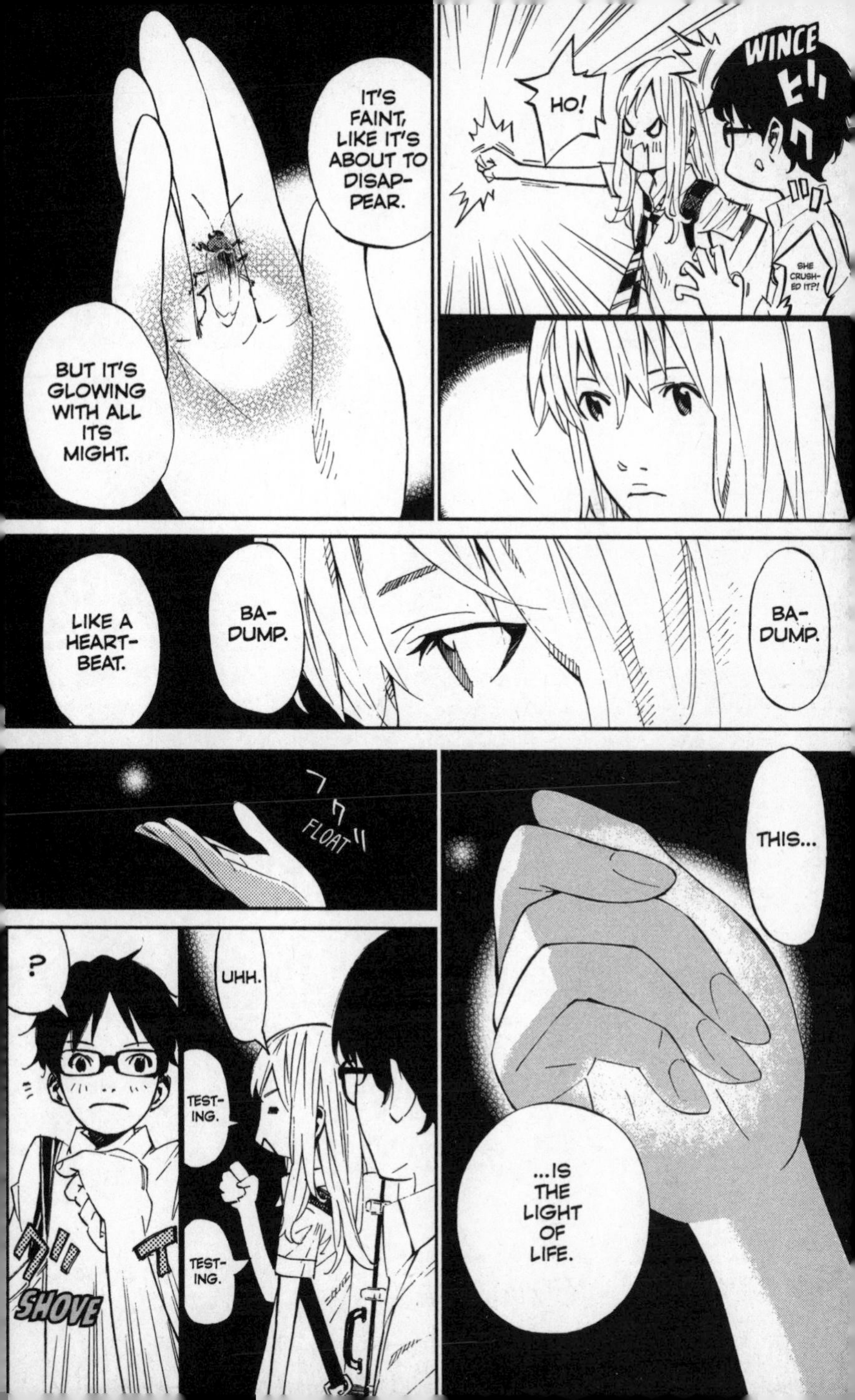
HO!
WINCE
SHE CRUSHED IT?!
IT'S FAINT, LIKE IT'S ABOUT TO DISAPPEAR.
BUT IT'S GLOWING WITH ALL ITS MIGHT.
BA-DUMP.
BA-DUMP.
LIKE A HEARTBEAT.
THIS...
...IS THE LIGHT OF LIFE.
FLOAT
UHH.
TESTING.
TESTING.
?
SHOVE

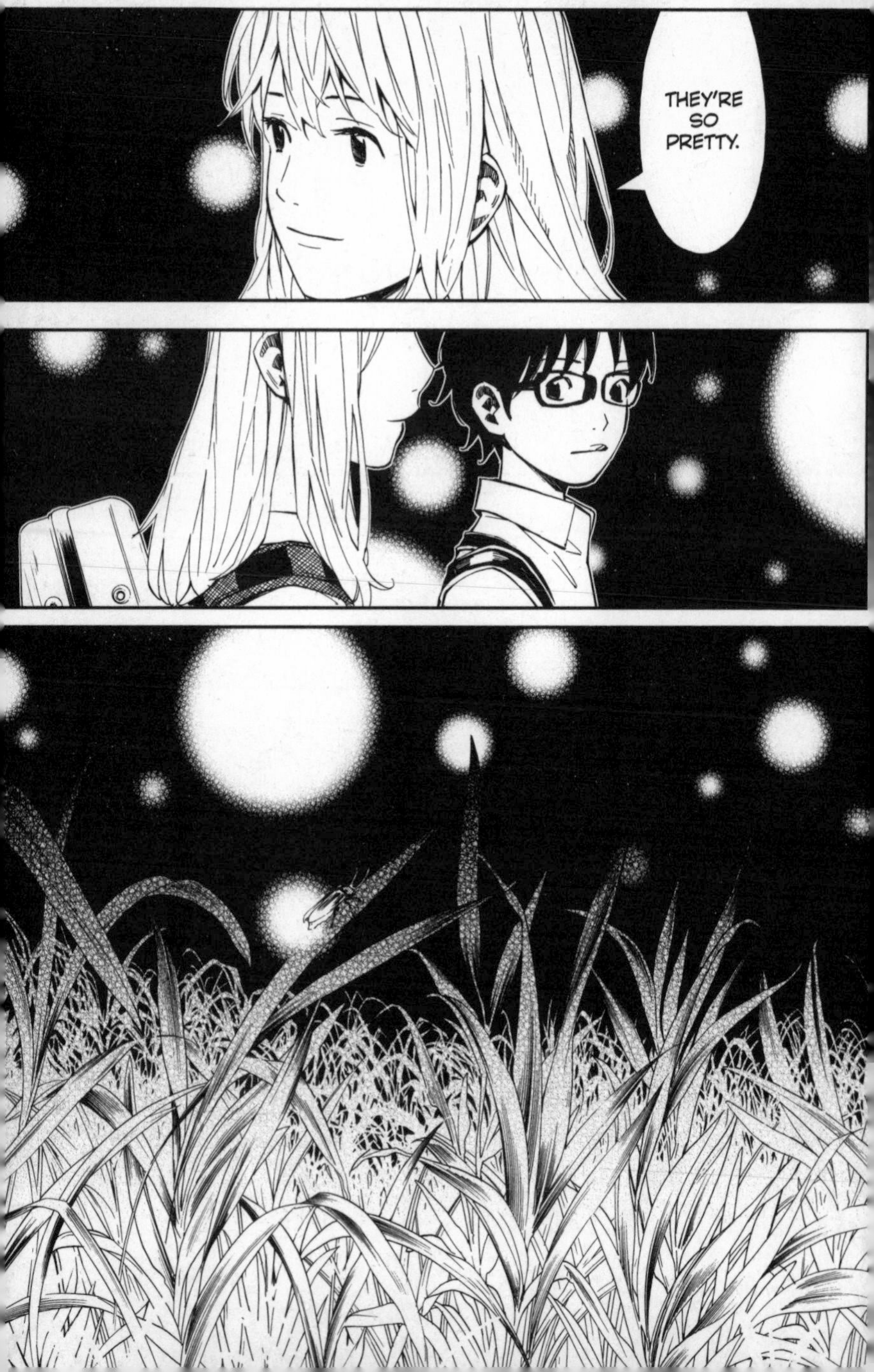
THEY'RE SO PRETTY.

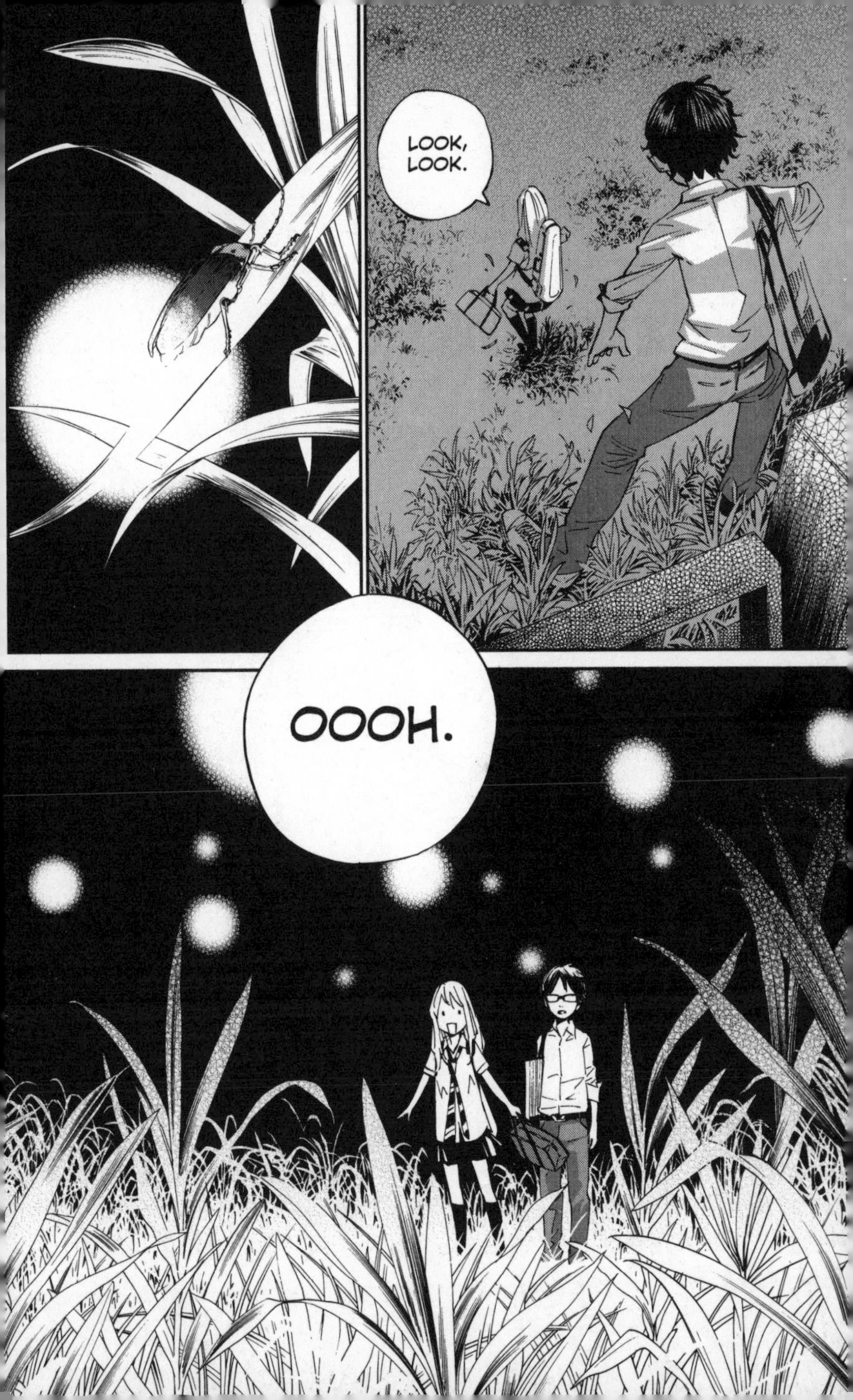
LOOK, LOOK.
OOOH.

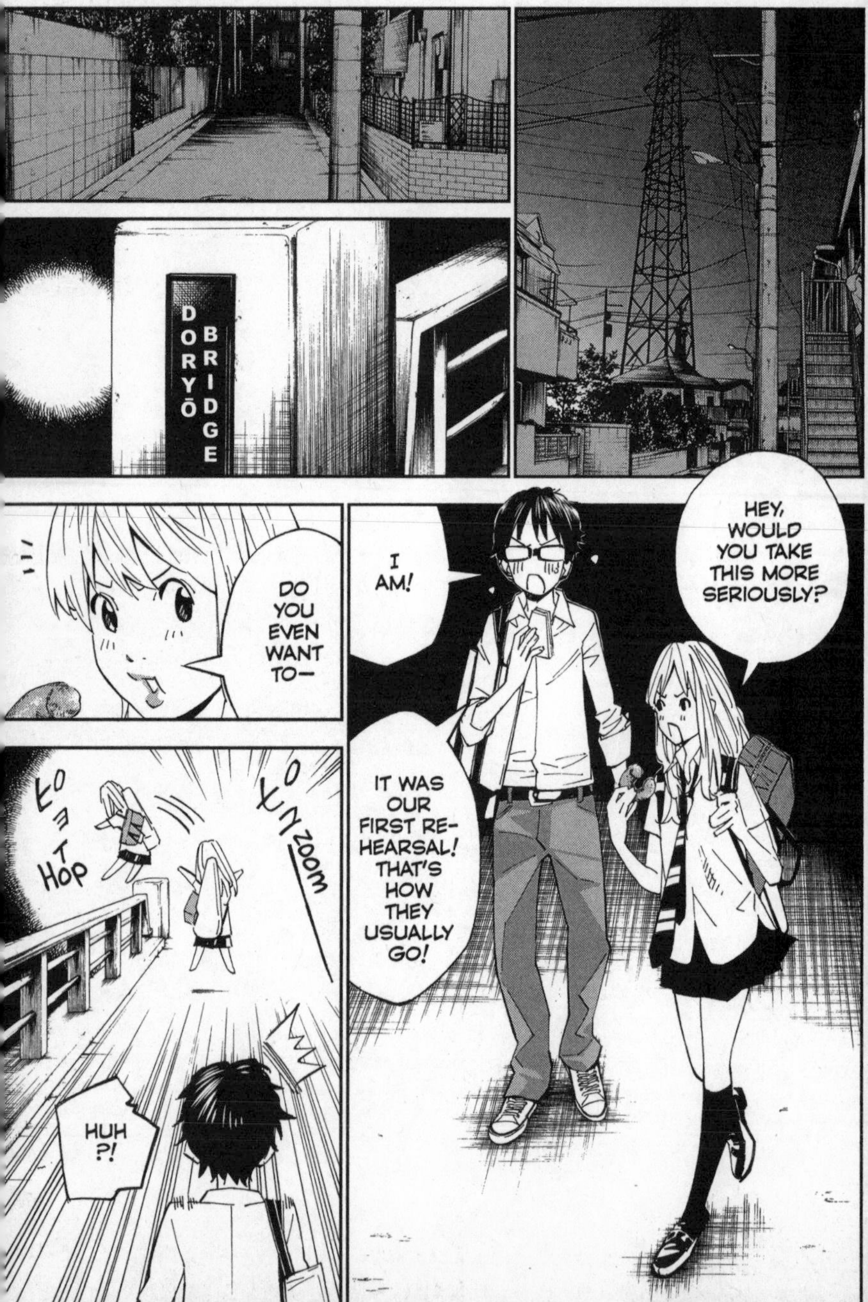
DORYŌ BRIDGE
HEY, WOULD YOU TAKE THIS MORE SERIOUSLY?
I AM!
IT WAS OUR FIRST RE-HEARSAL! THAT'S HOW THEY USUALLY GO!
DO YOU EVEN WANT TO—
HOP
ZOOM
HUH?!

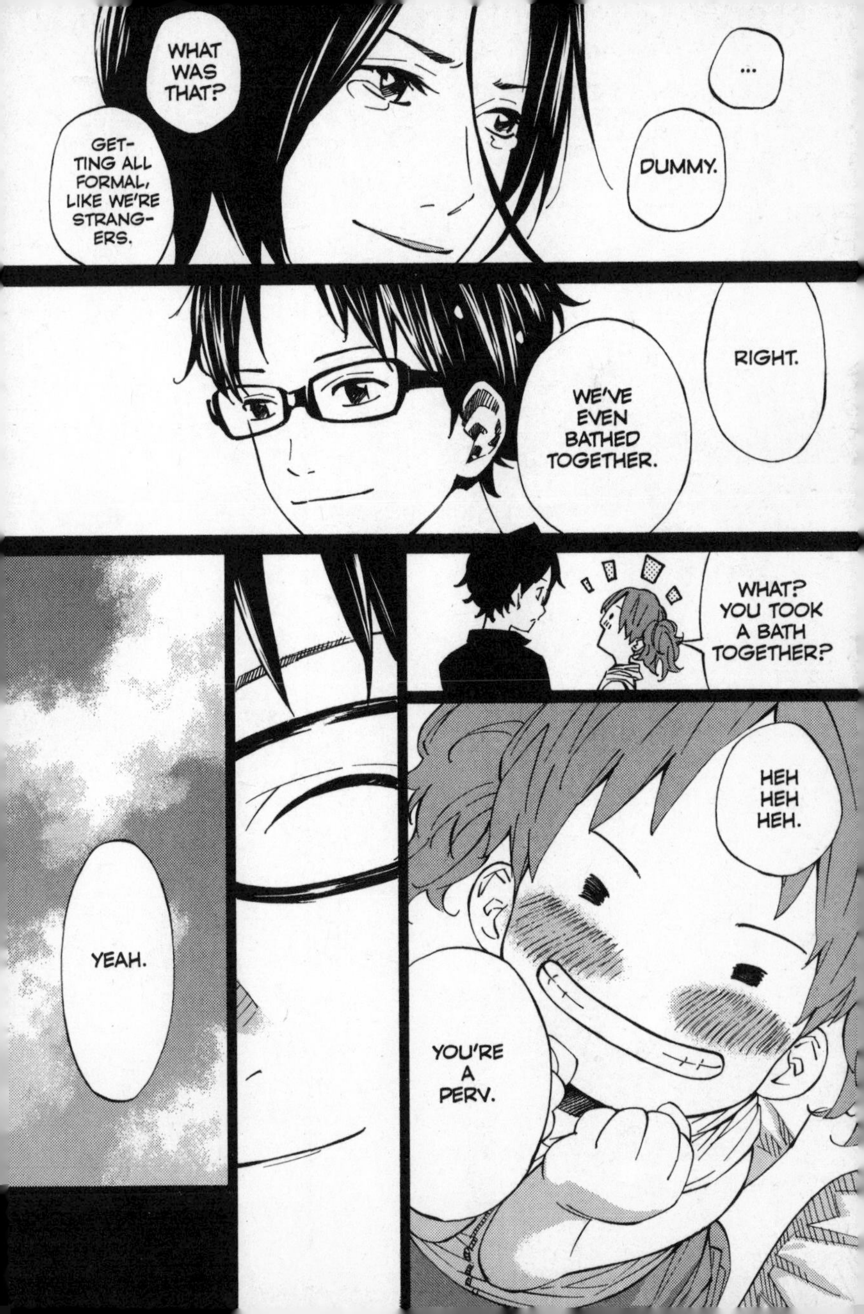
WHAT WAS THAT?
GET-TING ALL FORMAL, LIKE WE'RE STRANGERS.
...
DUMMY.
RIGHT.
WE'VE EVEN BATHED TOGETHER.
WHAT? YOU TOOK A BATH TOGETHER?
HEH HEH HEH.
YOU'RE A PERV.
YEAH.

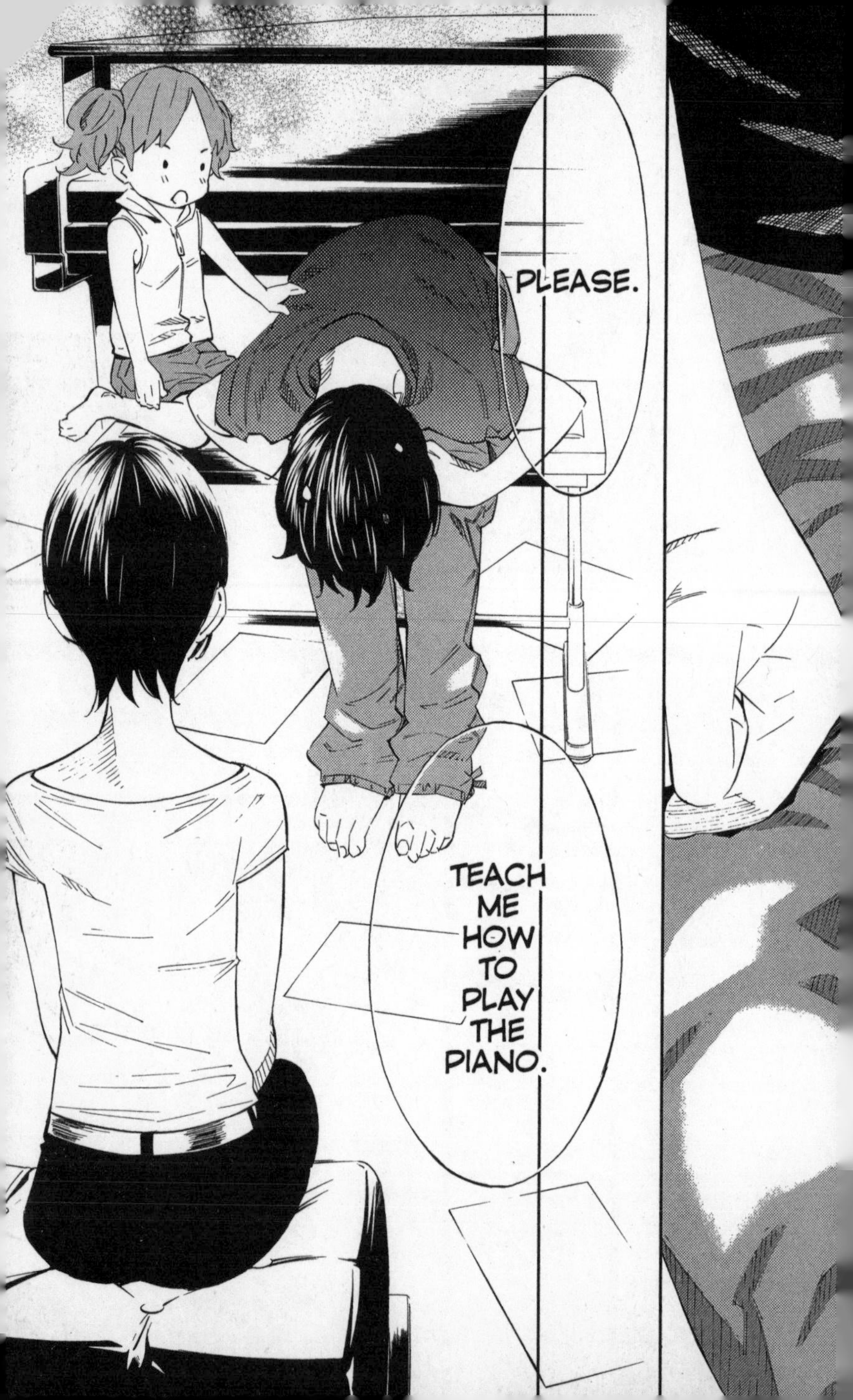
PLEASE.
TEACH ME HOW TO PLAY THE PIANO.

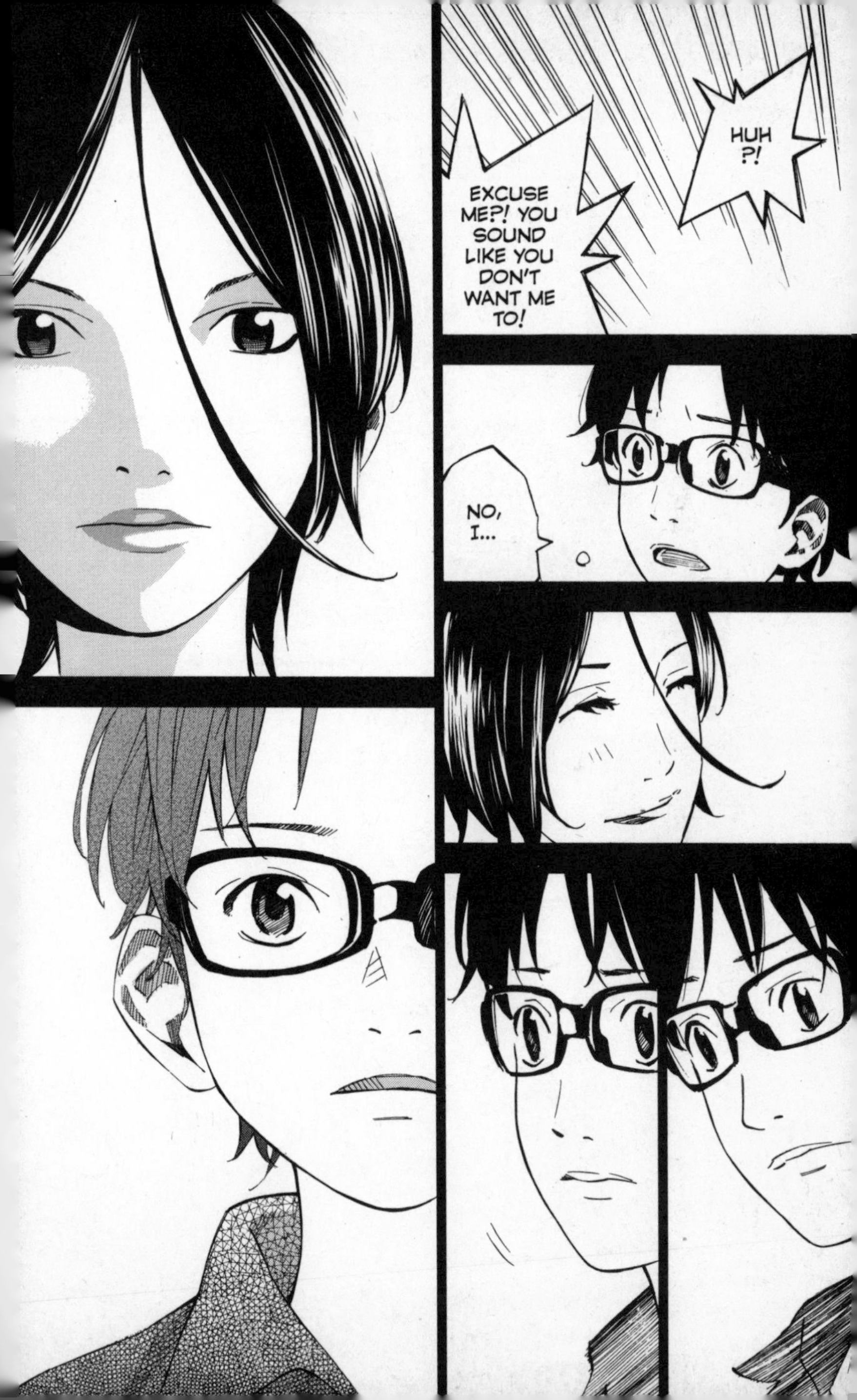
HUH ?!
EXCUSE ME?! YOU SOUND LIKE YOU DON'T WANT ME TO!
NO, I...

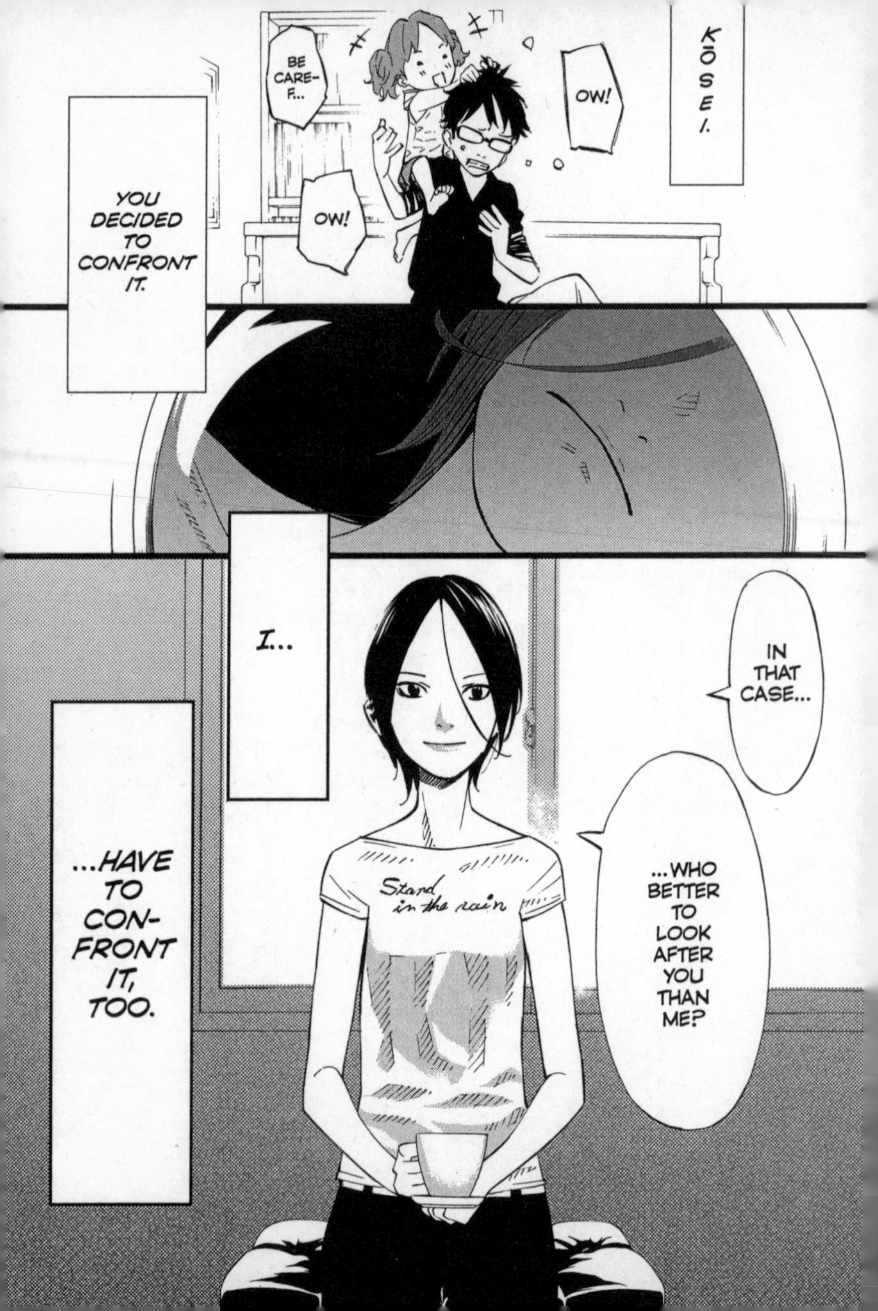
KŌSEI.
OW!
BE CARE-F...
OW!
YOU DECIDED TO CONFRONT IT.
IN THAT CASE...
...WHO BETTER TO LOOK AFTER YOU THAN ME?
Stand in the rain
I...
...HAVE TO CON-FRONT IT, TOO.

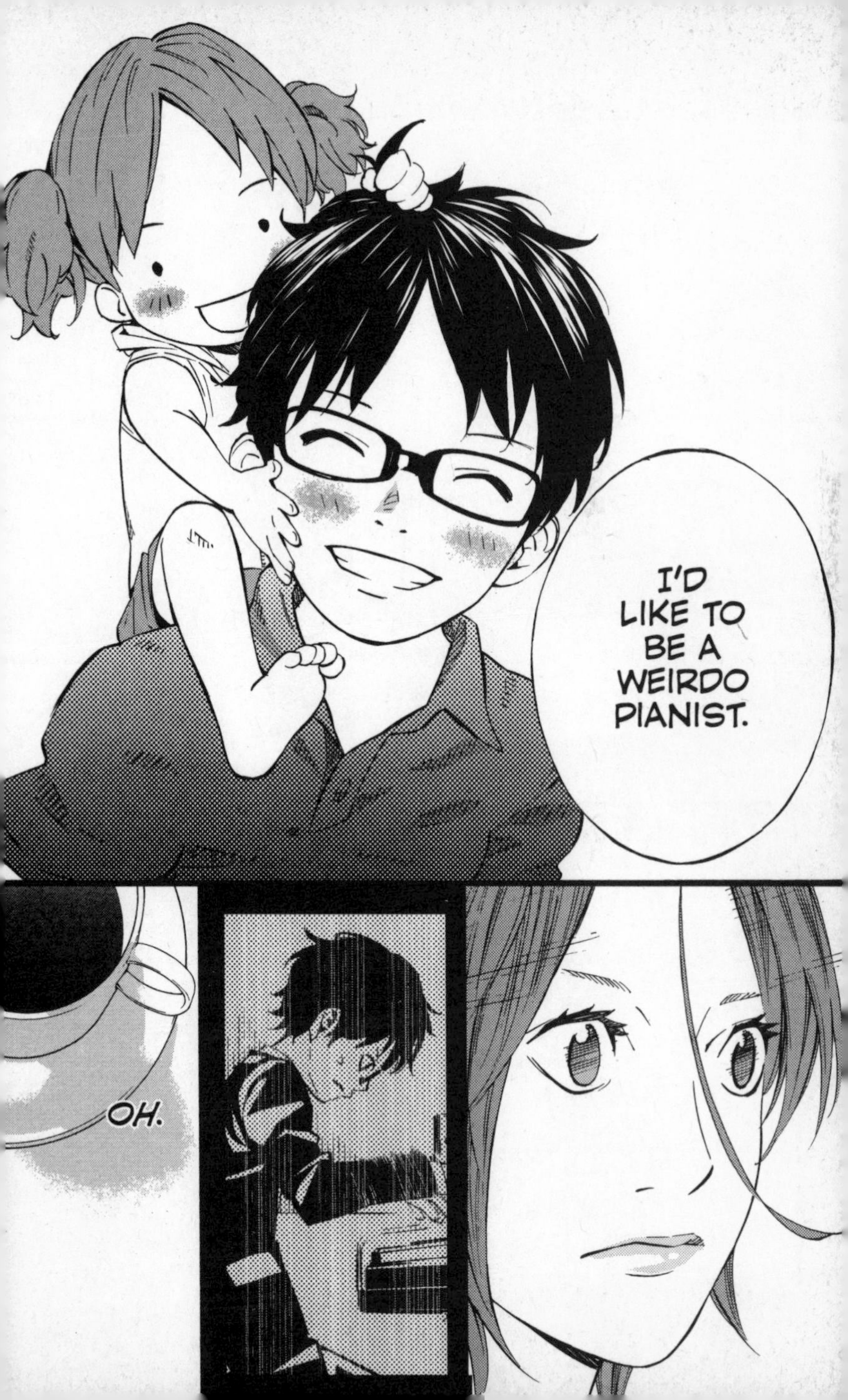
I'D LIKE TO BE A WEIRDO PIANIST.
OH.

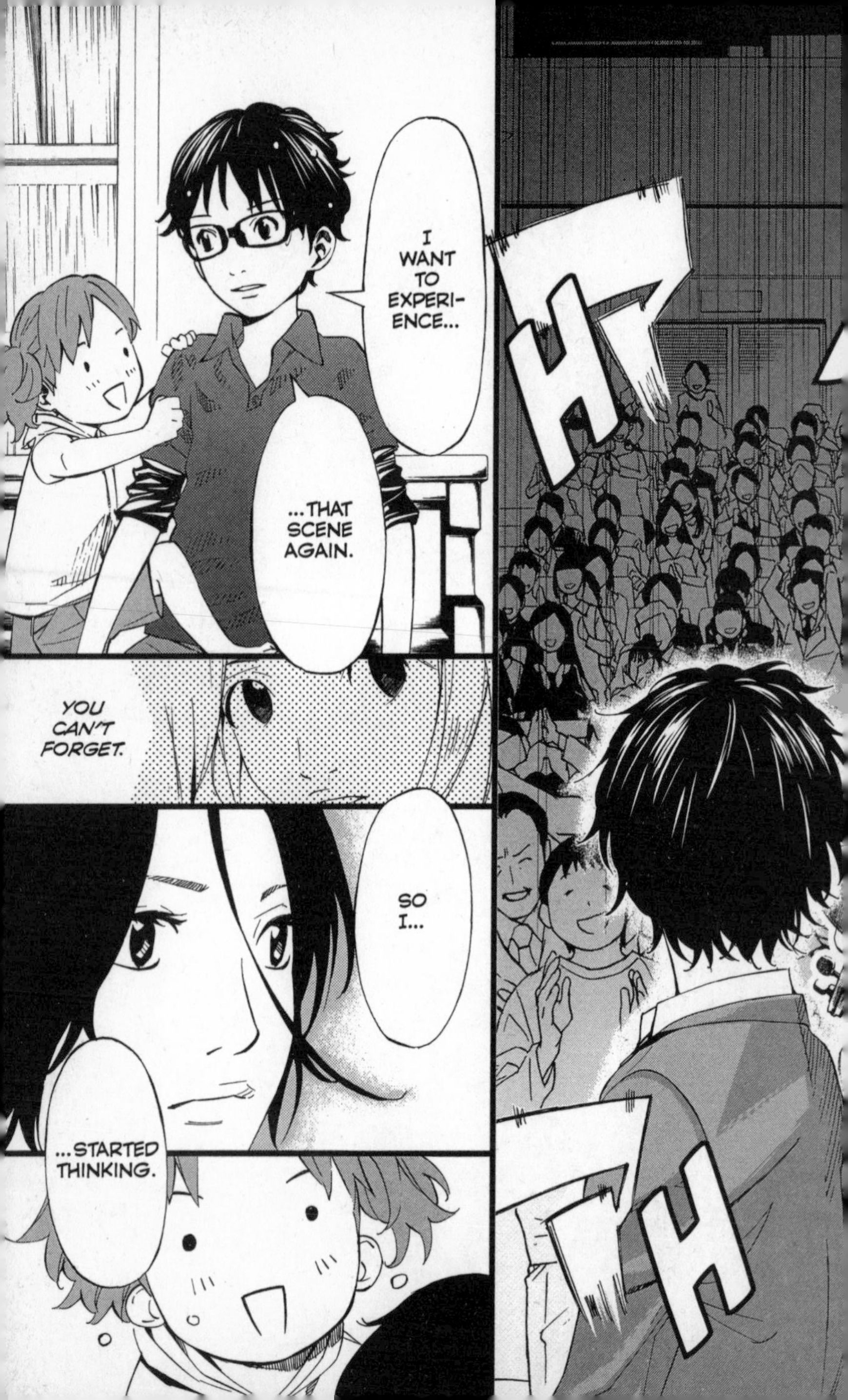
I WANT TO EXPERIENCE...
...THAT SCENE AGAIN.
YOU CAN'T FORGET.
SO I...
...STARTED THINKING.

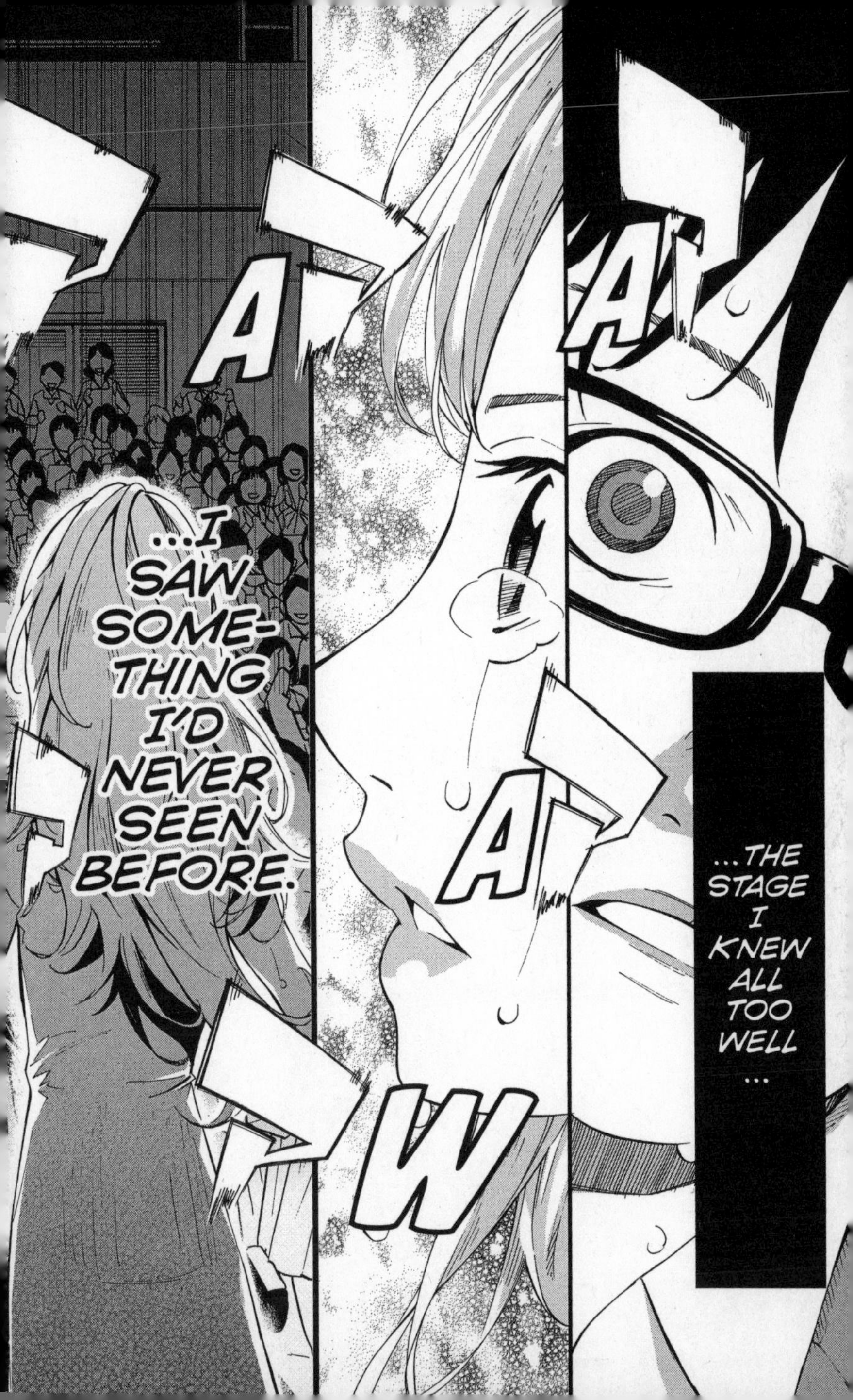
...THE STAGE I KNEW ALL TOO WELL...
AAAW
...I SAW SOME-THING I'D NEVER SEEN BEFORE.

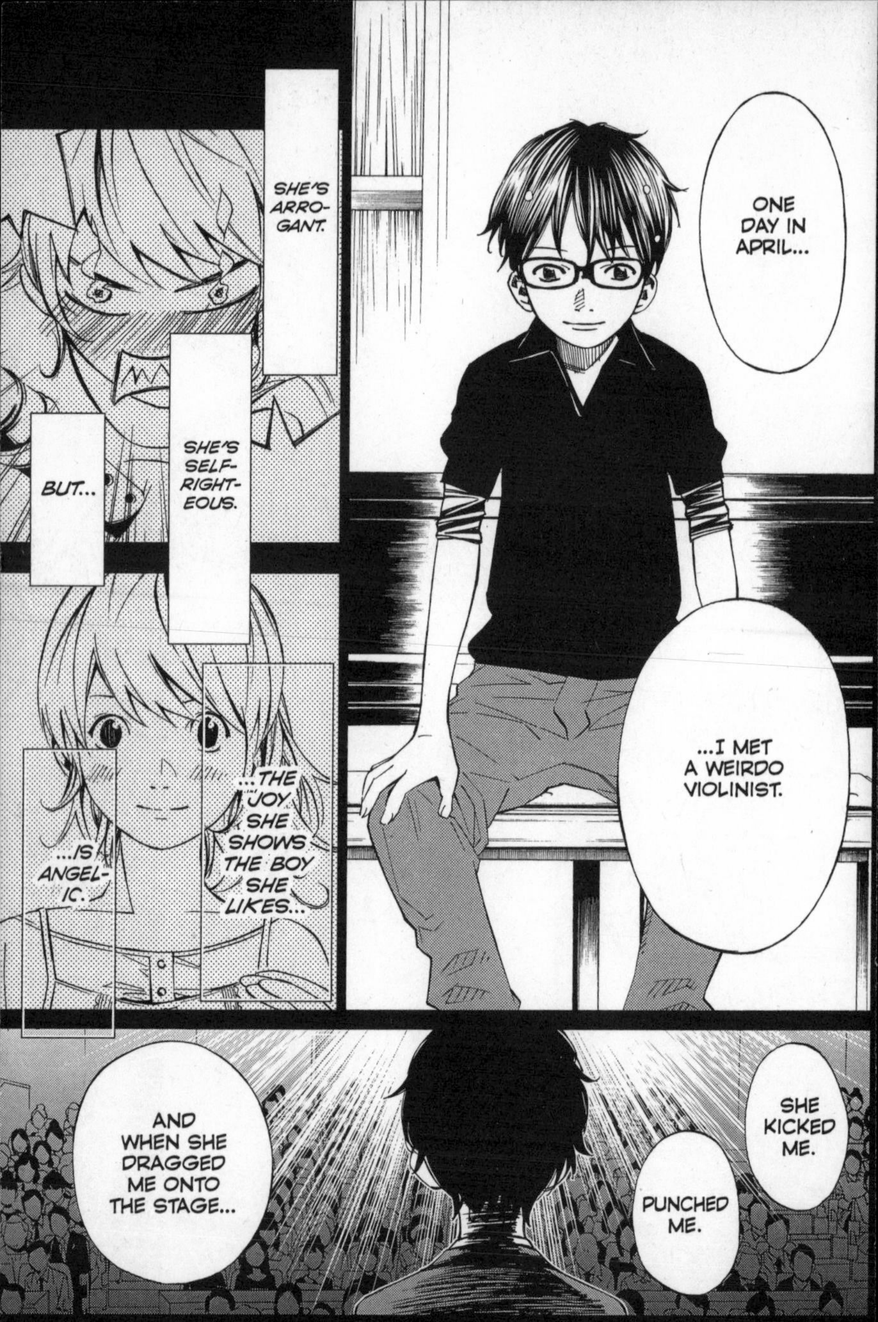
ONE DAY IN APRIL...
...I MET A WEIRDO VIOLINIST.
SHE'S ARRO-GANT.
SHE'S SELF-RIGHT-EOUS.
BUT...
...THE JOY SHE SHOWS THE BOY SHE LIKES...
...IS ANGEL-IC.
SHE KICKED ME.
PUNCHED ME.
AND WHEN SHE DRAGGED ME ONTO THE STAGE...

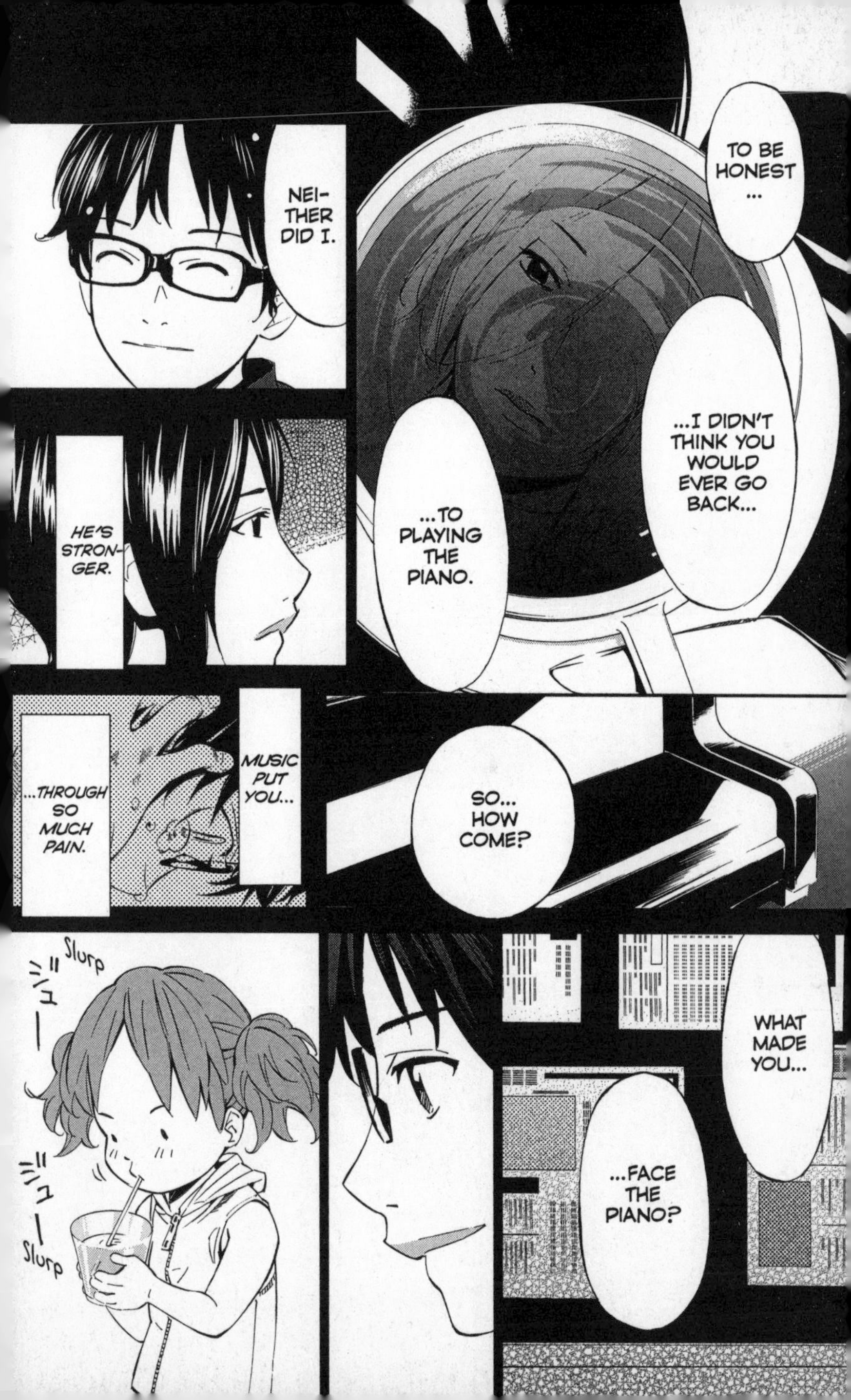
TO BE HONEST ...
...I DIDN'T THINK YOU WOULD EVER GO BACK...
...TO PLAYING THE PIANO.
NEI-THER DID I.
HE'S STRON-GER.
SO... HOW COME?
MUSIC PUT YOU...
...THROUGH SO MUCH PAIN.
WHAT MADE YOU...
...FACE THE PIANO?
ジュー Slurp
ジュー Slurp

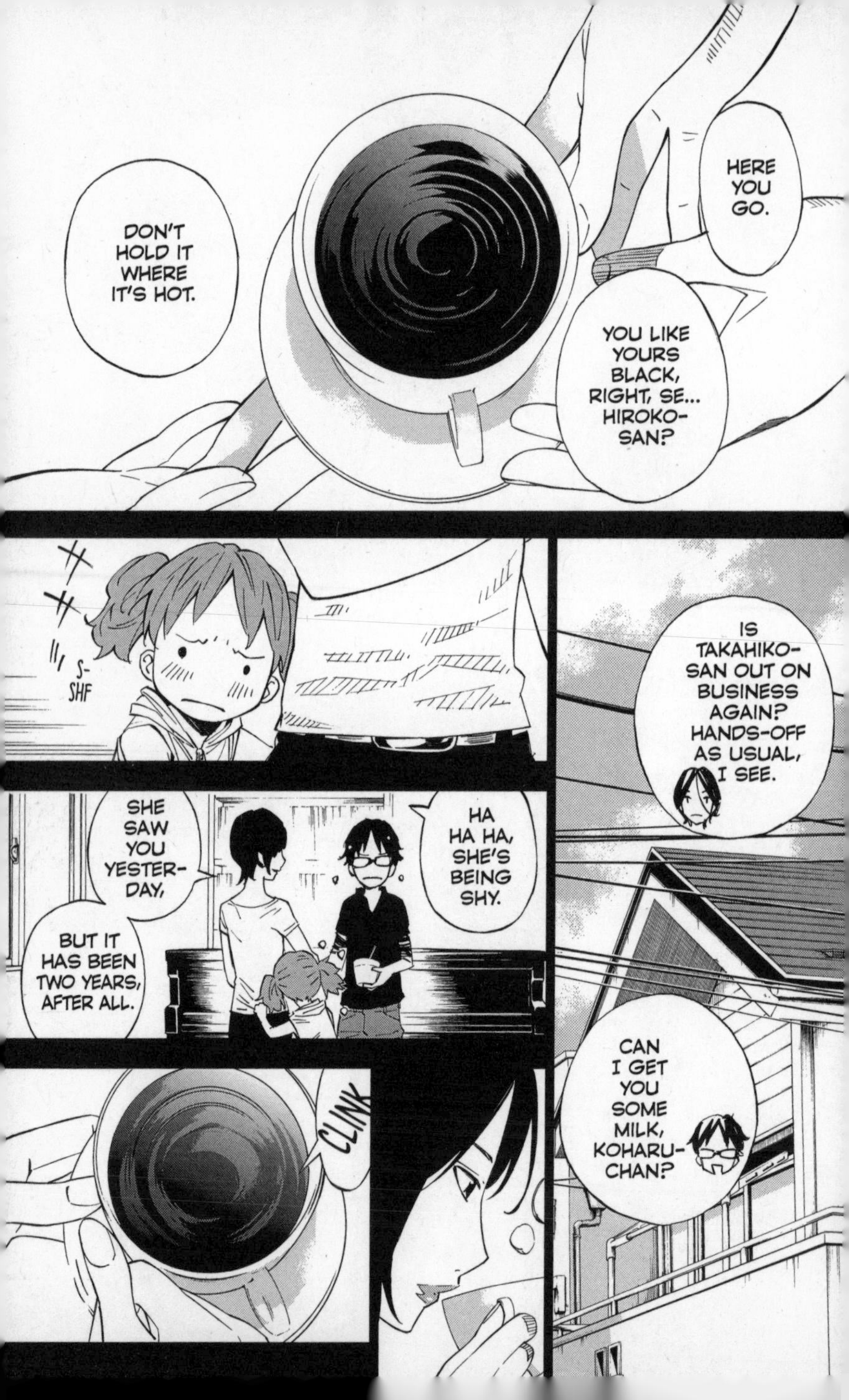
HERE YOU GO.
YOU LIKE YOURS BLACK, RIGHT, SE... HIROKO-SAN?
DON'T HOLD IT WHERE IT'S HOT.
IS TAKAHIKO-SAN OUT ON BUSINESS AGAIN? HANDS-OFF AS USUAL, I SEE.
CAN I GET YOU SOME MILK, KOHARU-CHAN?
S-SHF
HA HA HA, SHE'S BEING SHY.
SHE SAW YOU YESTER-DAY,
BUT IT HAS BEEN TWO YEARS, AFTER ALL.
CLINK

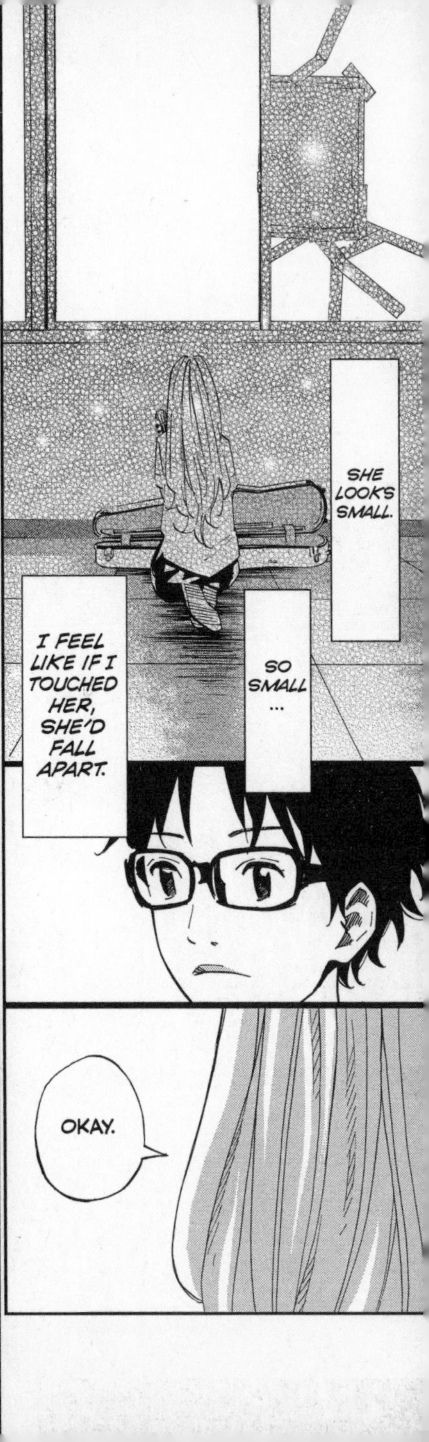
SHE LOOKS SMALL.
SO SMALL...
I FEEL LIKE IF I TOUCHED HER, SHE'D FALL APART.
OKAY.
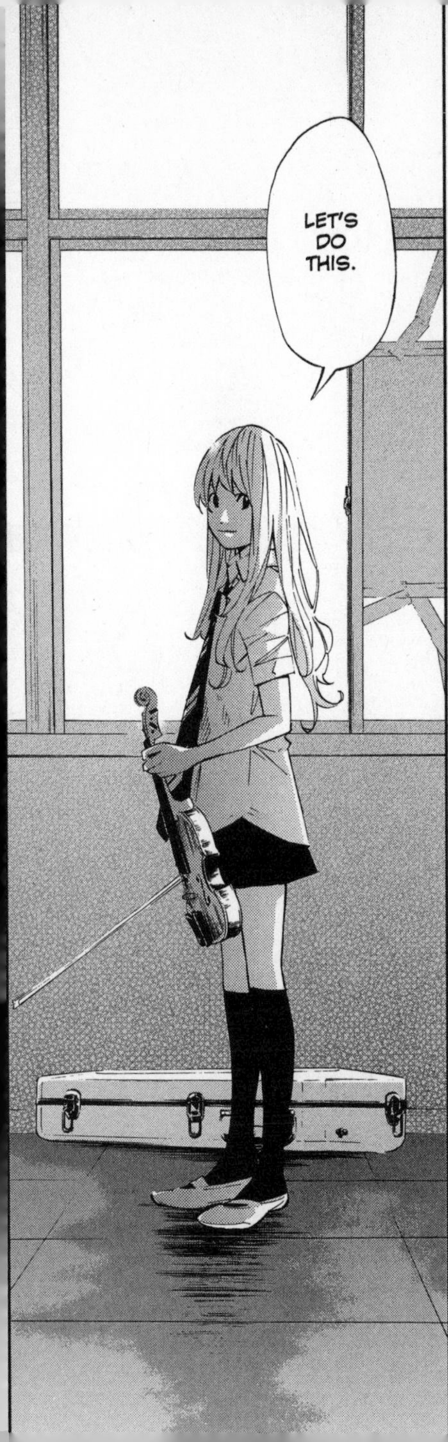
LET'S DO THIS.

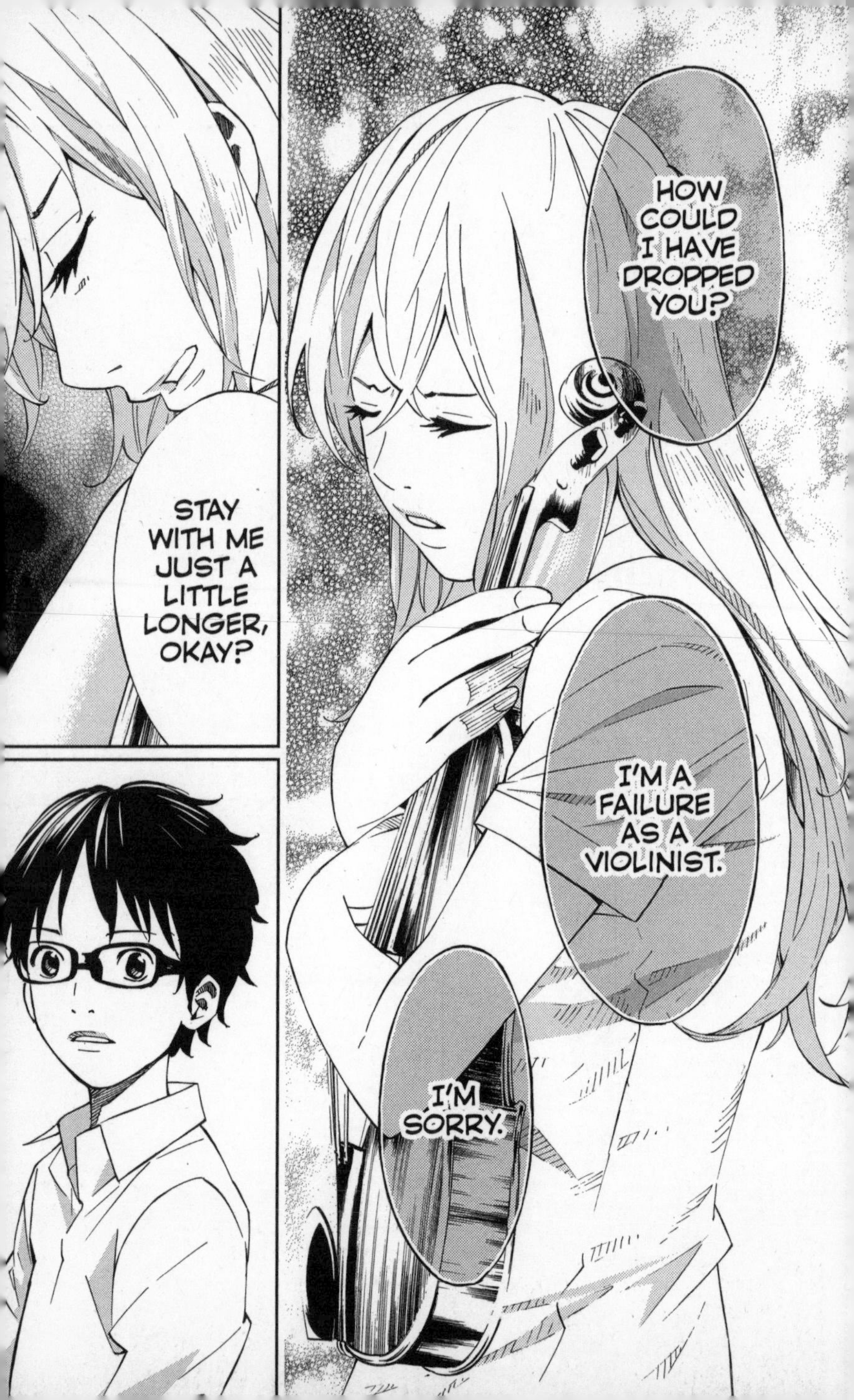
HOW COULD I HAVE DROPPED YOU?
I'M A FAILURE AS A VIOLINIST.
I'M SORRY.
STAY WITH ME JUST A LITTLE LONGER, OKAY?

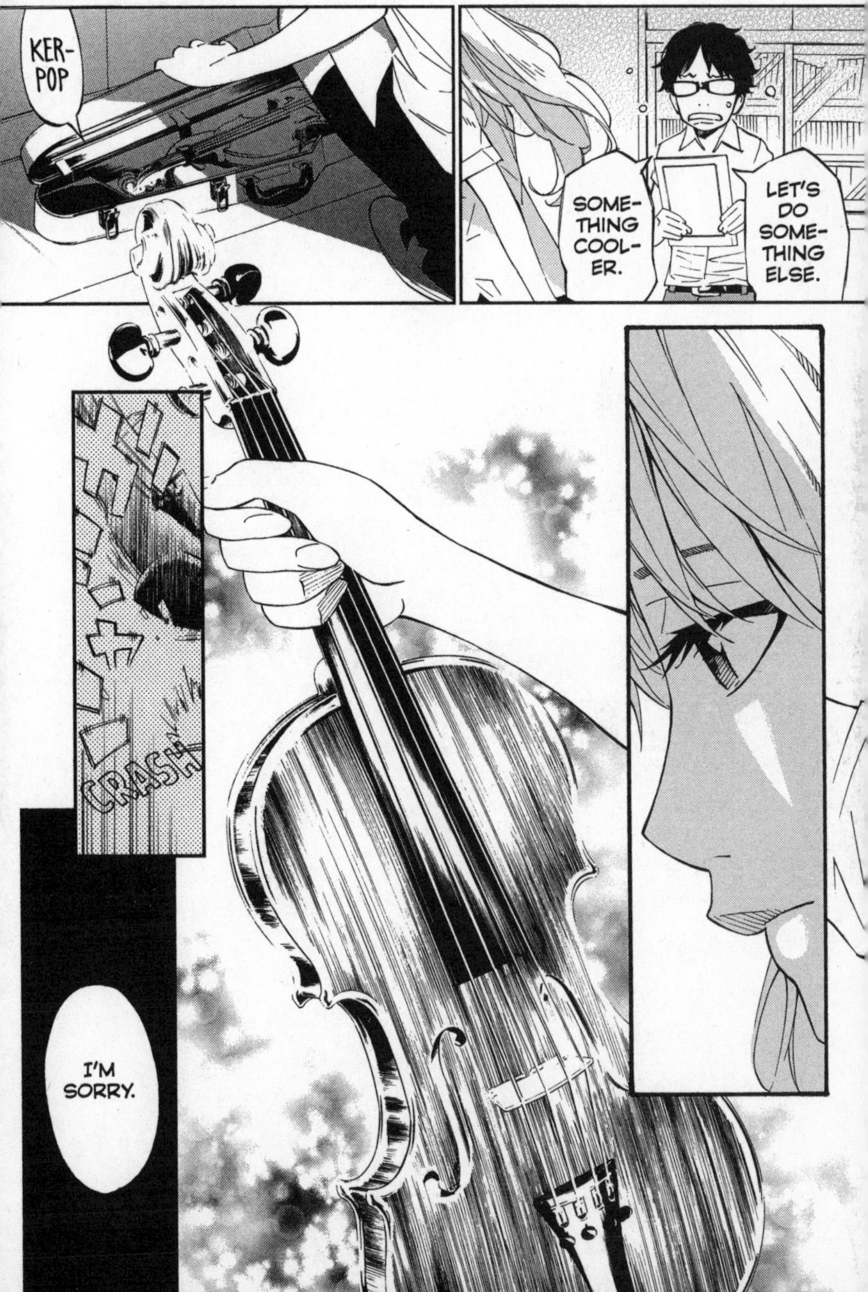
LET'S DO SOME-THING ELSE.
SOME-THING COOL-ER.
KER-POP
CRASH
I'M SORRY.

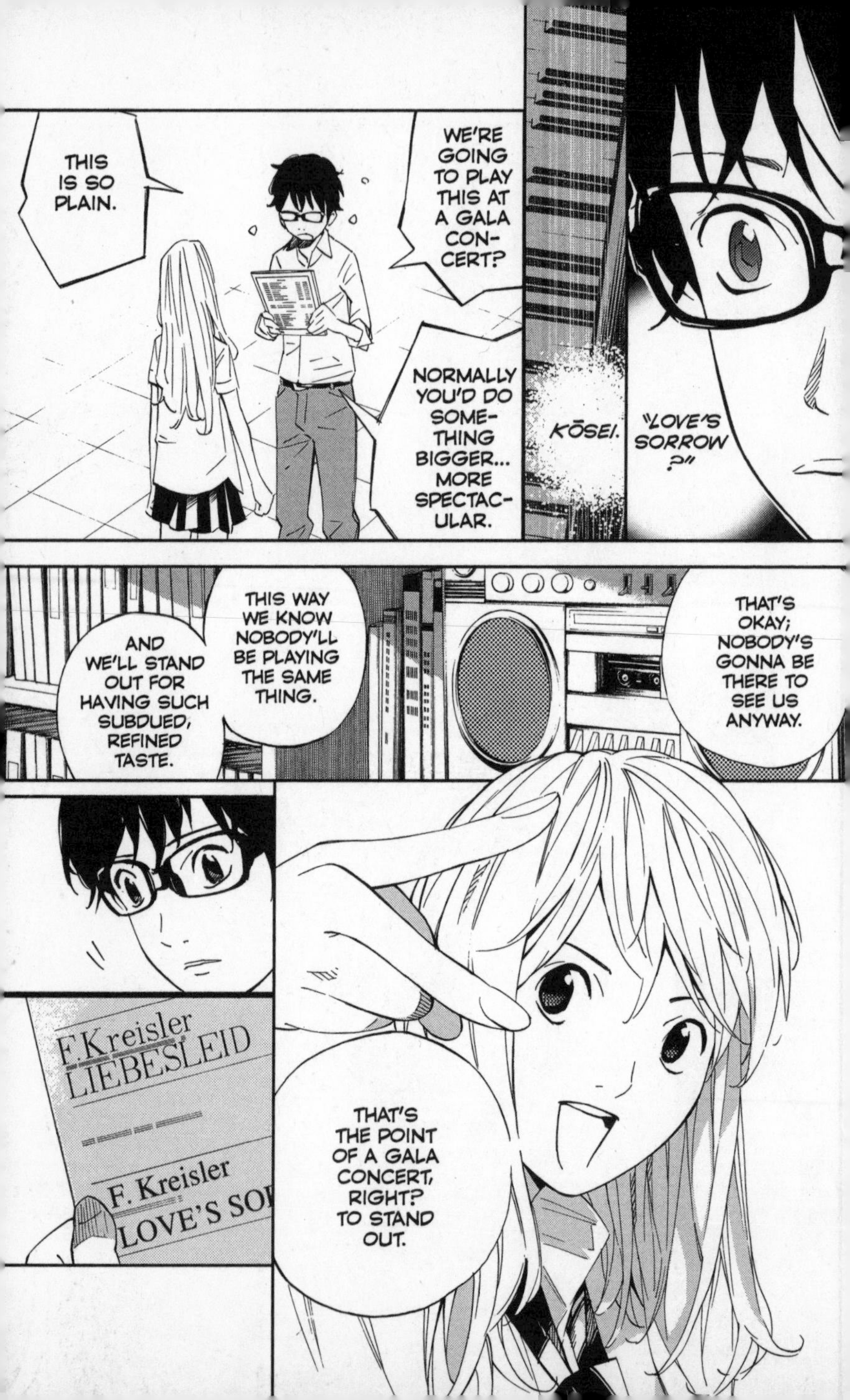
"LOVE'S SORROW?"
KŌSEI.
WE'RE GOING TO PLAY THIS AT A GALA CONCERT?
THIS IS SO PLAIN.
NORMALLY YOU'D DO SOMETHING BIGGER... MORE SPECTACULAR.
THAT'S OKAY; NOBODY'S GONNA BE THERE TO SEE US ANYWAY.
THIS WAY WE KNOW NOBODY'LL BE PLAYING THE SAME THING.
AND WE'LL STAND OUT FOR HAVING SUCH SUBDUED, REFINED TASTE.
THAT'S THE POINT OF A GALA CONCERT, RIGHT? TO STAND OUT.
F.Kreisler
LIEBESLEID
F. Kreisler
LOVE'S SO

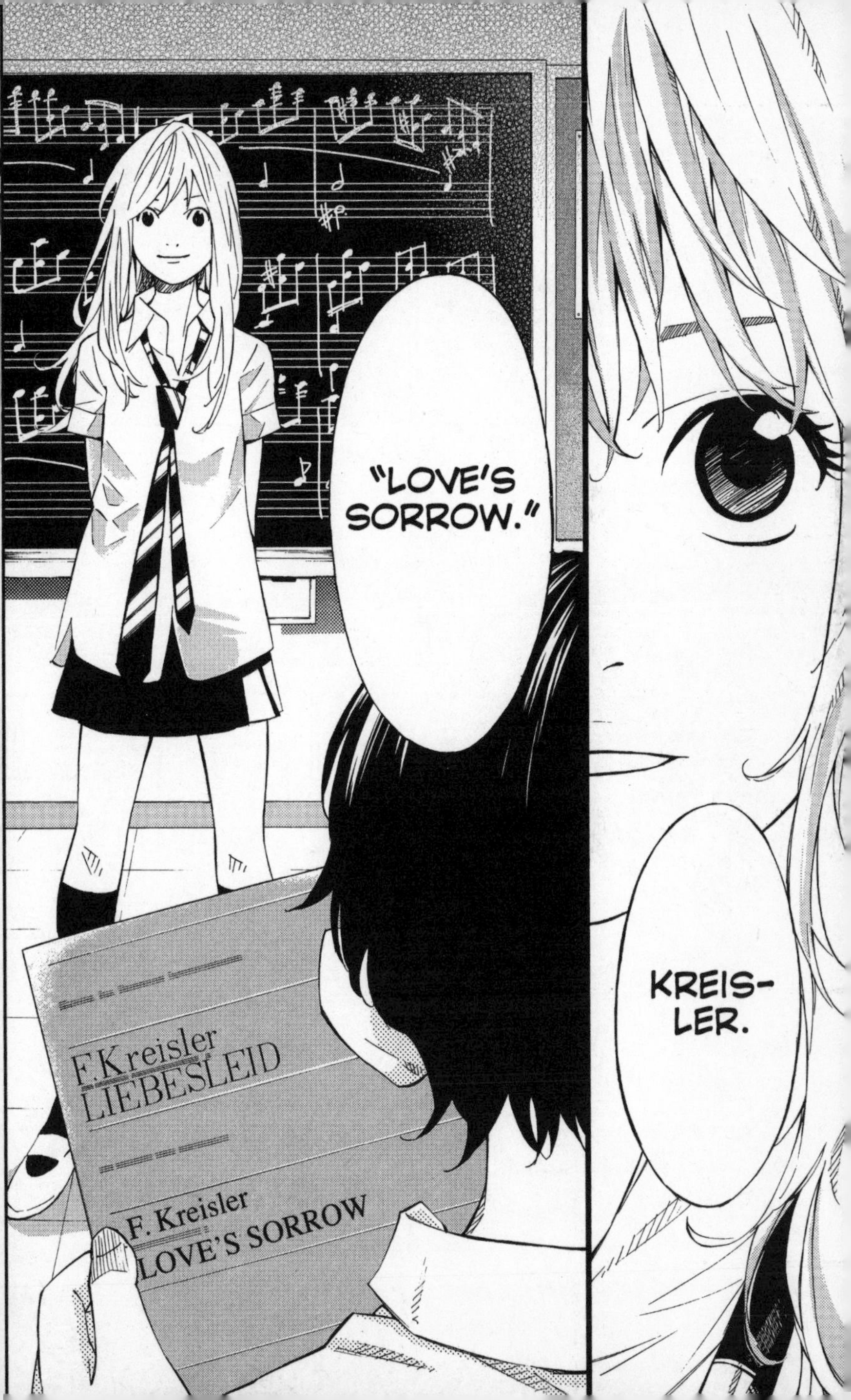
KREIS-
LER.
"LOVE'S
SORROW."
F.Kreisler
LIEBESLEID
F. Kreisler
LOVE'S SORROW

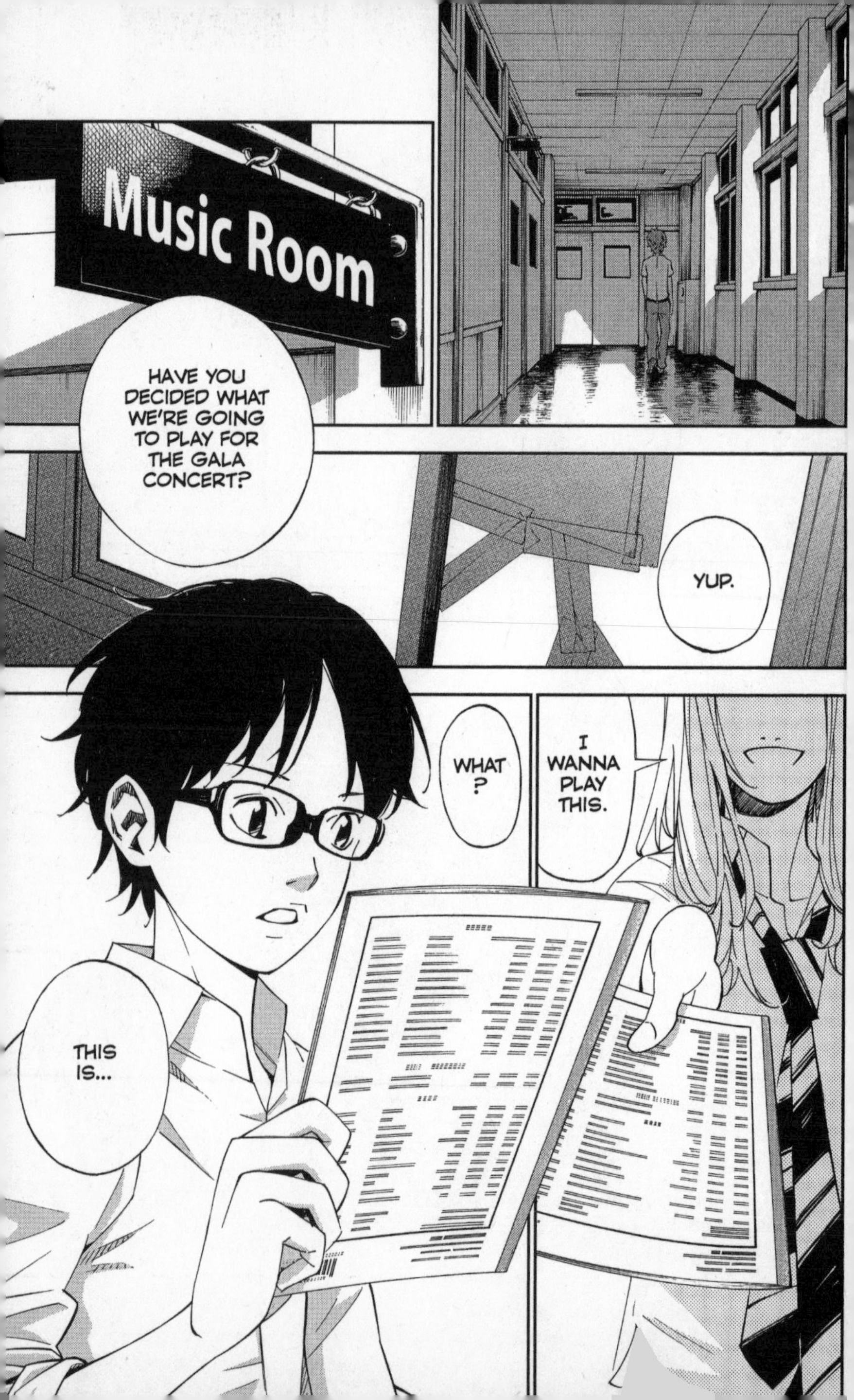
Music Room
HAVE YOU DECIDED WHAT WE'RE GOING TO PLAY FOR THE GALA CONCERT?
YUP.
I WANNA PLAY THIS.
WHAT?
THIS IS...

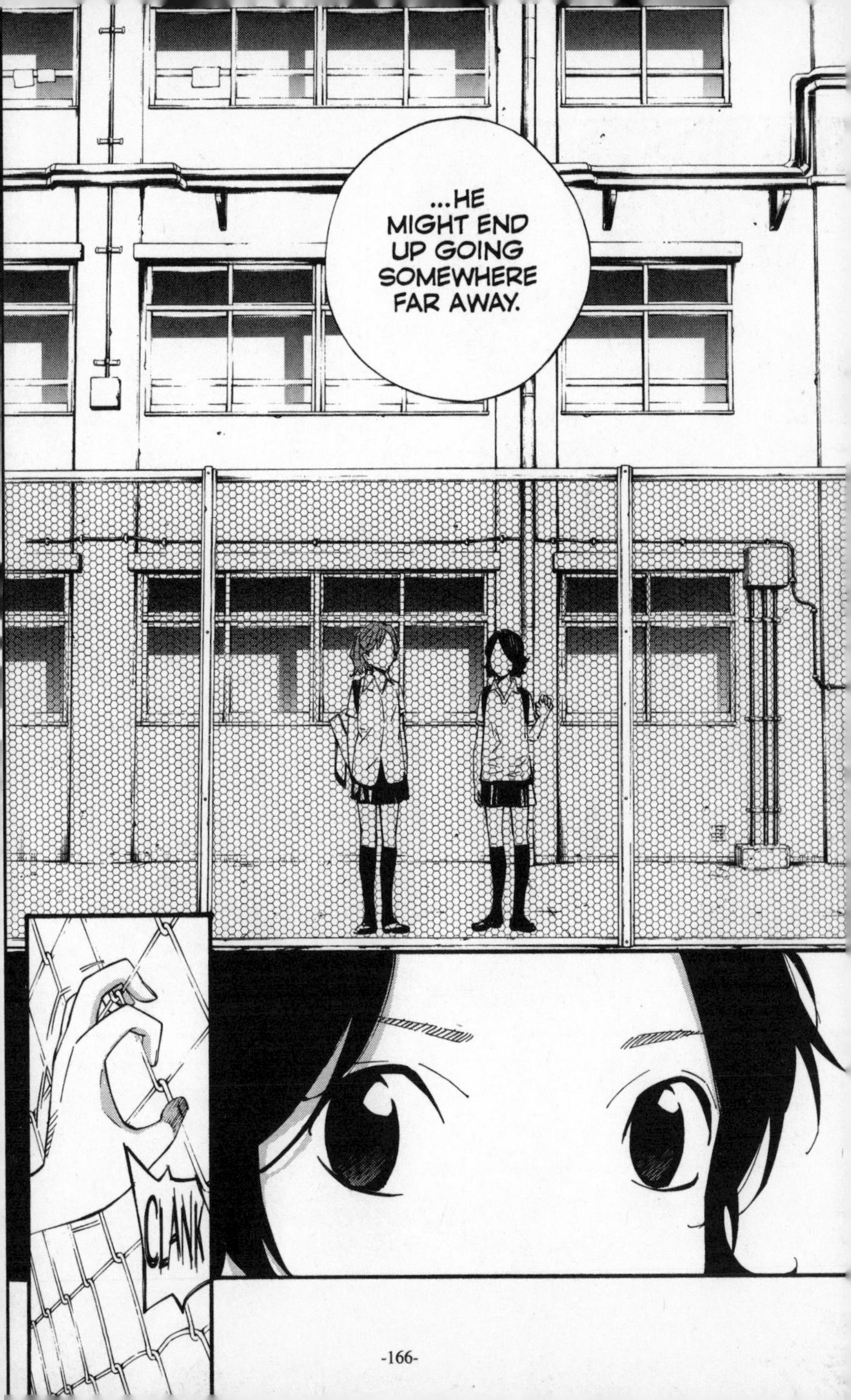
...HE MIGHT END UP GOING SOMEWHERE FAR AWAY.
CLANK

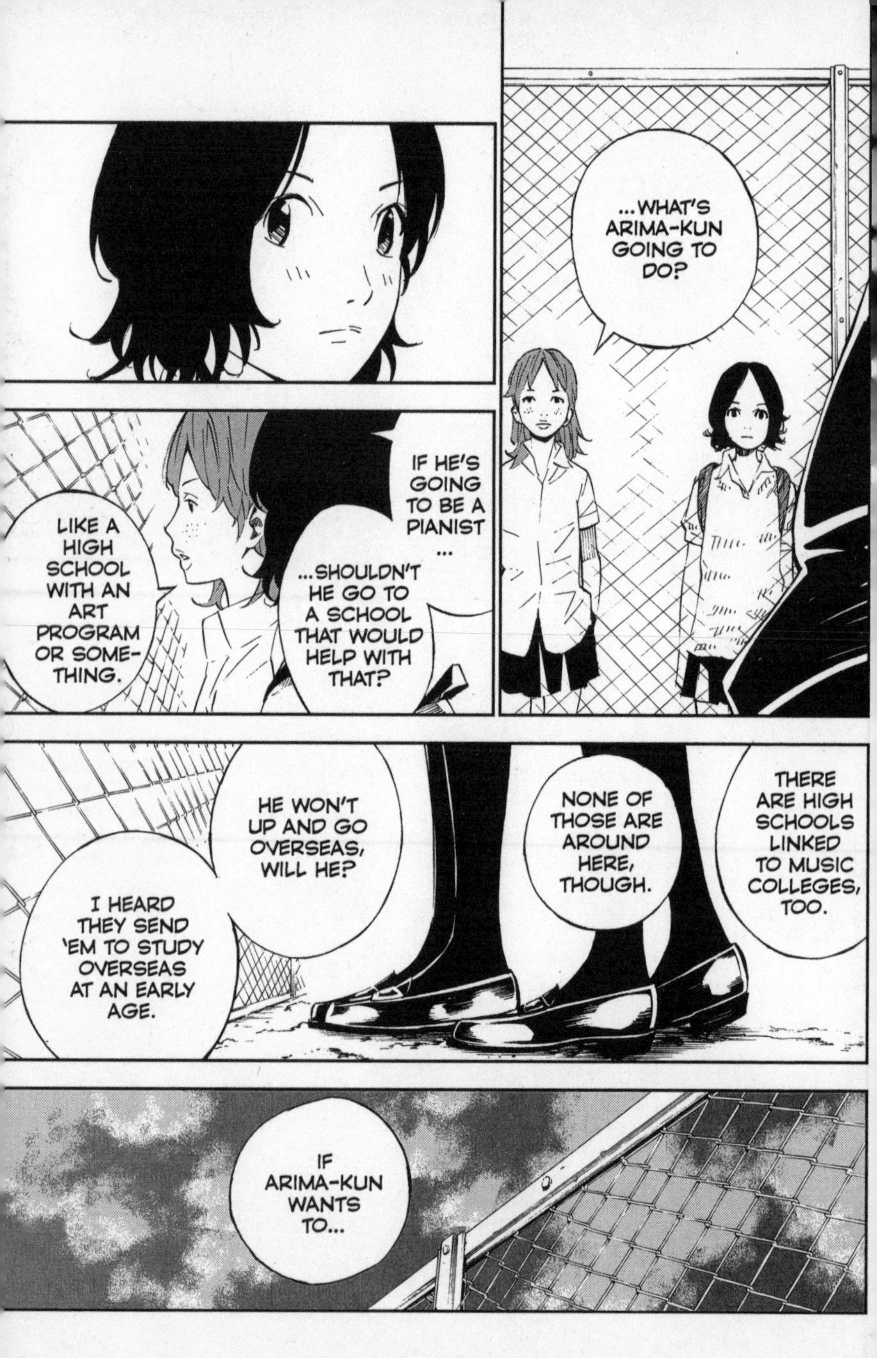
...WHAT'S ARIMA-KUN GOING TO DO?
IF HE'S GOING TO BE A PIANIST...
...SHOULDN'T HE GO TO A SCHOOL THAT WOULD HELP WITH THAT?
LIKE A HIGH SCHOOL WITH AN ART PROGRAM OR SOME-THING.
THERE ARE HIGH SCHOOLS LINKED TO MUSIC COLLEGES, TOO.
NONE OF THOSE ARE AROUND HERE, THOUGH.
HE WON'T UP AND GO OVERSEAS, WILL HE?
I HEARD THEY SEND 'EM TO STUDY OVERSEAS AT AN EARLY AGE.
IF ARIMA-KUN WANTS TO...

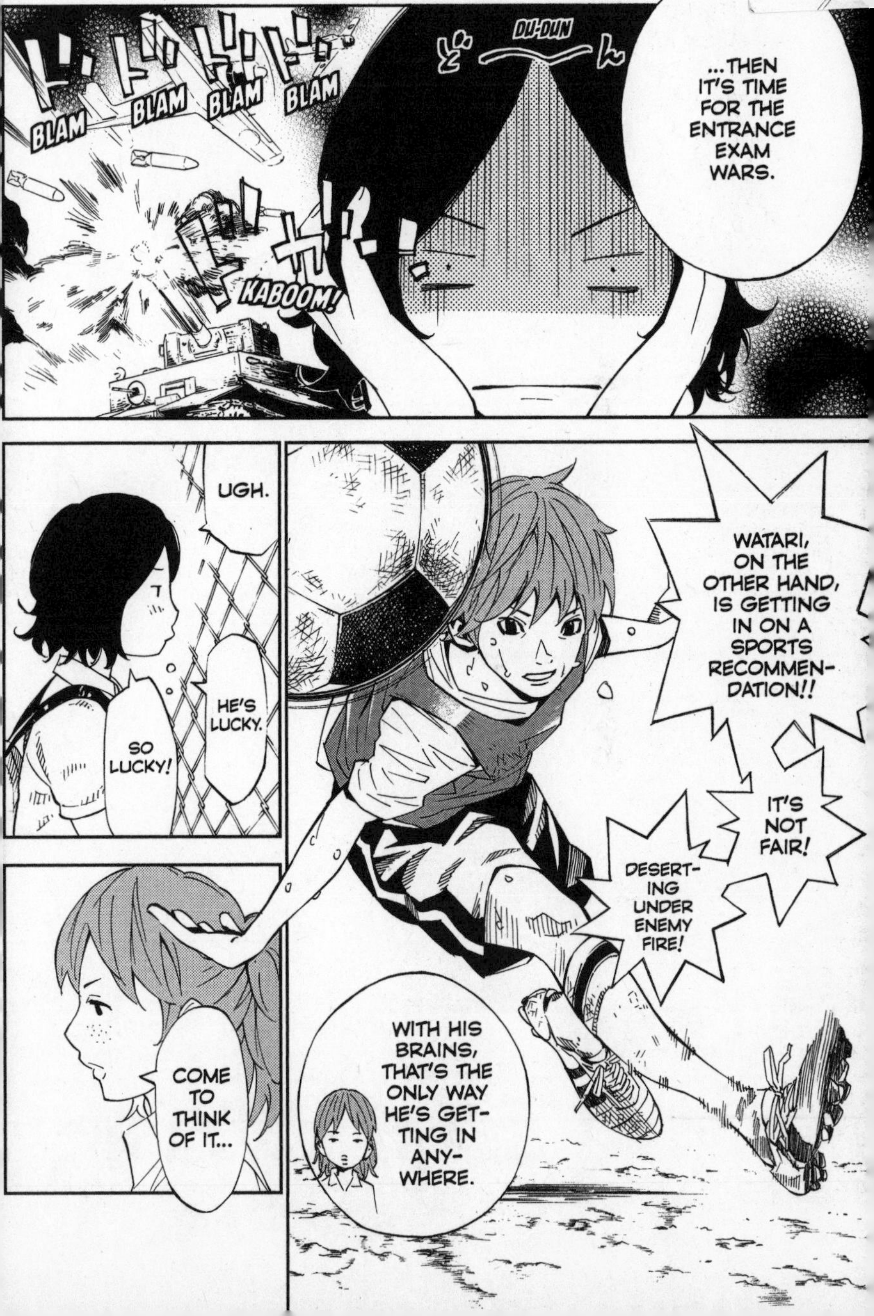
...THEN IT'S TIME FOR THE ENTRANCE EXAM WARS.
DU-DUN
BLAM BLAM BLAM BLAM
KABOOM!
WATARI, ON THE OTHER HAND, IS GETTING IN ON A SPORTS RECOMMENDATION!!
IT'S NOT FAIR!
DESERTING UNDER ENEMY FIRE!
WITH HIS BRAINS, THAT'S THE ONLY WAY HE'S GETTING IN ANYWHERE.
UGH.
HE'S LUCKY.
SO LUCKY!
COME TO THINK OF IT...

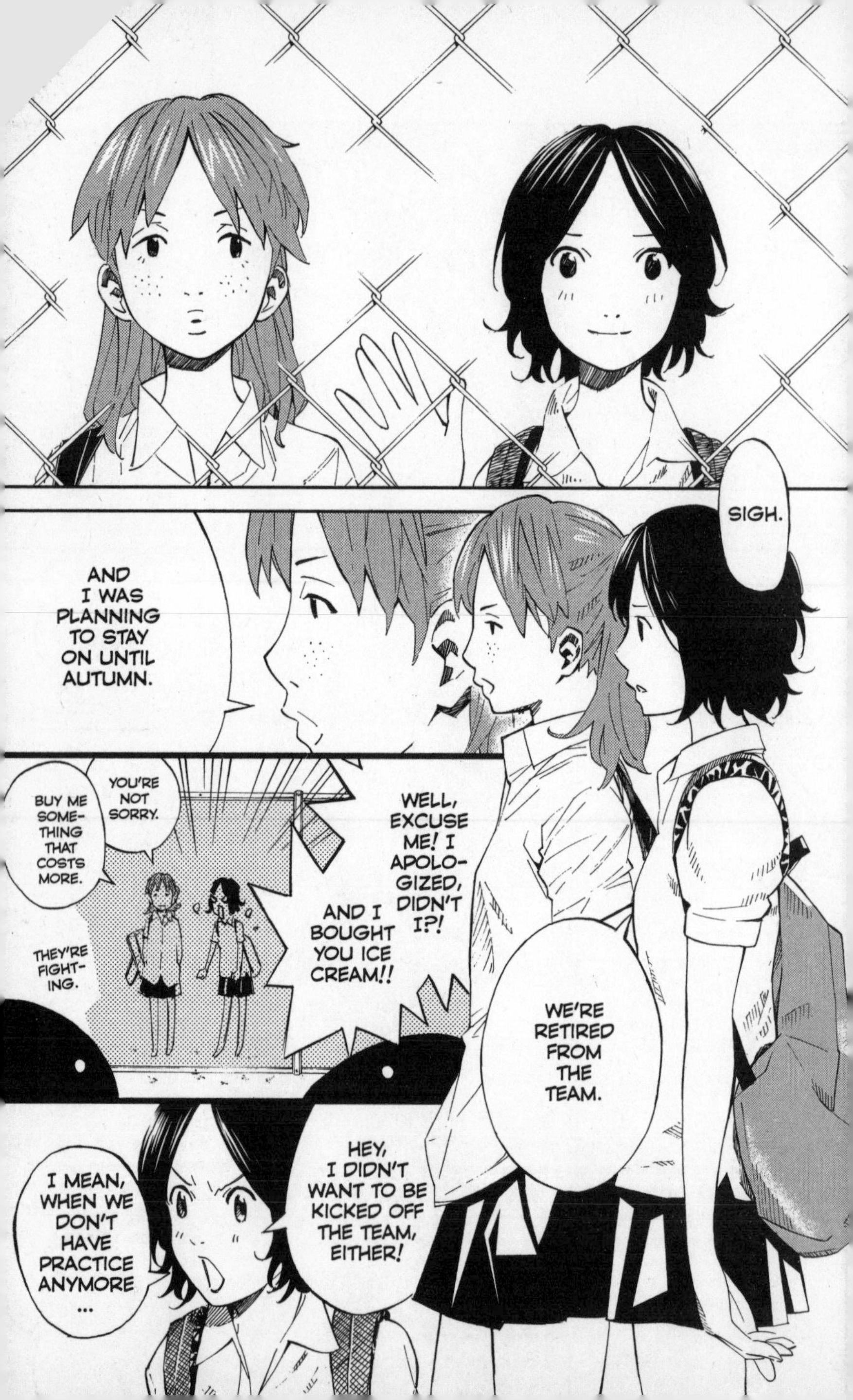
SIGH.
AND I WAS PLANNING TO STAY ON UNTIL AUTUMN.
WE'RE RETIRED FROM THE TEAM.
WELL, EXCUSE ME! I APOLOGIZED, DIDN'T I?!
AND I BOUGHT YOU ICE CREAM!!
YOU'RE NOT SORRY.
BUY ME SOME-THING THAT COSTS MORE.
THEY'RE FIGHT-ING.
HEY, I DIDN'T WANT TO BE KICKED OFF THE TEAM, EITHER!
I MEAN, WHEN WE DON'T HAVE PRACTICE ANYMORE ...

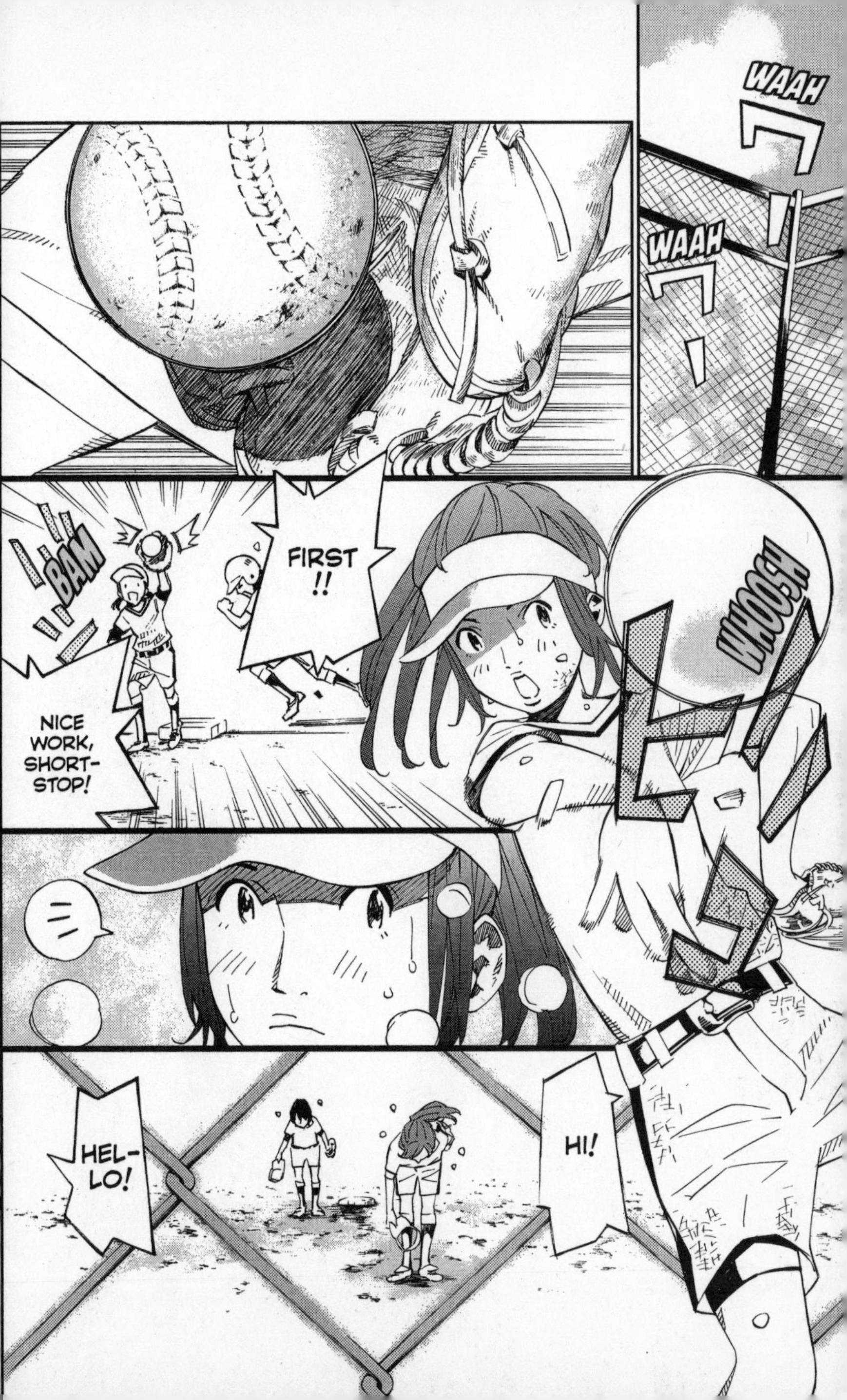
WAAH
WAAH
WHOOSH
FIRST !!
BAM
NICE WORK, SHORT-STOP!
HI!
HEL-LO!

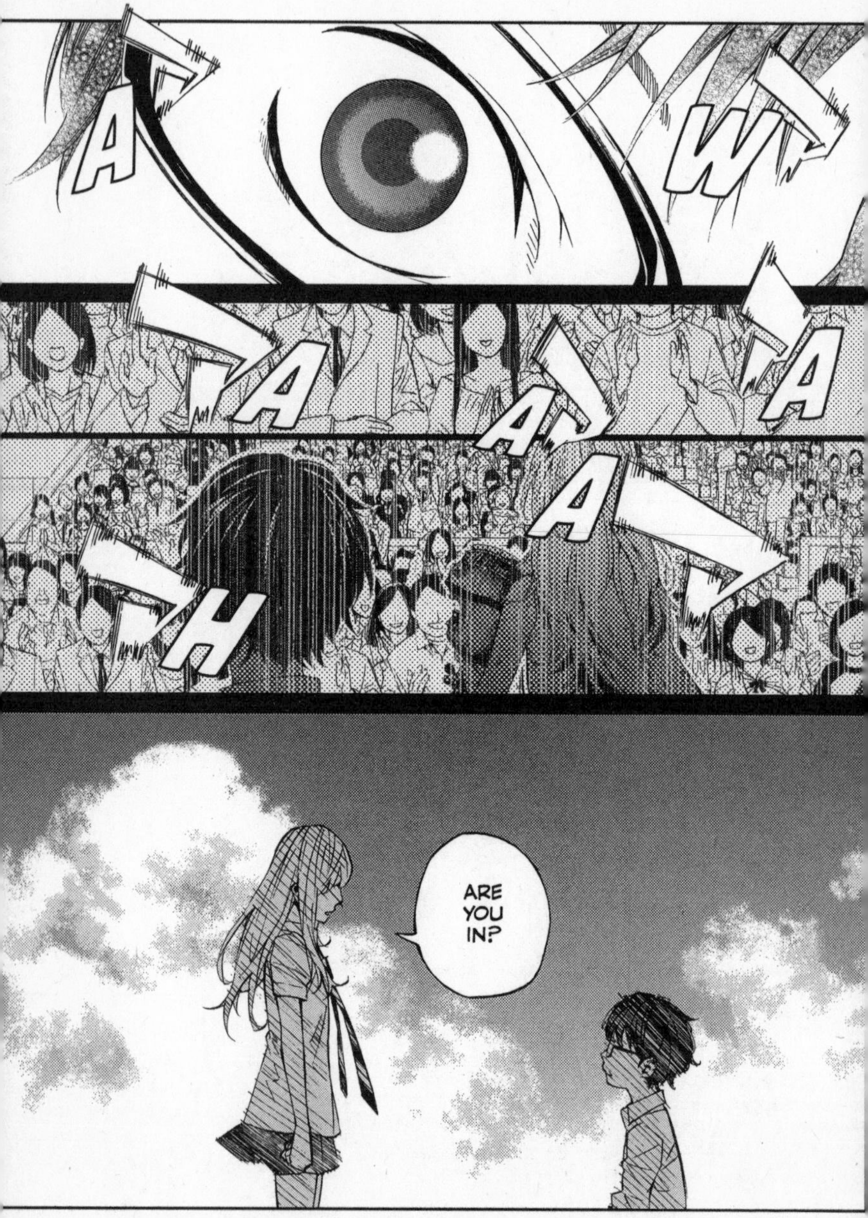
W
A
A
A
A
A
A
H
ARE YOU IN?

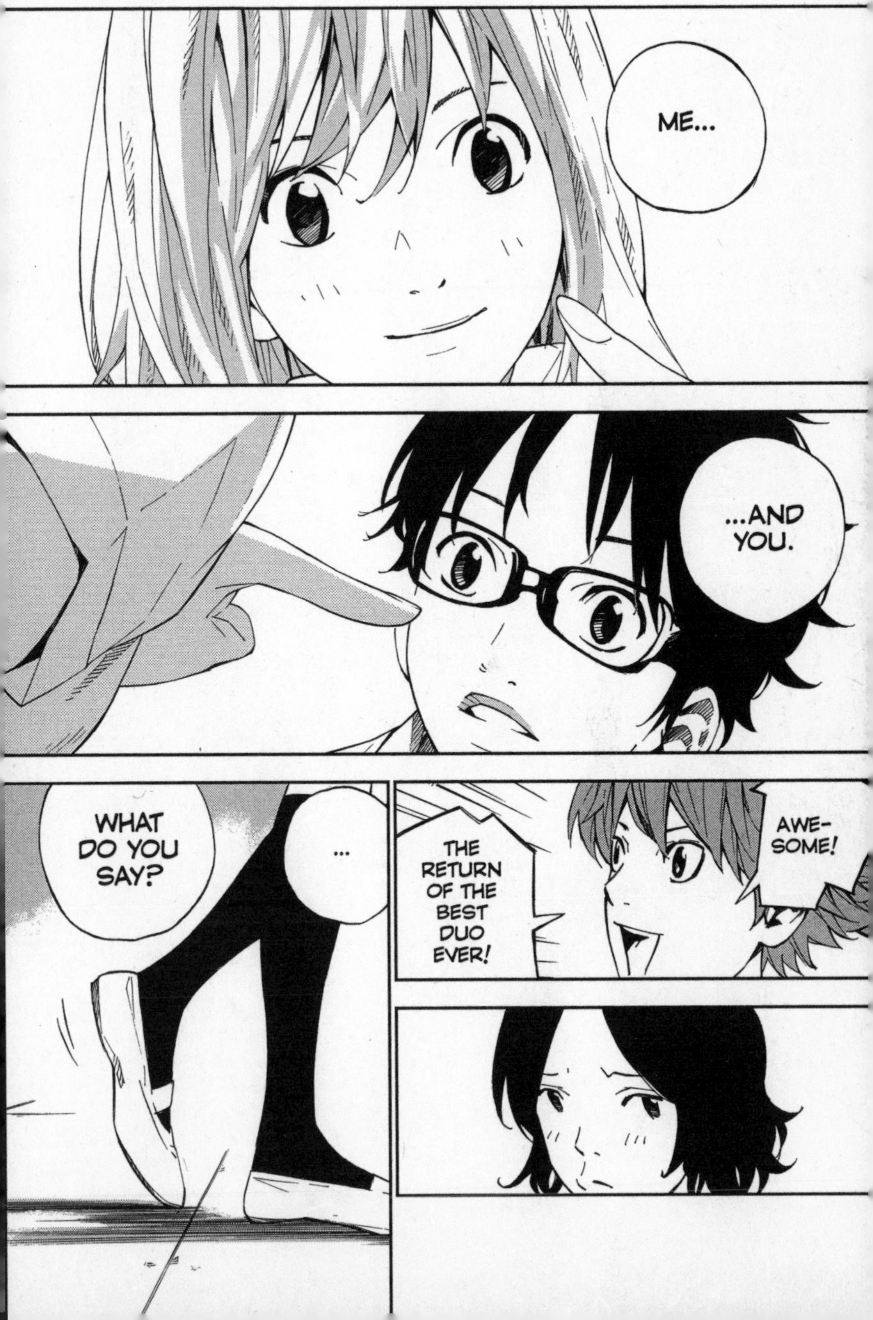
ME...
...AND YOU.
AWE-SOME!
THE RETURN OF THE BEST DUO EVER!
...
WHAT DO YOU SAY?

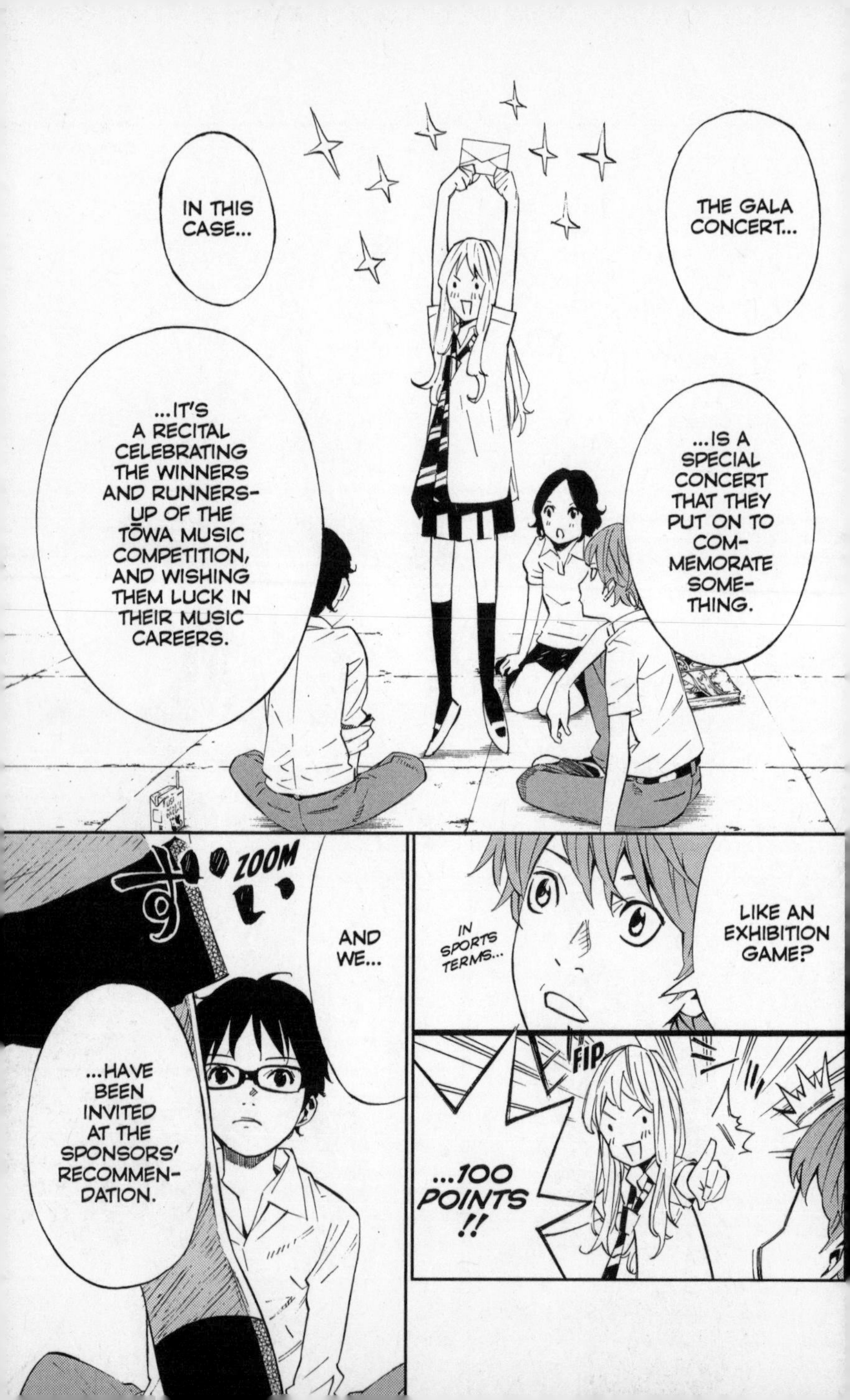
THE GALA CONCERT...
IN THIS CASE...
...IS A SPECIAL CONCERT THAT THEY PUT ON TO COM-MEMORATE SOME-THING.
...IT'S A RECITAL CELEBRATING THE WINNERS AND RUNNERS-UP OF THE TŌWA MUSIC COMPETITION, AND WISHING THEM LUCK IN THEIR MUSIC CAREERS.
IN SPORTS TERMS...
LIKE AN EXHIBITION GAME?
FIP
...100 POINTS !!
ZOOM
AND WE...
...HAVE BEEN INVITED AT THE SPONSORS' RECOMMEN-DATION.

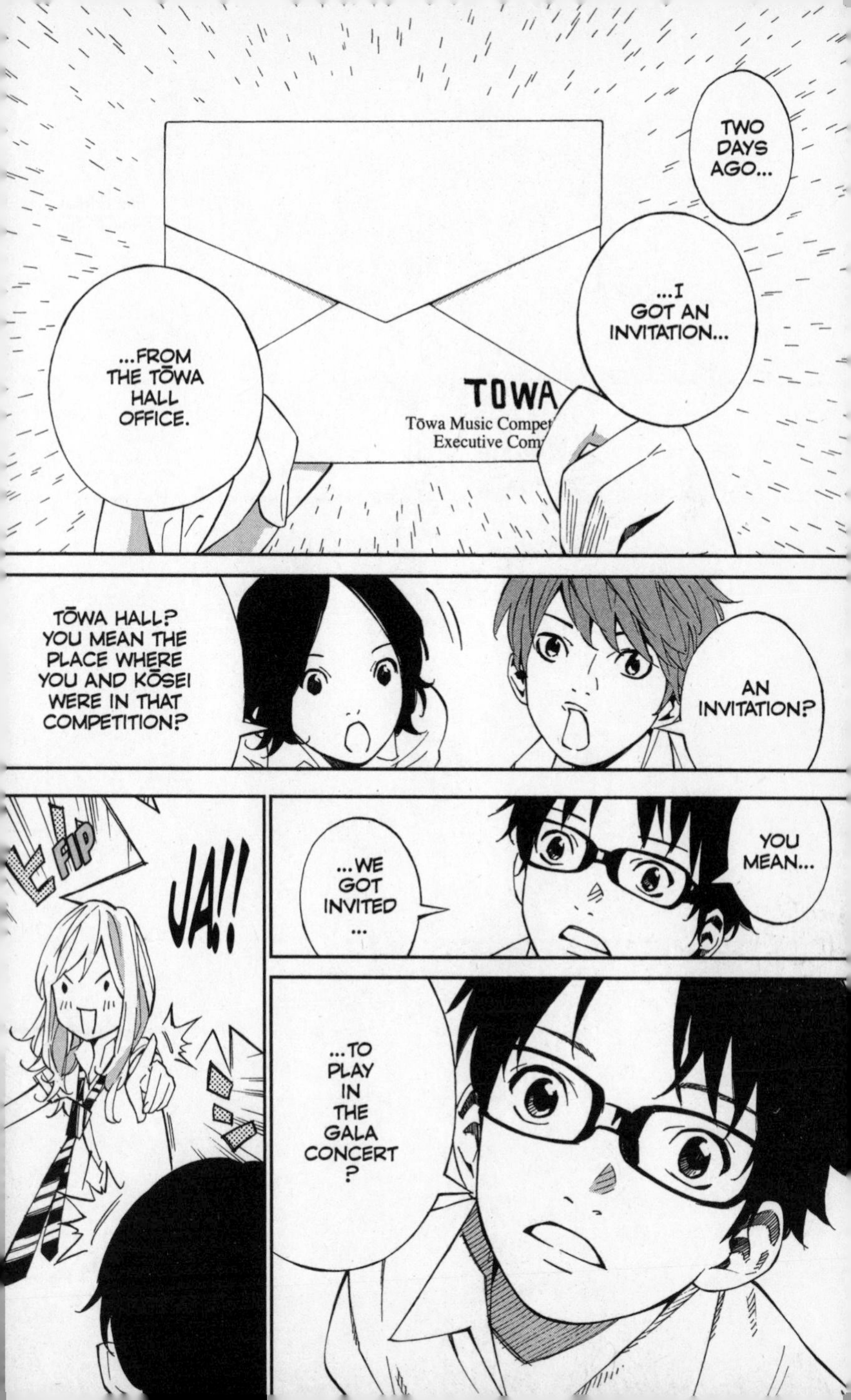
TWO DAYS AGO...
...I GOT AN INVITATION...
...FROM THE TŌWA HALL OFFICE.
TOWA
Tōwa Music Compet
Executive Com
AN INVITATION?
TŌWA HALL? YOU MEAN THE PLACE WHERE YOU AND KŌSEI WERE IN THAT COMPETITION?
YOU MEAN...
...WE GOT INVITED ...
...TO PLAY IN THE GALA CONCERT?
FIP
JA!!

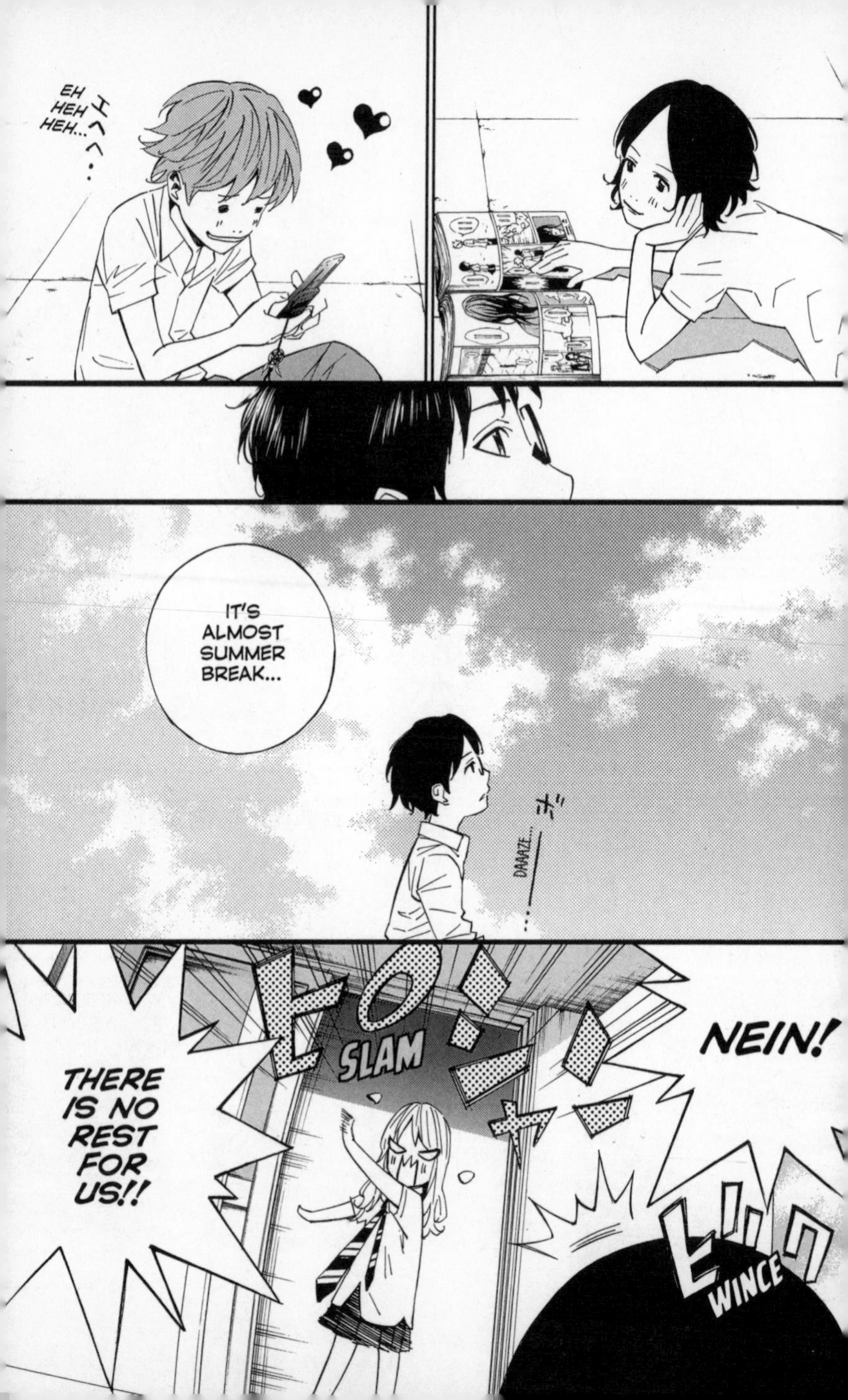
EH HEH HEH...
IT'S ALMOST SUMMER BREAK...
DAAAZE...
NEIN!
WINCE
SLAM
THERE IS NO REST FOR US!!

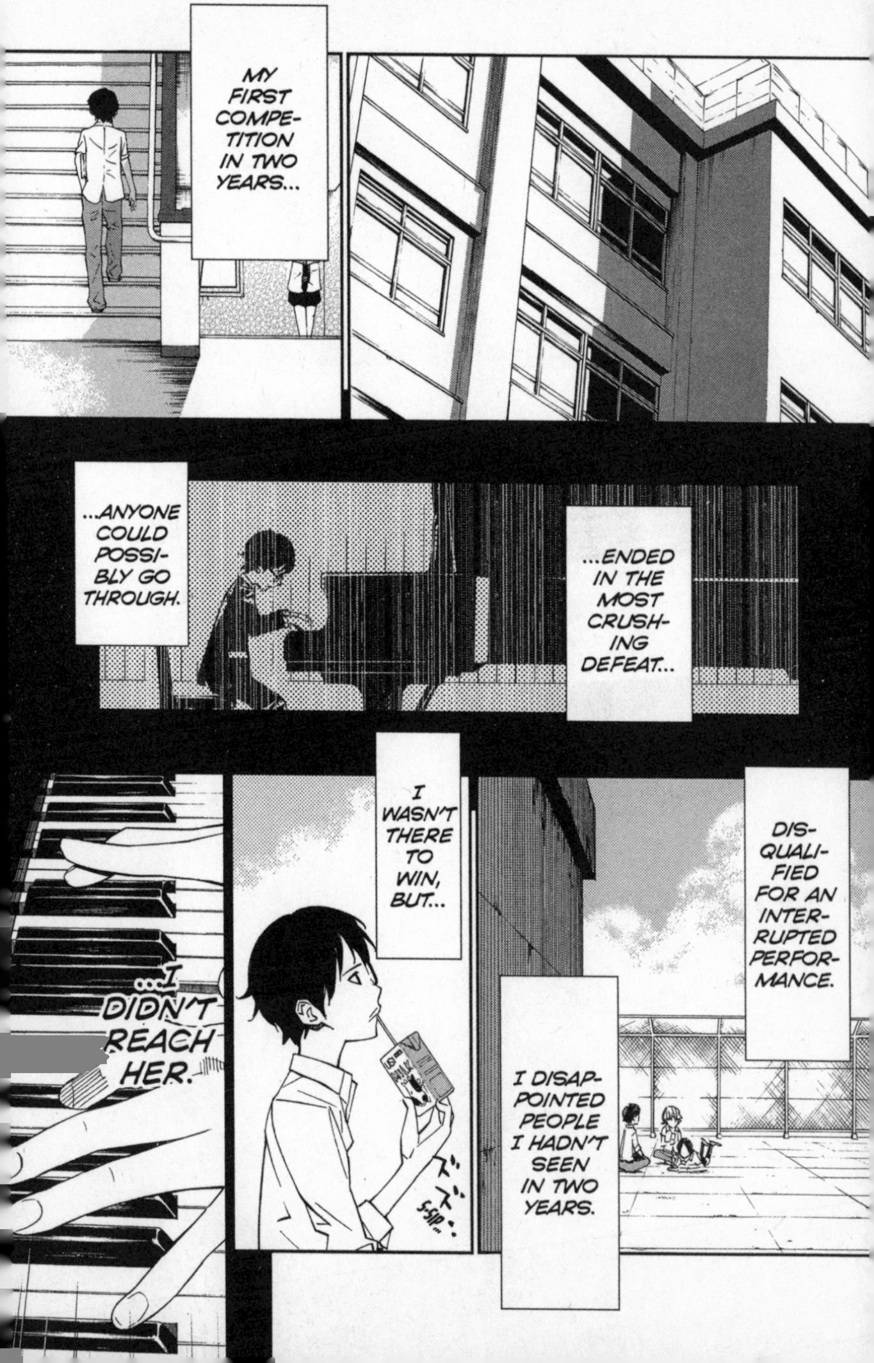
MY FIRST COMPETITION IN TWO YEARS...
...ENDED IN THE MOST CRUSHING DEFEAT...
...ANYONE COULD POSSIBLY GO THROUGH.
DISQUALIFIED FOR AN INTERRUPTED PERFORMANCE.
I DISAPPOINTED PEOPLE I HADN'T SEEN IN TWO YEARS.
I WASN'T THERE TO WIN, BUT...
S-SIP...
...I DIDN'T REACH HER.

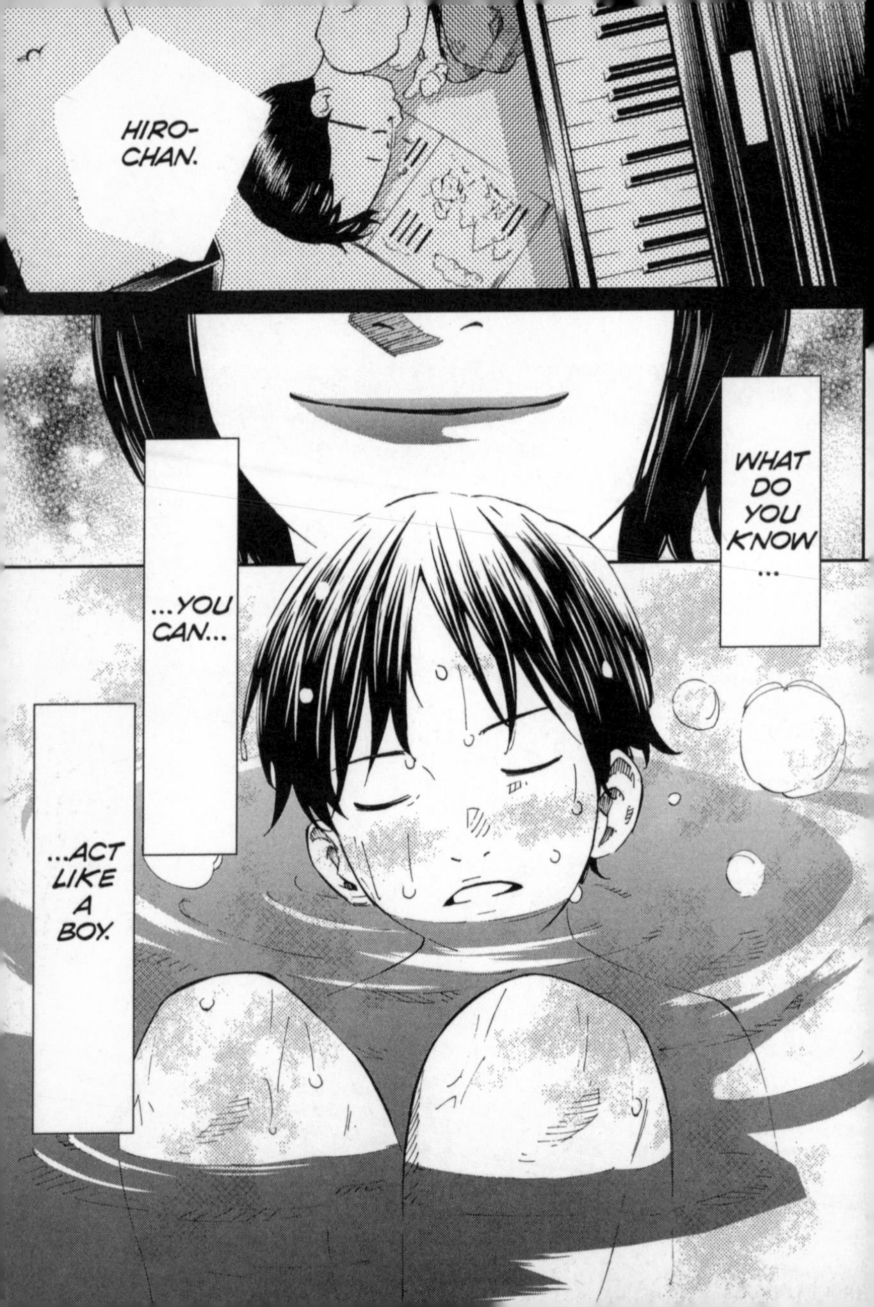
HIRO-CHAN.
WHAT DO YOU KNOW...
...YOU CAN...
...ACT LIKE A BOY.

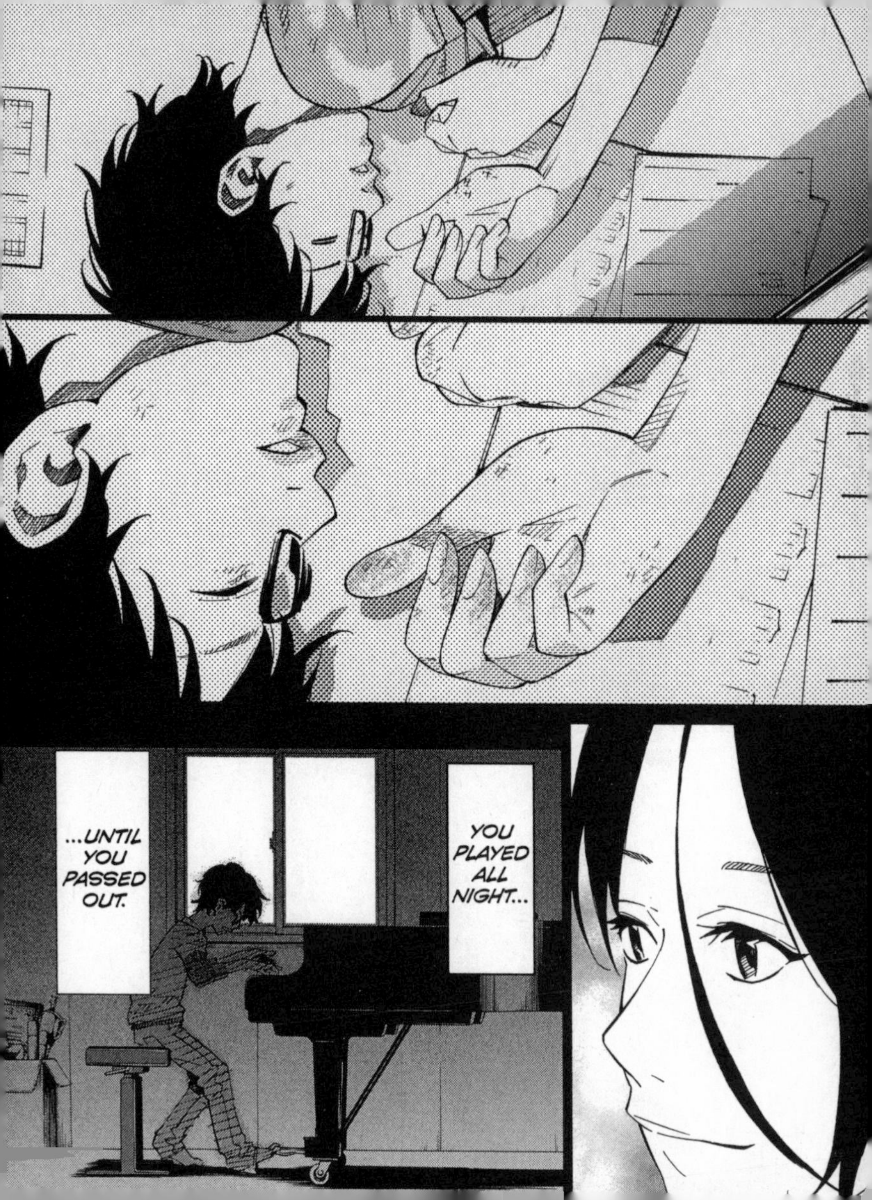
YOU PLAYED ALL NIGHT...
...UNTIL YOU PASSED OUT.

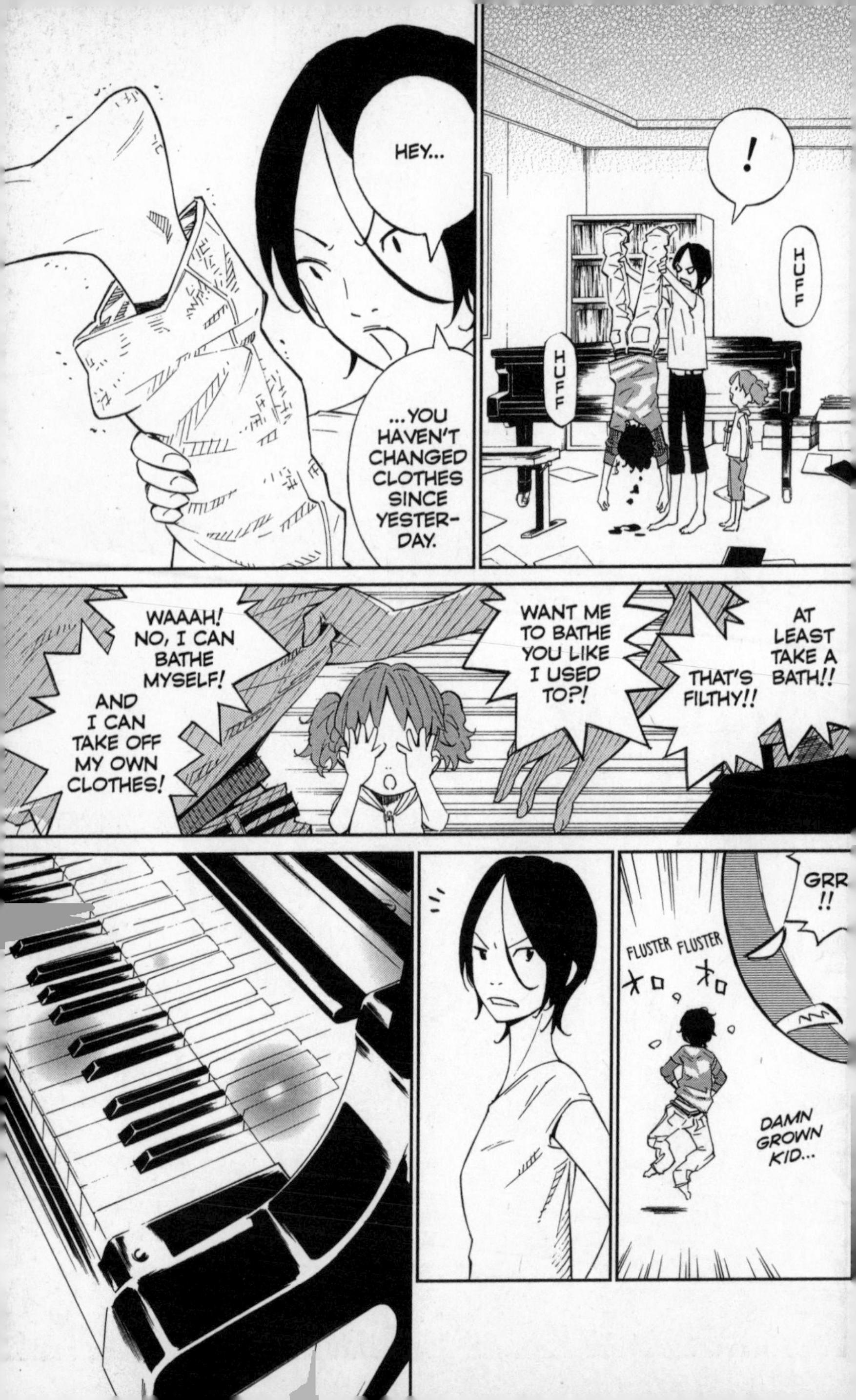
!
HUFF
HUFF
HEY...
...YOU HAVEN'T CHANGED CLOTHES SINCE YESTER-DAY.
AT LEAST TAKE A BATH!!
THAT'S FILTHY!!
WANT ME TO BATHE YOU LIKE I USED TO?!
WAAAH! NO, I CAN BATHE MYSELF!
AND I CAN TAKE OFF MY OWN CLOTHES!
GRR !!
FLUSTER FLUSTER
オロ オロ
DAMN GROWN KID...

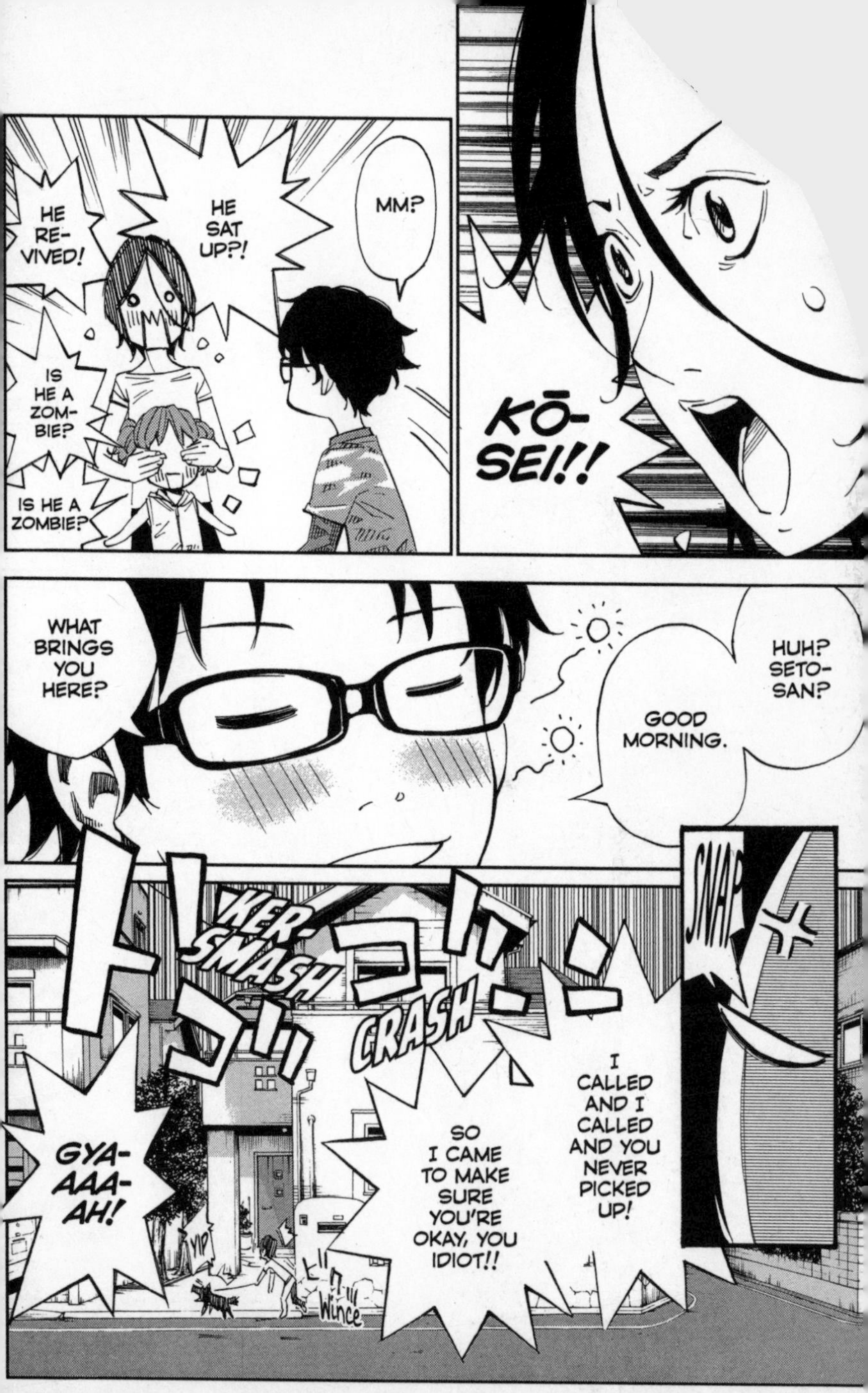
KŌ-SEI!!
MM?
HE SAT UP?!
HE RE-VIVED!
IS HE A ZOM-BIE?
IS HE A ZOMBIE?
HUH? SETO-SAN?
GOOD MORNING.
WHAT BRINGS YOU HERE?
SNAP
KER-SMASH
CRASH
I CALLED AND I CALLED AND YOU NEVER PICKED UP!
SO I CAME TO MAKE SURE YOU'RE OKAY, YOU IDIOT!!
GYA-AAA-AH!
YIP
Wince

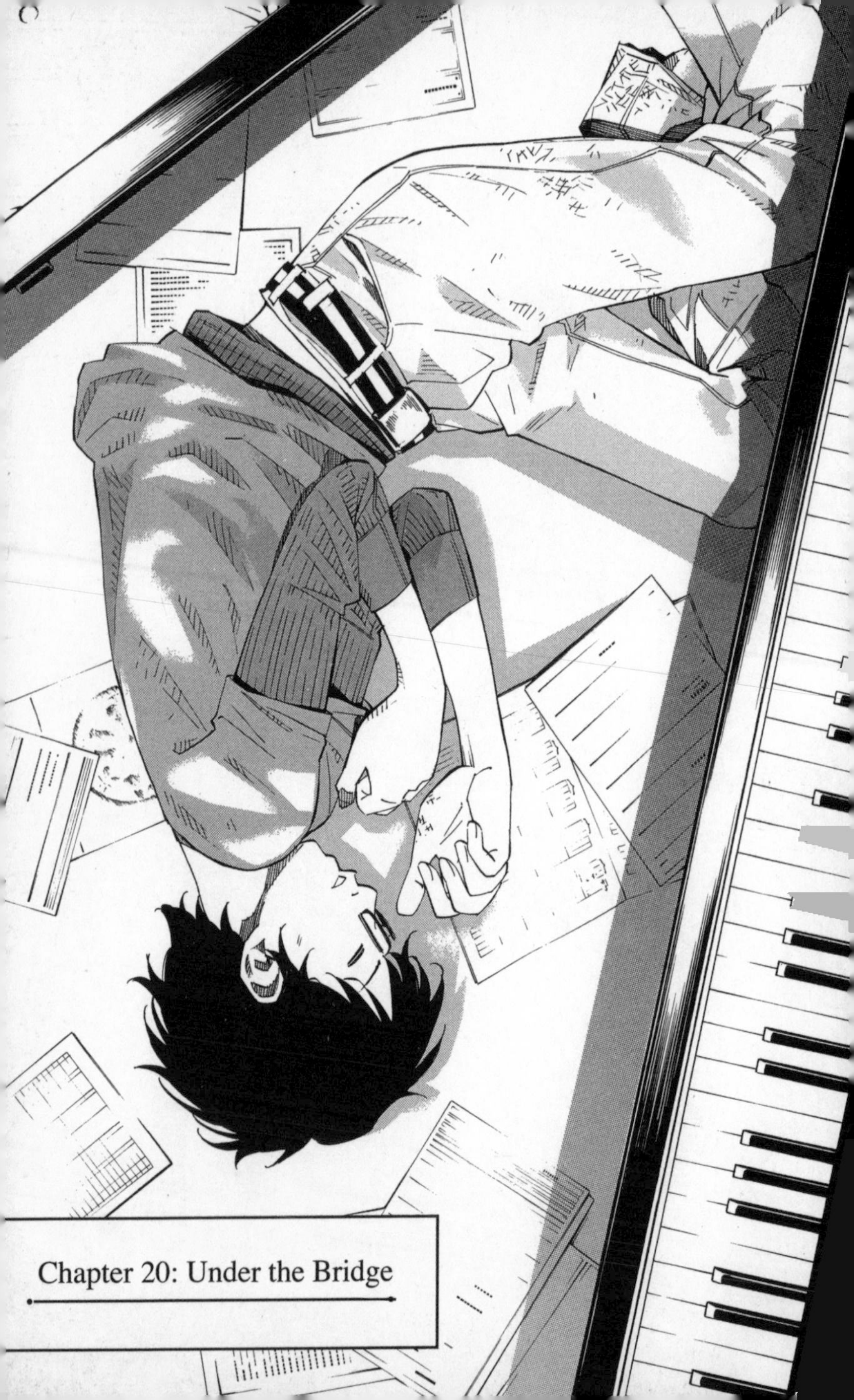

Chapter 20: Under the Bridge

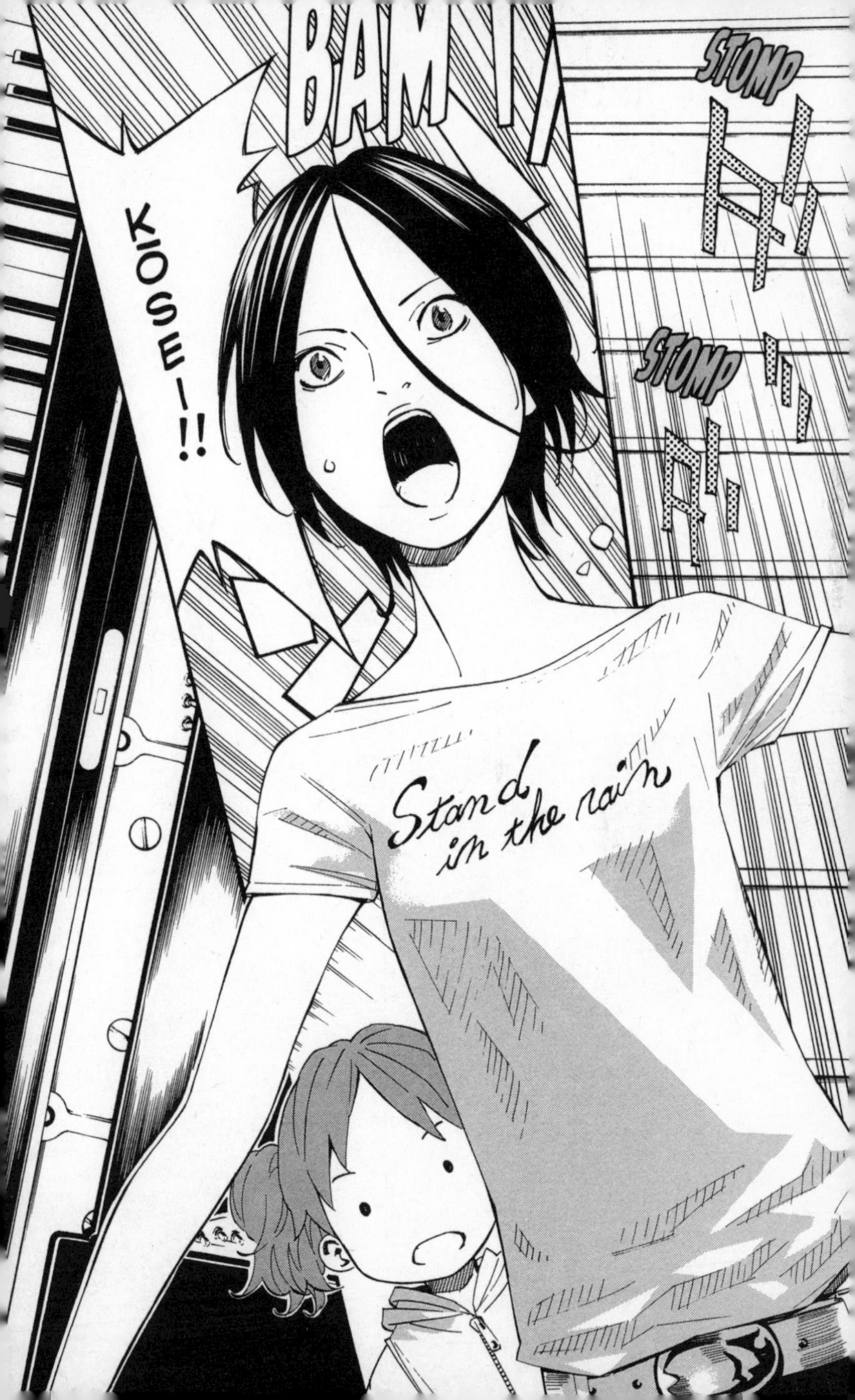
BAM!!
STOMP
STOMP
KOSEI!!
Stand in the rain

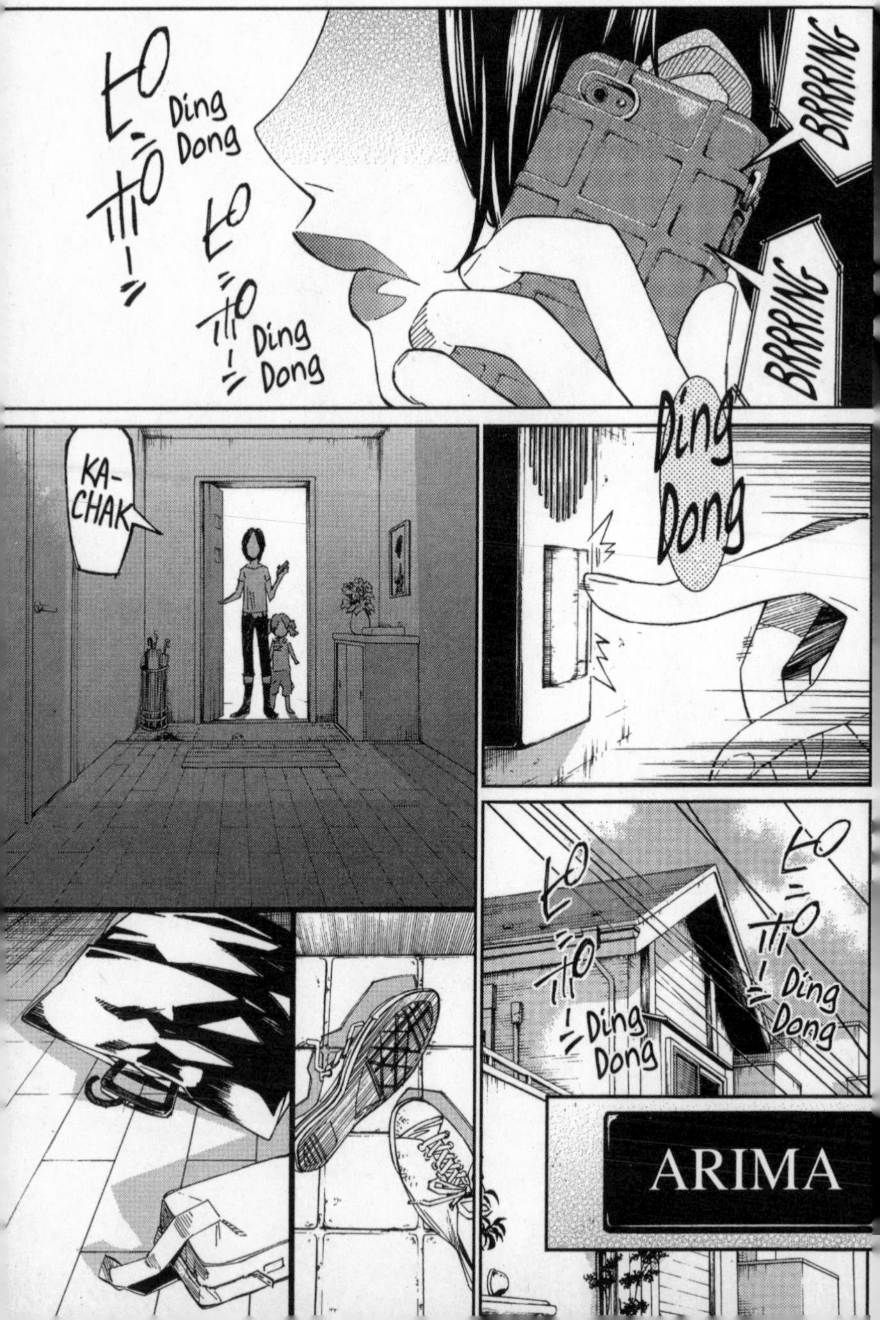
BRRRING
BRRRING
Ding Dong
Ding Dong
Ding Dong
KA-CHAK
Ding Dong
Ding Dong
ARIMA

Your Lie in April

I met the girl under full-bloomed cherry blossoms, and my fate has begun to change.

Your Lie in April

I met the girl under full-bloomed cherry blossoms, and my fate has begun to change.

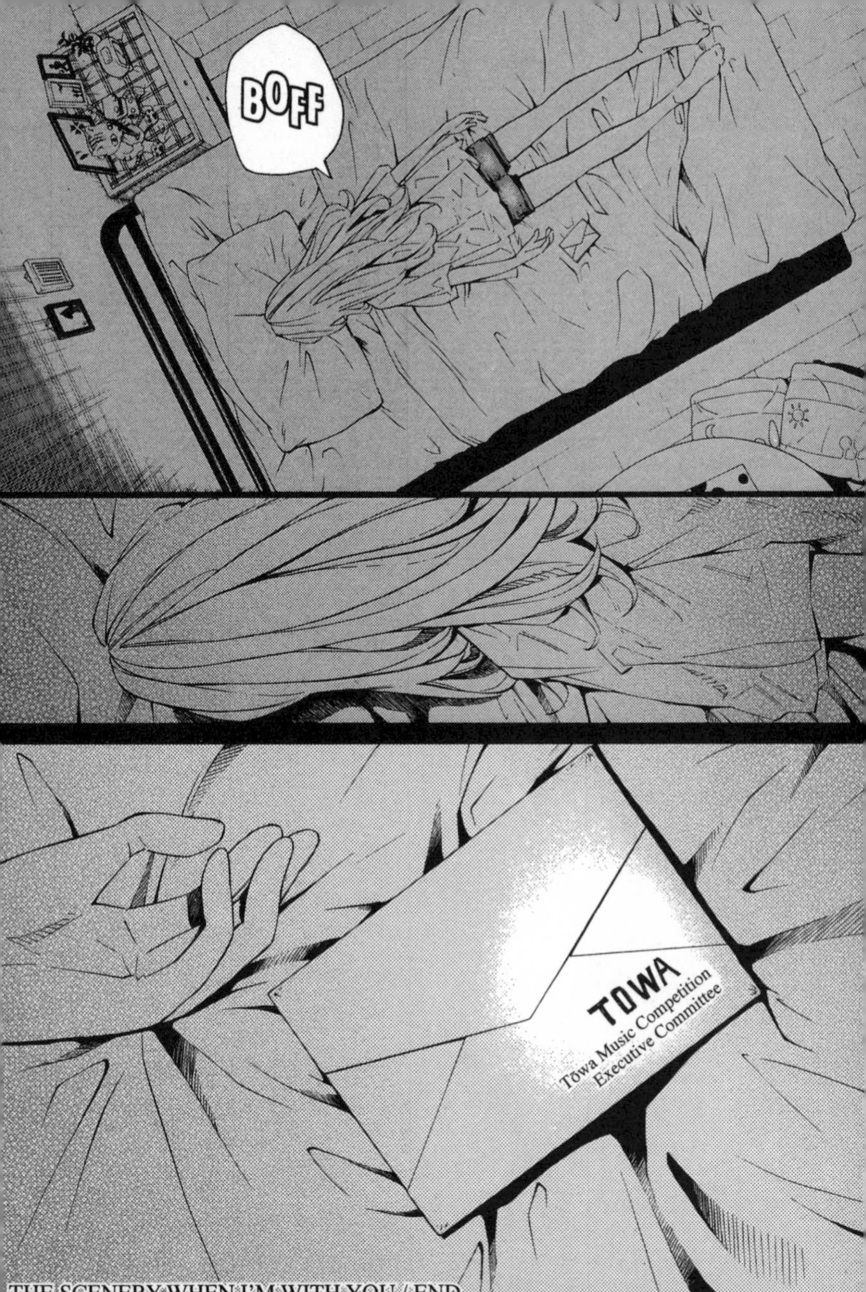
BOFF
TOWA
Tōwa Music Competition
Executive Committee

THE SCENERY WHEN I'M WITH YOU / END

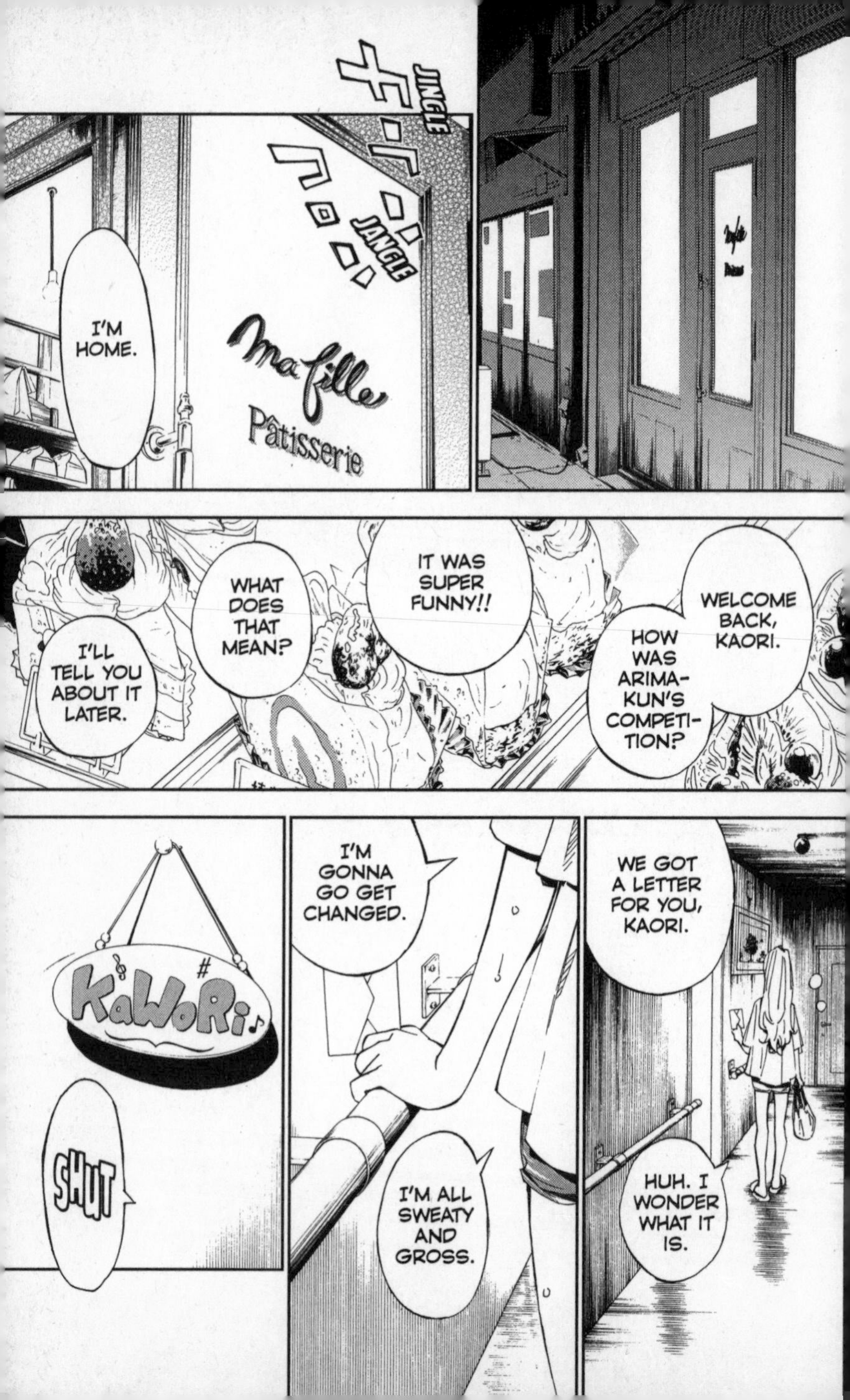
JINGLE
JANGLE
ma fille
Pâtisserie
I'M HOME.
WELCOME BACK, KAORI.
HOW WAS ARIMA-KUN'S COMPETITION?
IT WAS SUPER FUNNY!!
WHAT DOES THAT MEAN?
I'LL TELL YOU ABOUT IT LATER.
WE GOT A LETTER FOR YOU, KAORI.
HUH. I WONDER WHAT IT IS.
I'M GONNA GO GET CHANGED.
I'M ALL SWEATY AND GROSS.
KaWoRi
SHUT

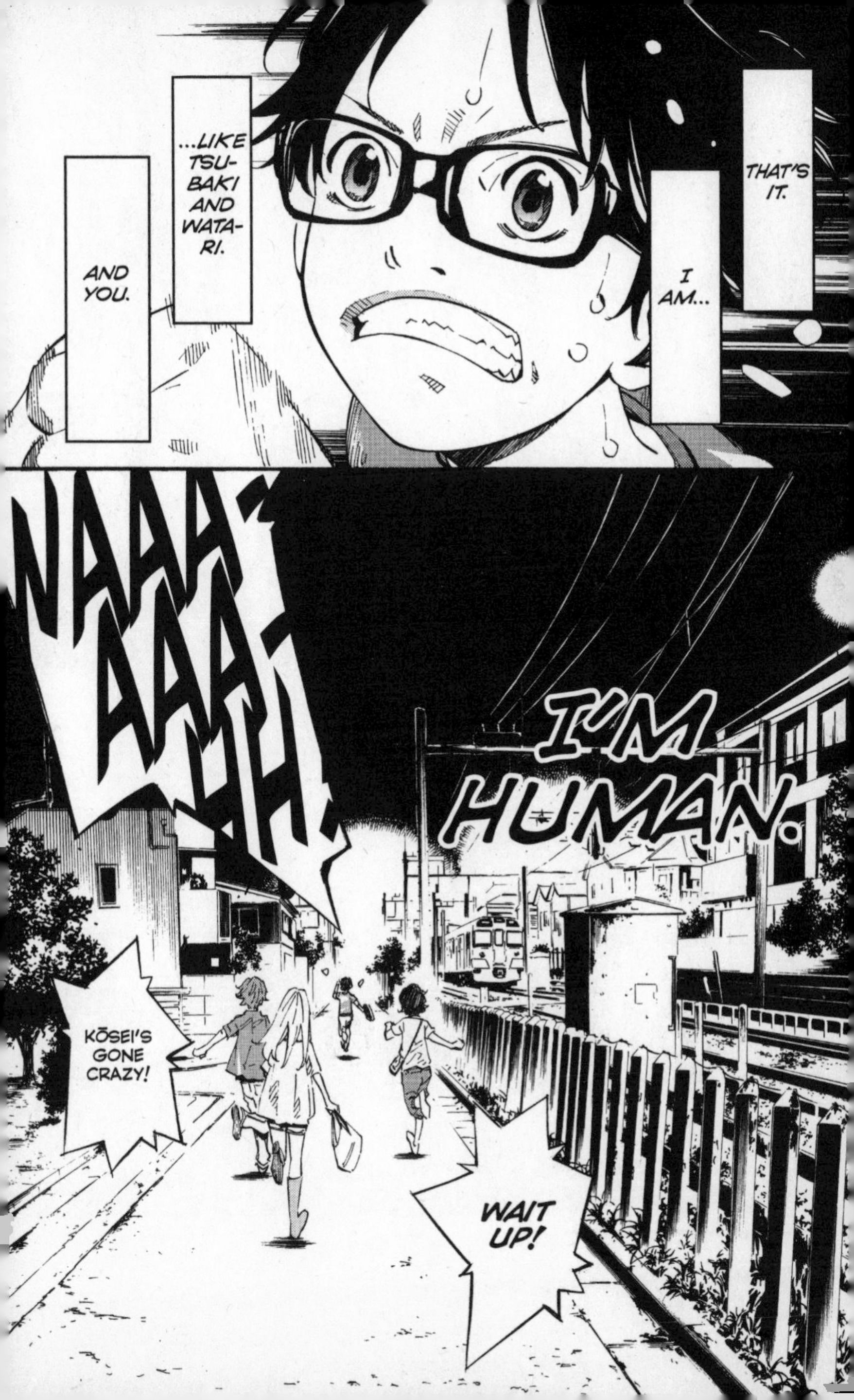
THAT'S IT.
I AM...
...LIKE TSUBAKI AND WATARI.
AND YOU.
I'M HUMAN.
NAAAAAAAH!
KŌSEI'S GONE CRAZY!
WAIT UP!

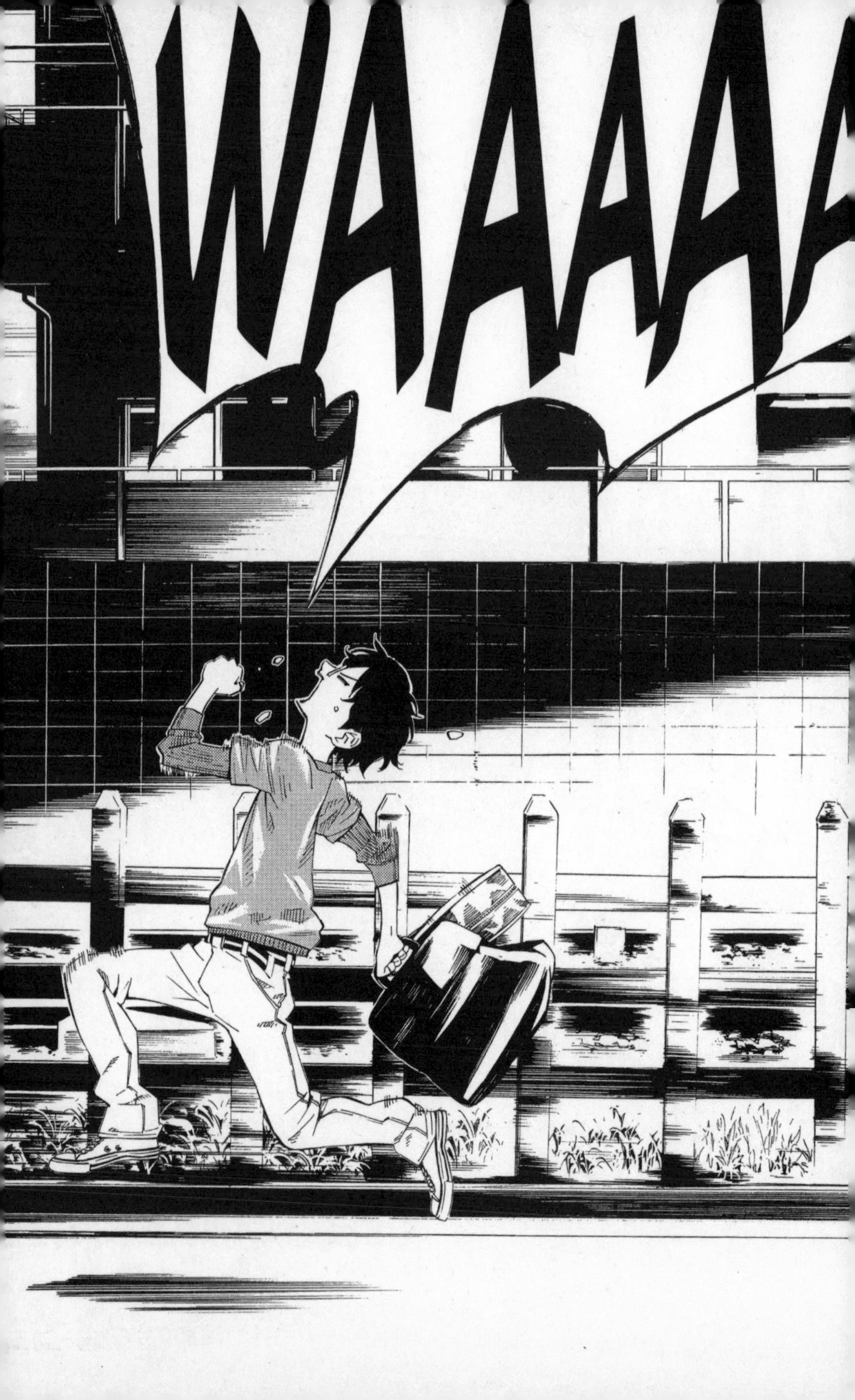
WAAAA

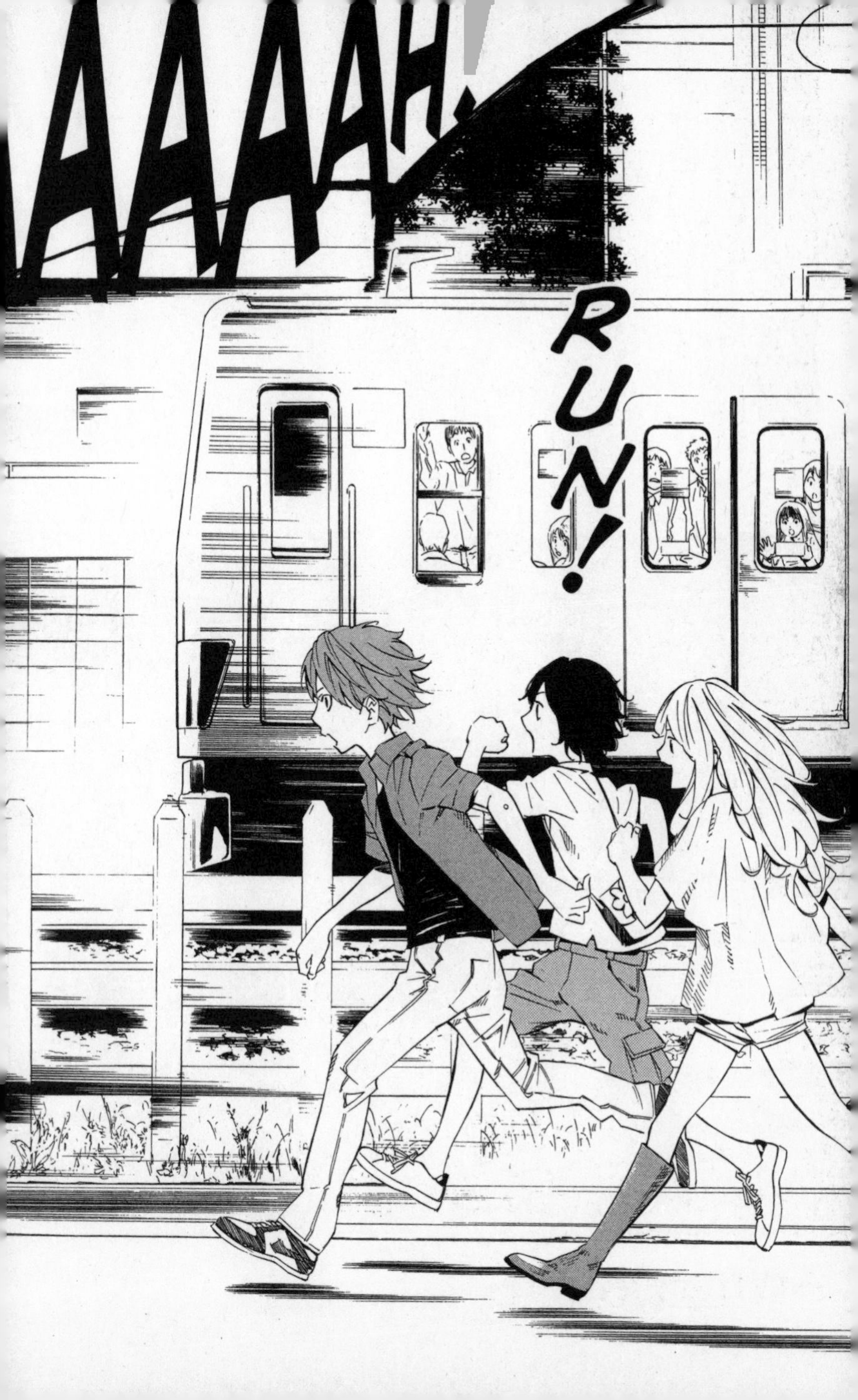
AAAAH!
RUN!

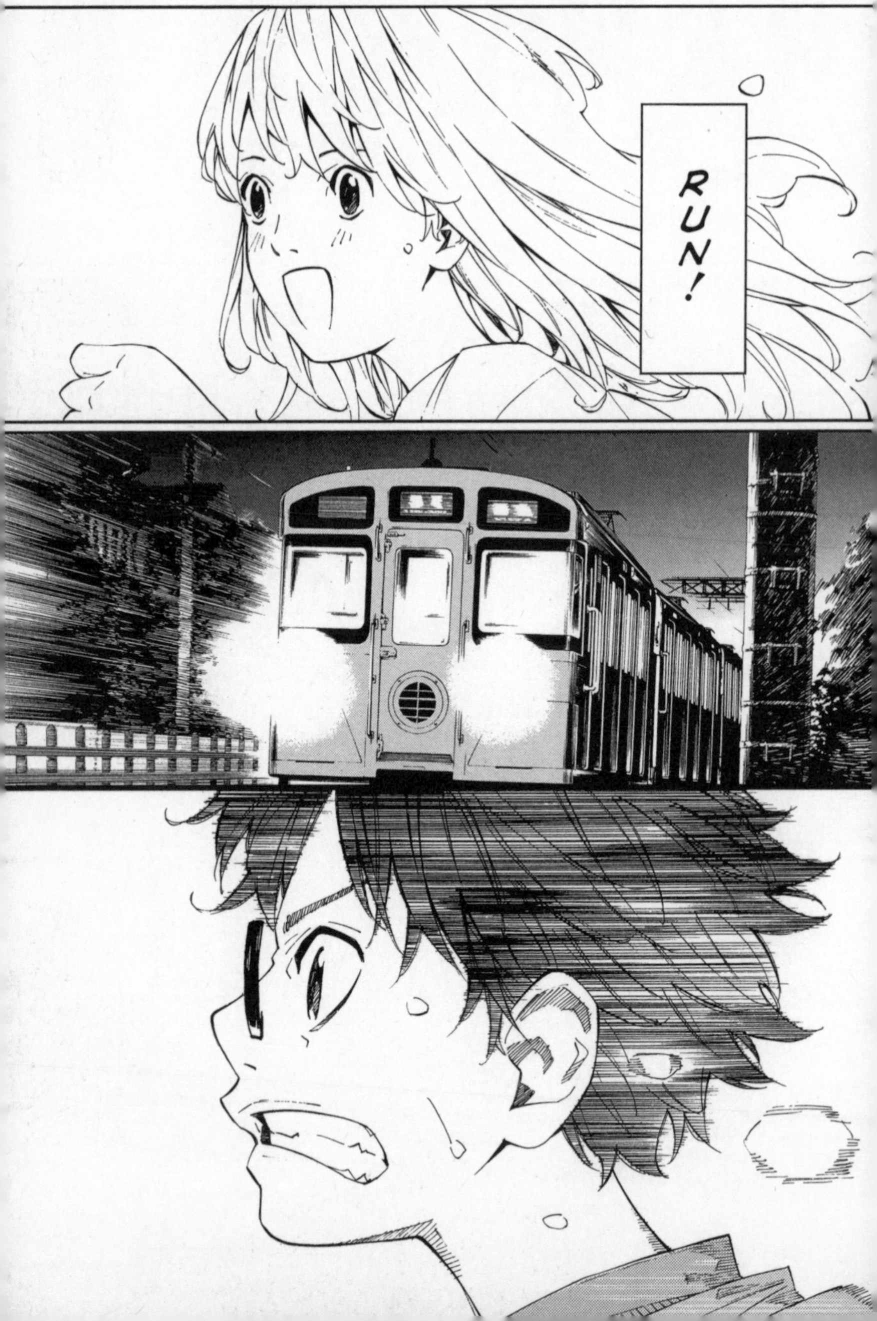
RUN!

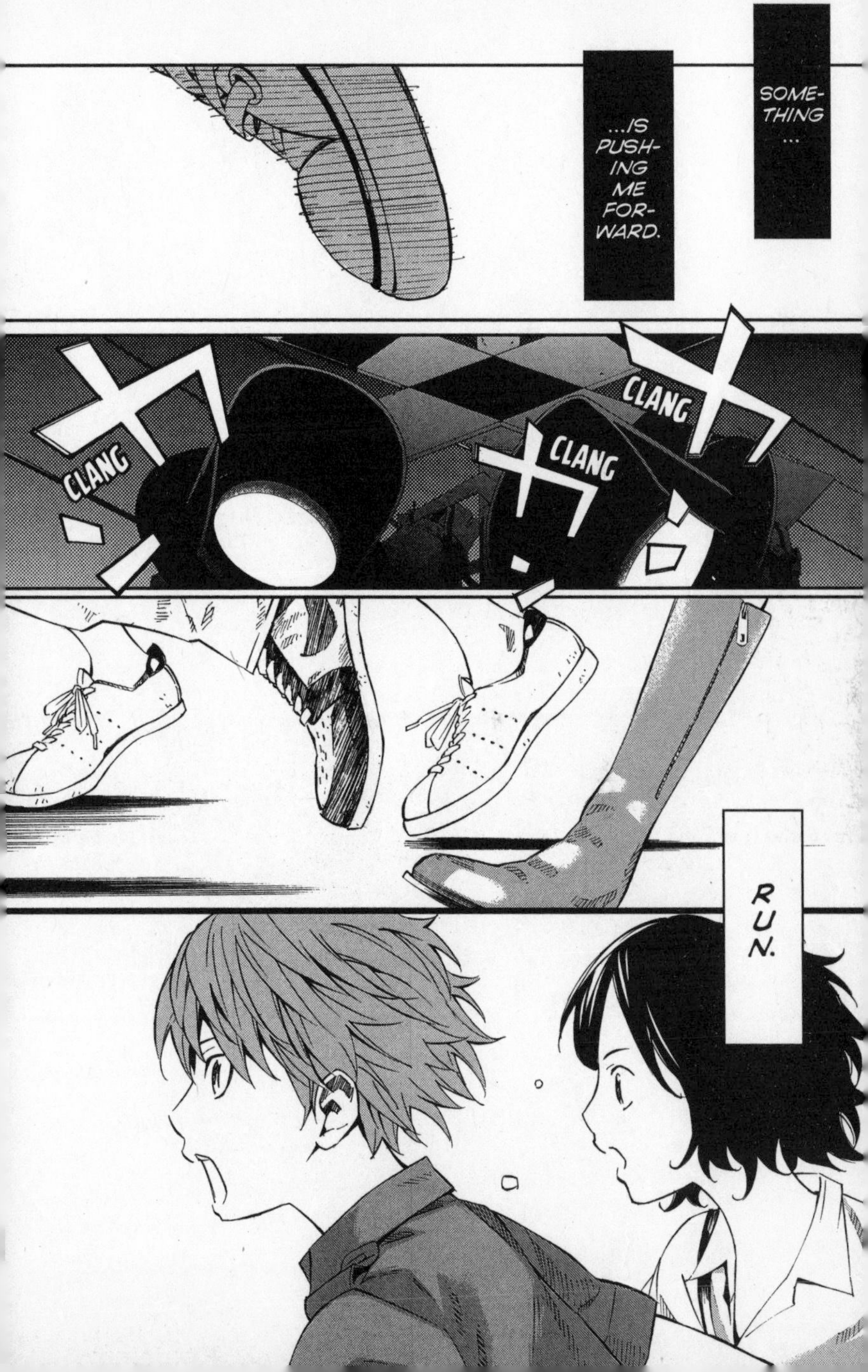
SOMETHING...
...IS PUSHING ME FORWARD.
CLANG
CLANG
CLANG
RUN.

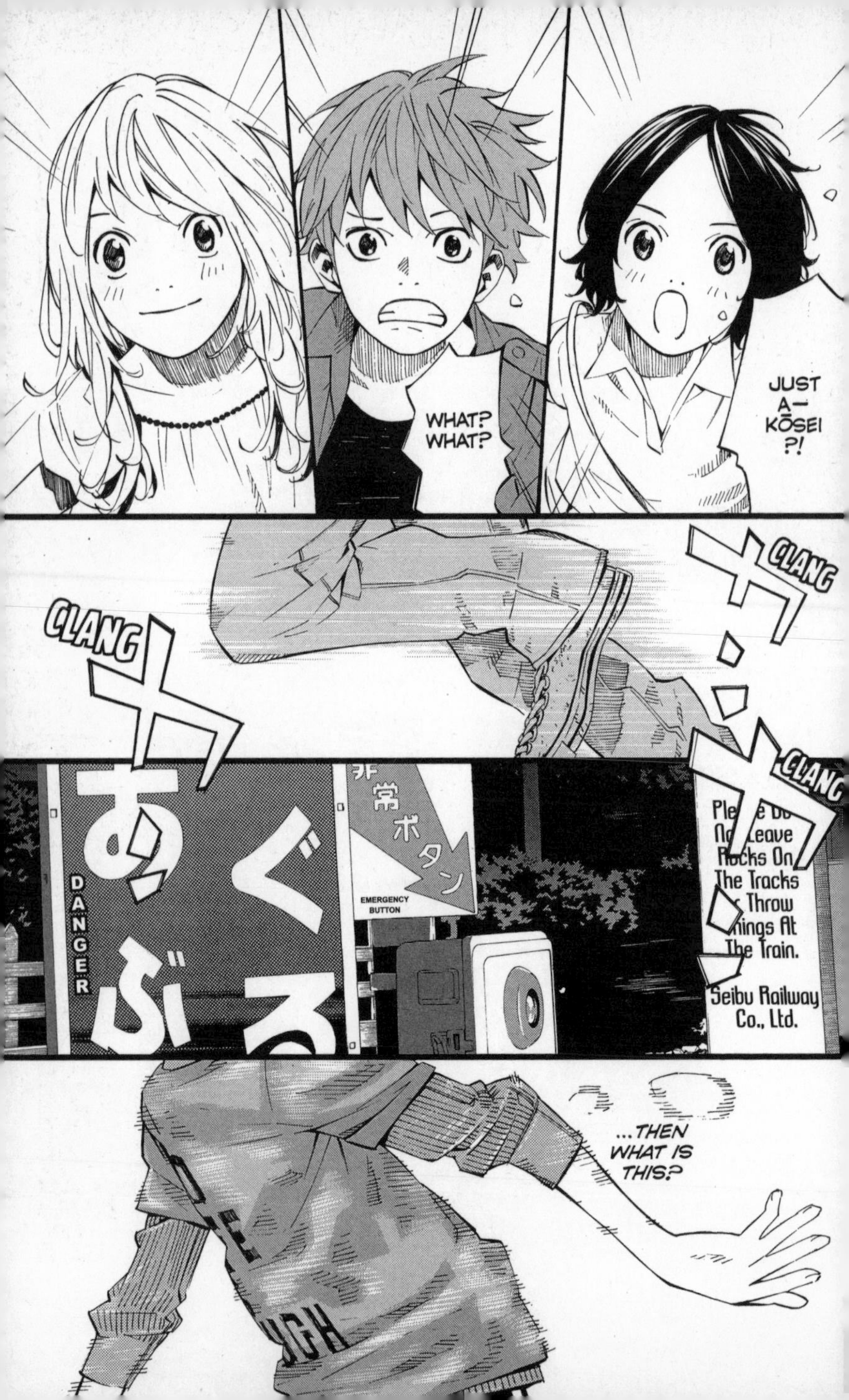
JUST A— KŌSEI ?!
WHAT? WHAT?
CLANG
CLANG
CLANG
The Tracks
The Train.
Seibu Railway Co., Ltd.
非常ボタン
EMERGENCY BUTTON
DANGER
...THEN WHAT IS THIS?

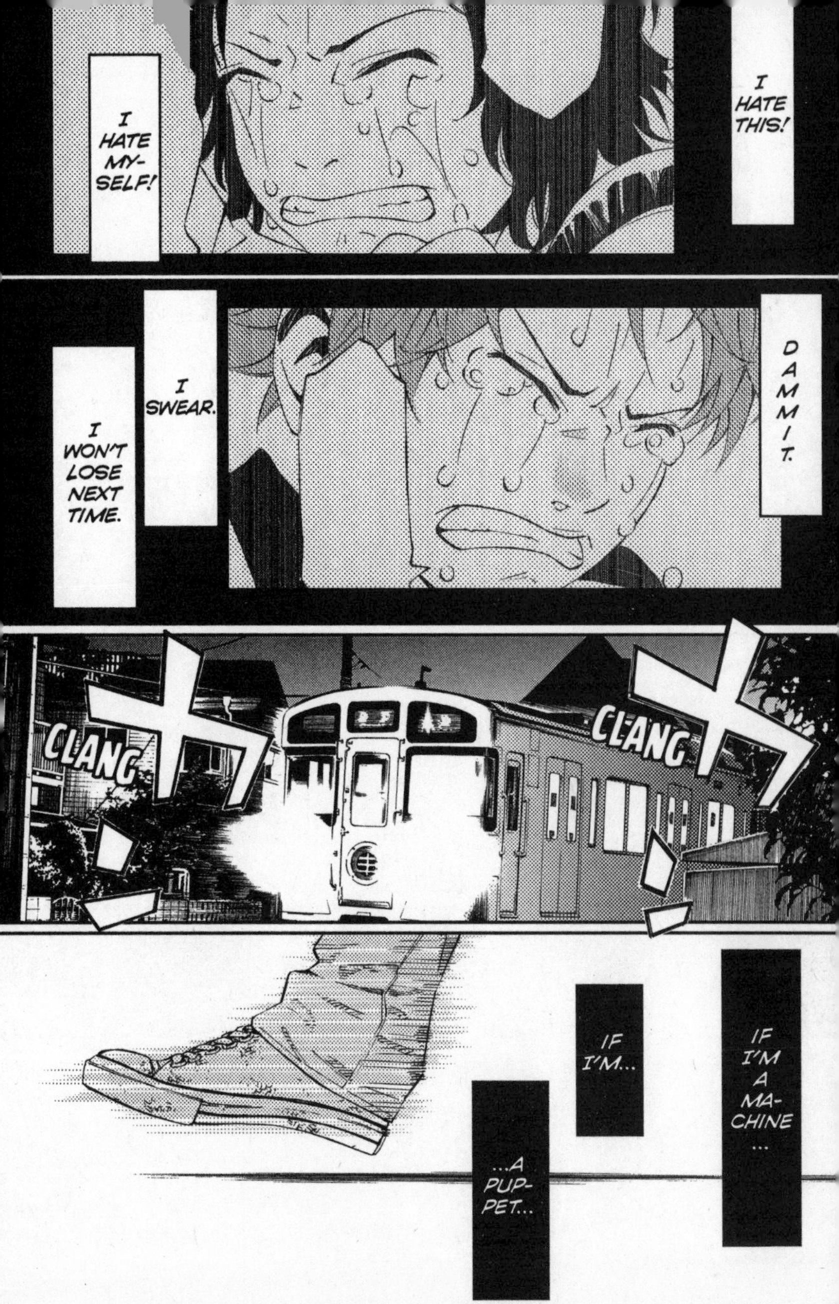
I HATE THIS!
I HATE MYSELF!
DAMMIT.
I SWEAR.
I WON'T LOSE NEXT TIME.
CLANG
CLANG
IF I'M A MACHINE...
IF I'M...
...A PUPPET...

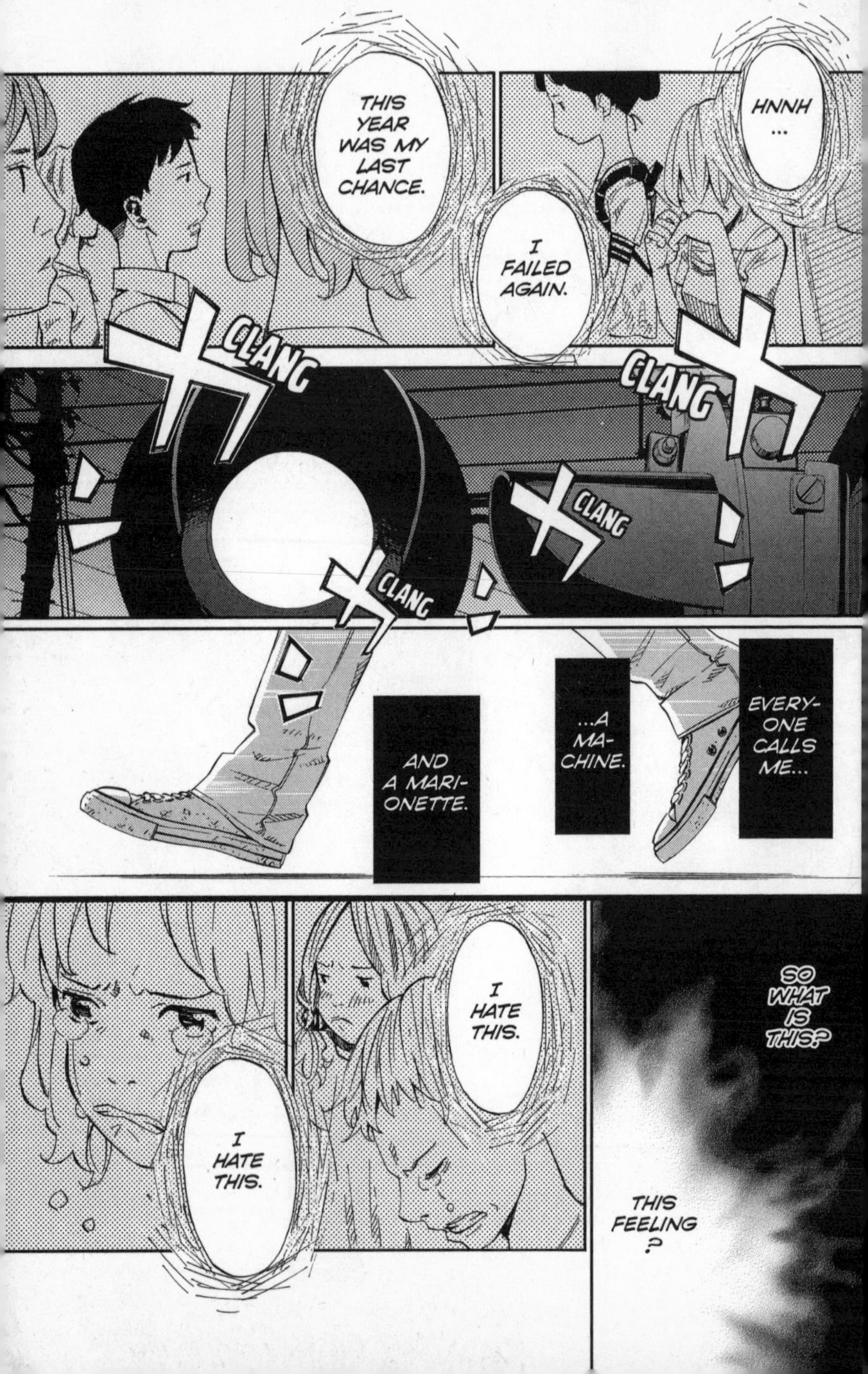
HNNH ...
I FAILED AGAIN.
THIS YEAR WAS MY LAST CHANCE.
CLANG
CLANG
CLANG
CLANG
EVERY-ONE CALLS ME...
...A MA-CHINE.
AND A MARI-ONETTE.
SO WHAT IS THIS?
THIS FEELING ?
I HATE THIS.
I HATE THIS.

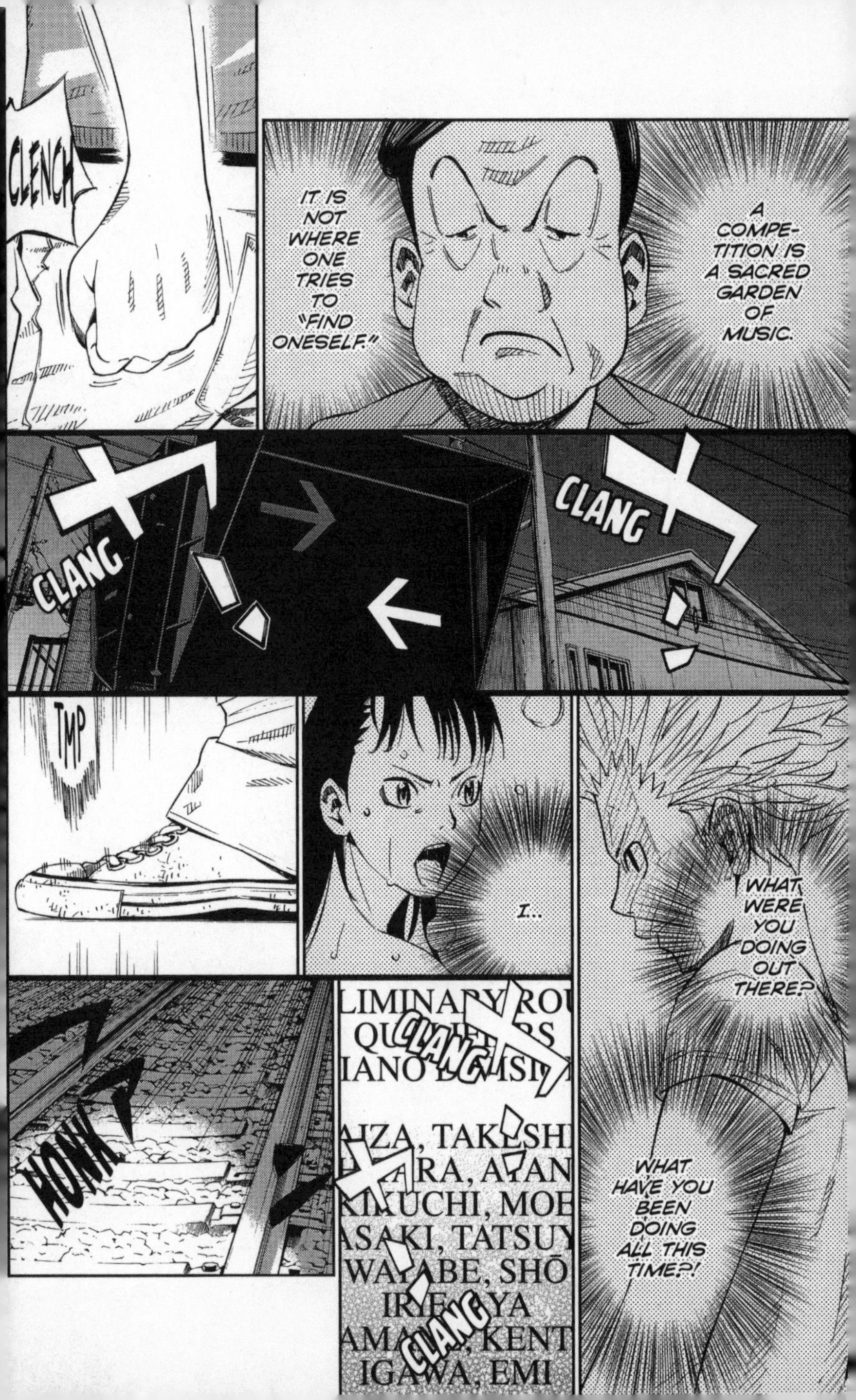
A COMPETITION IS A SACRED GARDEN OF MUSIC.
IT IS NOT WHERE ONE TRIES TO "FIND ONESELF."
CLENCH
CLANG
CLANG
WHAT WERE YOU DOING OUT THERE?
WHAT HAVE YOU BEEN DOING ALL THIS TIME?!
I...
TMP
LIMINARY ROU
IANO DIVISI
AIZA, TAKESHI
ARA, AYAN
KIKUCHI, MOE
ASAKI, TATSUY
WATABE, SHŌ
IRIE, AYA
IGAWA, EMI
CLANG
CLANG
HONK

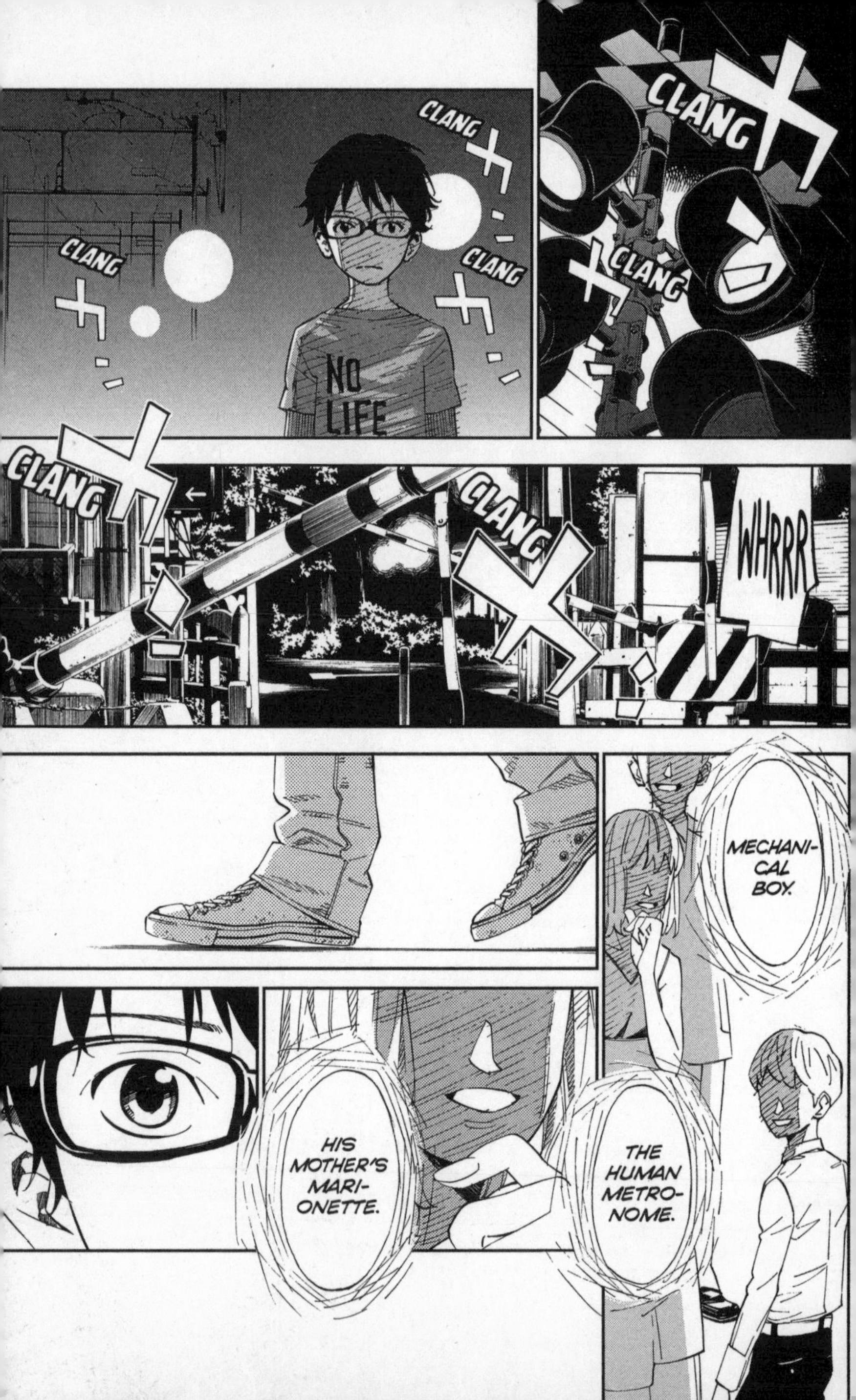
CLANG
CLANG
CLANG
CLANG
CLANG
NO LIFE
WHRRR
CLANG
CLANG
MECHANI-CAL BOY.
THE HUMAN METRO-NOME.
HIS MOTHER'S MARI-ONETTE.

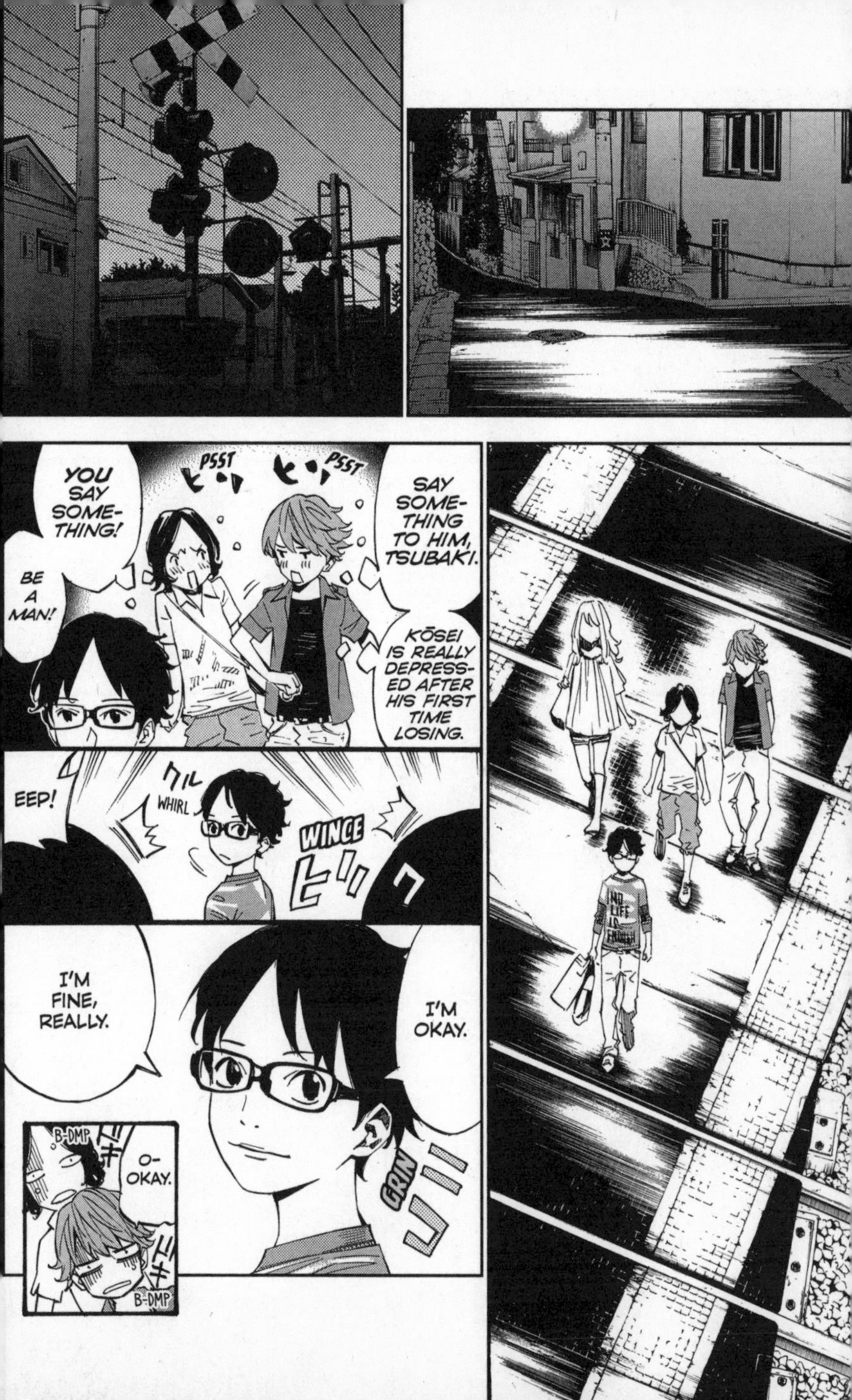
SAY SOME-THING TO HIM, TSUBAKI.
KŌSEI IS REALLY DEPRESS-ED AFTER HIS FIRST TIME LOSING.
PSST
PSST
YOU SAY SOME-THING!
BE A MAN!
WINCE
WHIRL
EEP!
I'M OKAY.
I'M FINE, REALLY.
GRIN
O-OKAY.
B-DMP
B-DMP

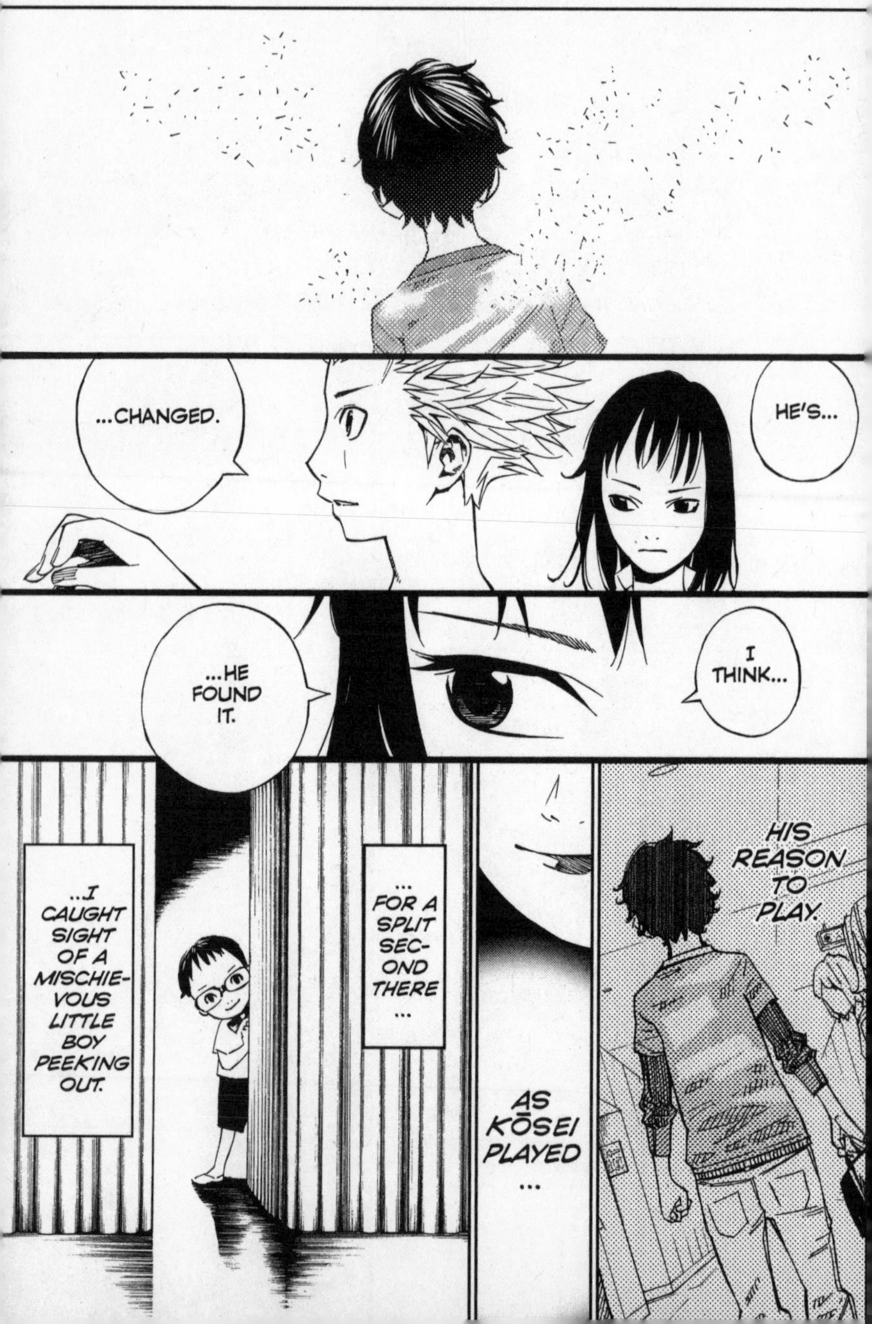
HE'S...
...CHANGED.
I THINK...
...HE FOUND IT.
HIS REASON TO PLAY.
AS KŌSEI PLAYED...
...FOR A SPLIT SECOND THERE...
...I CAUGHT SIGHT OF A MISCHIEVOUS LITTLE BOY PEEKING OUT.

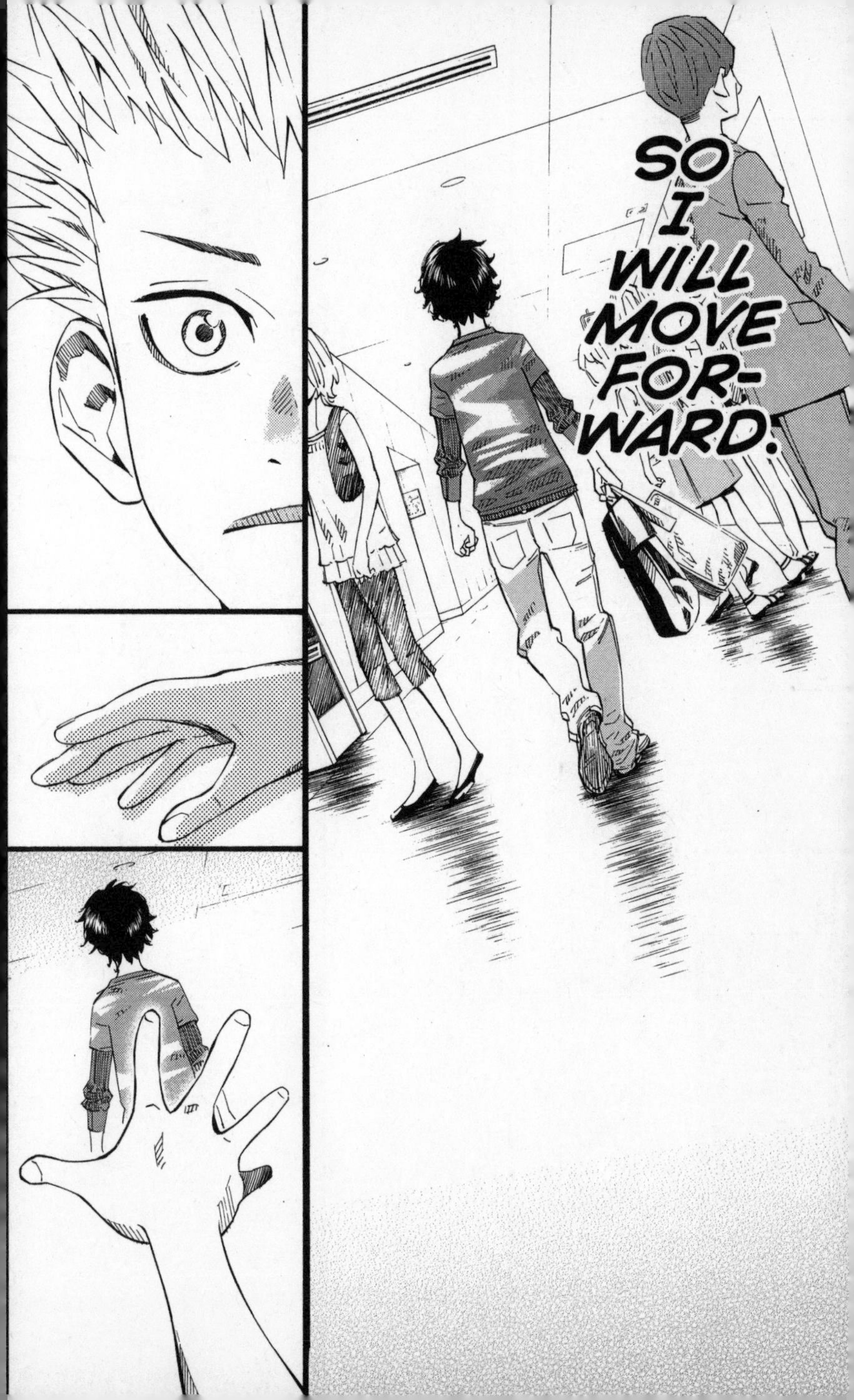
SO I WILL MOVE FOR-WARD.

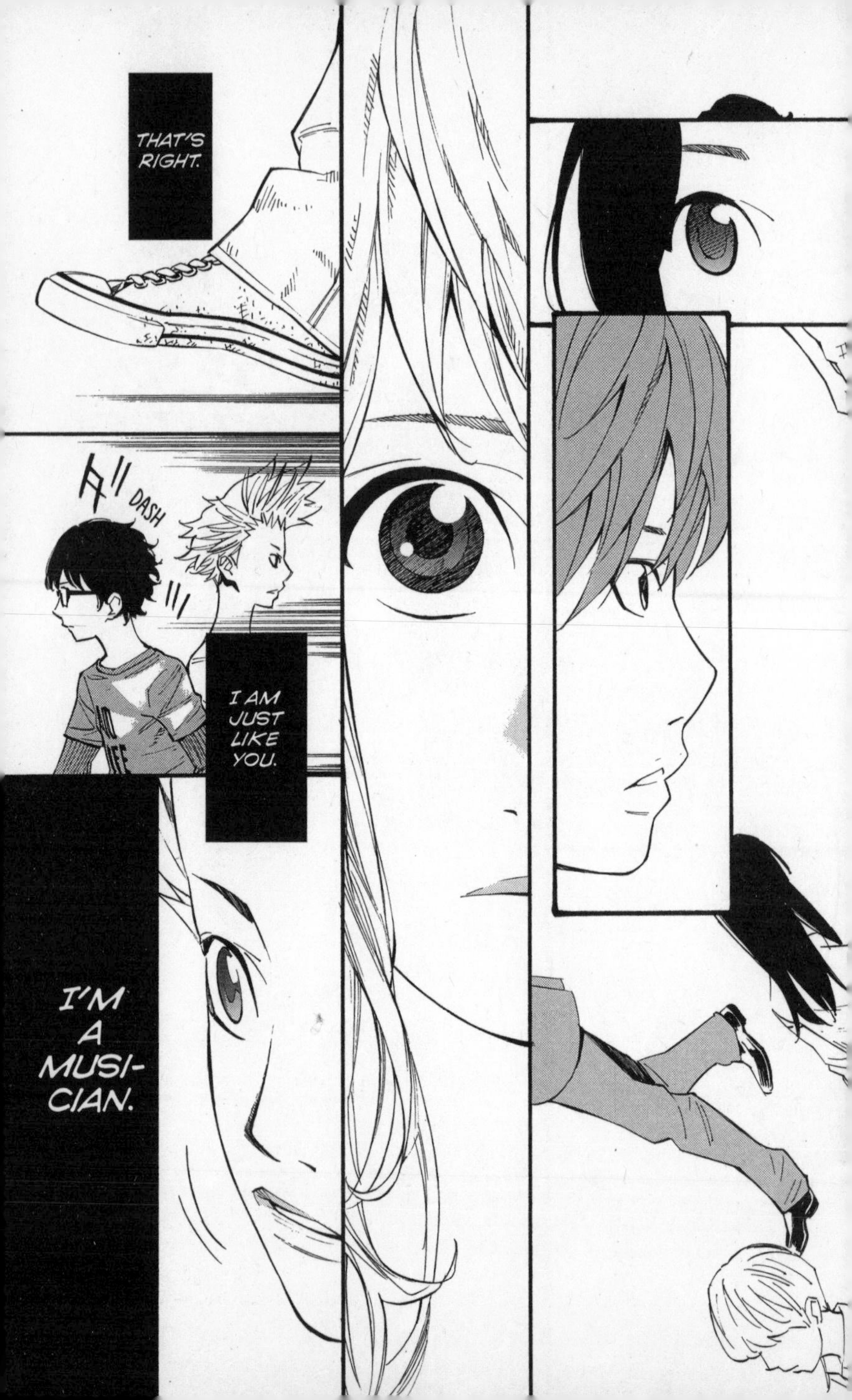
THAT'S RIGHT.
DASH
I AM JUST LIKE YOU.
I'M A MUSICIAN.

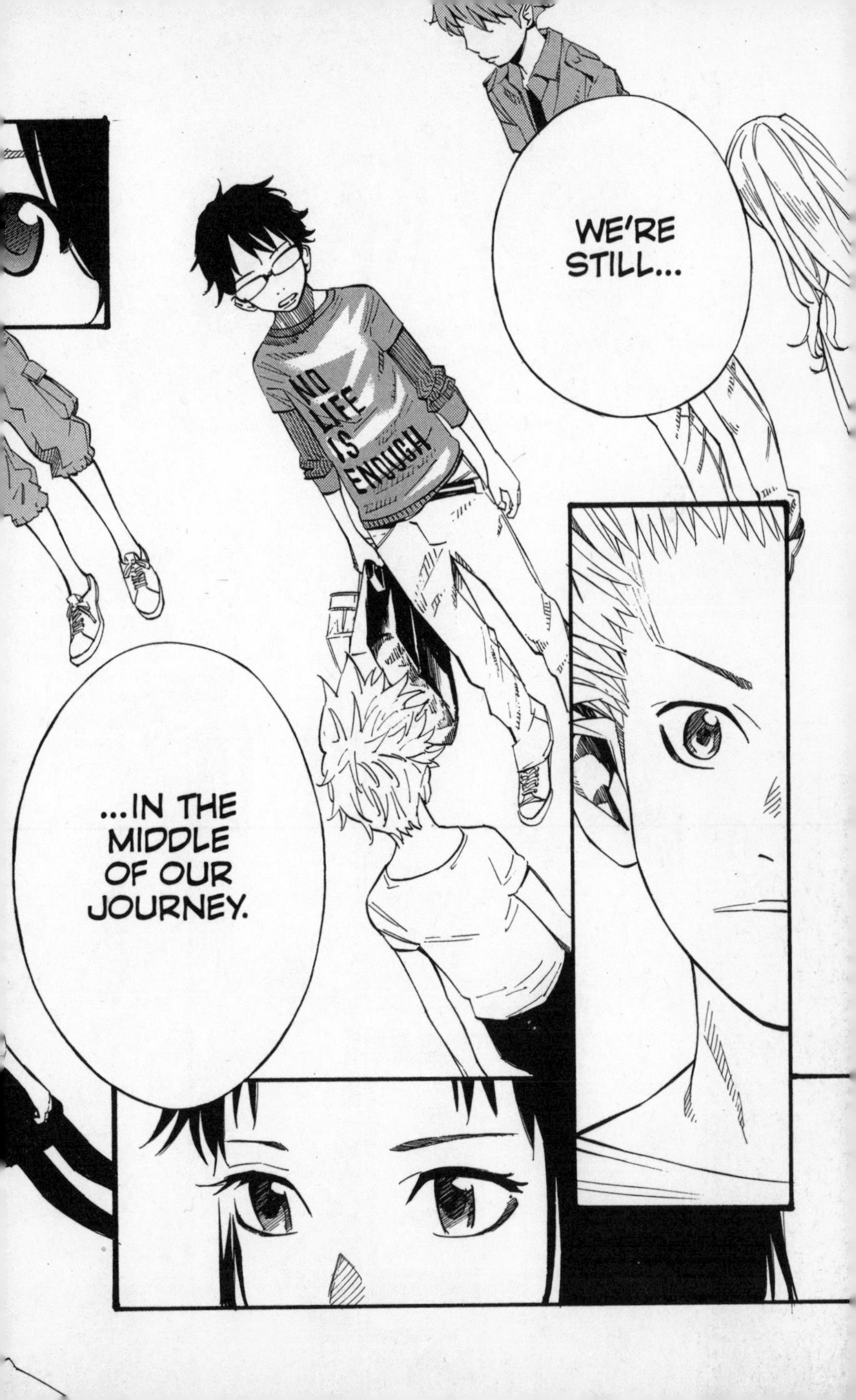
WE'RE STILL...
NO LIFE IS ENOUGH
...IN THE MIDDLE OF OUR JOURNEY.

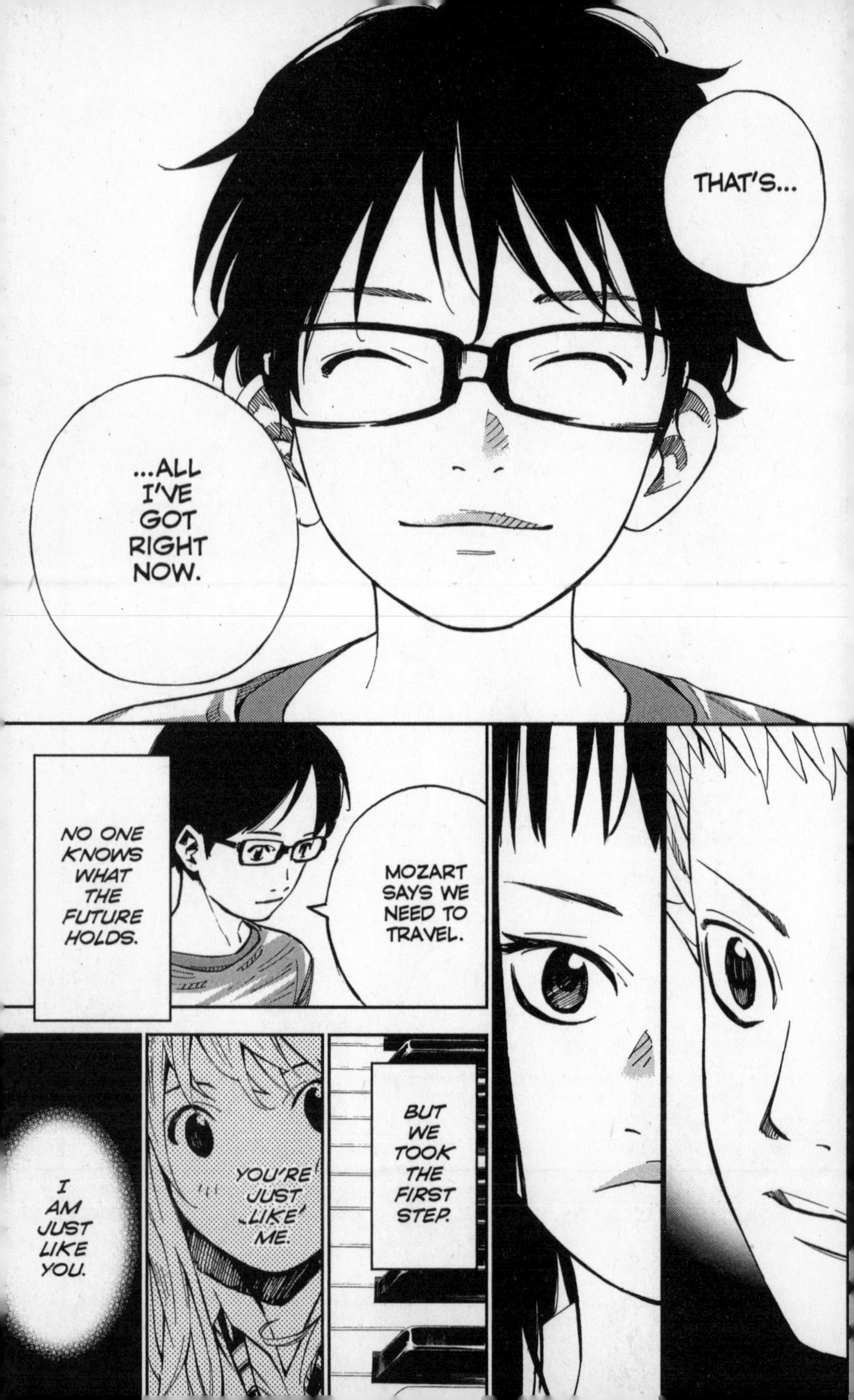
THAT'S...
...ALL I'VE GOT RIGHT NOW.
MOZART SAYS WE NEED TO TRAVEL.
NO ONE KNOWS WHAT THE FUTURE HOLDS.
BUT WE TOOK THE FIRST STEP.
YOU'RE JUST LIKE ME.
I AM JUST LIKE YOU.

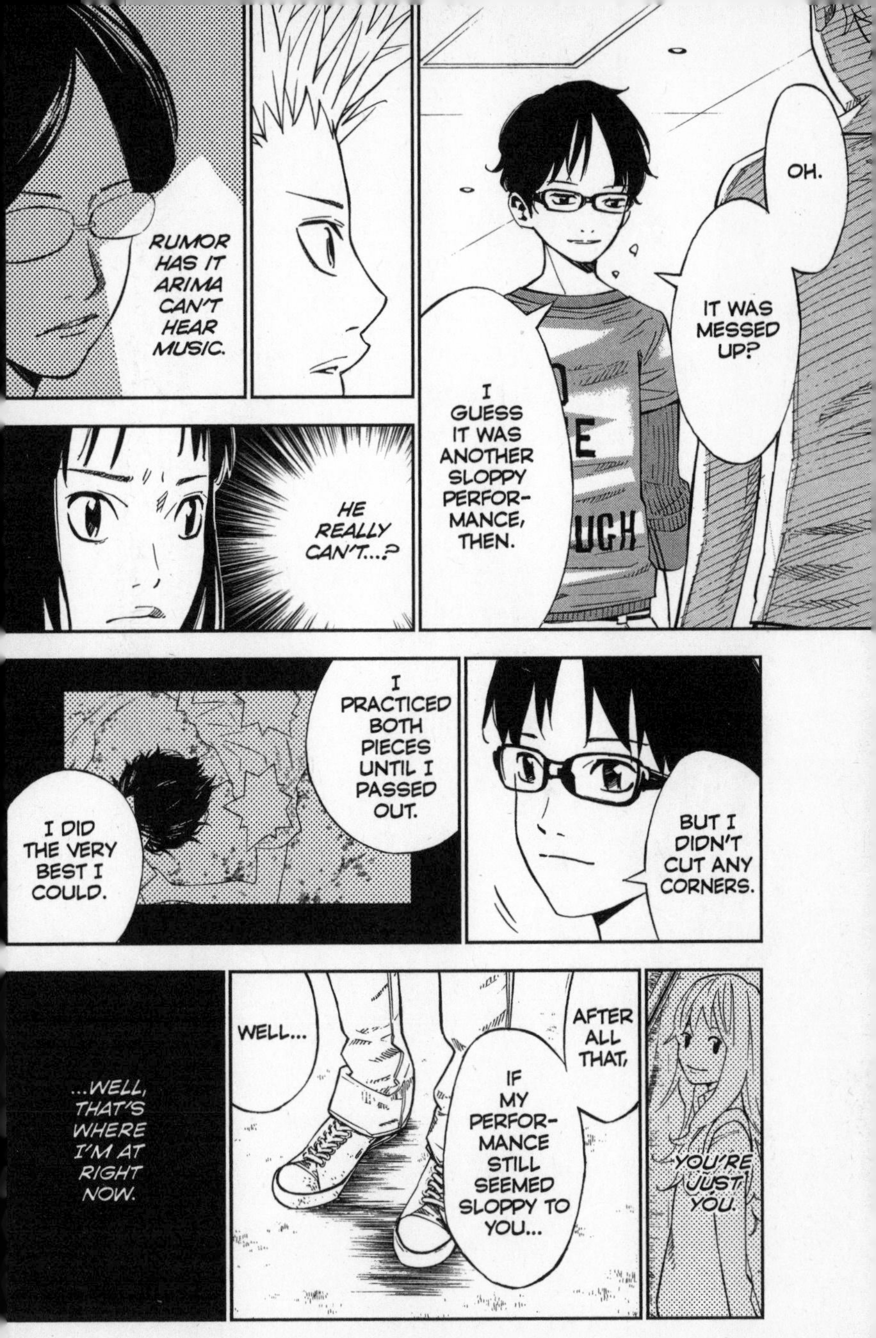
OH.
IT WAS MESSED UP?
I GUESS IT WAS ANOTHER SLOPPY PERFORMANCE, THEN.
RUMOR HAS IT ARIMA CAN'T HEAR MUSIC.
HE REALLY CAN'T...?
BUT I DIDN'T CUT ANY CORNERS.
I PRACTICED BOTH PIECES UNTIL I PASSED OUT.
I DID THE VERY BEST I COULD.
YOU'RE JUST YOU.
AFTER ALL THAT,
IF MY PERFORMANCE STILL SEEMED SLOPPY TO YOU...
WELL...
...WELL, THAT'S WHERE I'M AT RIGHT NOW.

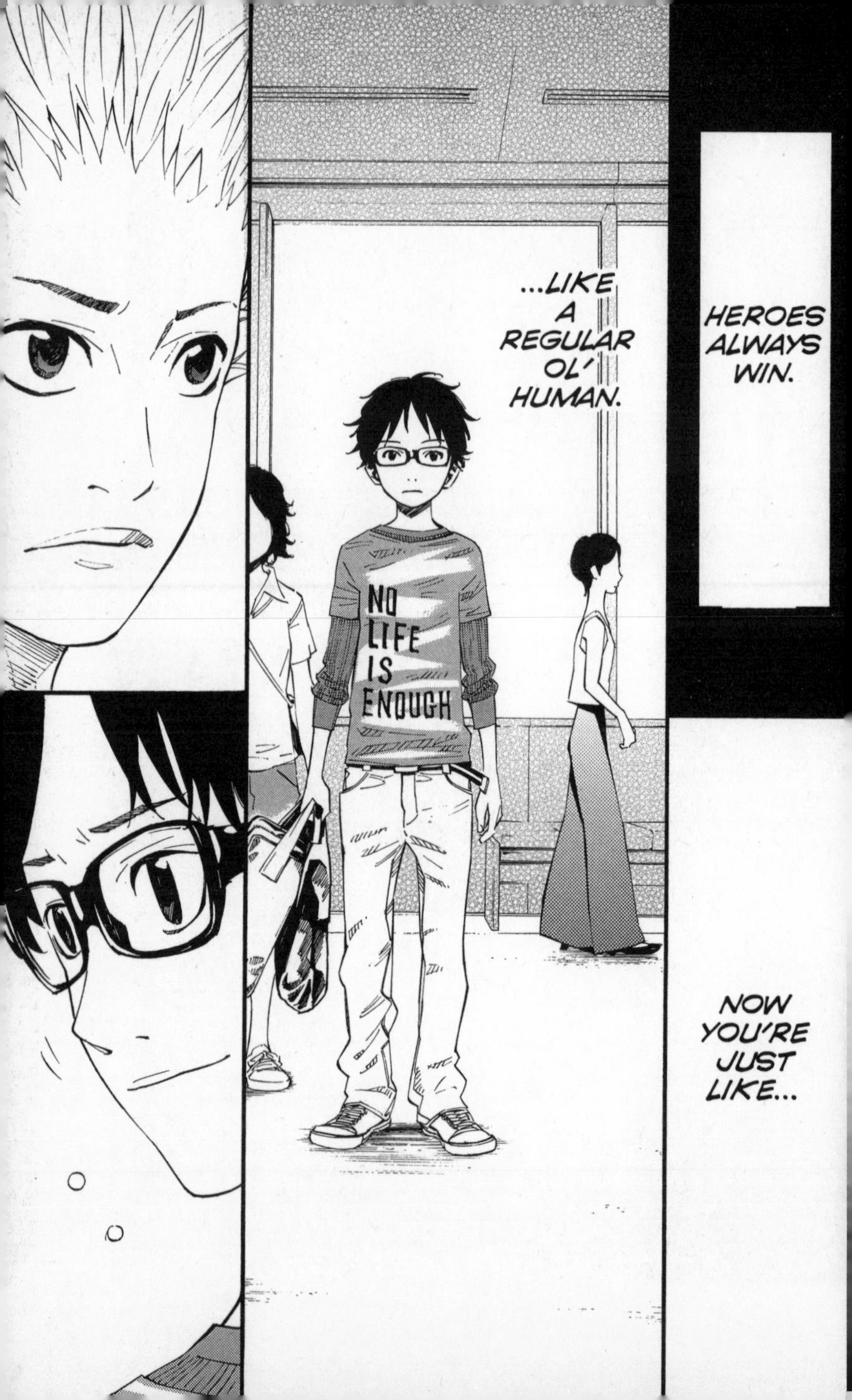
HEROES ALWAYS WIN.
NOW YOU'RE JUST LIKE...
...LIKE A REGULAR OL' HUMAN.
NO LIFE IS ENOUGH

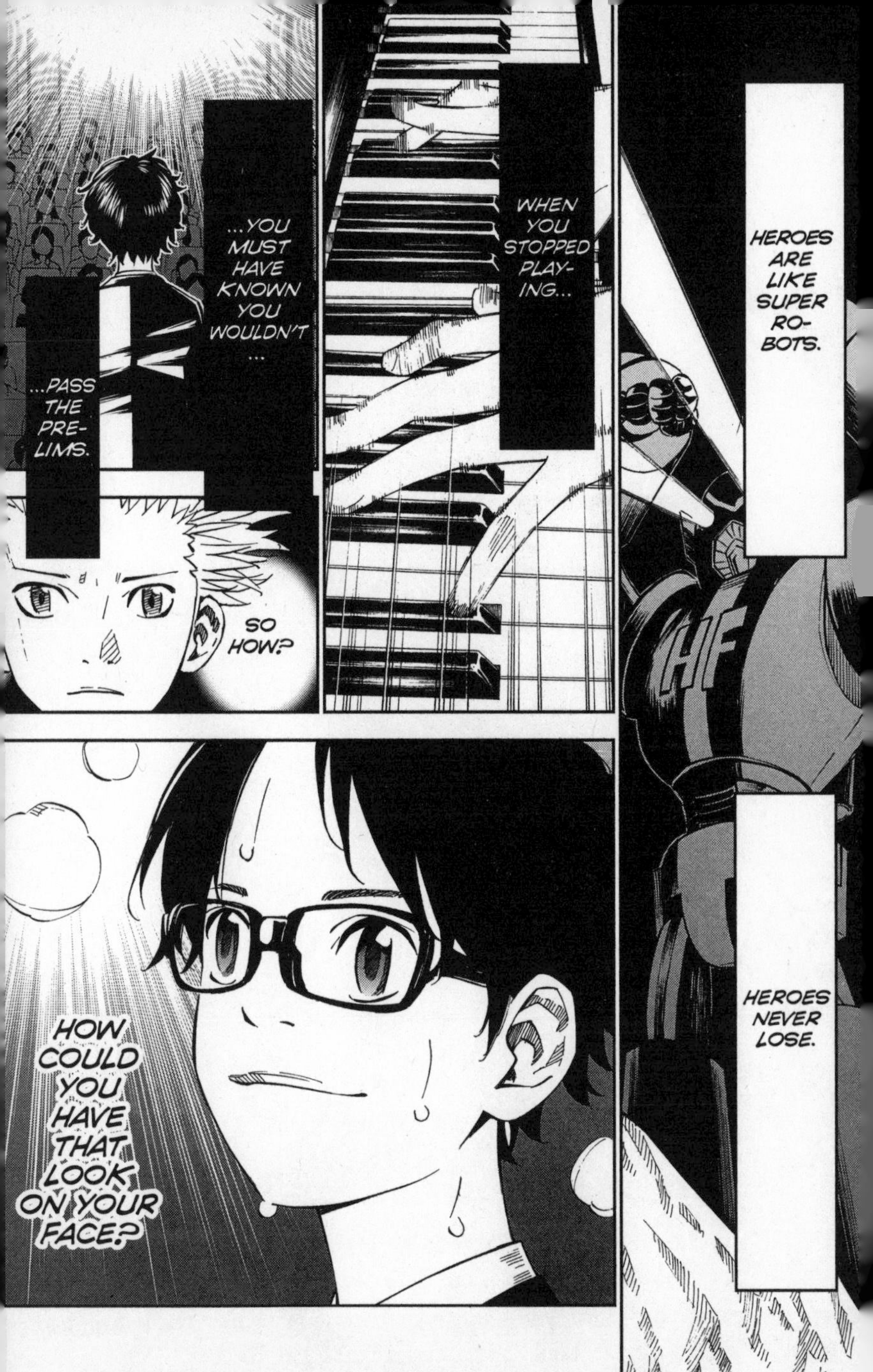
HEROES ARE LIKE SUPER ROBOTS.
HEROES NEVER LOSE.
WHEN YOU STOPPED PLAYING...
...YOU MUST HAVE KNOWN YOU WOULDN'T ...
...PASS THE PRELIMS.
SO HOW?
HOW COULD YOU HAVE THAT LOOK ON YOUR FACE?

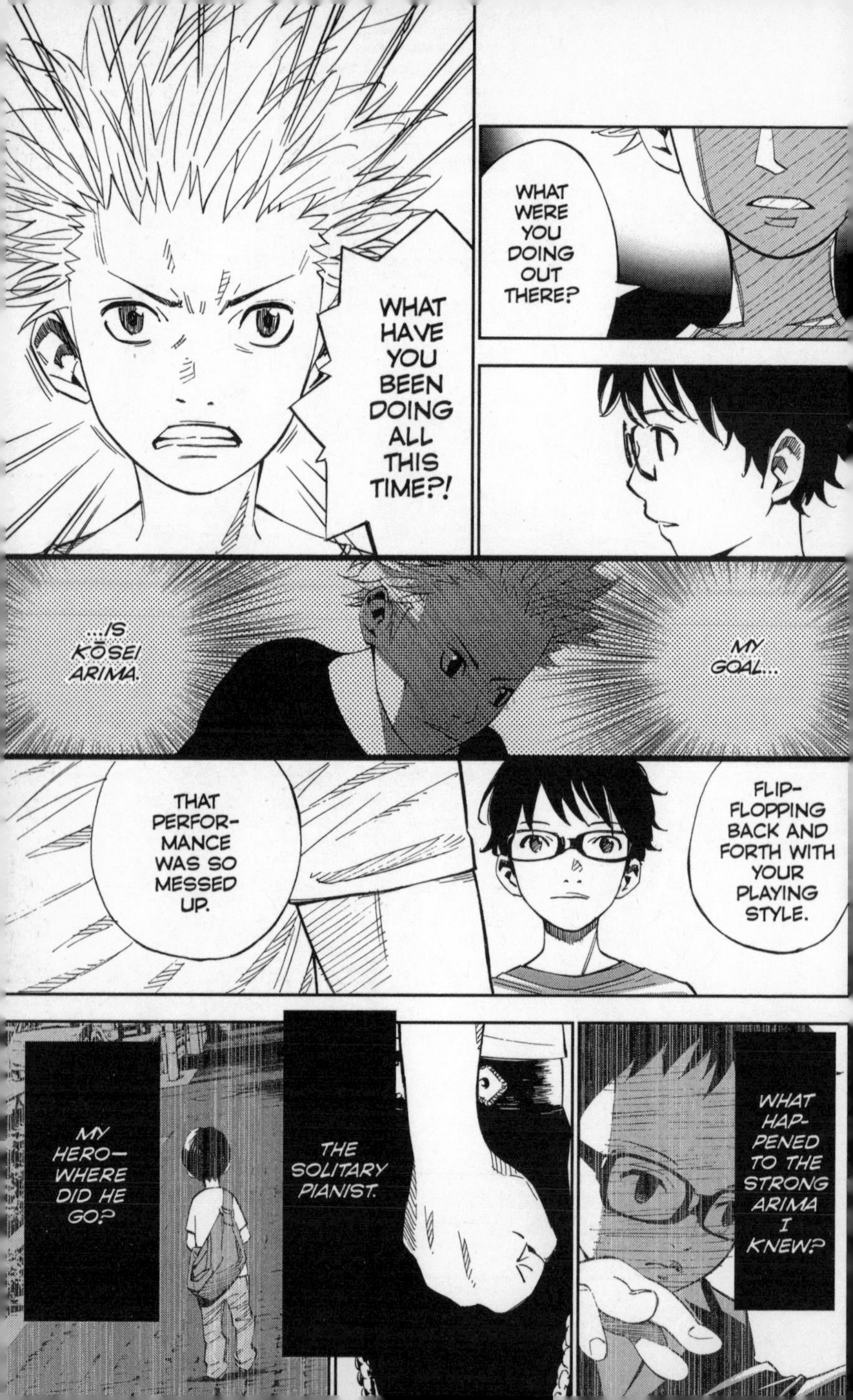
WHAT WERE YOU DOING OUT THERE?
WHAT HAVE YOU BEEN DOING ALL THIS TIME?!
MY GOAL...
...IS KŌSEI ARIMA.
FLIP-FLOPPING BACK AND FORTH WITH YOUR PLAYING STYLE.
THAT PERFORMANCE WAS SO MESSED UP.
WHAT HAPPENED TO THE STRONG ARIMA I KNEW?
THE SOLITARY PIANIST.
MY HERO—WHERE DID HE GO?

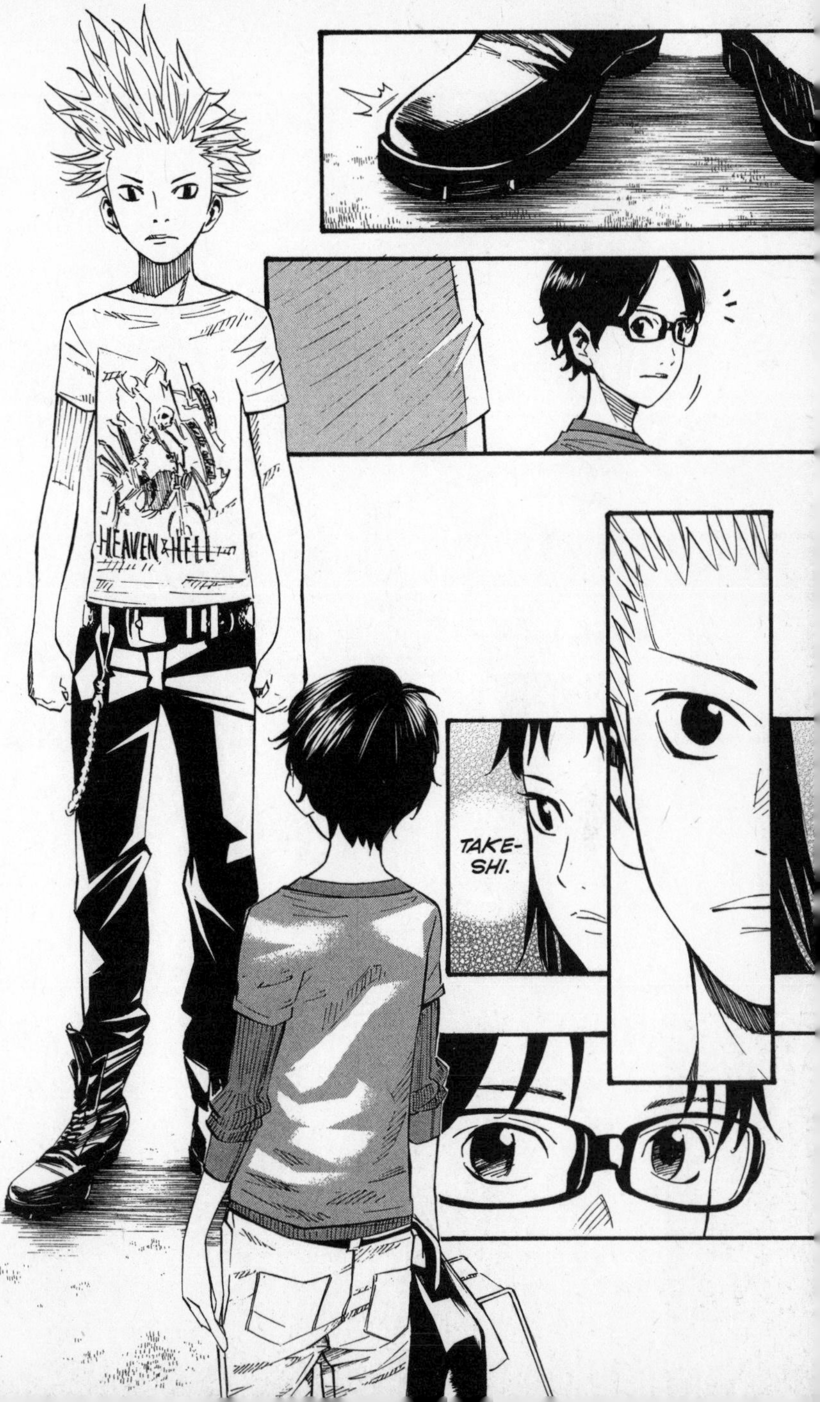
HEAVEN & HELL
TAKE-SHI.

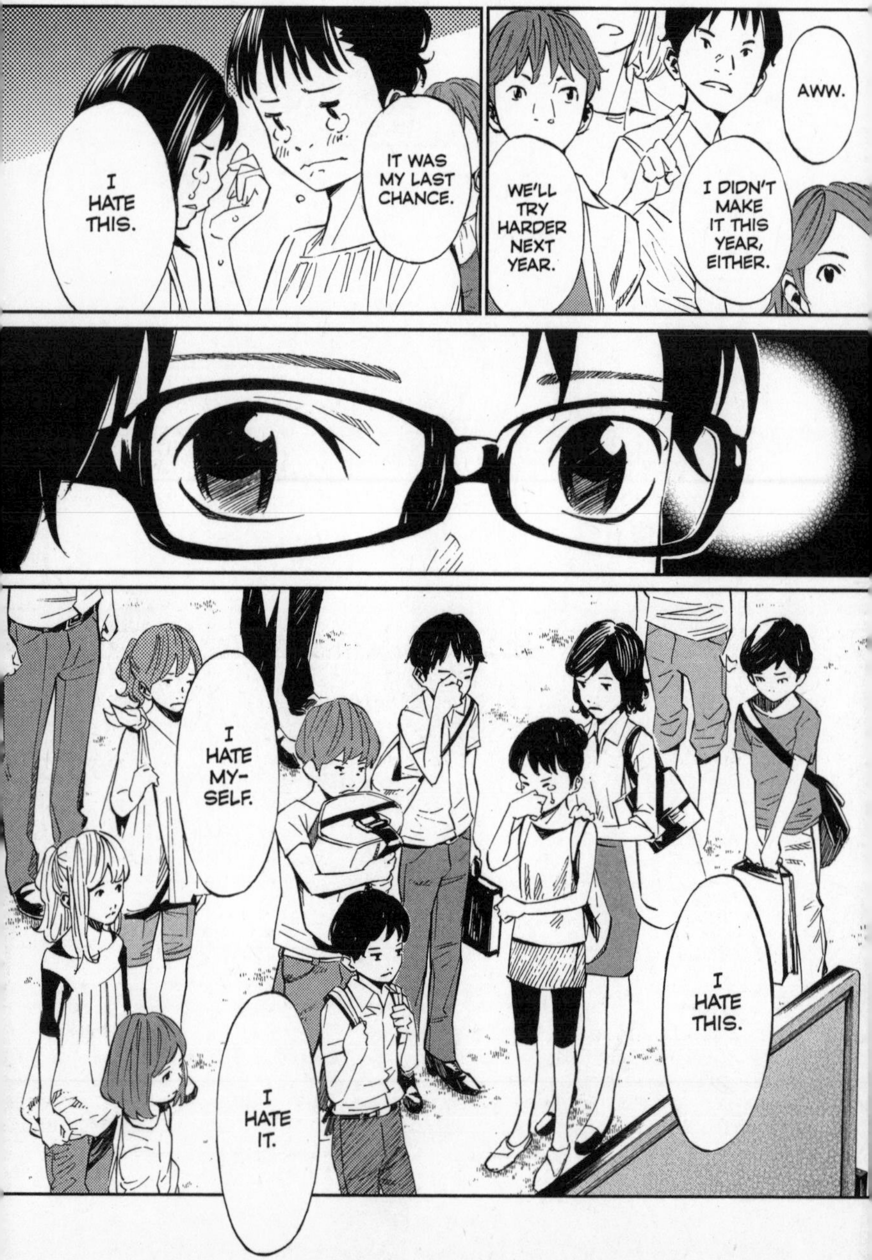
AWW.
I DIDN'T MAKE IT THIS YEAR, EITHER.
WE'LL TRY HARDER NEXT YEAR.
IT WAS MY LAST CHANCE.
I HATE THIS.
I HATE THIS.
I HATE IT.
I HATE MY-SELF.

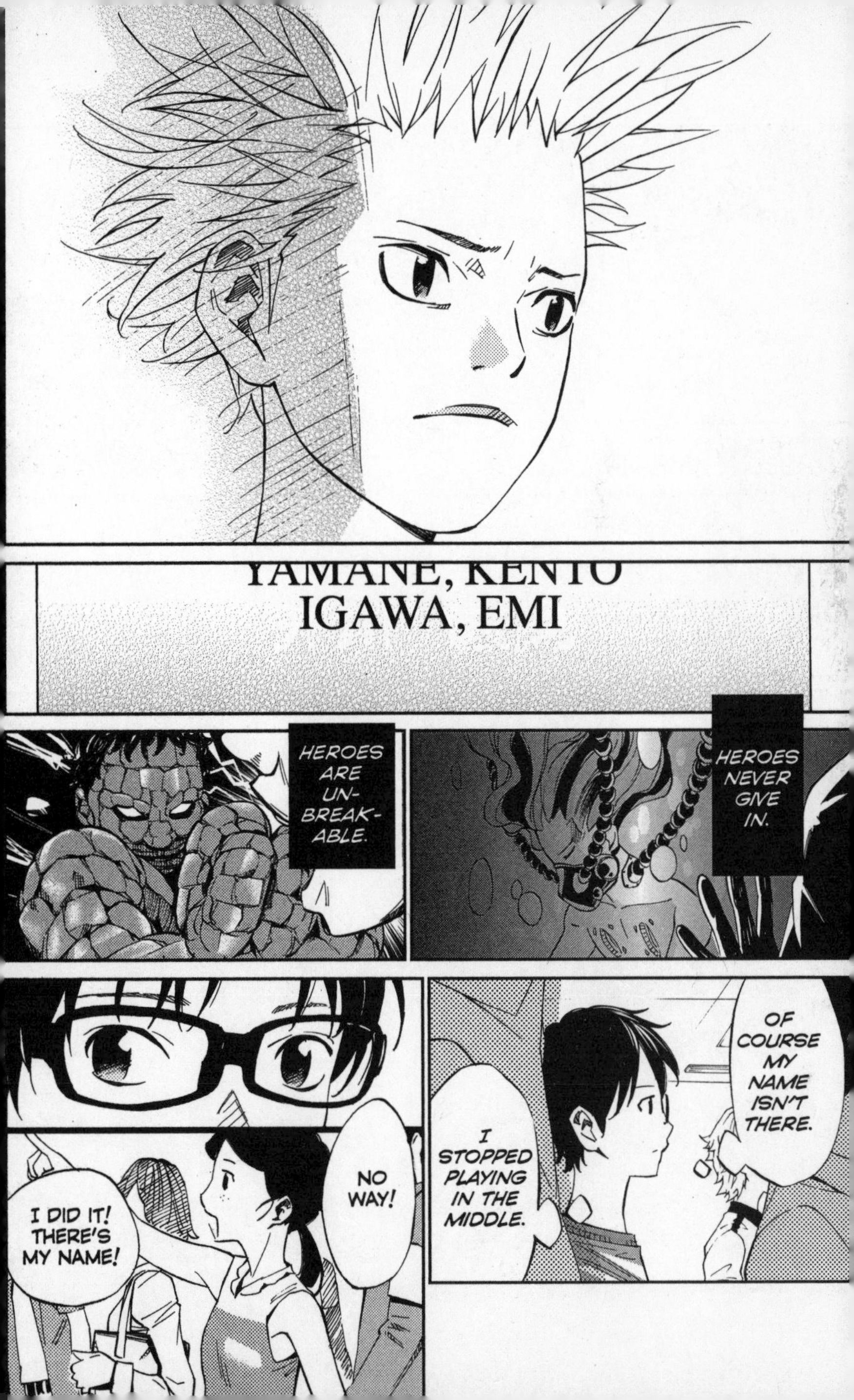
YAMANE, KENTO
IGAWA, EMI
HEROES NEVER GIVE IN.
HEROES ARE UN-BREAK-ABLE.
OF COURSE MY NAME ISN'T THERE.
I STOPPED PLAYING IN THE MIDDLE.
NO WAY!
I DID IT! THERE'S MY NAME!

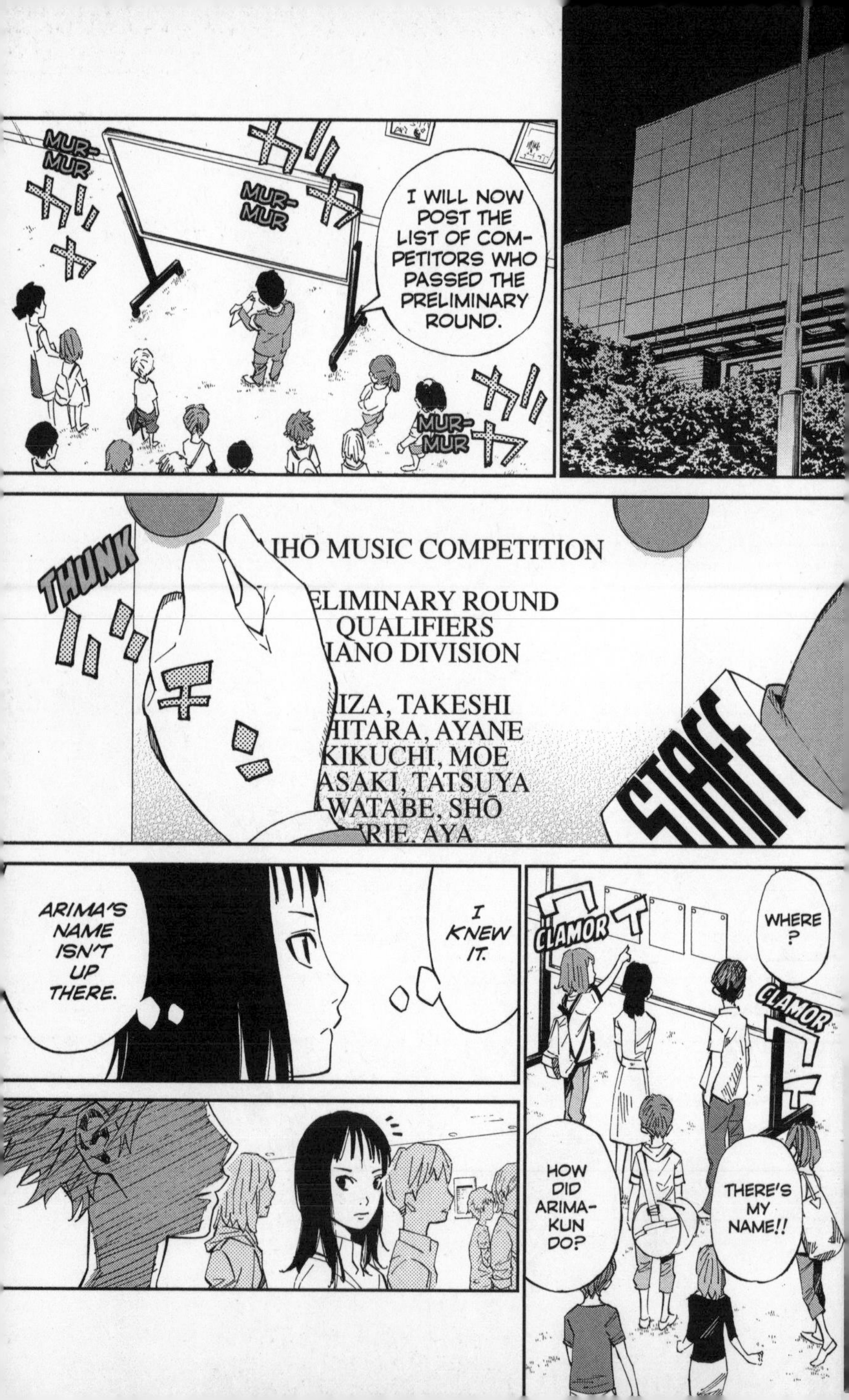
I WILL NOW POST THE LIST OF COMPETITORS WHO PASSED THE PRELIMINARY ROUND.
MUR-MUR
MUR-MUR
MUR-MUR
STAFF
THUNK
IHŌ MUSIC COMPETITION
ELIMINARY ROUND
QUALIFIERS
IANO DIVISION
IZA, TAKESHI
HITARA, AYANE
KIKUCHI, MOE
ASAKI, TATSUYA
WATABE, SHŌ
WHERE?
CLAMOR
CLAMOR
THERE'S MY NAME!!
HOW DID ARIMA-KUN DO?
I KNEW IT.
ARIMA'S NAME ISN'T UP THERE.

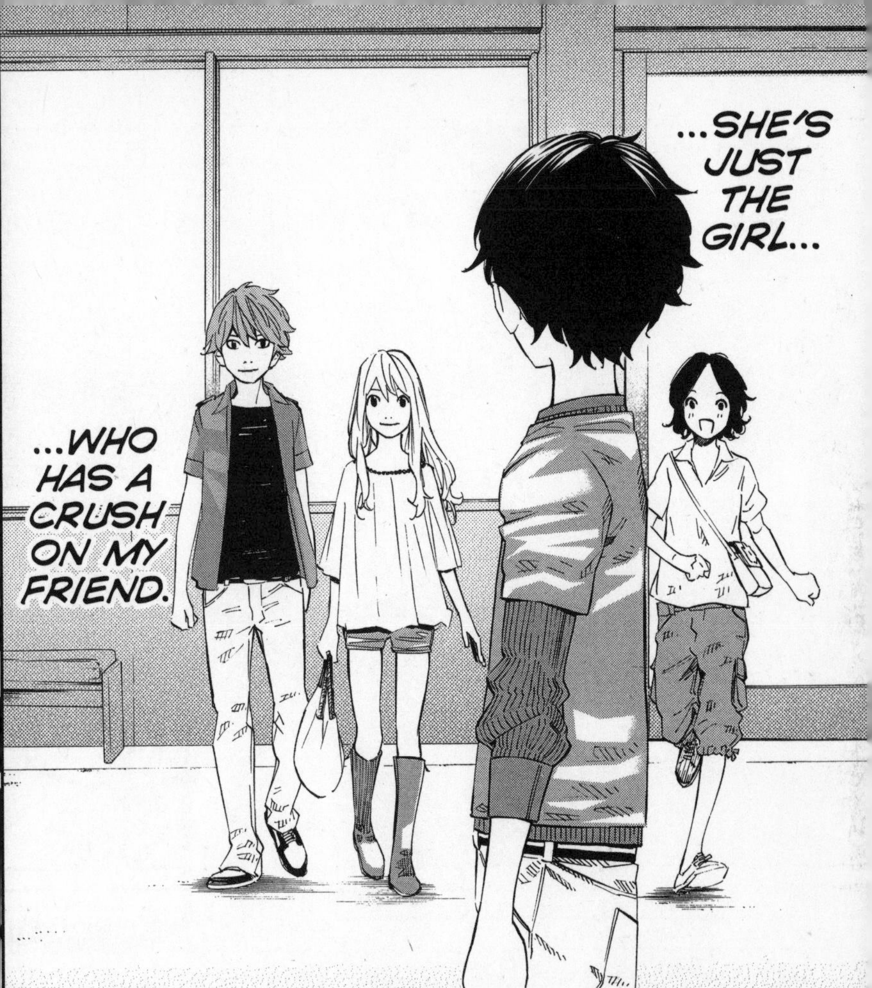
...SHE'S JUST THE GIRL...
...WHO HAS A CRUSH ON MY FRIEND.
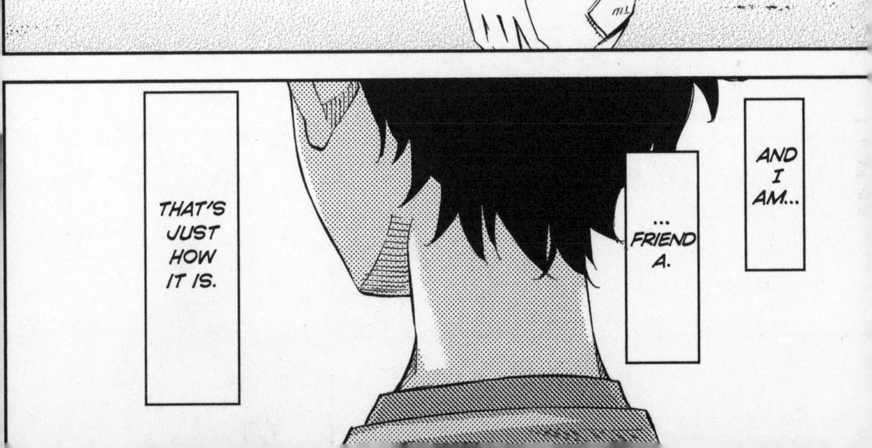
AND I AM...
...FRIEND A.
THAT'S JUST HOW IT IS.

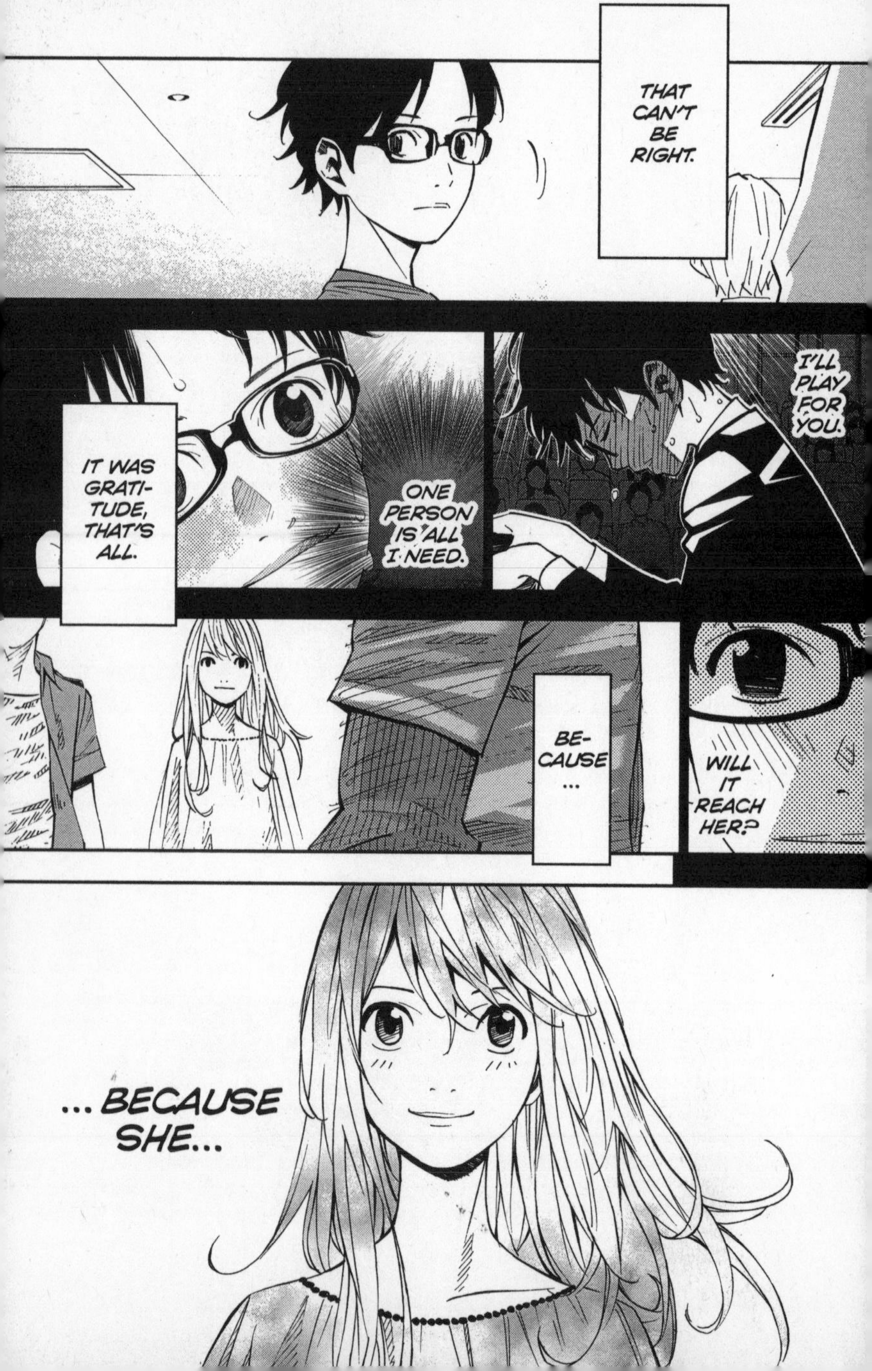
THAT CAN'T BE RIGHT.
I'LL PLAY FOR YOU.
ONE PERSON IS ALL I NEED.
IT WAS GRATI-TUDE, THAT'S ALL.
WILL IT REACH HER?
BE-CAUSE ...
... BECAUSE SHE...

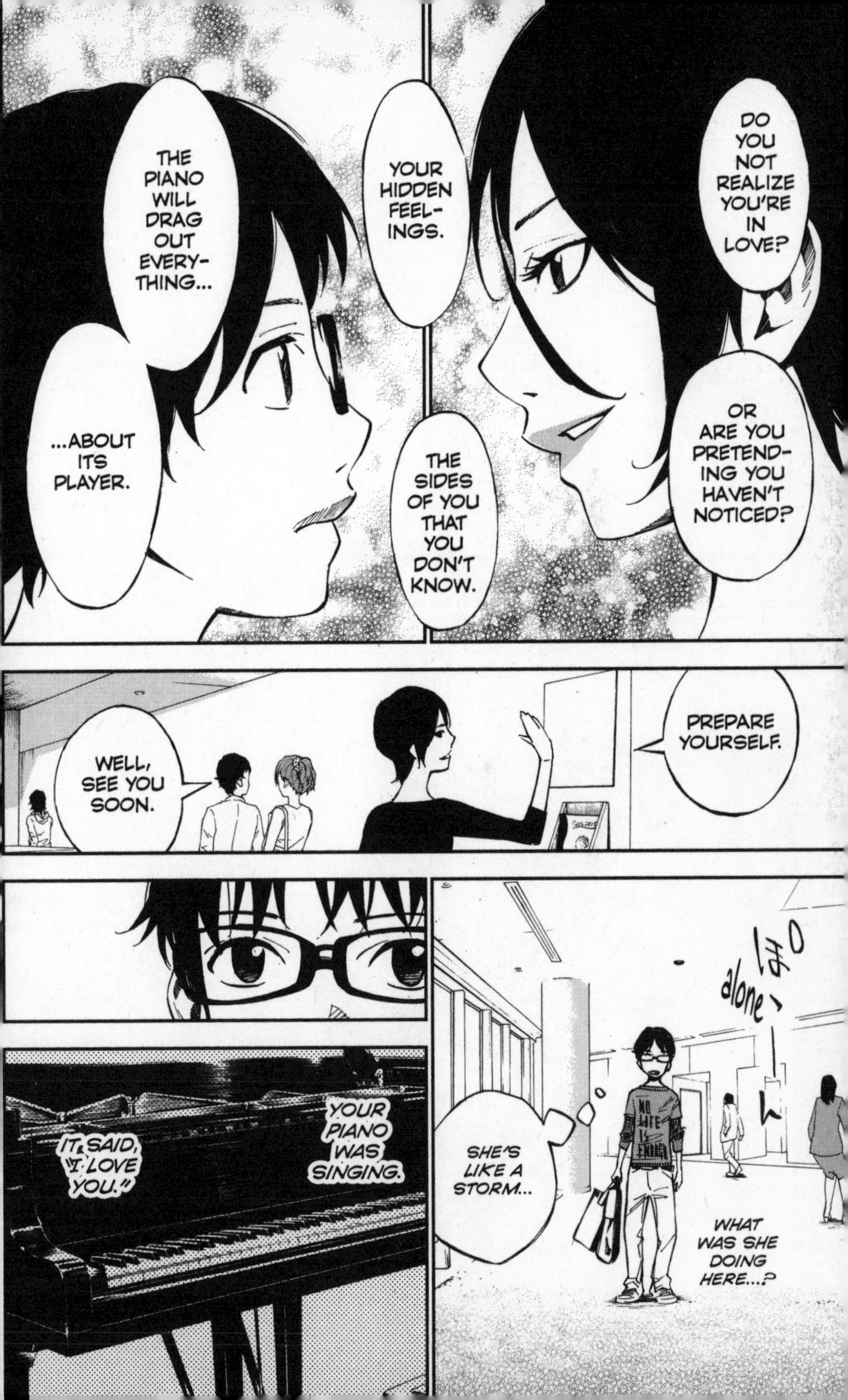
DO YOU NOT REALIZE YOU'RE IN LOVE?
OR ARE YOU PRETENDING YOU HAVEN'T NOTICED?
THE PIANO WILL DRAG OUT EVERYTHING...
...ABOUT ITS PLAYER.
YOUR HIDDEN FEELINGS.
THE SIDES OF YOU THAT YOU DON'T KNOW.
PREPARE YOURSELF.
WELL, SEE YOU SOON.
alone
WHAT WAS SHE DOING HERE...?
SHE'S LIKE A STORM...
YOUR PIANO WAS SINGING.
IT SAID, "I LOVE YOU."

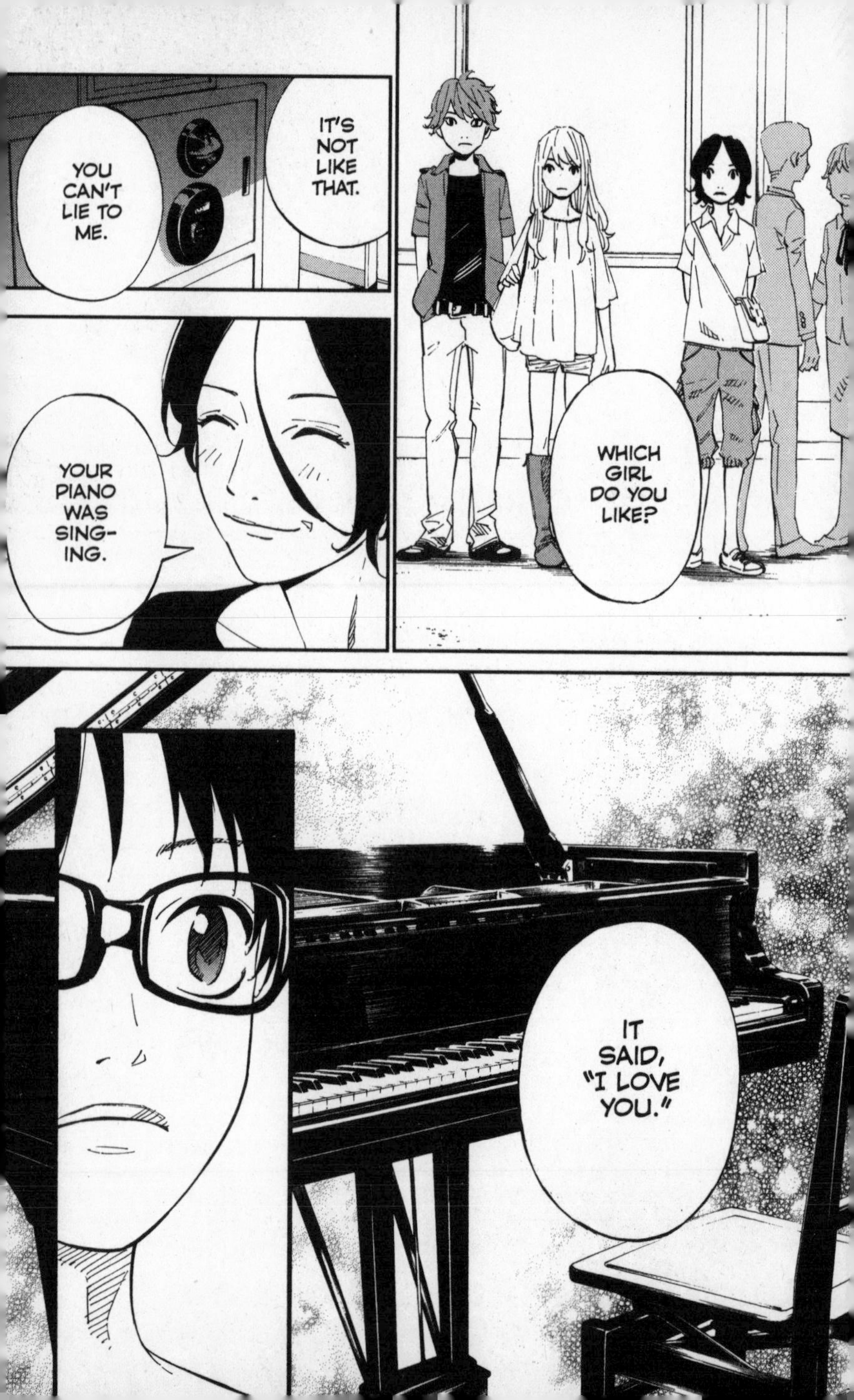
WHICH GIRL DO YOU LIKE?
IT'S NOT LIKE THAT.
YOU CAN'T LIE TO ME.
YOUR PIANO WAS SING-ING.
IT SAID, "I LOVE YOU."

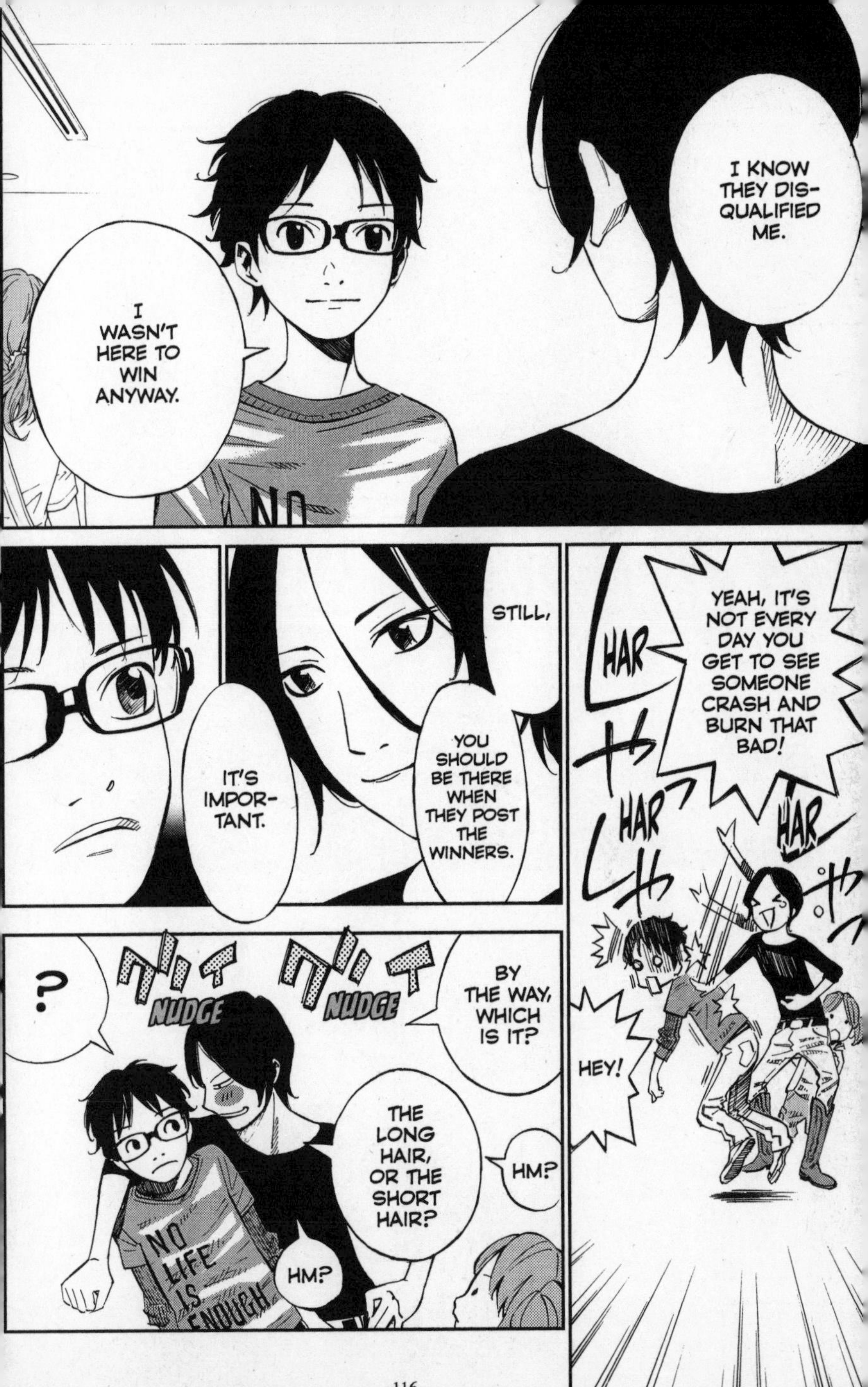

I KNOW THEY DIS-QUALIFIED ME.
I WASN'T HERE TO WIN ANYWAY.
NO
HAR
YEAH, IT'S NOT EVERY DAY YOU GET TO SEE SOMEONE CRASH AND BURN THAT BAD!
HAR
HAR
HEY!
STILL,
YOU SHOULD BE THERE WHEN THEY POST THE WINNERS.
IT'S IMPOR-TANT.
BY THE WAY, WHICH IS IT?
NUDGE
NUDGE
?
HM?
THE LONG HAIR, OR THE SHORT HAIR?
HM?
NO LIFE IS ENOUGH

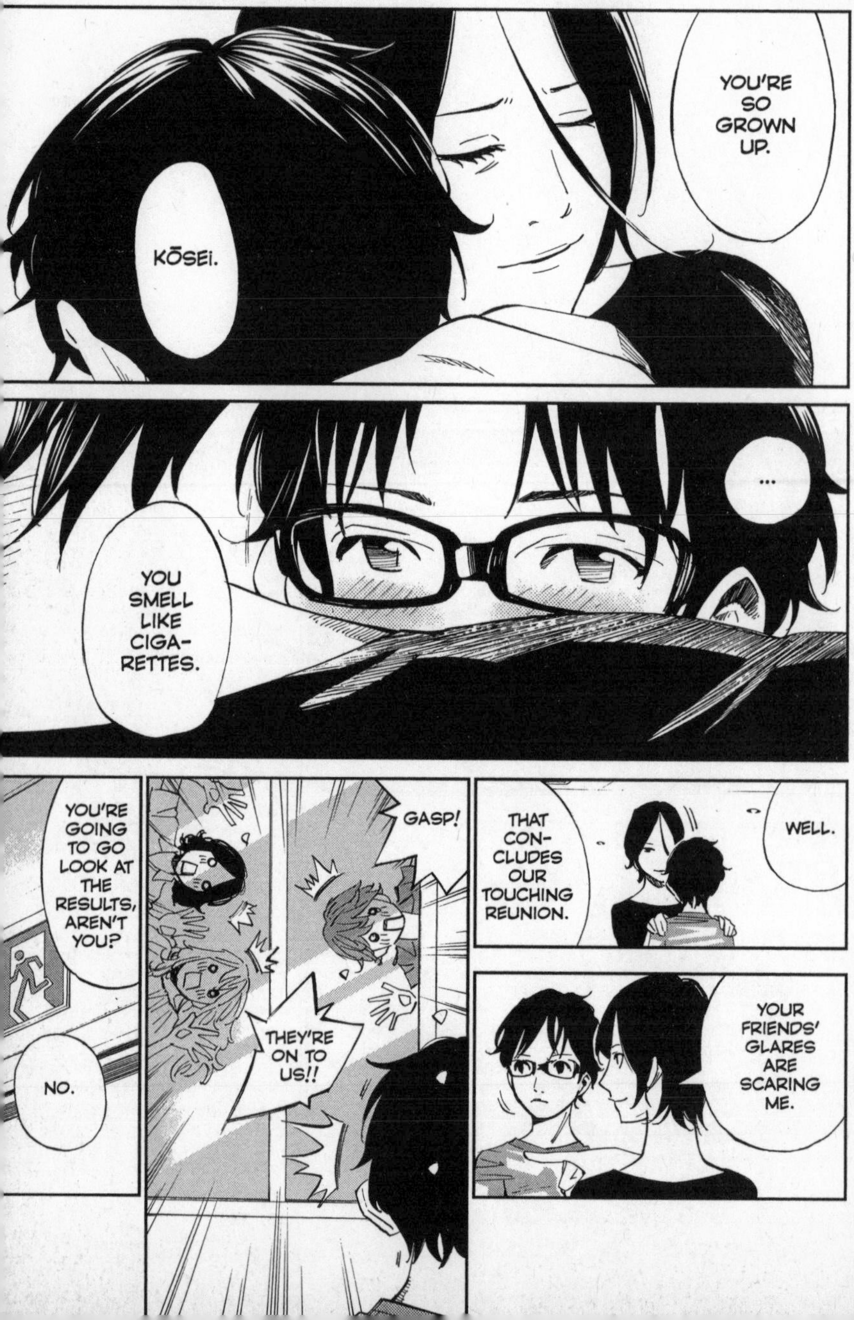
YOU'RE SO GROWN UP.
KŌSEI.
...
YOU SMELL LIKE CIGA-RETTES.
WELL.
THAT CON-CLUDES OUR TOUCHING REUNION.
YOUR FRIENDS' GLARES ARE SCARING ME.
GASP!
THEY'RE ON TO US!!
YOU'RE GOING TO GO LOOK AT THE RESULTS, AREN'T YOU?
NO.

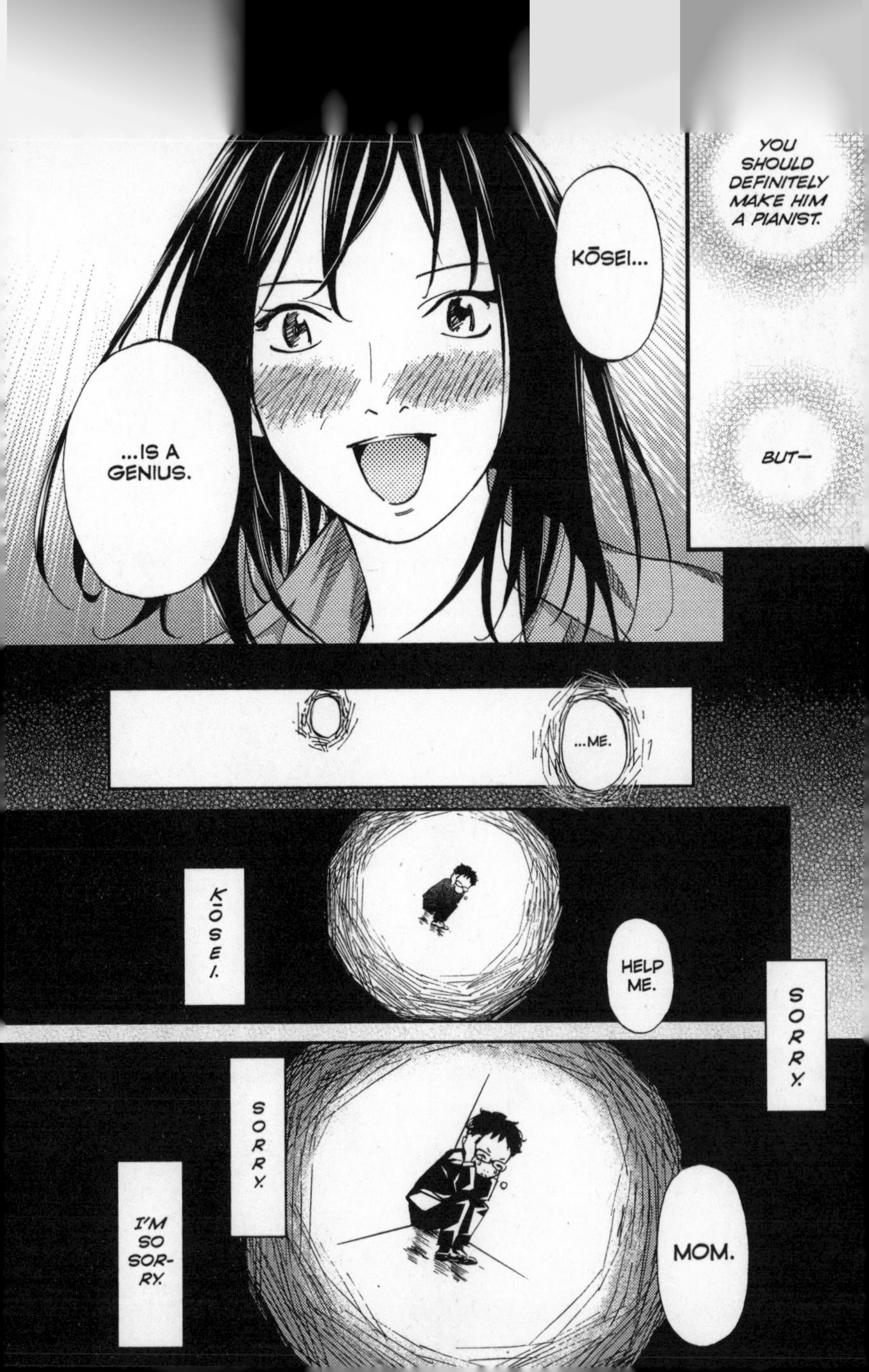
YOU SHOULD DEFINITELY MAKE HIM A PIANIST.
BUT—
KŌSEI...
...IS A GENIUS.
...ME.
HELP ME.
KŌSEI!
SORRY.
MOM.
SORRY.
I'M SO SORRY.

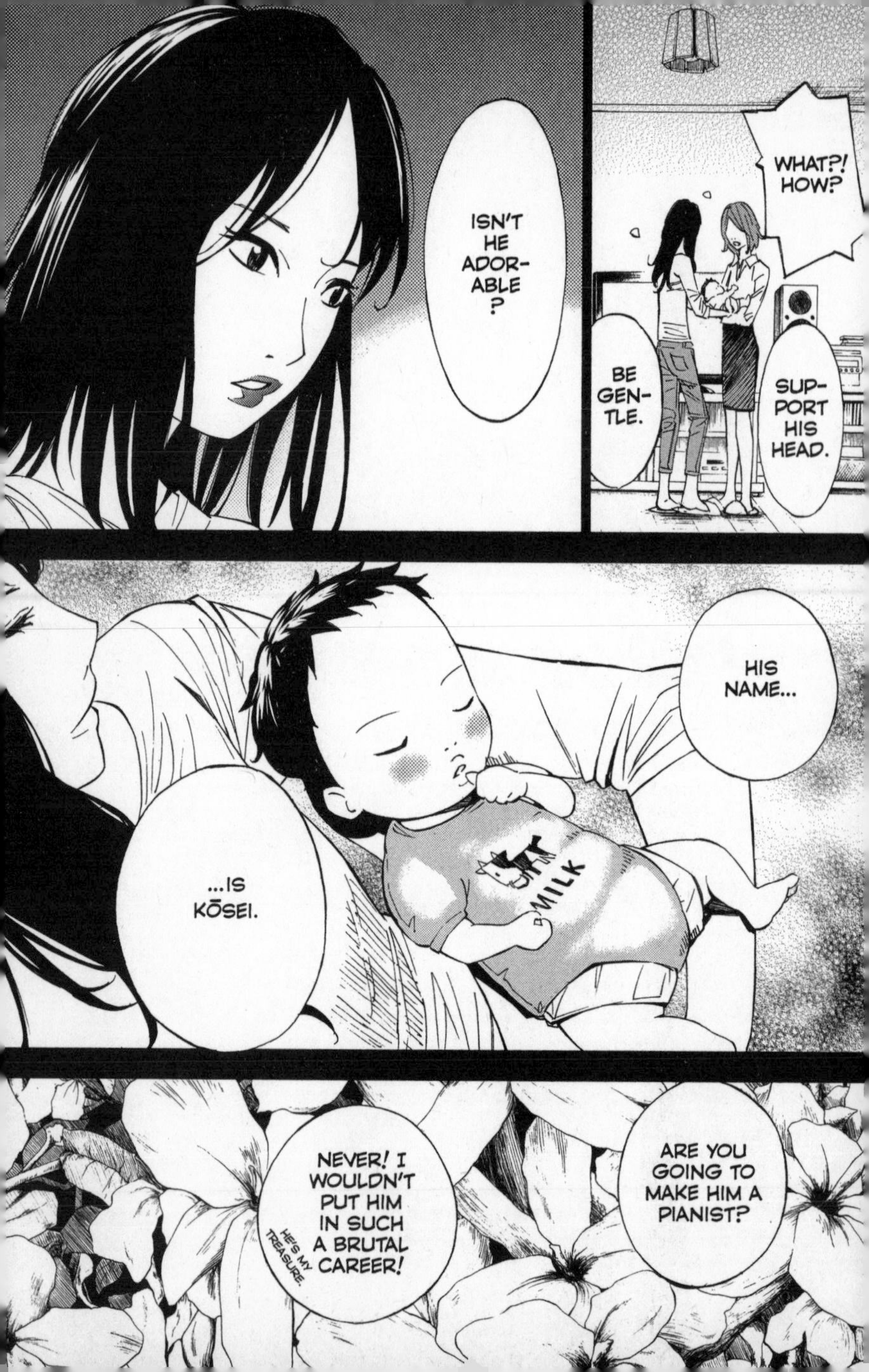
WHAT?! HOW?
SUPPORT HIS HEAD.
BE GENTLE.
ISN'T HE ADORABLE?
HIS NAME...
...IS KŌSEI.
ARE YOU GOING TO MAKE HIM A PIANIST?
NEVER! I WOULDN'T PUT HIM IN SUCH A BRUTAL CAREER!
HE'S MY TREASURE.

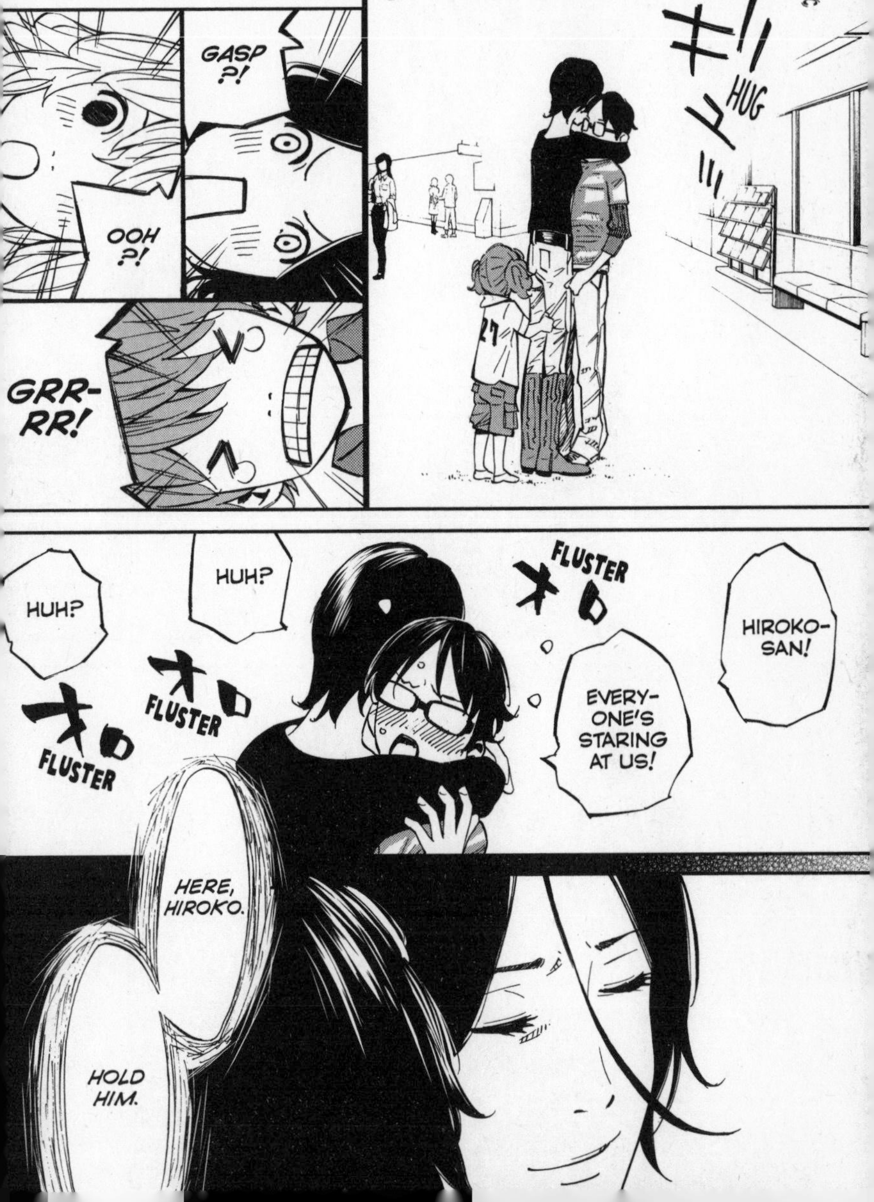
HUG
GASP ?!
OOH ?!
GRR-RR!
HIROKO-SAN!
FLUSTER
EVERY-ONE'S STARING AT US!
HUH?
HUH?
FLUSTER
FLUSTER
HERE, HIROKO.
HOLD HIM.

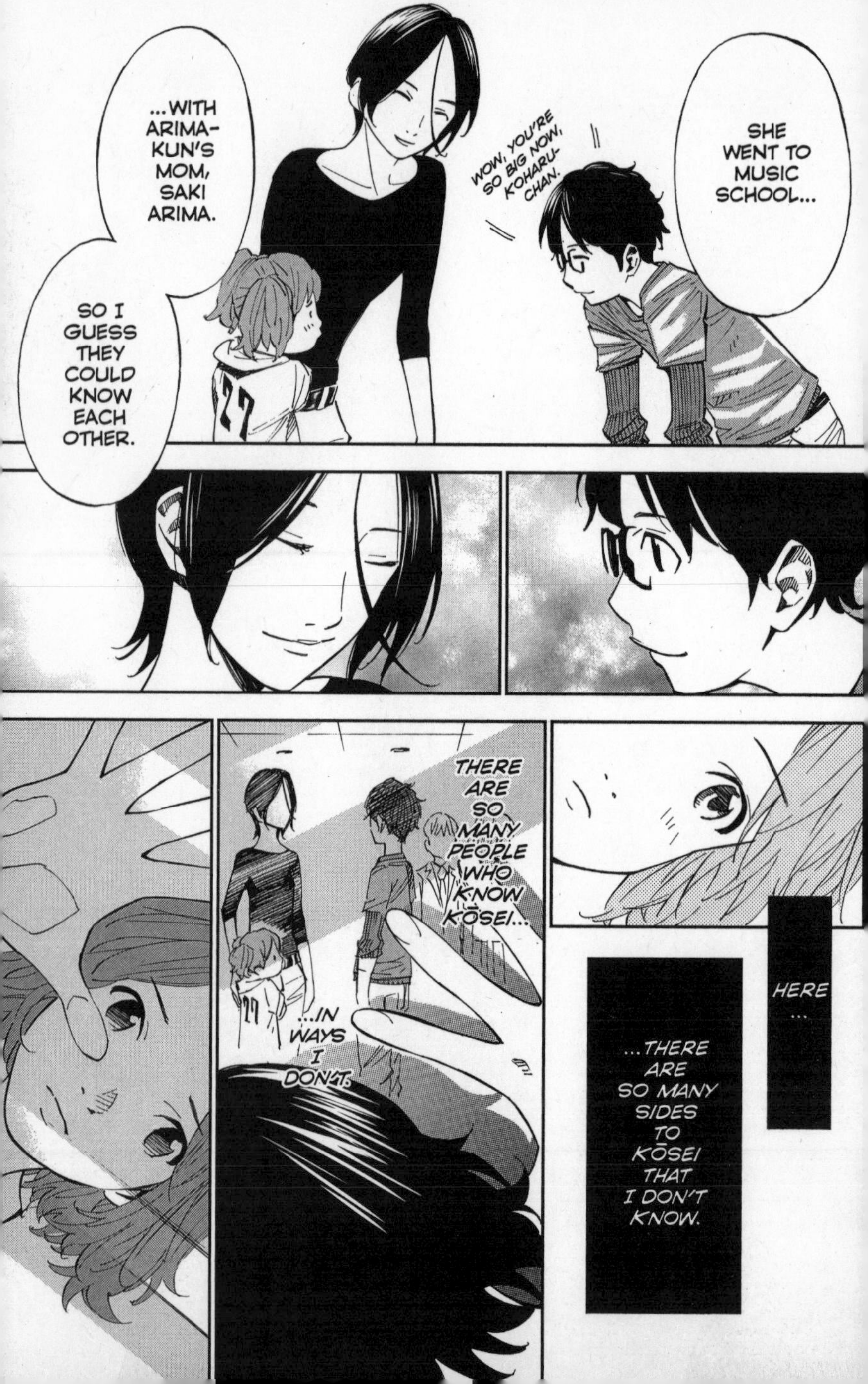
SHE WENT TO MUSIC SCHOOL...
WOW, YOU'RE SO BIG NOW, KOHARU-CHAN.
...WITH ARIMA-KUN'S MOM, SAKI ARIMA.
SO I GUESS THEY COULD KNOW EACH OTHER.
THERE ARE SO MANY PEOPLE WHO KNOW KŌSEI...
...IN WAYS I DON'T.
HERE...
...THERE ARE SO MANY SIDES TO KŌSEI THAT I DON'T KNOW.

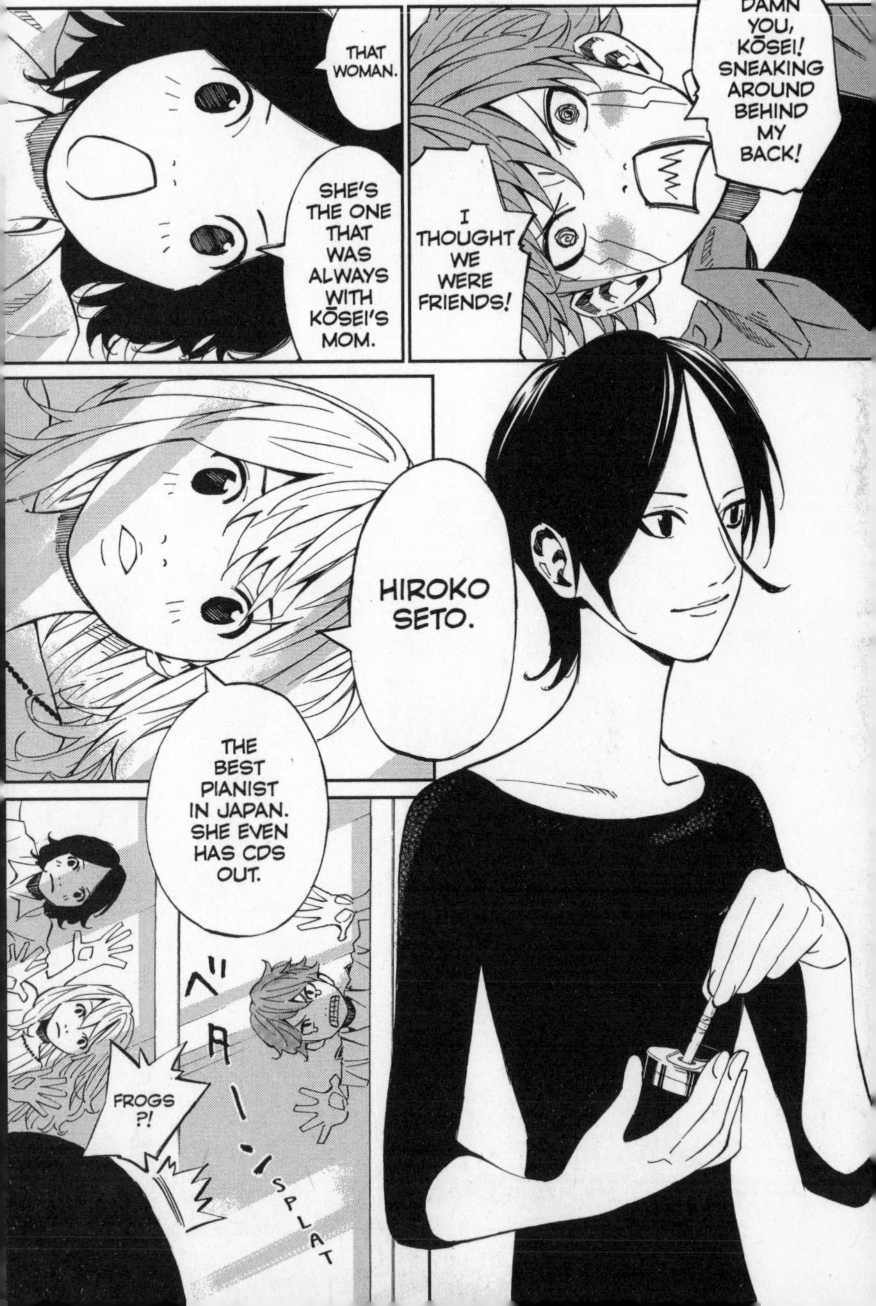
DAMN YOU, KŌSEI! SNEAKING AROUND BEHIND MY BACK!
I THOUGHT WE WERE FRIENDS!
THAT WOMAN.
SHE'S THE ONE THAT WAS ALWAYS WITH KŌSEI'S MOM.
HIROKO SETO.
THE BEST PIANIST IN JAPAN. SHE EVEN HAS CDS OUT.
FROGS ?!
SPLAT

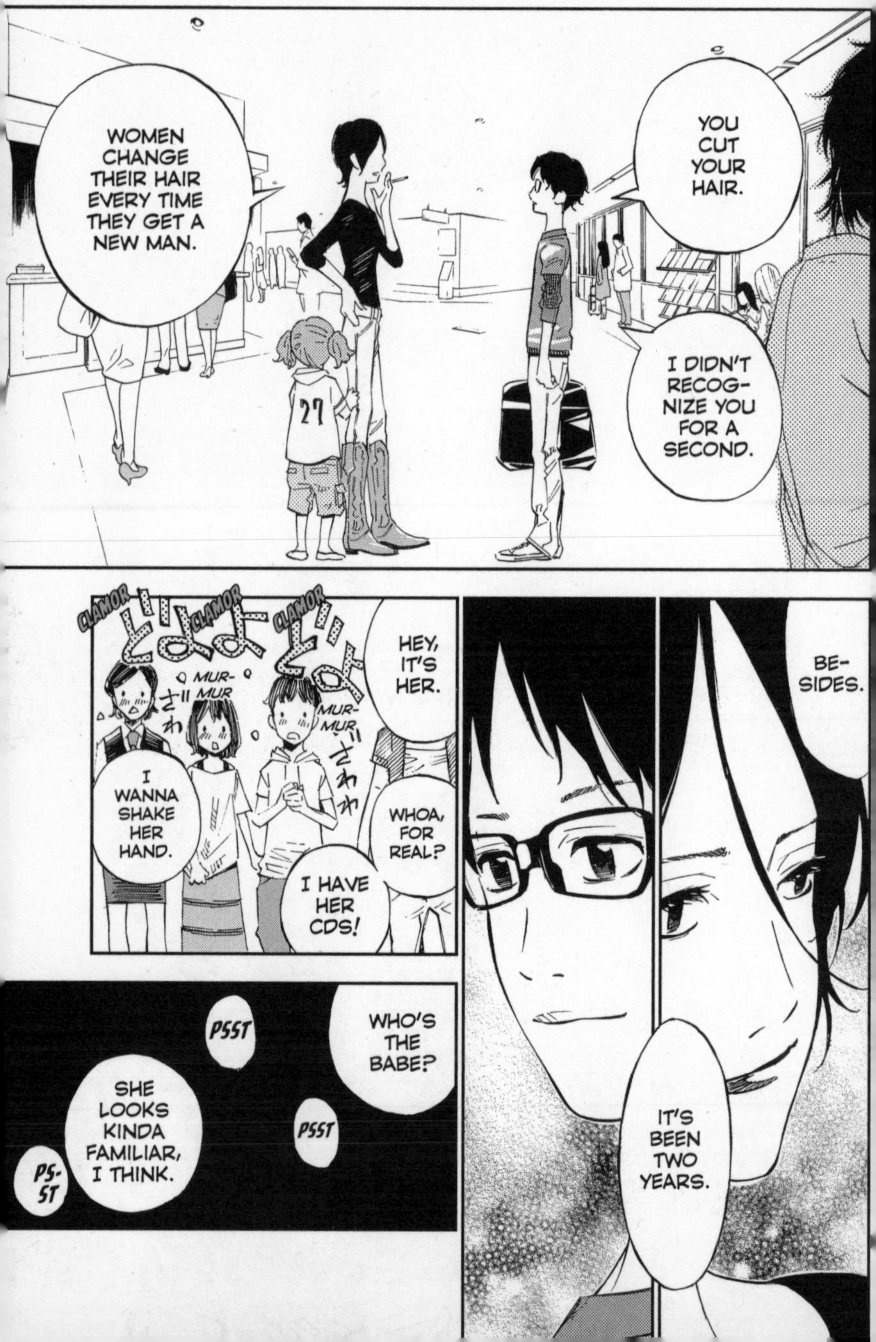

YOU CUT YOUR HAIR.
I DIDN'T RECOGNIZE YOU FOR A SECOND.
WOMEN CHANGE THEIR HAIR EVERY TIME THEY GET A NEW MAN.
BE-SIDES.
IT'S BEEN TWO YEARS.
HEY, IT'S HER.
CLAMOR
CLAMOR
CLAMOR
MUR-MUR
MUR-MUR
WHOA, FOR REAL?
I WANNA SHAKE HER HAND.
I HAVE HER CDS!
WHO'S THE BABE?
PSST
PSST
SHE LOOKS KINDA FAMILIAR, I THINK.
PS-ST

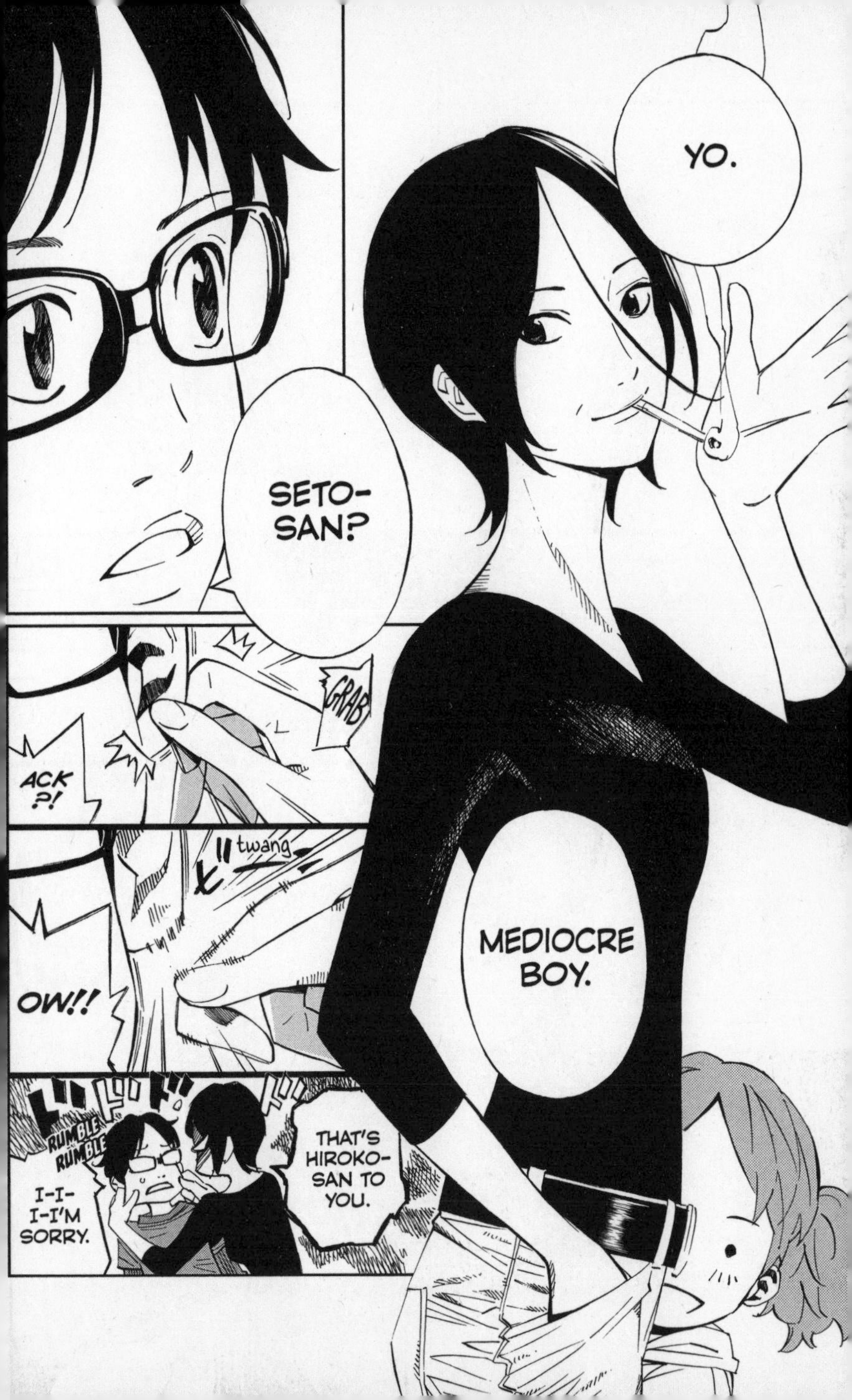
YO.
MEDIOCRE BOY.
SETO-SAN?
GRAB
ACK ?!
twang
OW!!
RUMBLE RUMBLE
THAT'S HIROKO-SAN TO YOU.
I-I-I-I'M SORRY.

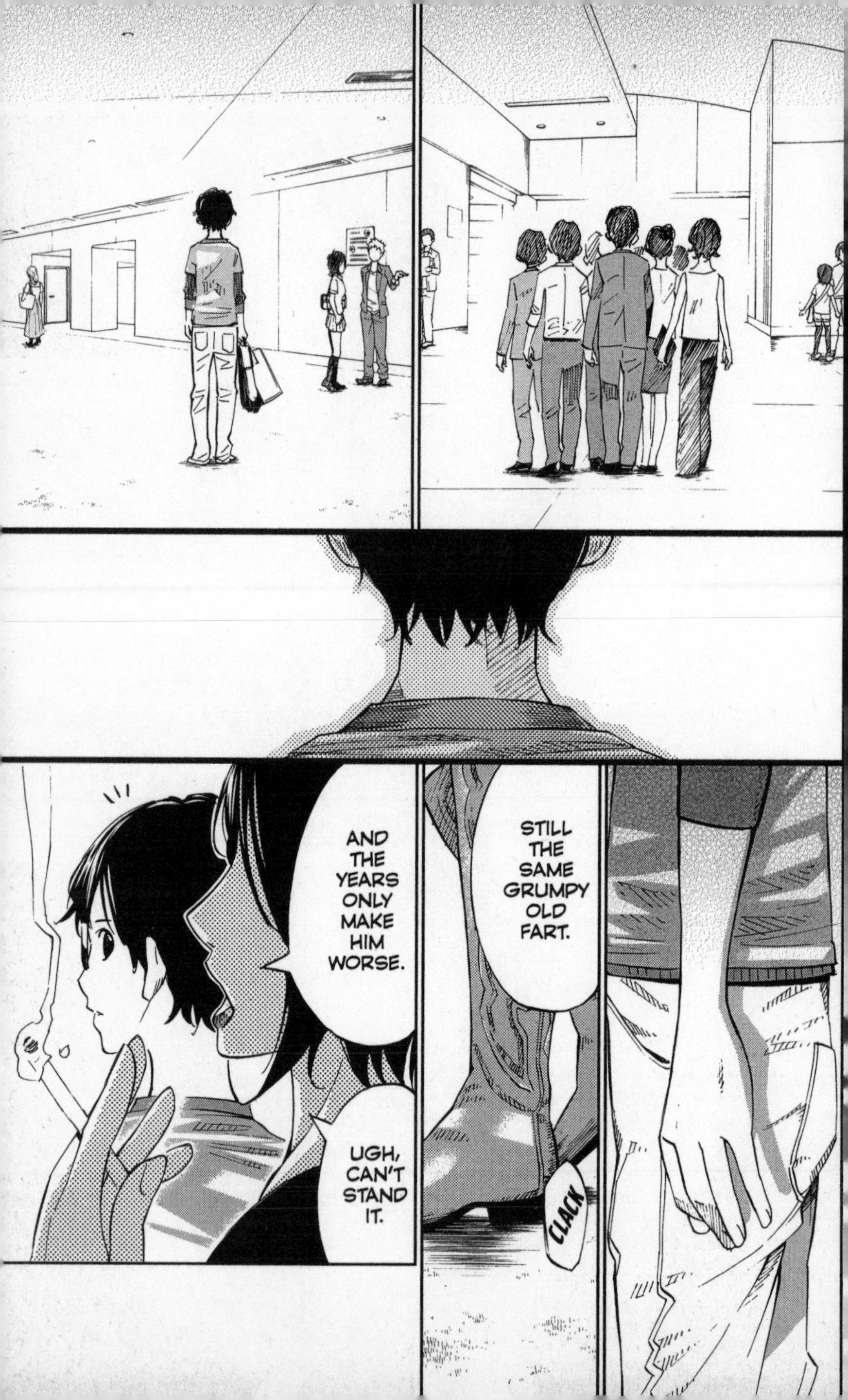
STILL THE SAME GRUMPY OLD FART.
CLACK
AND THE YEARS ONLY MAKE HIM WORSE.
UGH, CAN'T STAND IT.

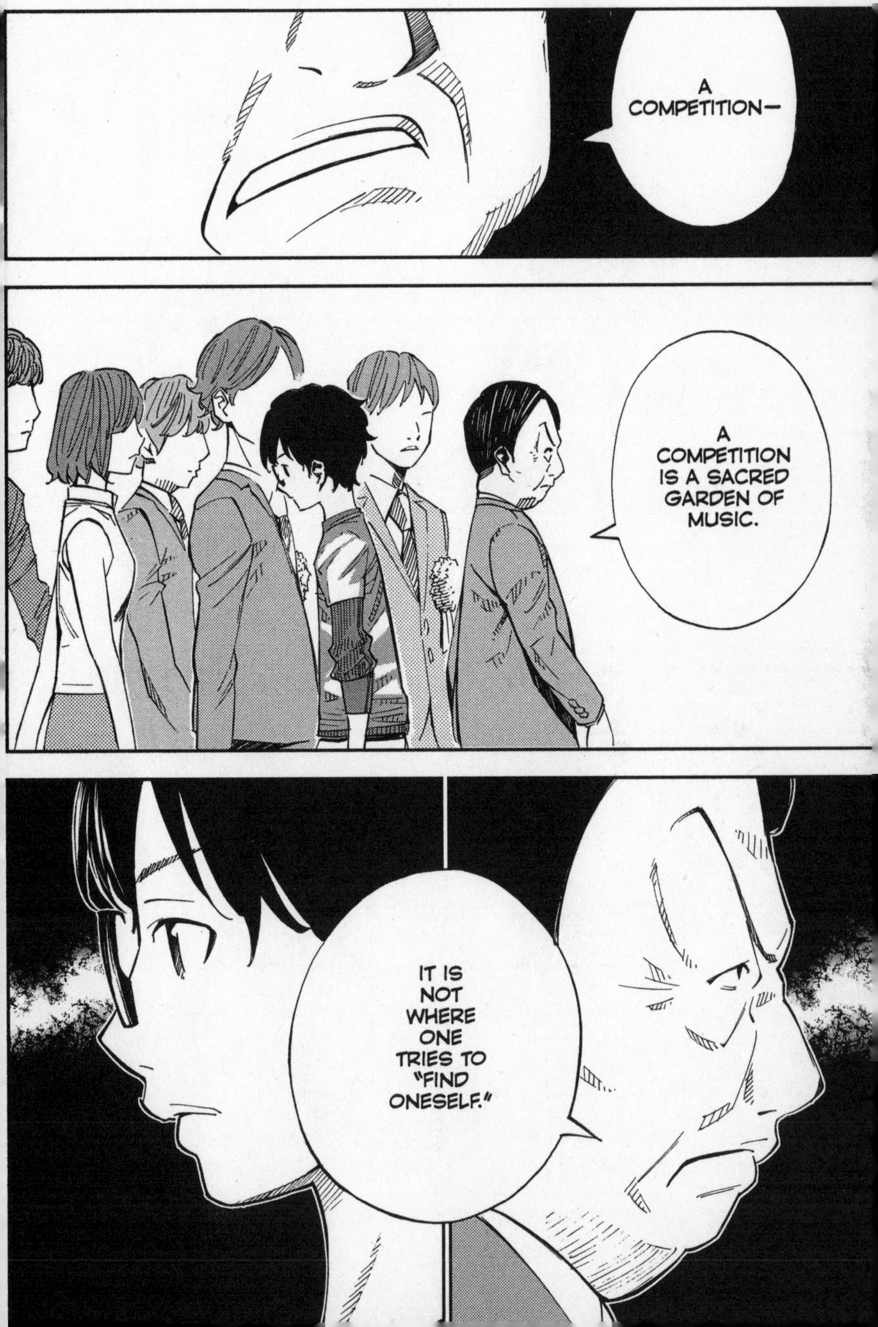
A COMPETITION—
A COMPETITION IS A SACRED GARDEN OF MUSIC.
IT IS NOT WHERE ONE TRIES TO "FIND ONESELF."

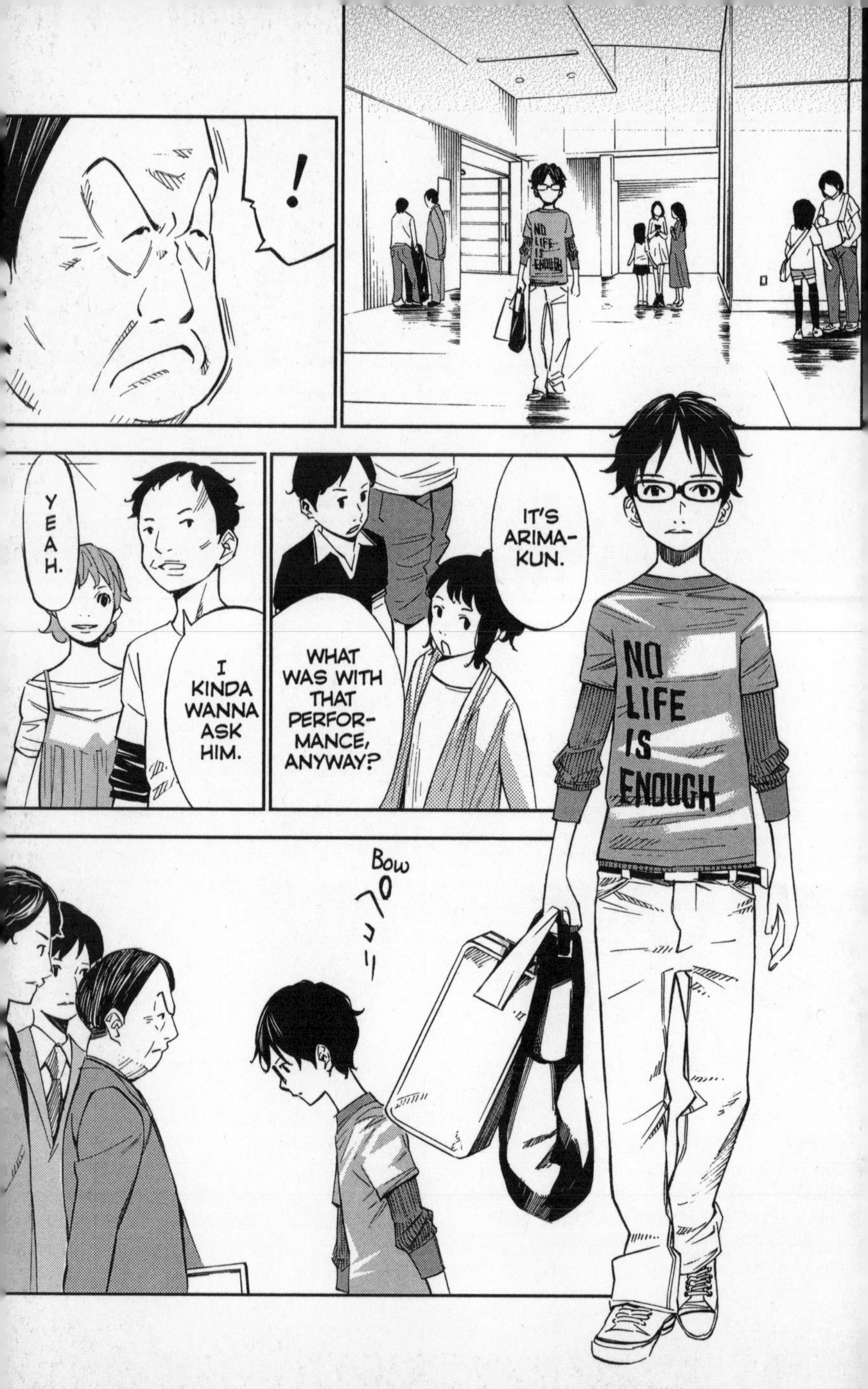
!
IT'S ARIMA-KUN.
WHAT WAS WITH THAT PERFORMANCE, ANYWAY?
I KINDA WANNA ASK HIM.
YEAH.
Bow

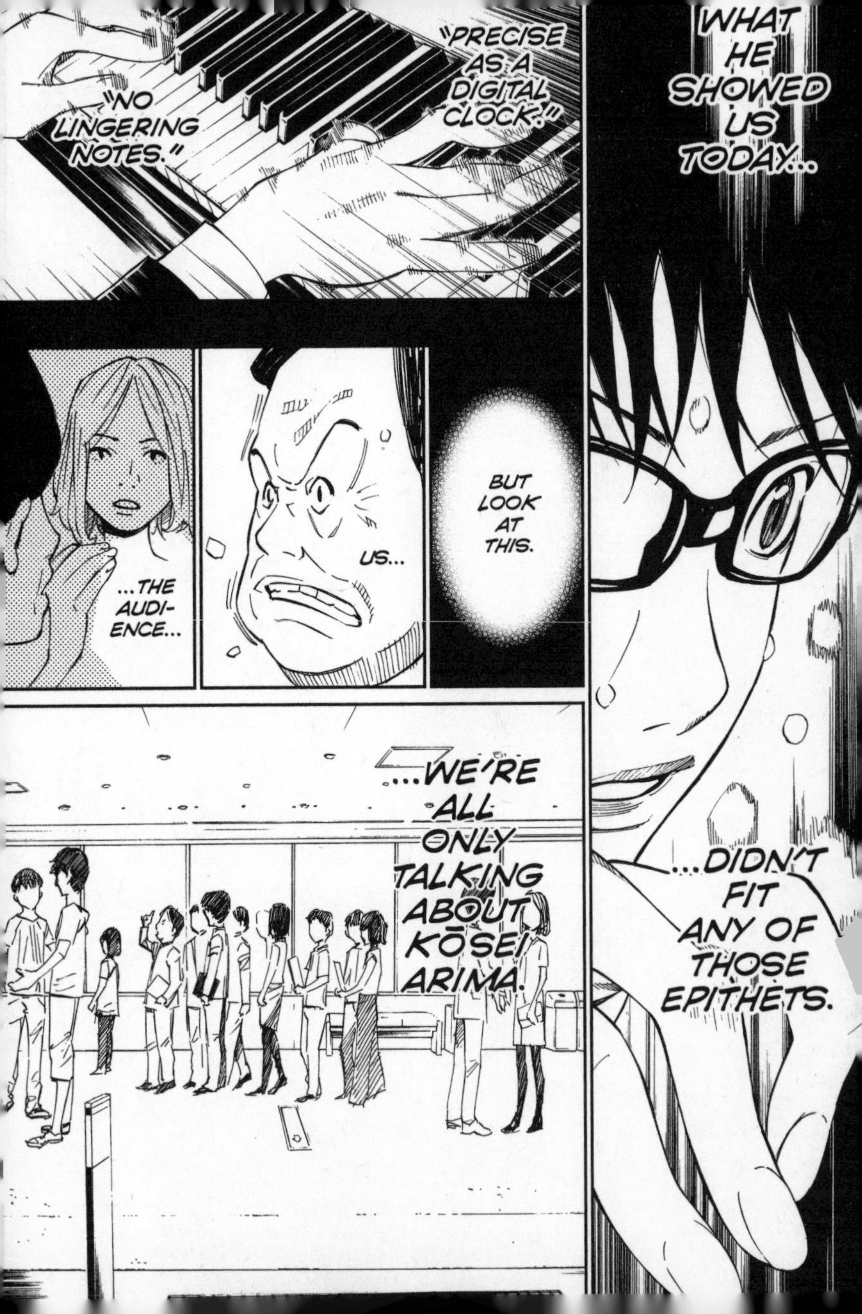
WHAT HE SHOWED US TODAY...
...DIDN'T FIT ANY OF THOSE EPITHETS.
"PRECISE AS A DIGITAL CLOCK."
"NO LINGERING NOTES."
BUT LOOK AT THIS.
US...
...THE AUDI-ENCE...
...WE'RE ALL ONLY TALKING ABOUT KŌSEI ARIMA.

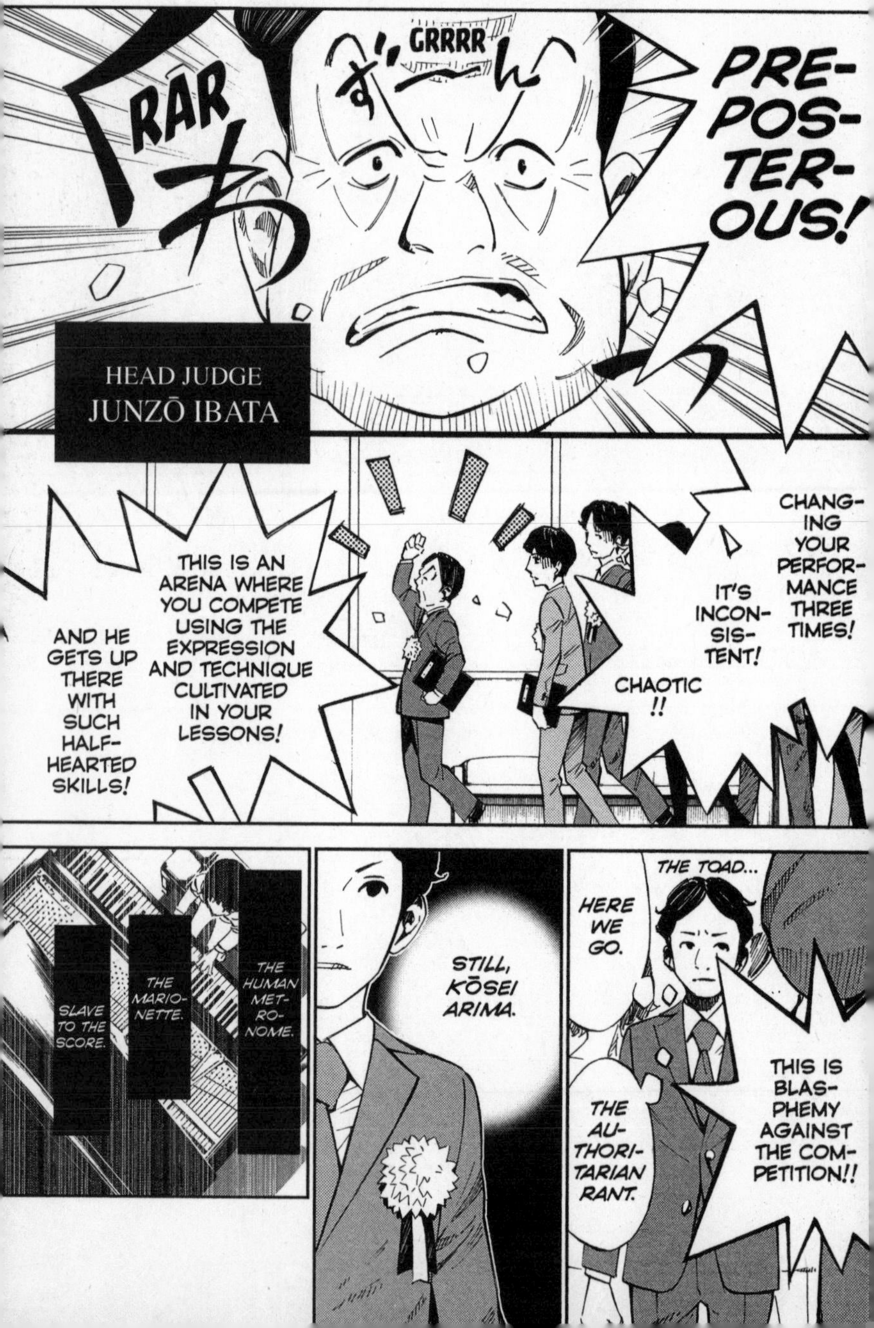
PREPOSTEROUS!
GRRRR
RAR
HEAD JUDGE JUNZŌ IBATA
CHANGING YOUR PERFORMANCE THREE TIMES!
IT'S INCONSISTENT!
CHAOTIC!!
THIS IS AN ARENA WHERE YOU COMPETE USING THE EXPRESSION AND TECHNIQUE CULTIVATED IN YOUR LESSONS!
AND HE GETS UP THERE WITH SUCH HALF-HEARTED SKILLS!
THE TOAD...
HERE WE GO.
THIS IS BLASPHEMY AGAINST THE COMPETITION!!
THE AUTHORITARIAN RANT.
STILL, KŌSEI ARIMA.
THE HUMAN METRONOME.
THE MARIONETTE.
SLAVE TO THE SCORE.

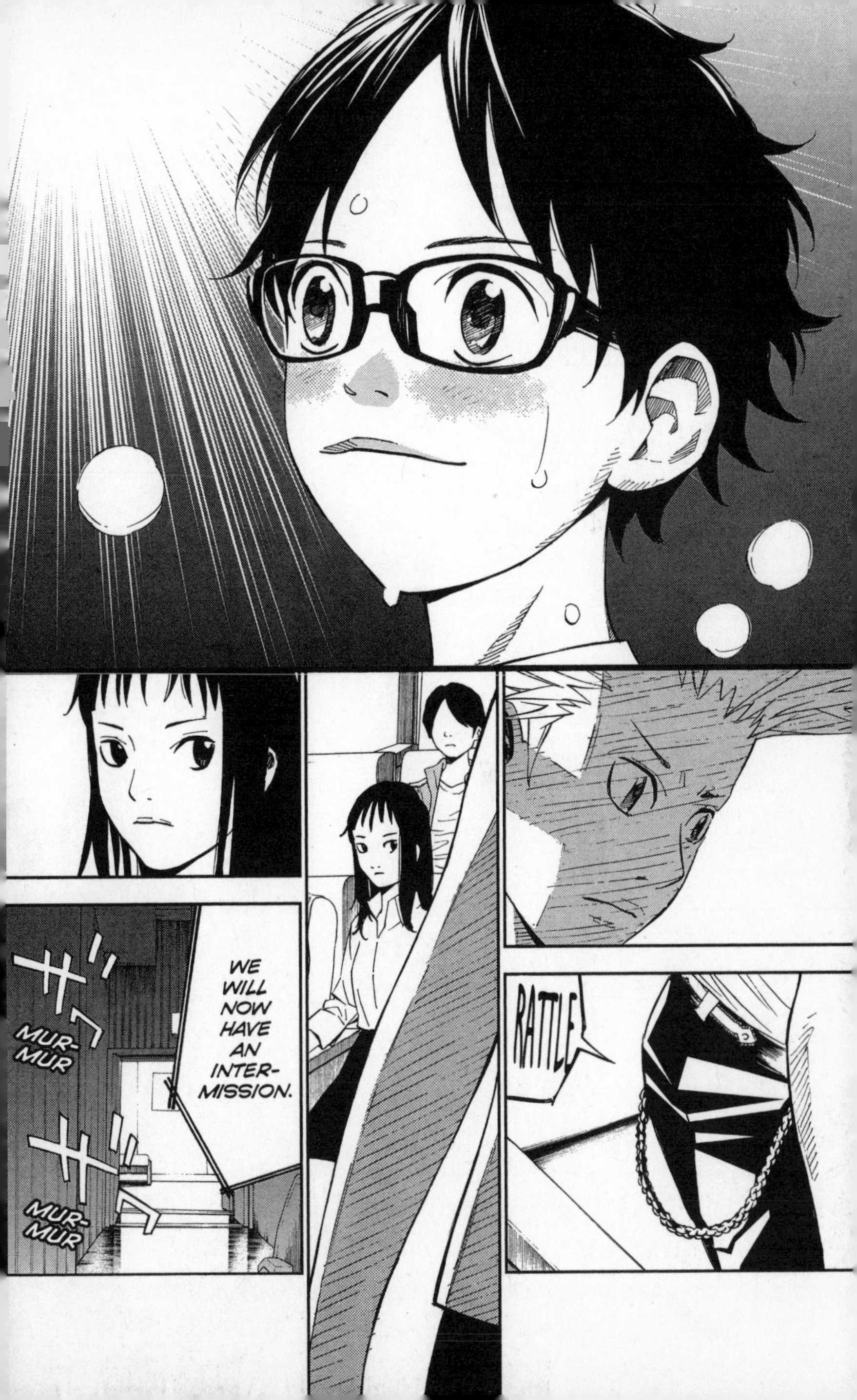
RATTLE
WE WILL NOW HAVE AN INTER-MISSION.
MUR-MUR
MUR-MUR

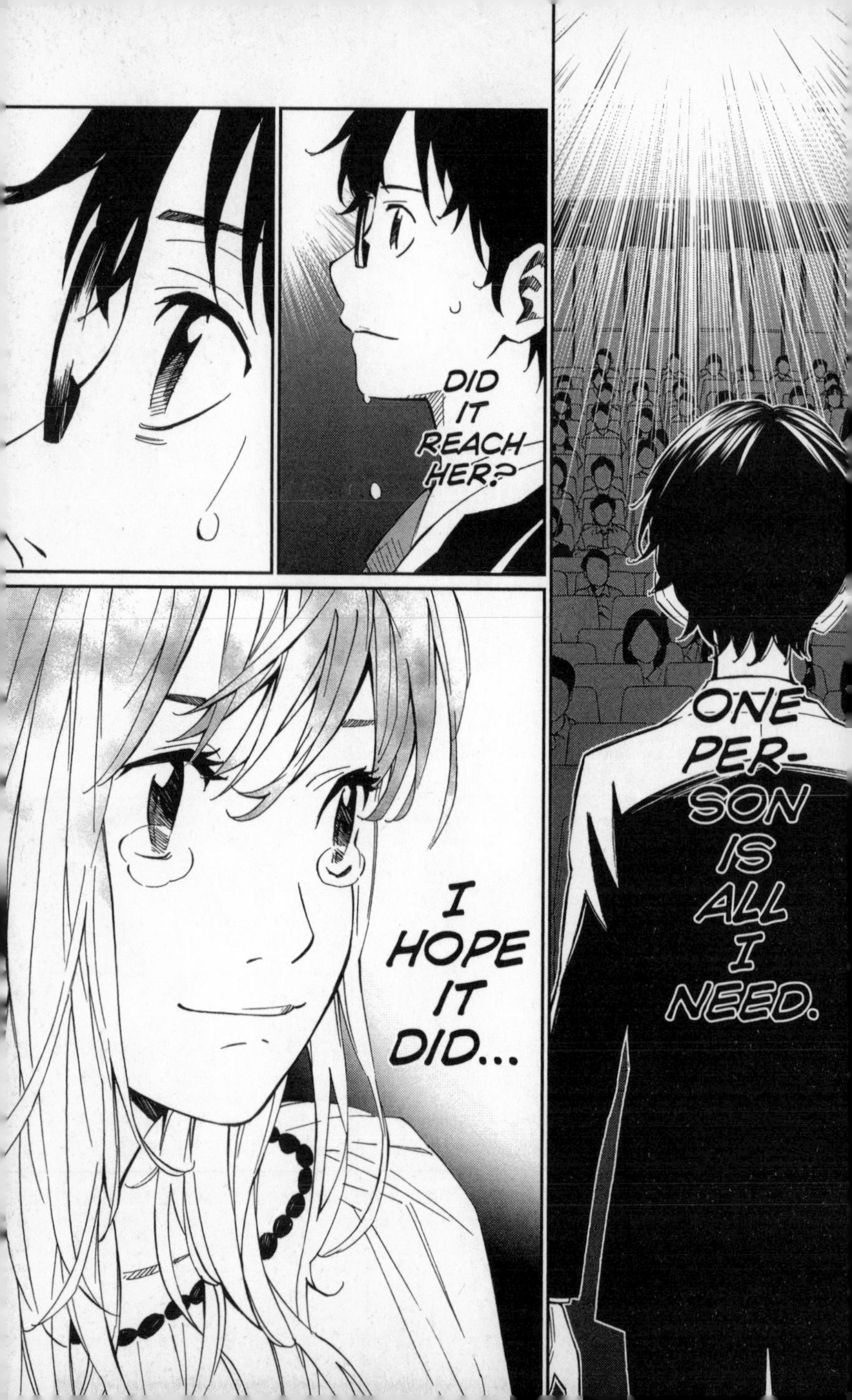
ONE PER-SON IS ALL I NEED.
DID IT REACH HER?
I HOPE IT DID...

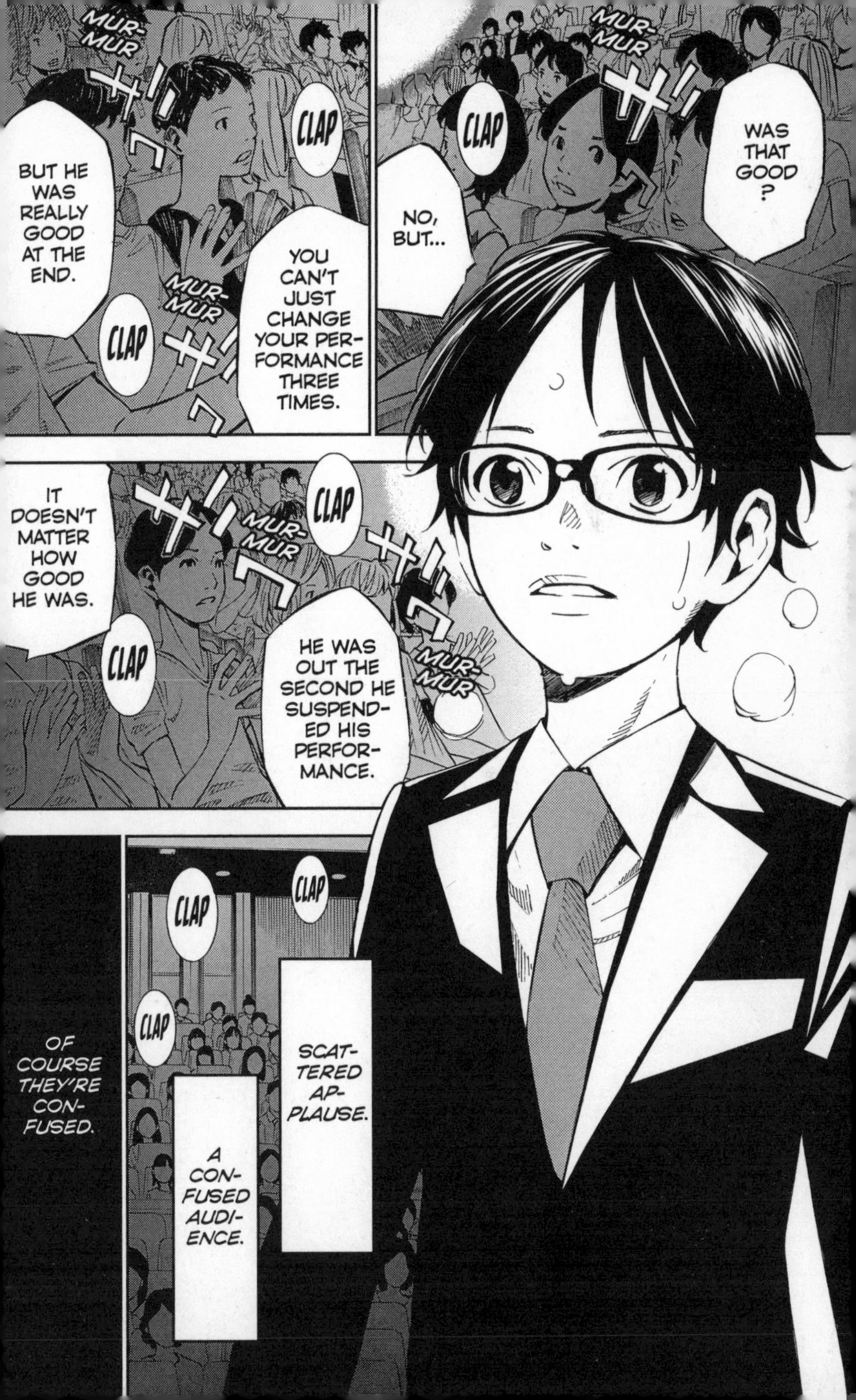
MUR-MUR
WAS THAT GOOD?
CLAP
NO, BUT...
MUR-MUR
CLAP
BUT HE WAS REALLY GOOD AT THE END.
YOU CAN'T JUST CHANGE YOUR PERFORMANCE THREE TIMES.
MUR-MUR
CLAP
CLAP
MUR-MUR
IT DOESN'T MATTER HOW GOOD HE WAS.
HE WAS OUT THE SECOND HE SUSPENDED HIS PERFORMANCE.
MUR-MUR
CLAP
CLAP
CLAP
SCATTERED APPLAUSE.
A CONFUSED AUDIENCE.
CLAP
OF COURSE THEY'RE CONFUSED.

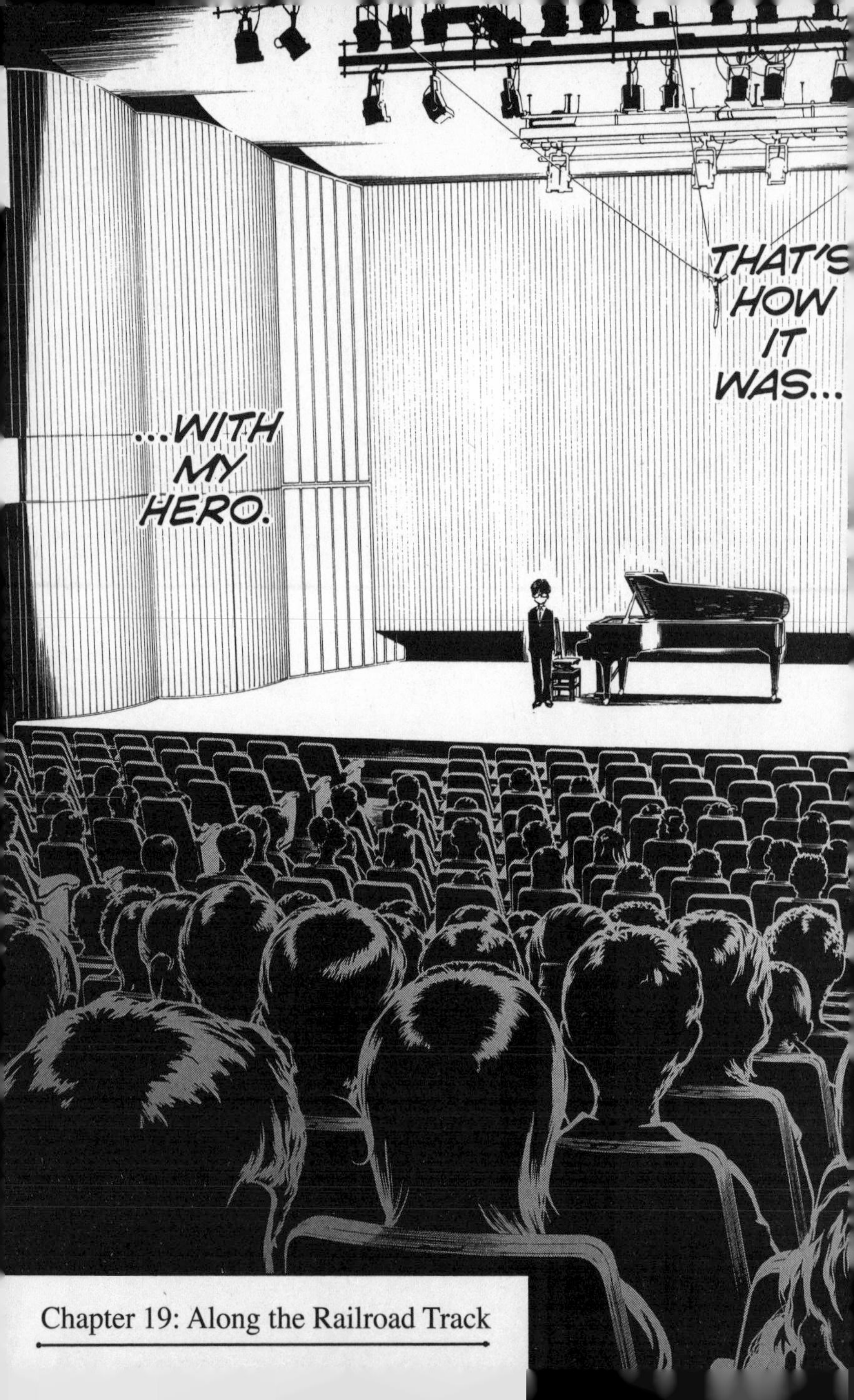
THAT'S HOW IT WAS...
...WITH MY HERO.

Chapter 19: Along the Railroad Track

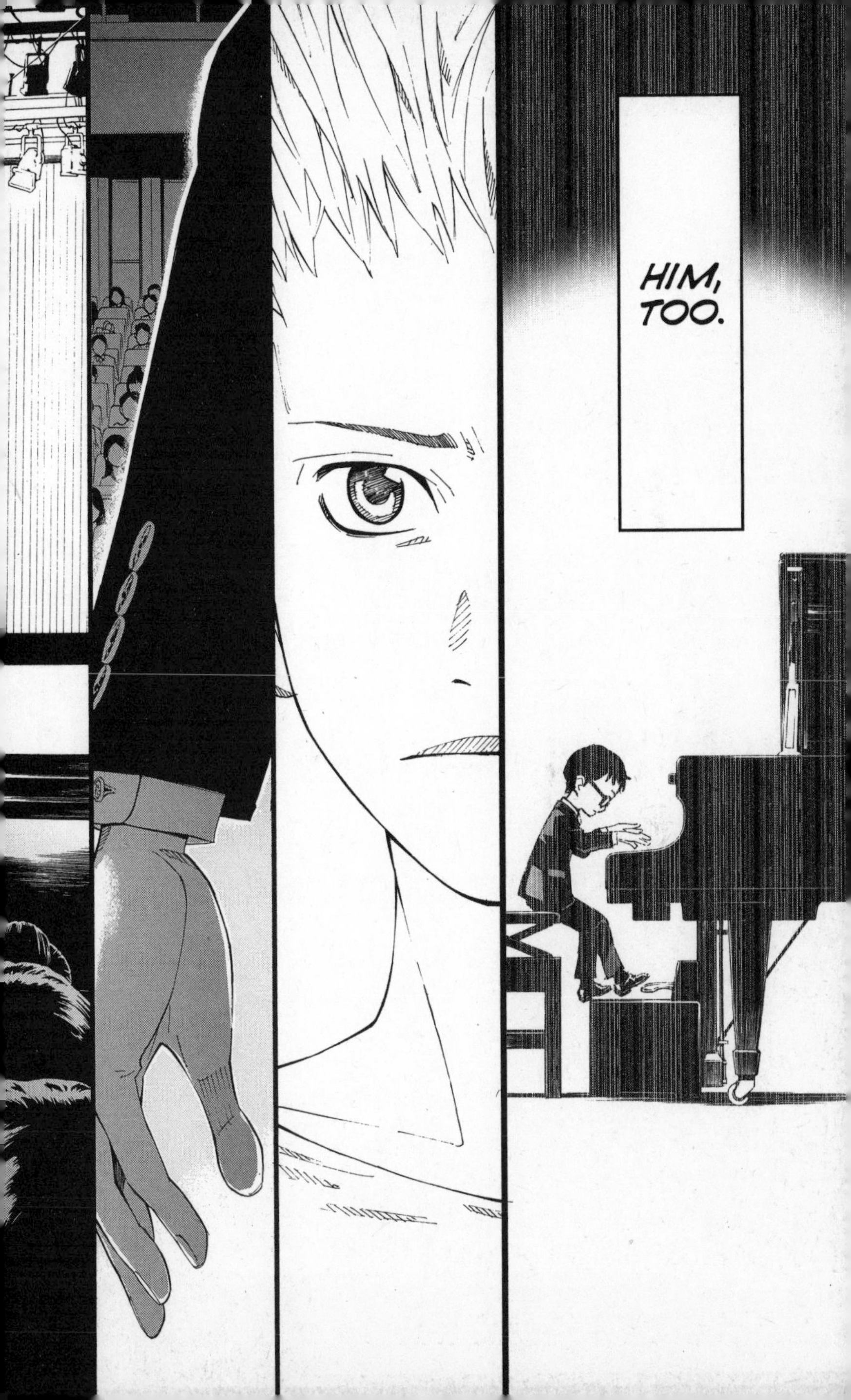
HIM, TOO.

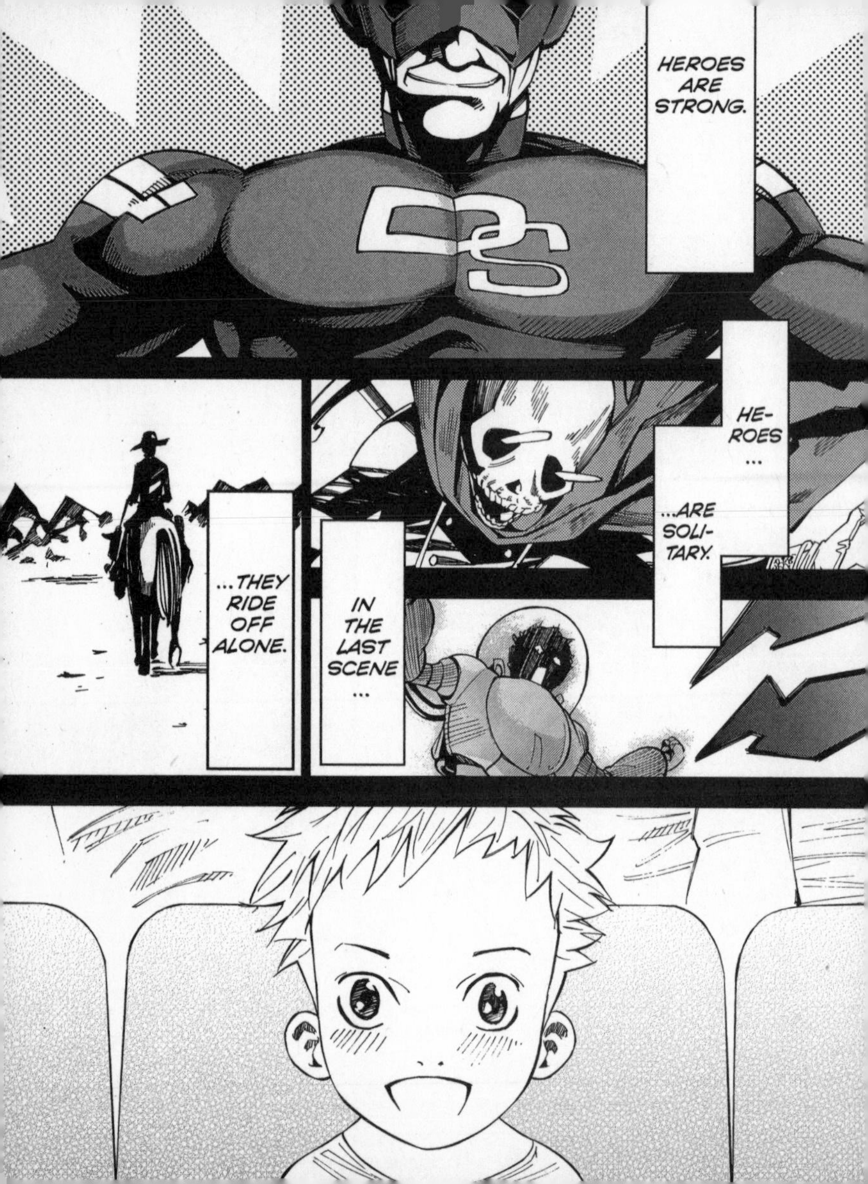
HEROES ARE STRONG.
HE-ROES...
...ARE SOLI-TARY.
IN THE LAST SCENE...
...THEY RIDE OFF ALONE.

YOUR LIE IN APRIL FEATURED MUSIC

CHOPIN'S ÉTUDES OP. 25, NO. 5 IN E MINOR

The most memorable part of this piece is its middle section, with a sweet, beautiful melody that makes it a hidden gem of music, beloved by many pianists. In this middle section, the melodies of the right and left hand intertwine, revealing a beautiful flower of romanticism that is the epitome of Chopin.

The beginning, which at first glance seems to repeat the same pattern again and again, starts with the right hand playing a light rhythm and is then directed through subtle changes in the rhythm and phrasing. To convey these subtle changes of expression, the movement of the hands and fingers must be flexible and precise.

It doesn't have any of the grandiose finesse of Op. 10 No. 4 or Op. 25, No. 11 "Winter Wind," but you could say that this piece does demand delicate technique, as well as mature musicianship, in order to control the sounds of the piano.

(Pianist Masanori Sugano, lecturer at Tokyo University of the Arts and Musashino Academia Musicae)

Watch it on YouTube (Search "Monthly Shonen Magazine Your Lie in April Featured Music")

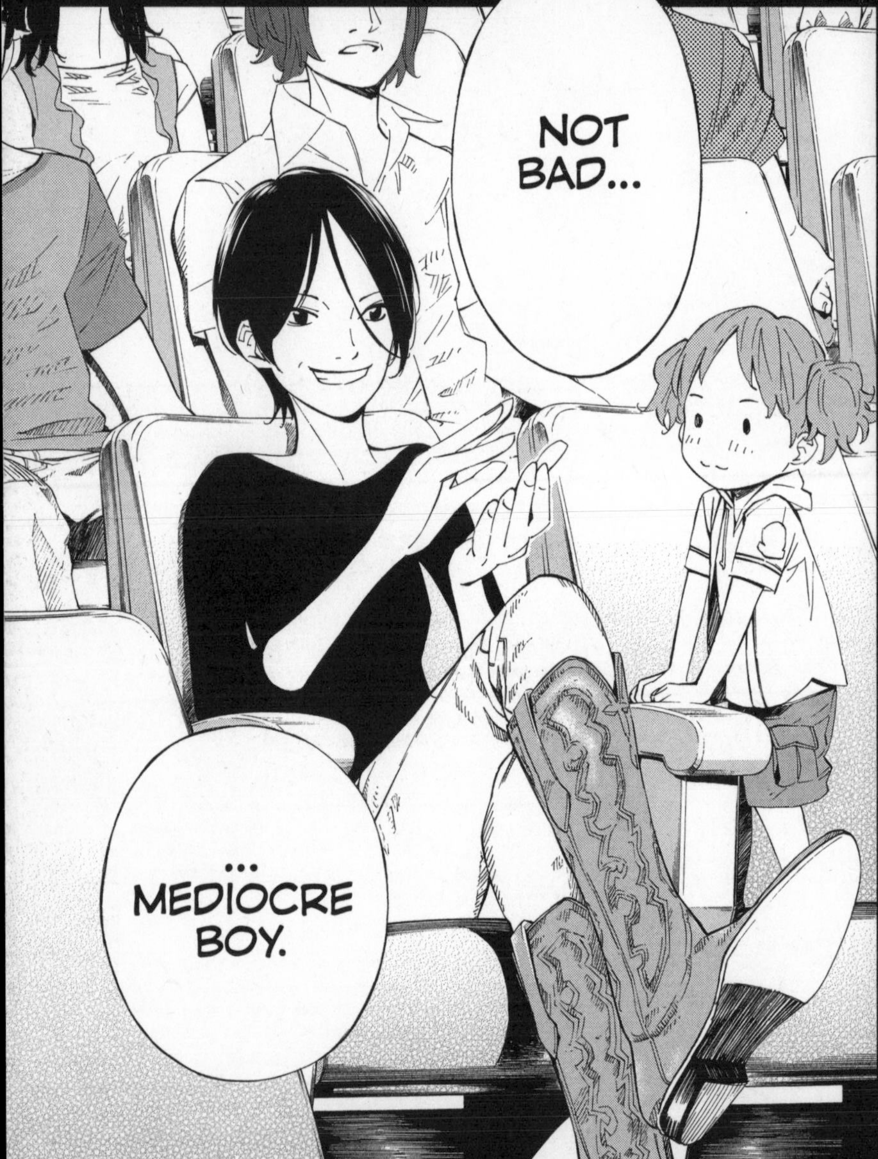
NOT BAD...
... MEDIOCRE BOY.

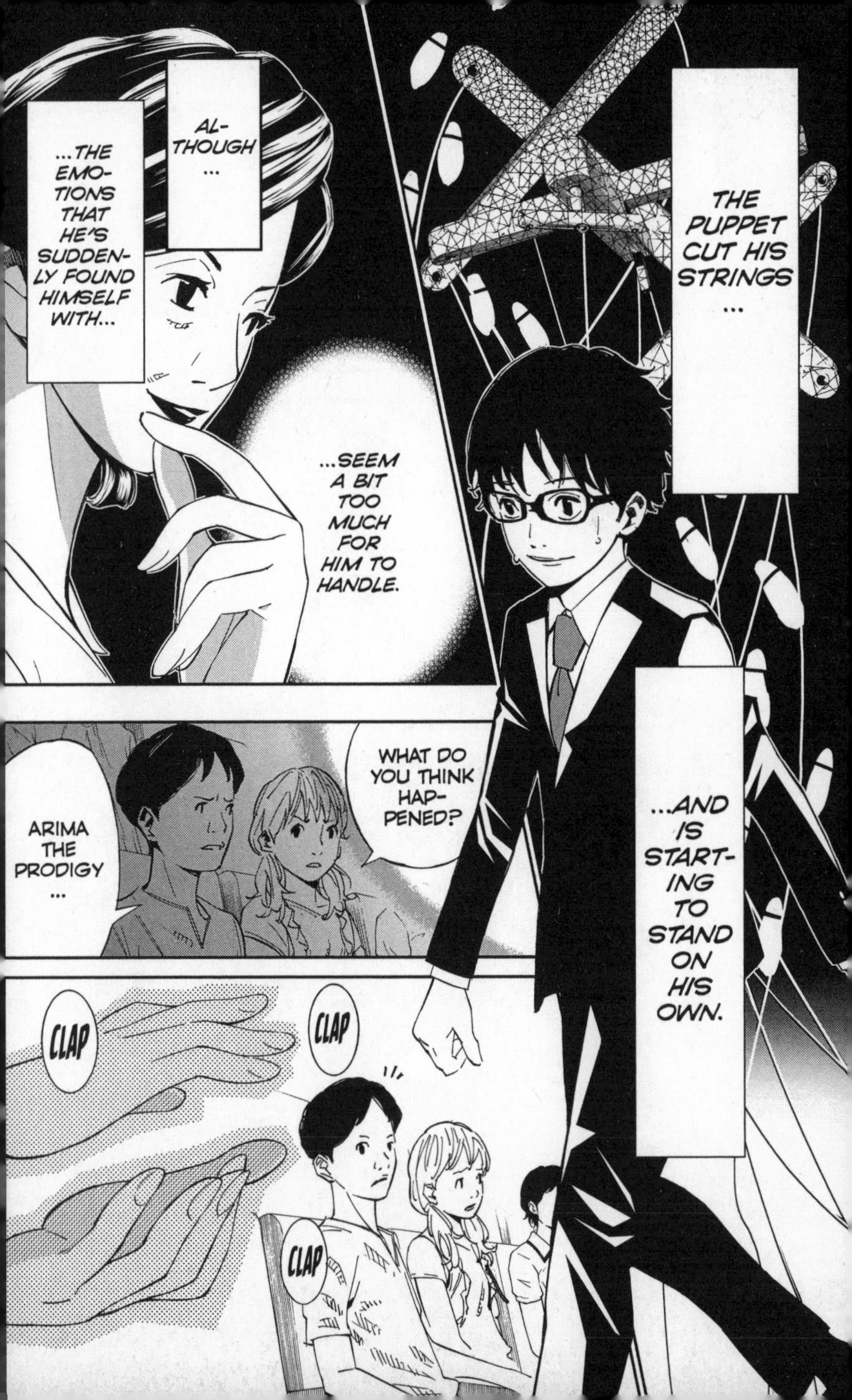
THE PUPPET CUT HIS STRINGS...
...AND IS STARTING TO STAND ON HIS OWN.
ALTHOUGH...
...THE EMOTIONS THAT HE'S SUDDENLY FOUND HIMSELF WITH...
...SEEM A BIT TOO MUCH FOR HIM TO HANDLE.
WHAT DO YOU THINK HAPPENED?
ARIMA THE PRODIGY...
CLAP
CLAP
CLAP

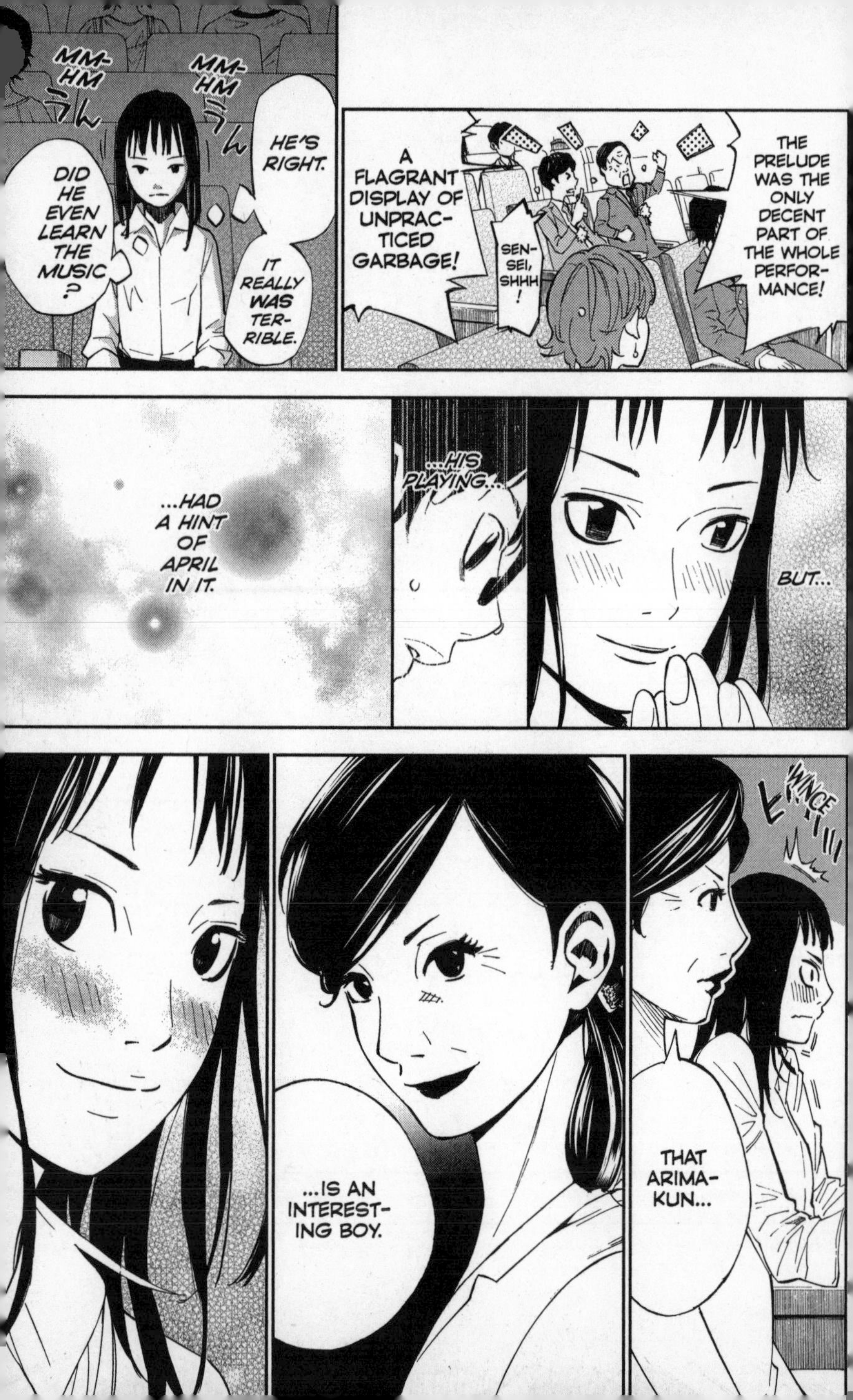
THE PRELUDE WAS THE ONLY DECENT PART OF THE WHOLE PERFORMANCE!
A FLAGRANT DISPLAY OF UNPRAC-TICED GARBAGE!
SEN-SEI, SHHH!
MM-HM うん
HE'S RIGHT.
IT REALLY WAS TER-RIBLE.
MM-HM うん
DID HE EVEN LEARN THE MUSIC?
BUT...
...HIS PLAYING...
...HAD A HINT OF APRIL IN IT.
WINCE
THAT ARIMA-KUN...
...IS AN INTEREST-ING BOY.

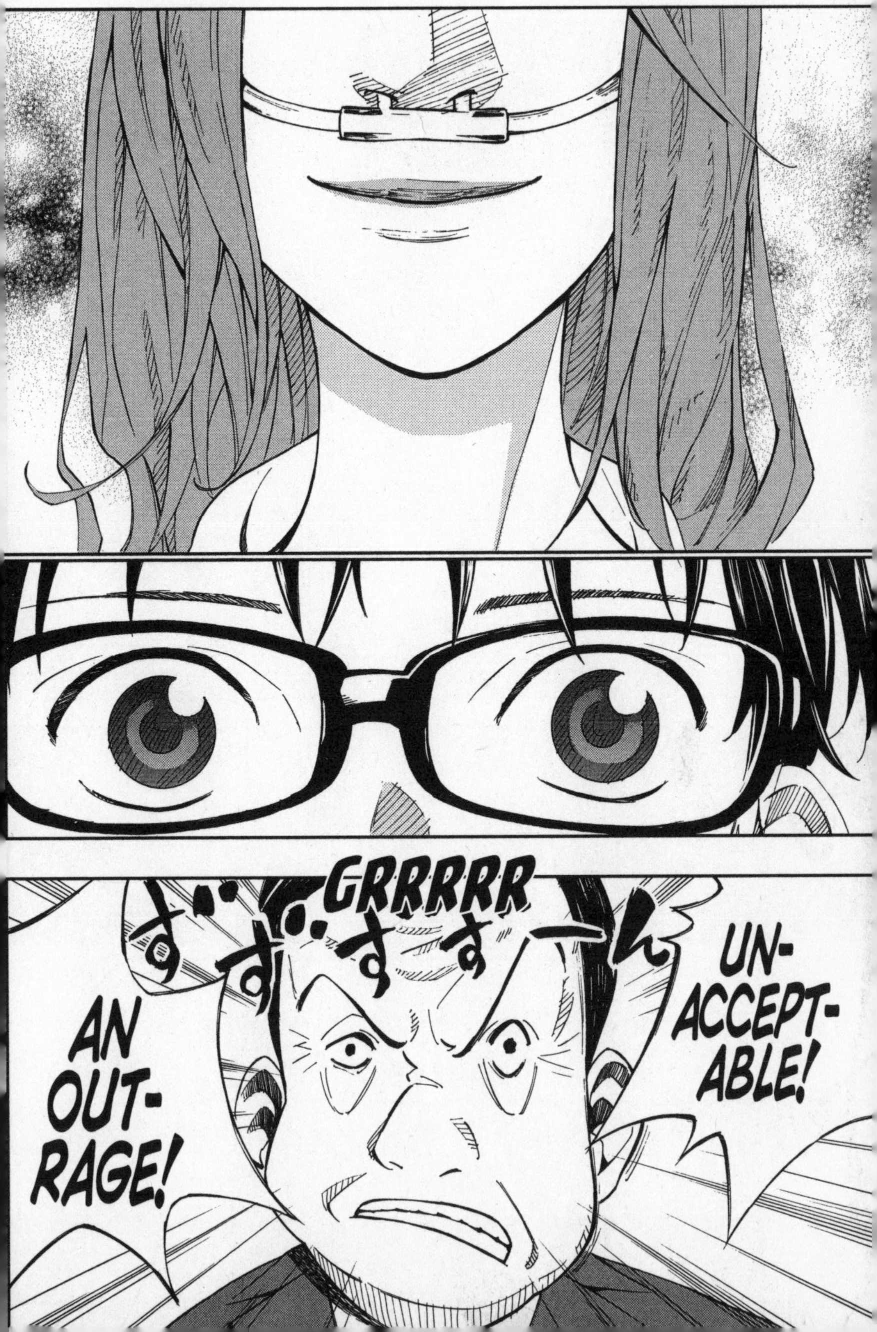
UN-ACCEPT-ABLE!
GRRRRRR
AN OUT-RAGE!

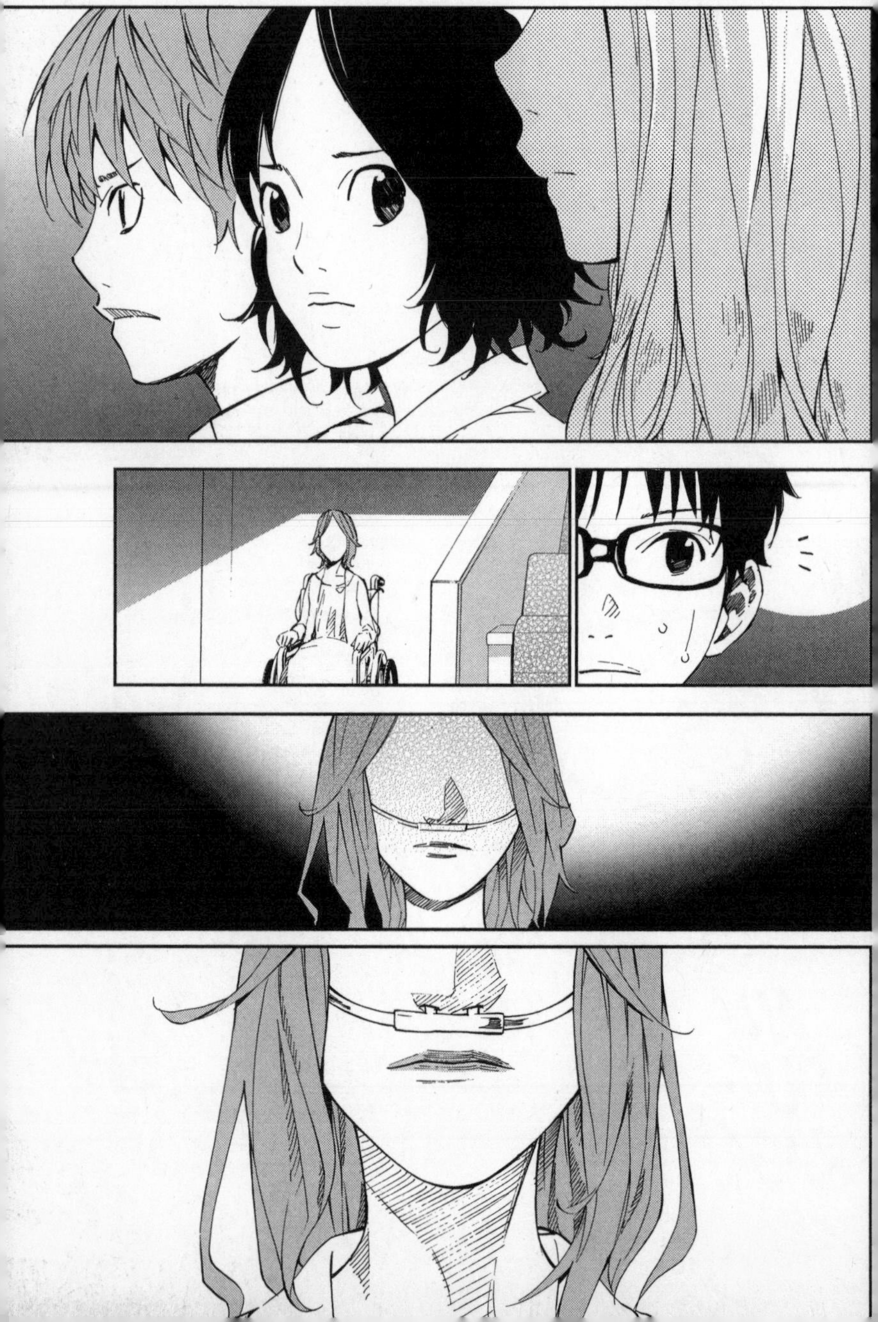

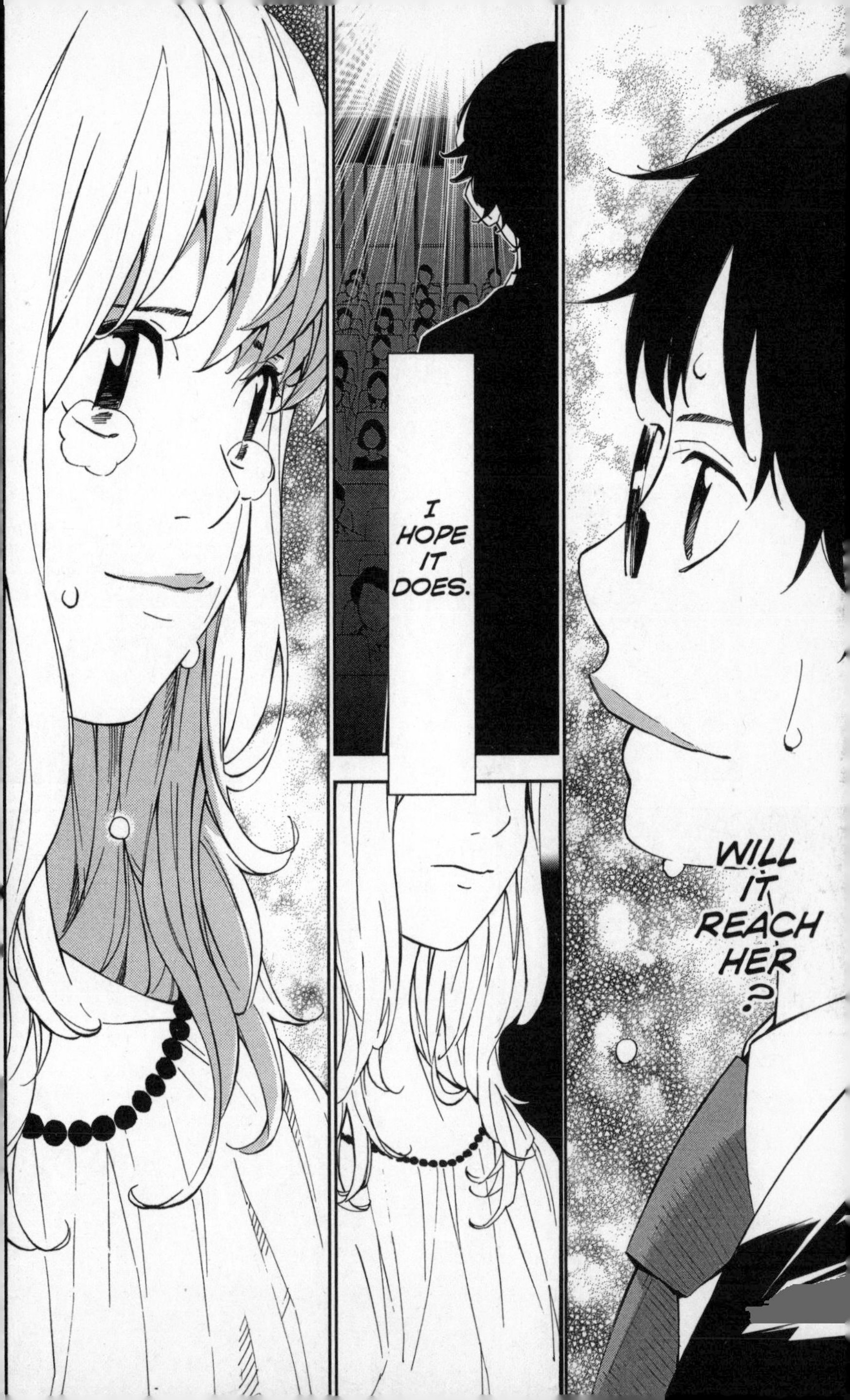
WILL IT REACH HER?
I HOPE IT DOES.

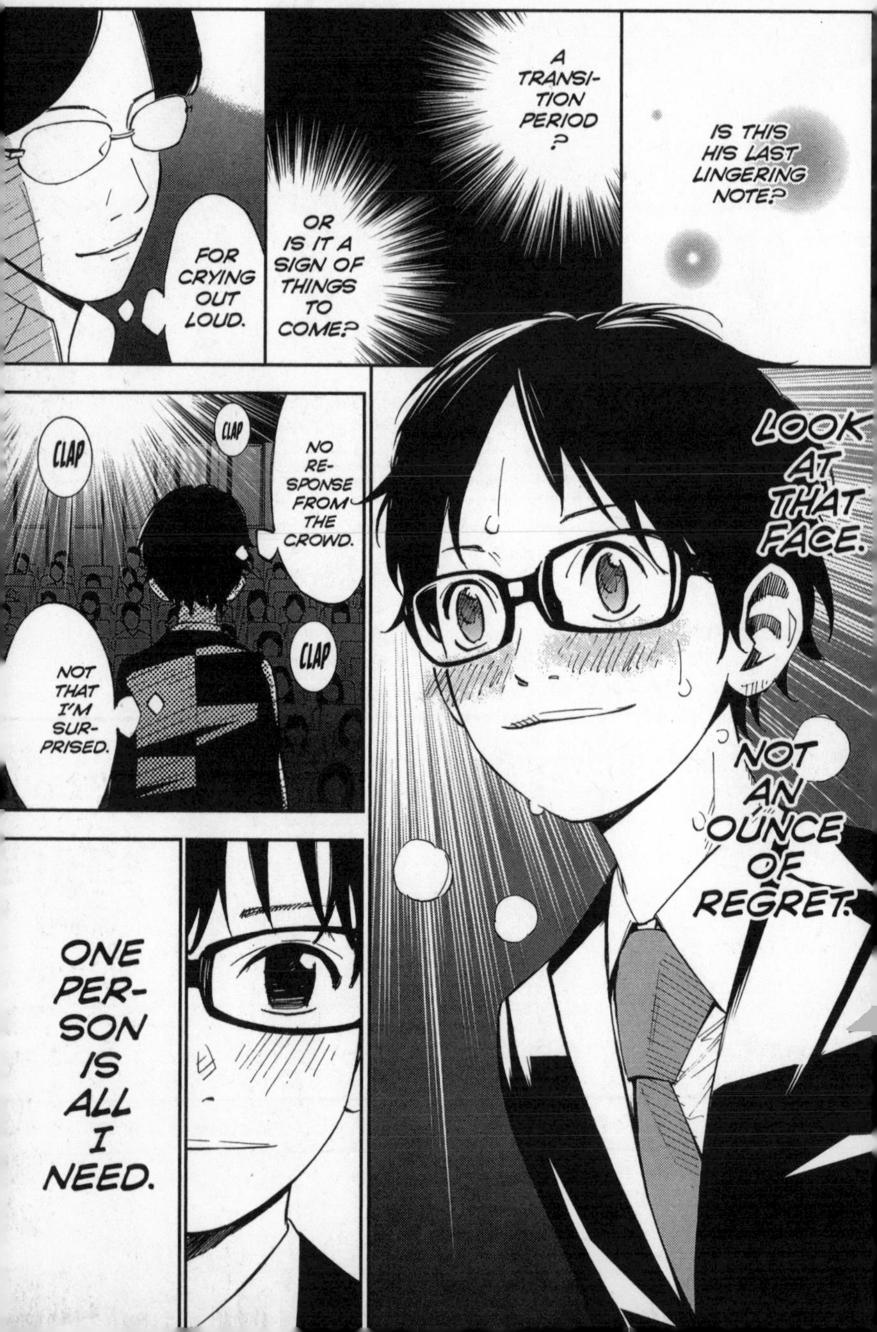
IS THIS HIS LAST LINGERING NOTE?
A TRANSITION PERIOD?
OR IS IT A SIGN OF THINGS TO COME?
FOR CRYING OUT LOUD.
LOOK AT THAT FACE.
NOT AN OUNCE OF REGRET.
CLAP
NO RESPONSE FROM THE CROWD.
CLAP
CLAP
NOT THAT I'M SURPRISED.
ONE PERSON IS ALL I NEED.

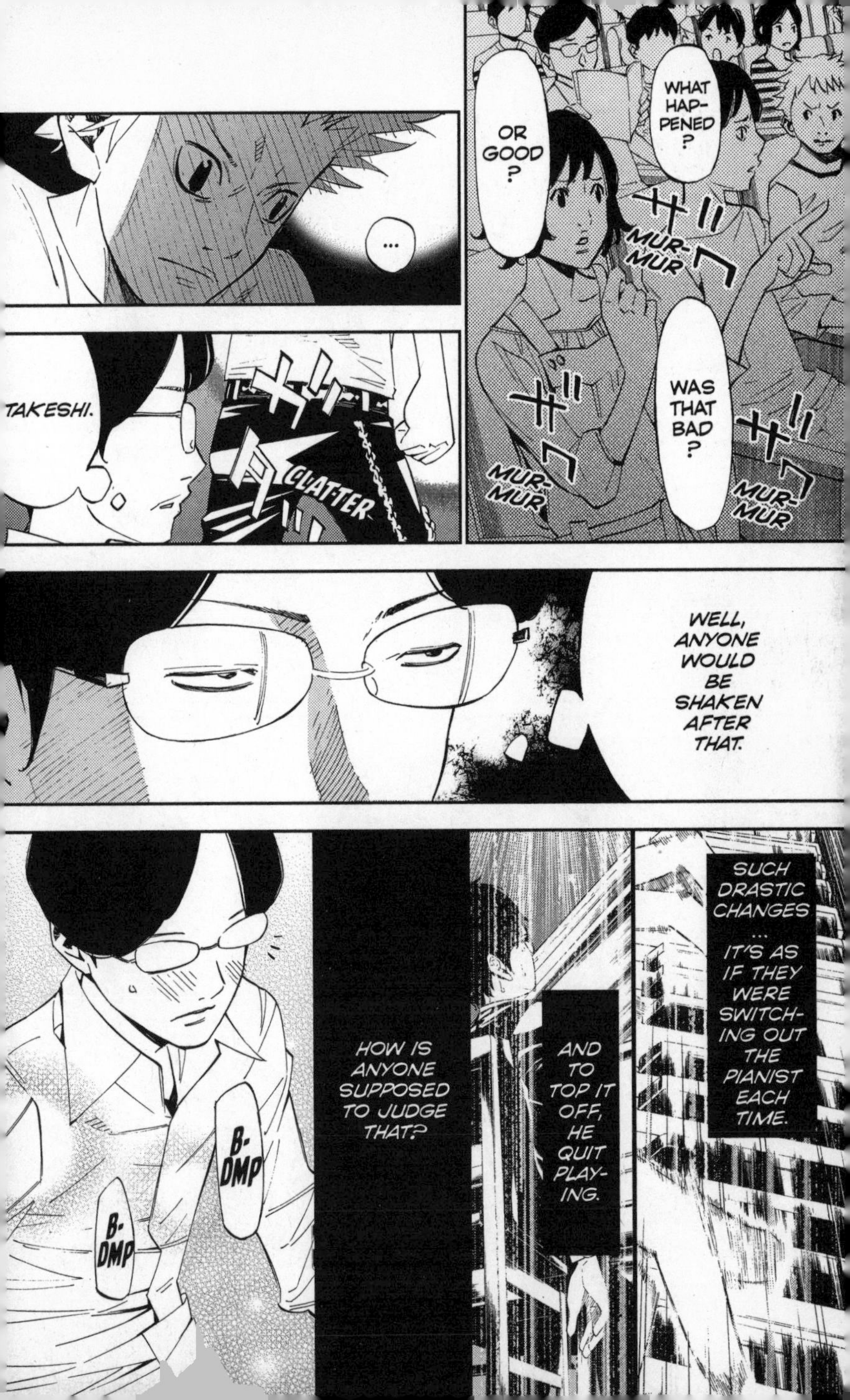
WHAT HAPPENED?
MUR-MUR
WAS THAT BAD?
OR GOOD?
MUR-MUR
MUR-MUR
...
TAKESHI.
CLAT-TER
WELL, ANYONE WOULD BE SHAKEN AFTER THAT.
SUCH DRASTIC CHANGES... IT'S AS IF THEY WERE SWITCHING OUT THE PIANIST EACH TIME.
AND TO TOP IT OFF, HE QUIT PLAYING.
HOW IS ANYONE SUPPOSED TO JUDGE THAT?
B-DMP
B-DMP

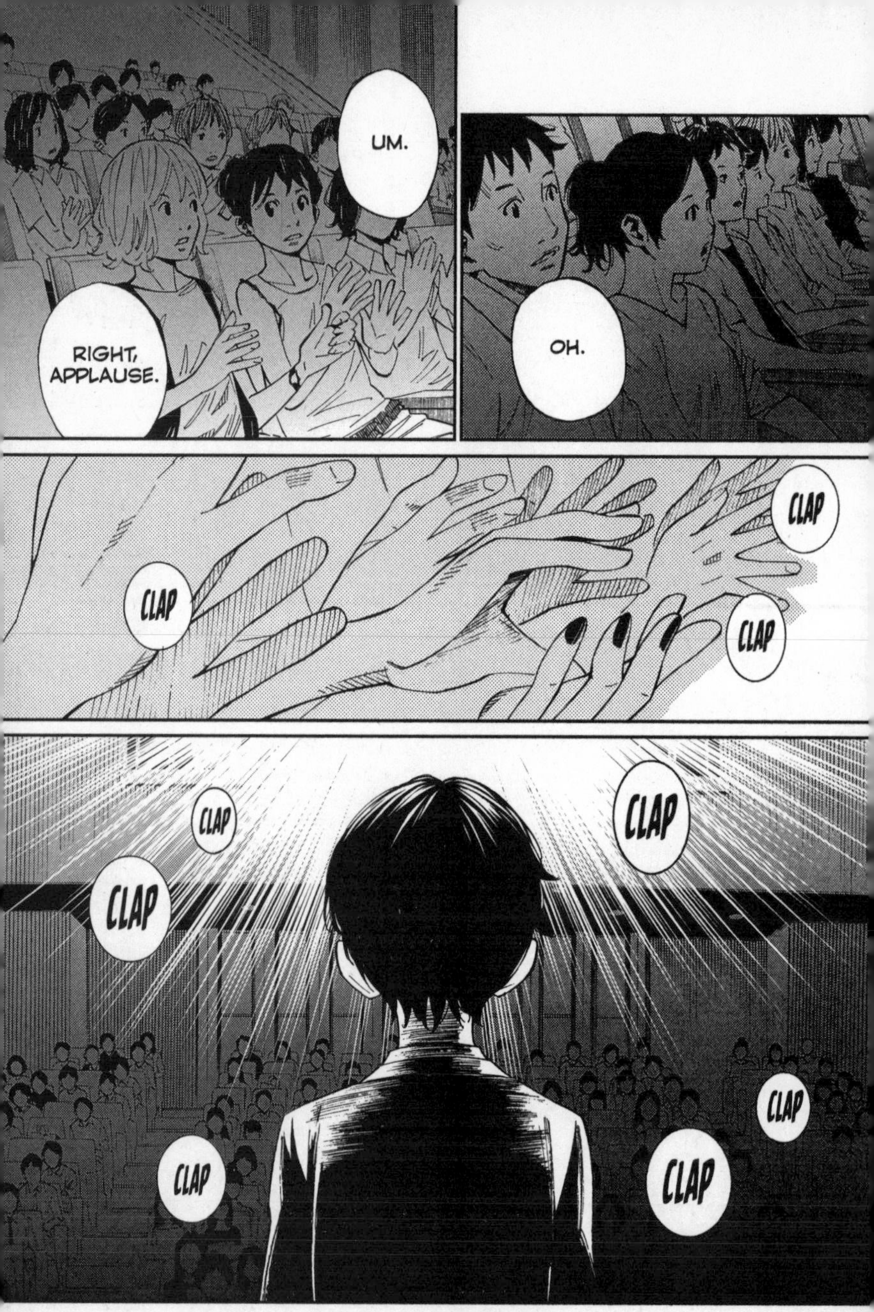
OH.
UM.
RIGHT, APPLAUSE.
CLAP
CLAP
CLAP
CLAP
CLAP
CLAP
CLAP
CLAP
CLAP

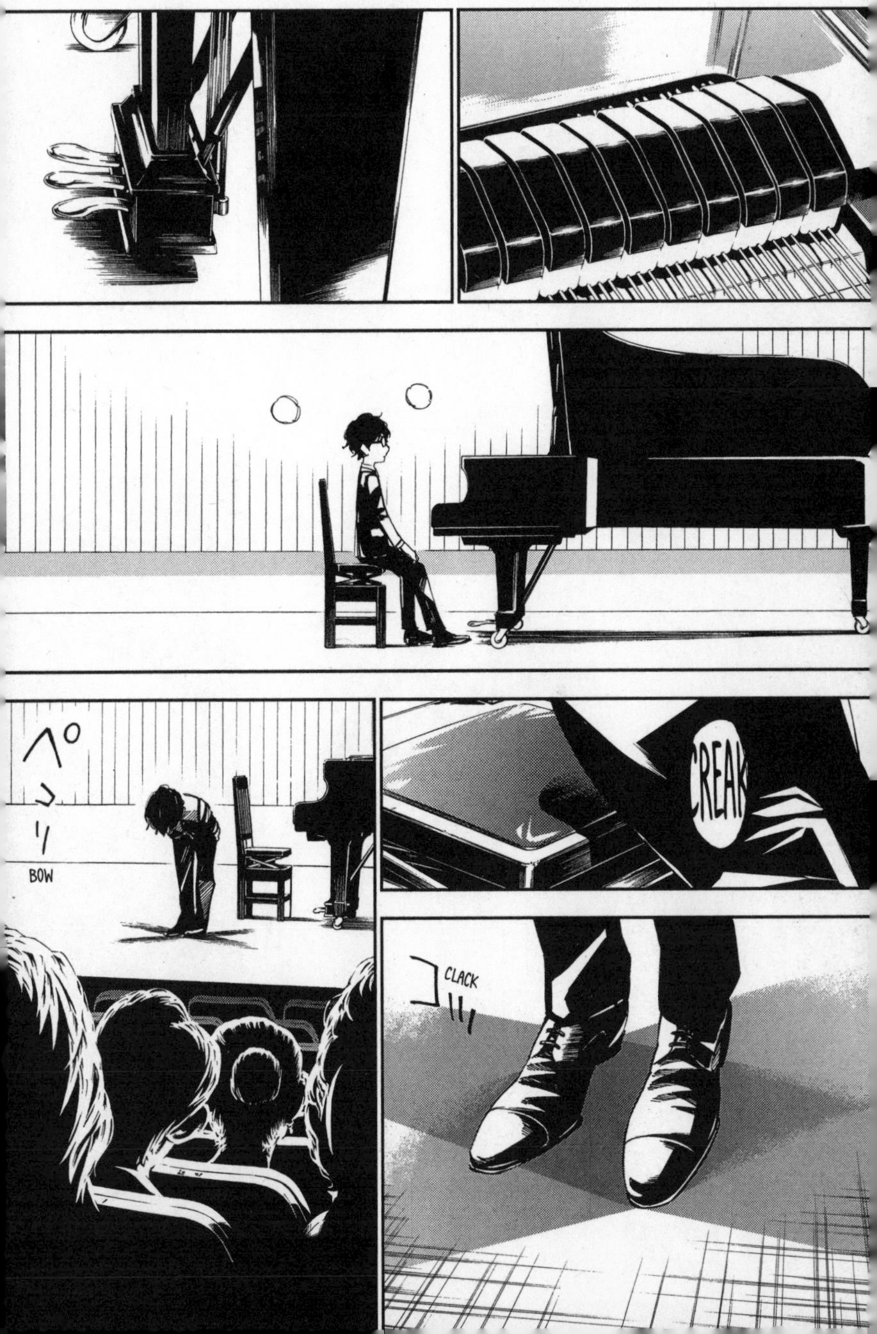
CREAK
CLACK
BOW

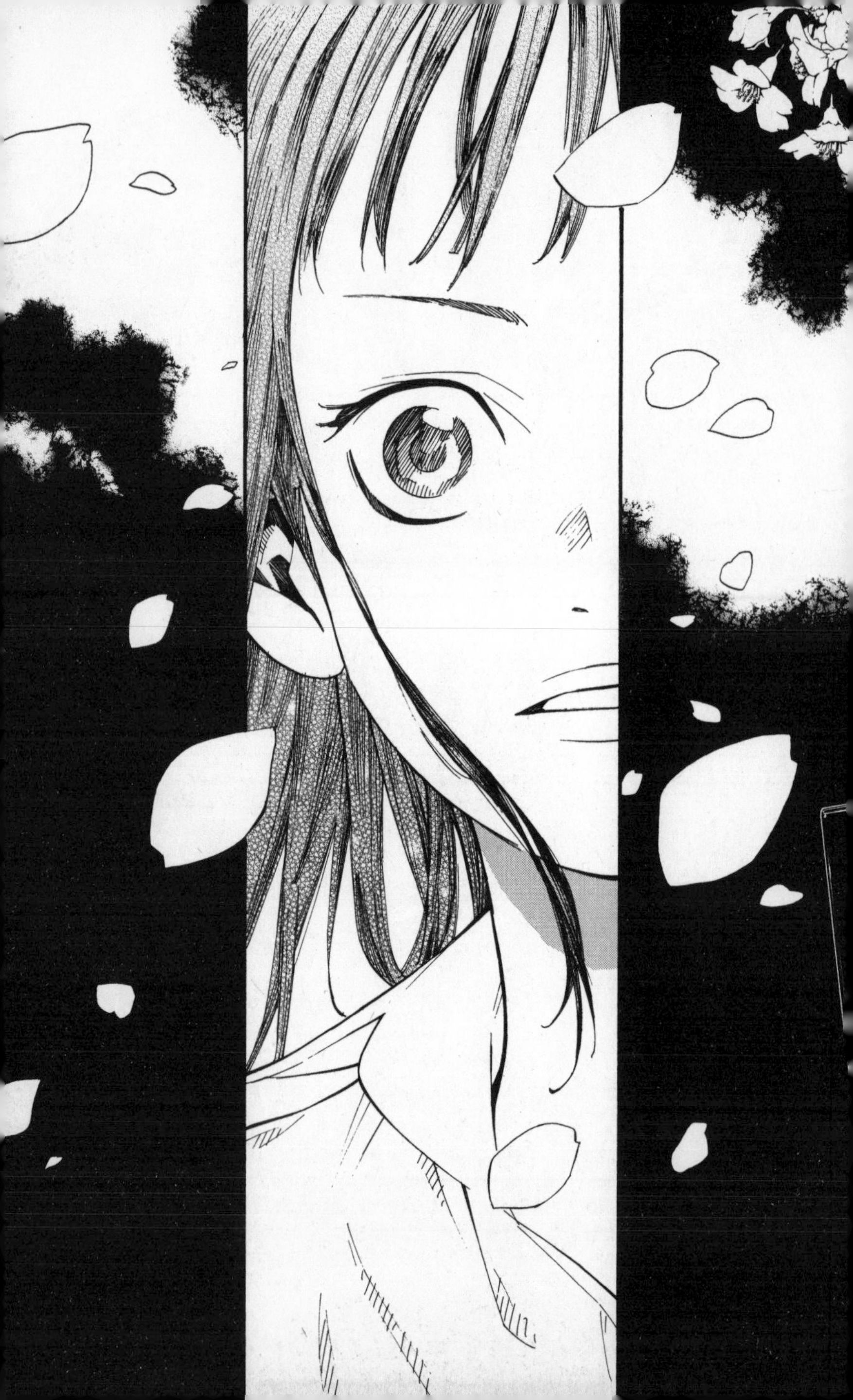

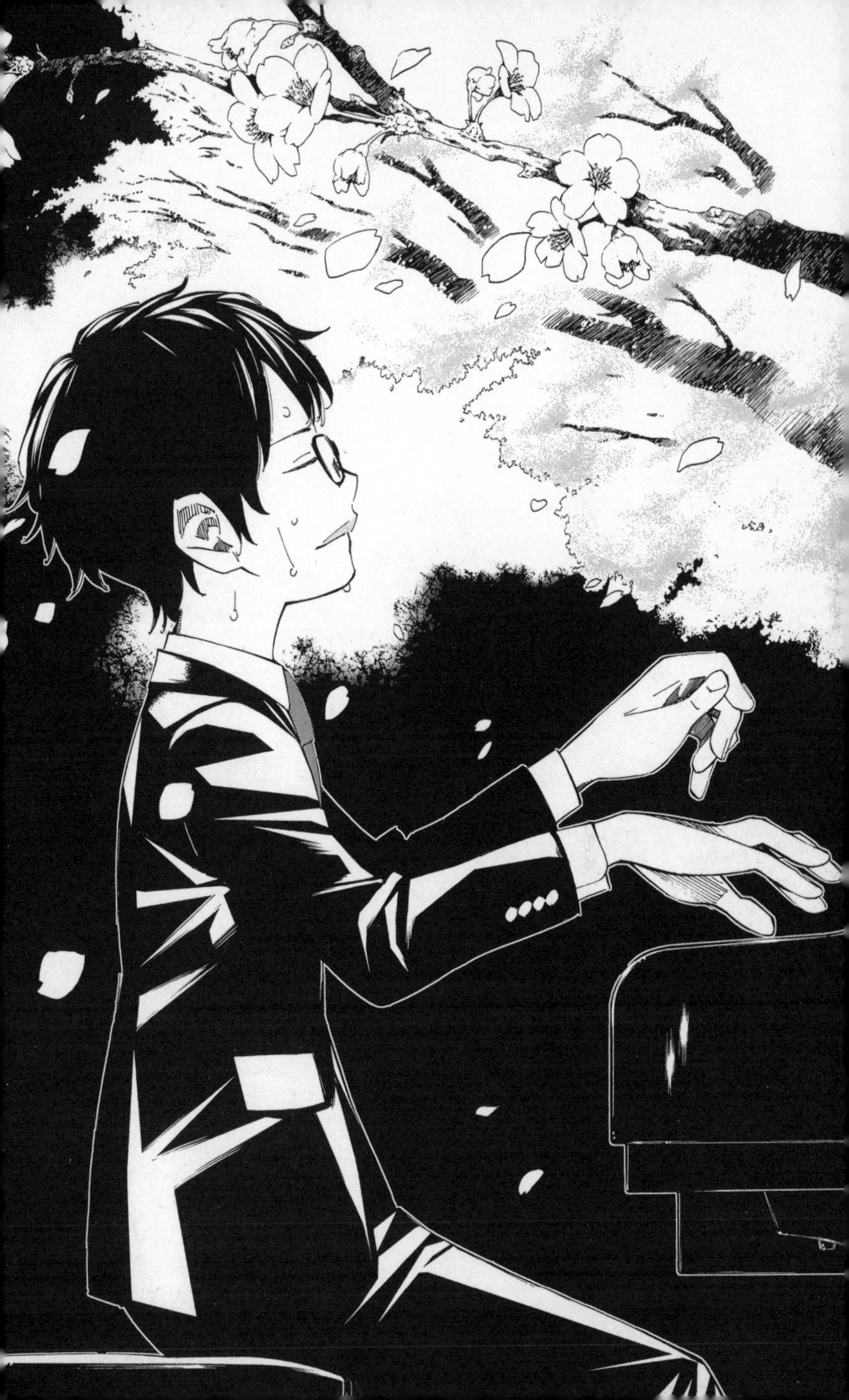

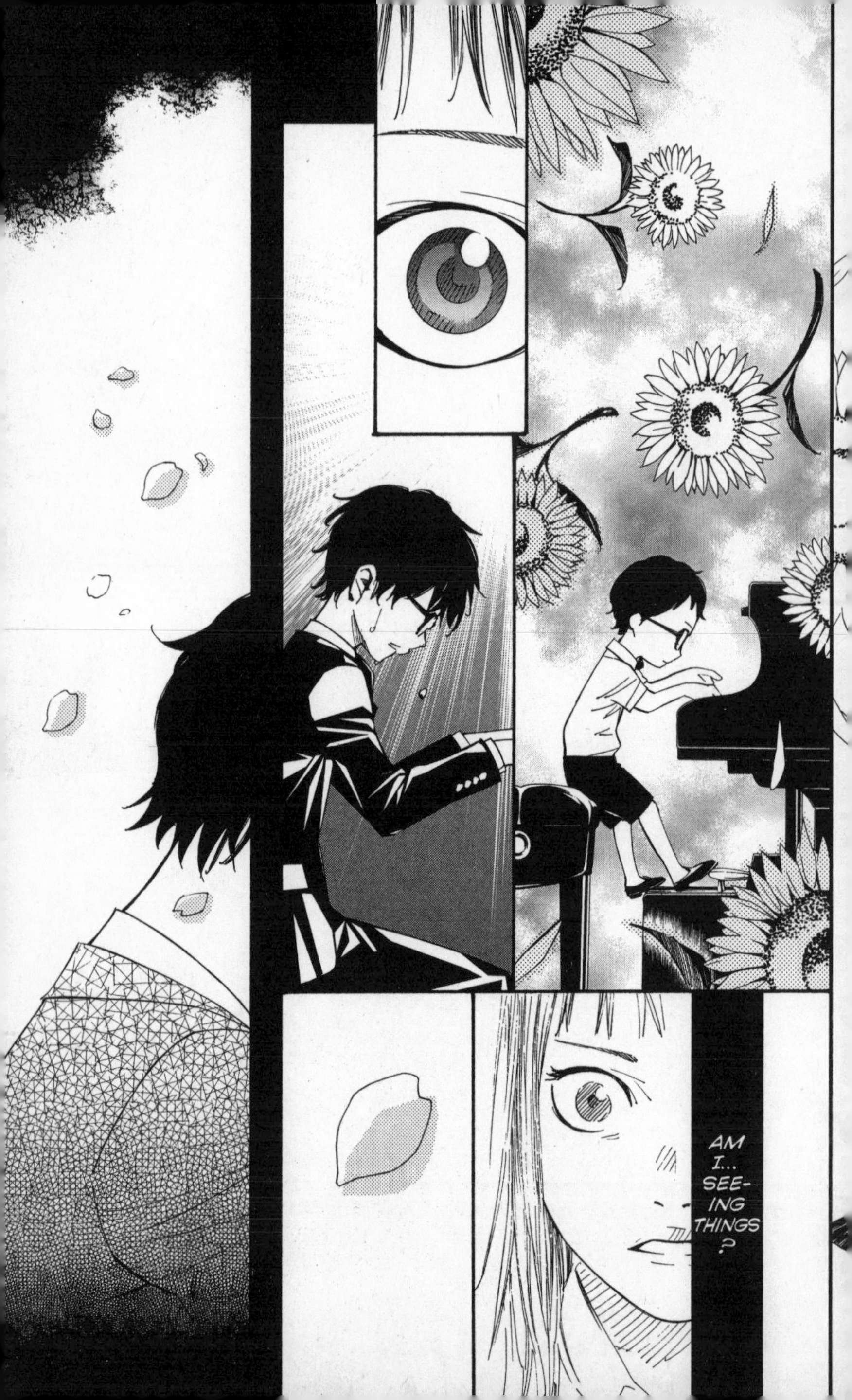
AM I... SEE-ING THINGS?

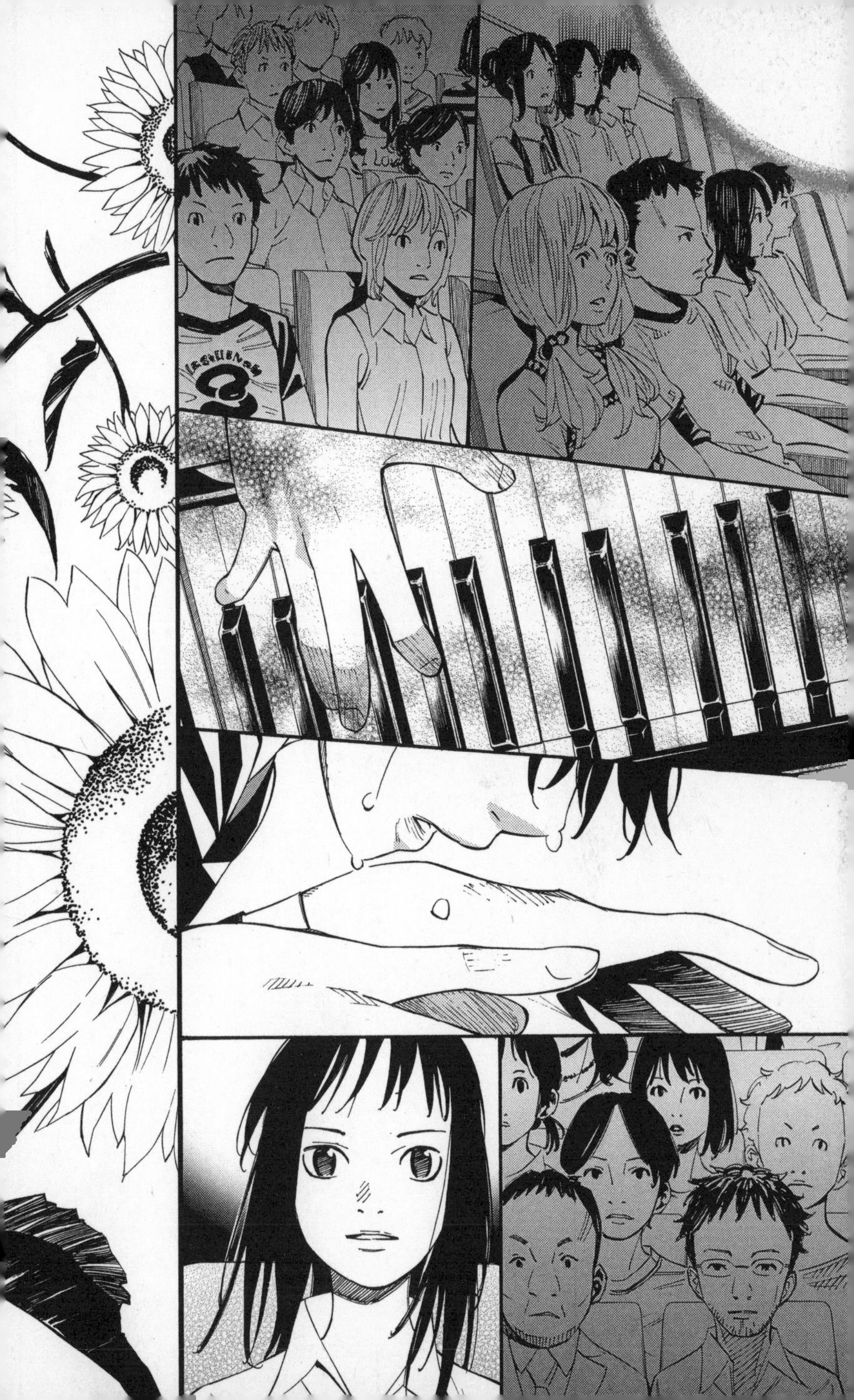

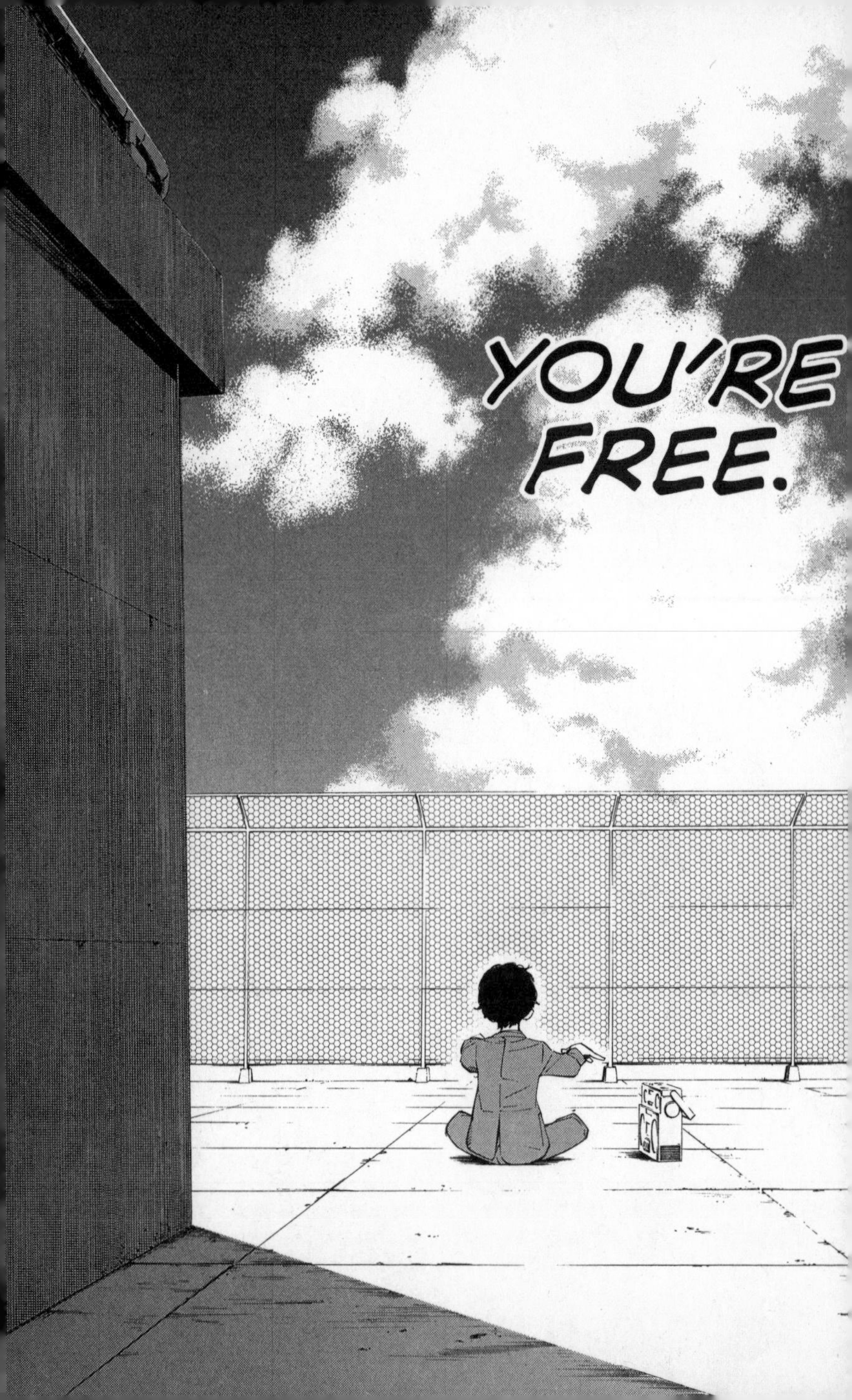
YOU'RE FREE.

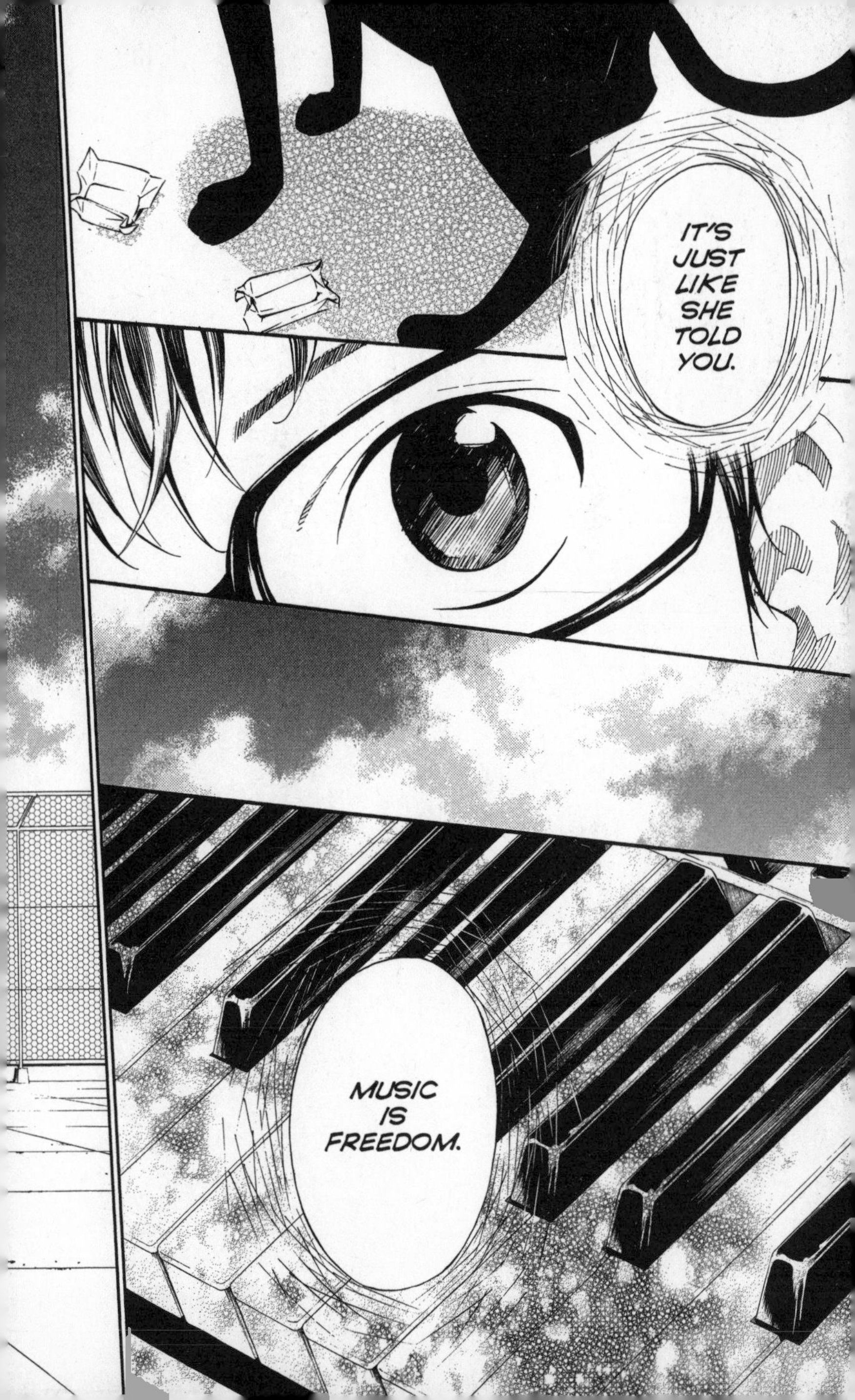
IT'S JUST LIKE SHE TOLD YOU.
MUSIC IS FREEDOM.

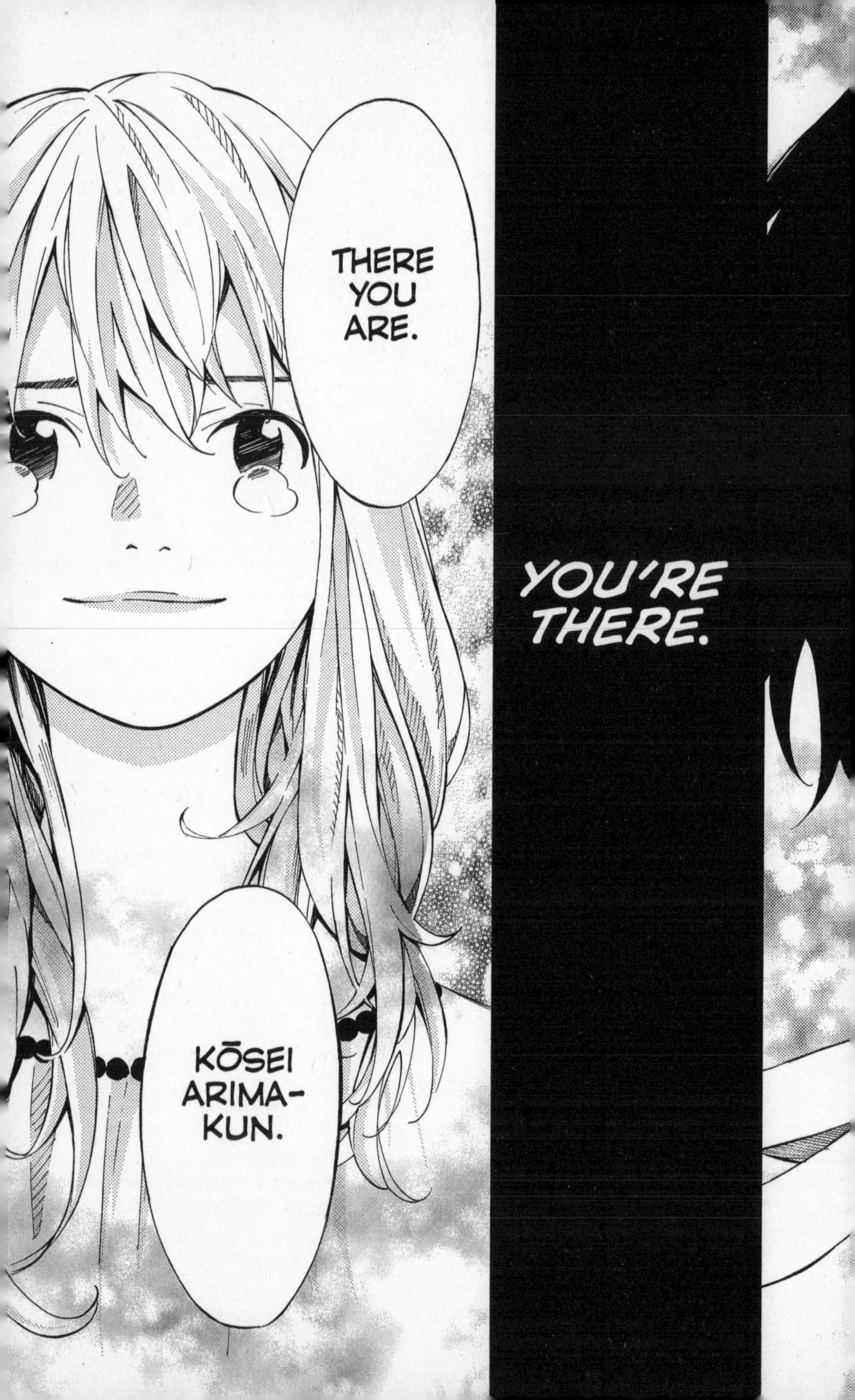
YOU'RE THERE.
THERE YOU ARE.
KŌSEI ARIMA-KUN.

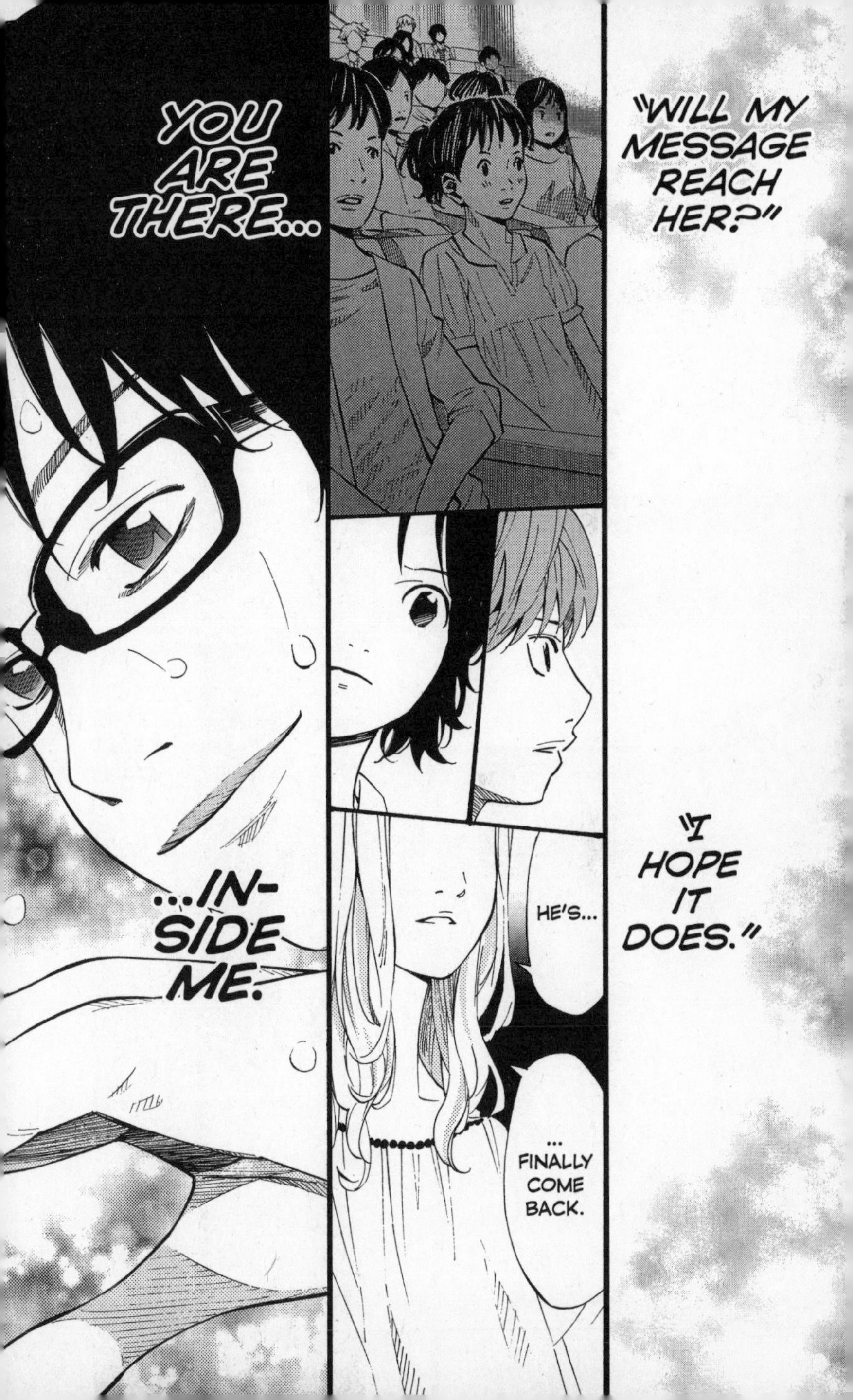
"WILL MY MESSAGE REACH HER?"
"I HOPE IT DOES."
HE'S...
...FINALLY COME BACK.
YOU ARE THERE...
...IN-SIDE ME.

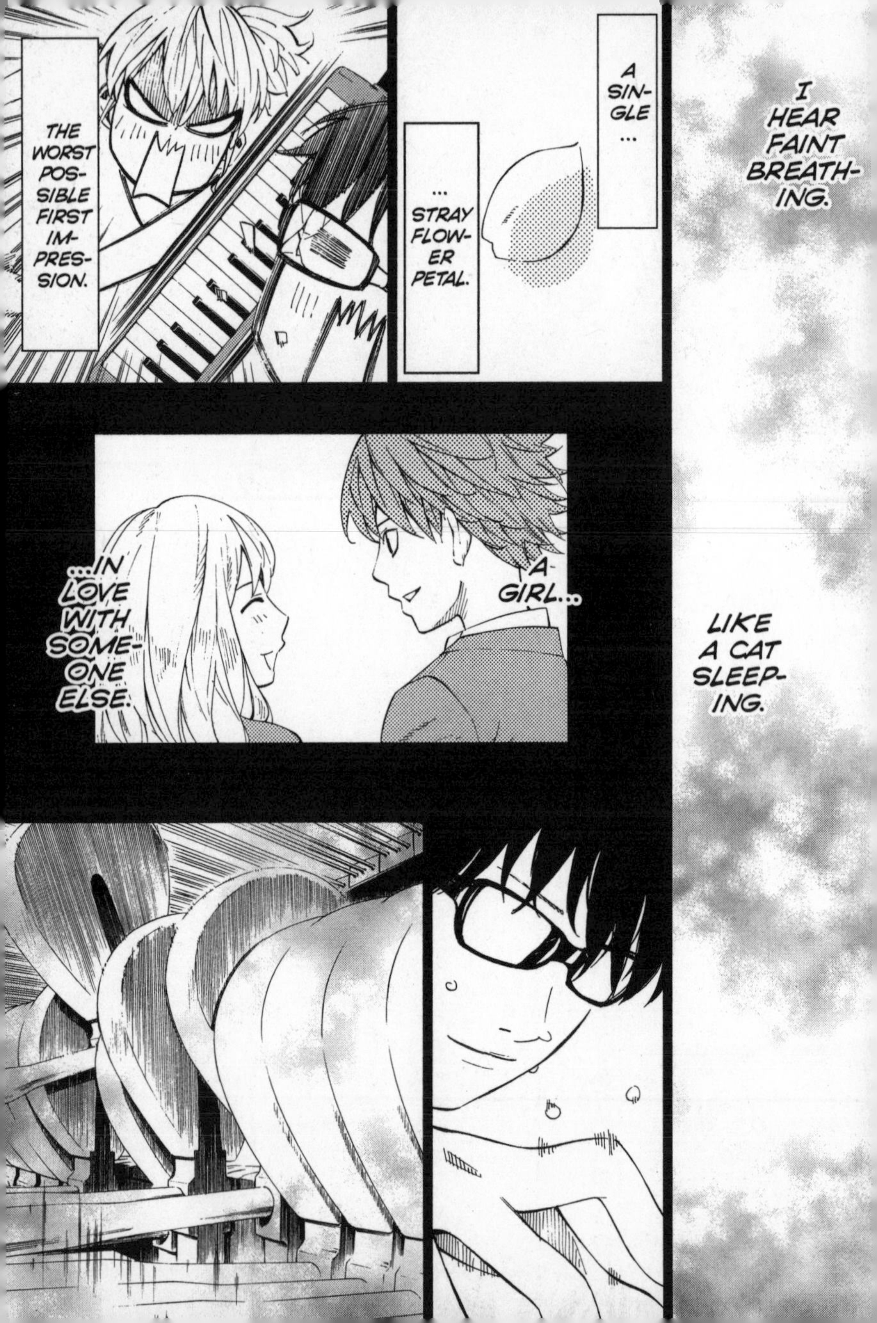
I HEAR FAINT BREATHING.
LIKE A CAT SLEEPING.
A SINGLE ...
... STRAY FLOWER PETAL.
THE WORST POSSIBLE FIRST IMPRESSION.
A GIRL...
...IN LOVE WITH SOMEONE ELSE.

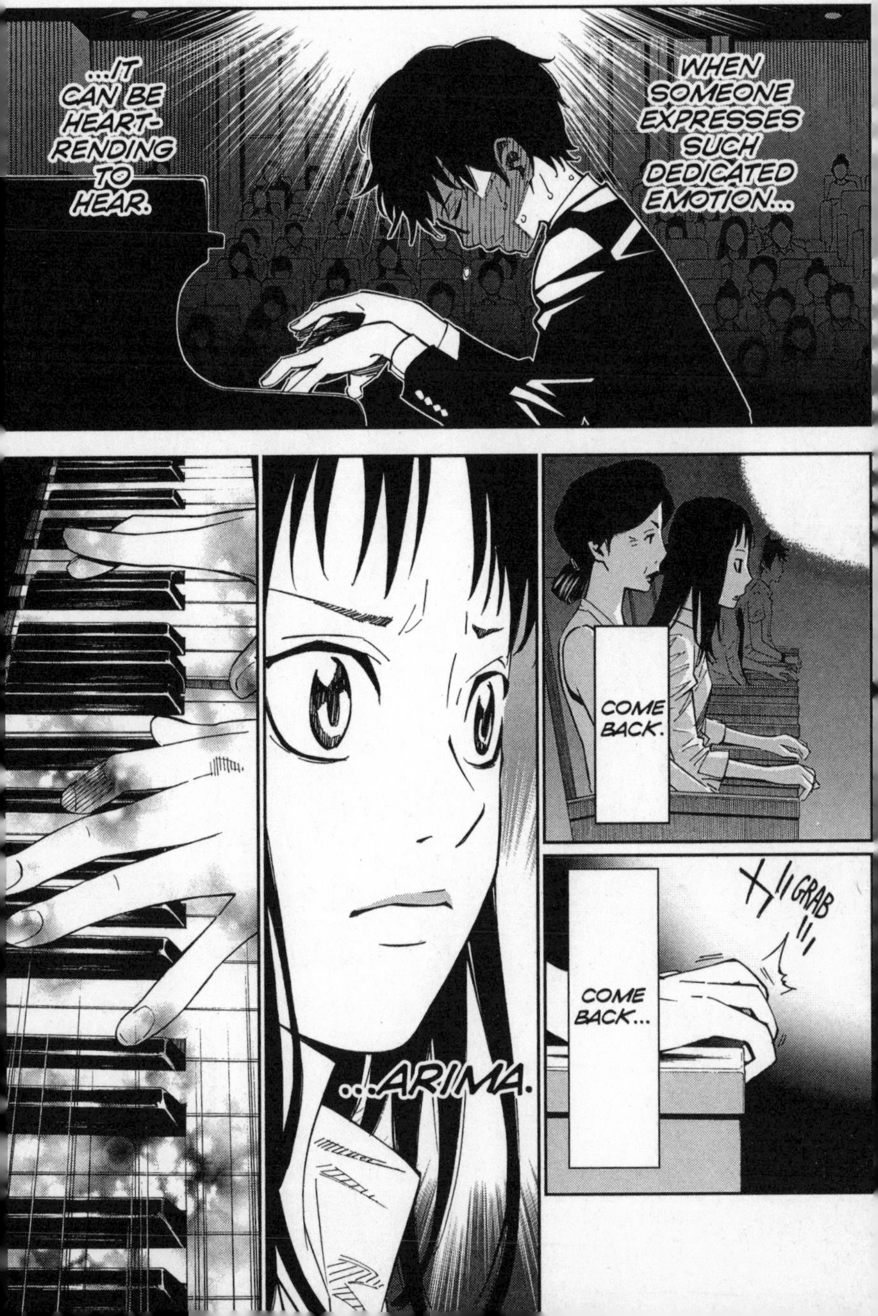
WHEN SOMEONE EXPRESSES SUCH DEDICATED EMOTION...
...IT CAN BE HEART-RENDING TO HEAR.
COME BACK.
GRAB
COME BACK...
...ARIMA.

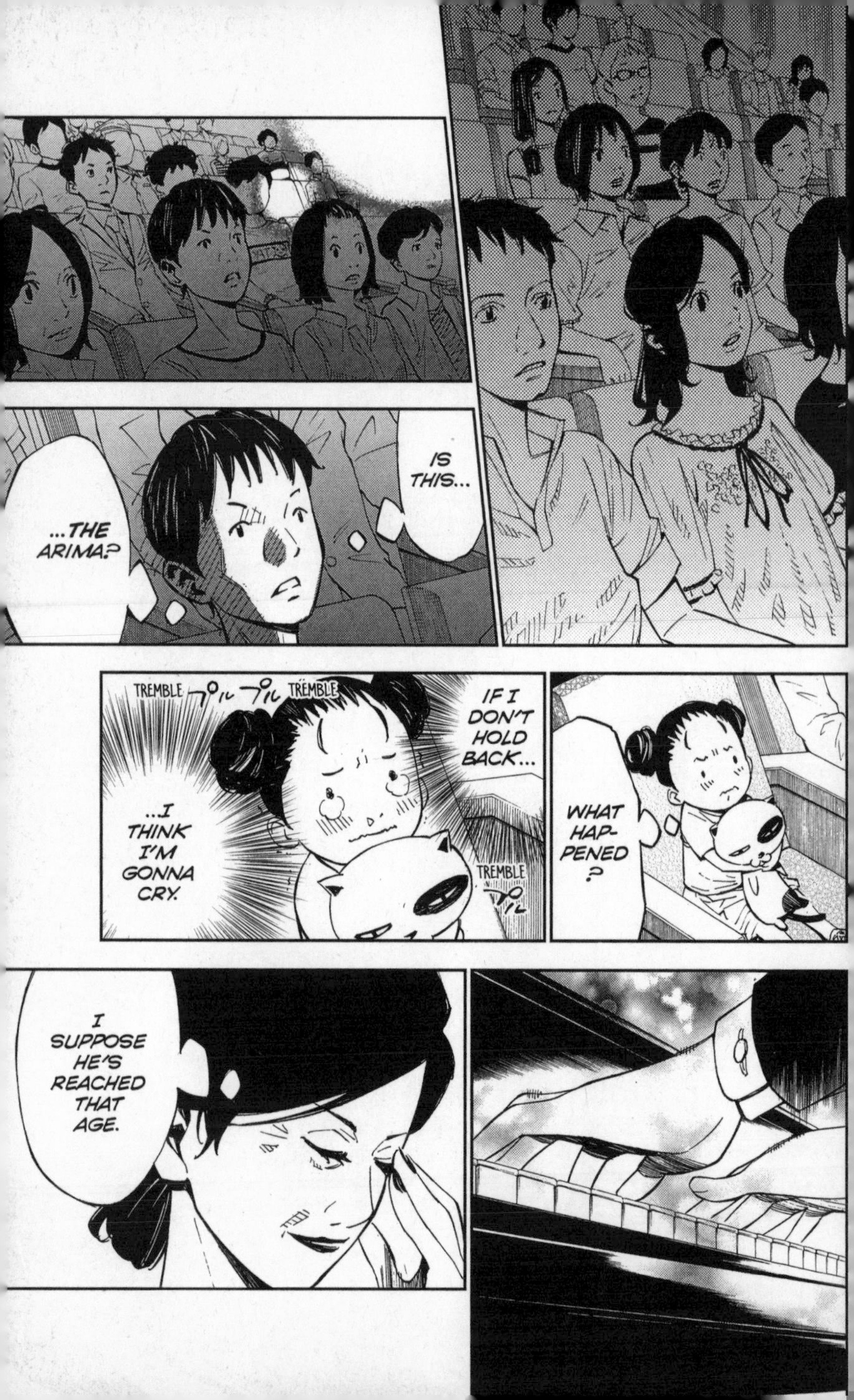
IS THIS...
...THE ARIMA?
WHAT HAPPENED?
IF I DON'T HOLD BACK...
TREMBLE プルプル TREMBLE
...I THINK I'M GONNA CRY.
TREMBLE プル
I SUPPOSE HE'S REACHED THAT AGE.

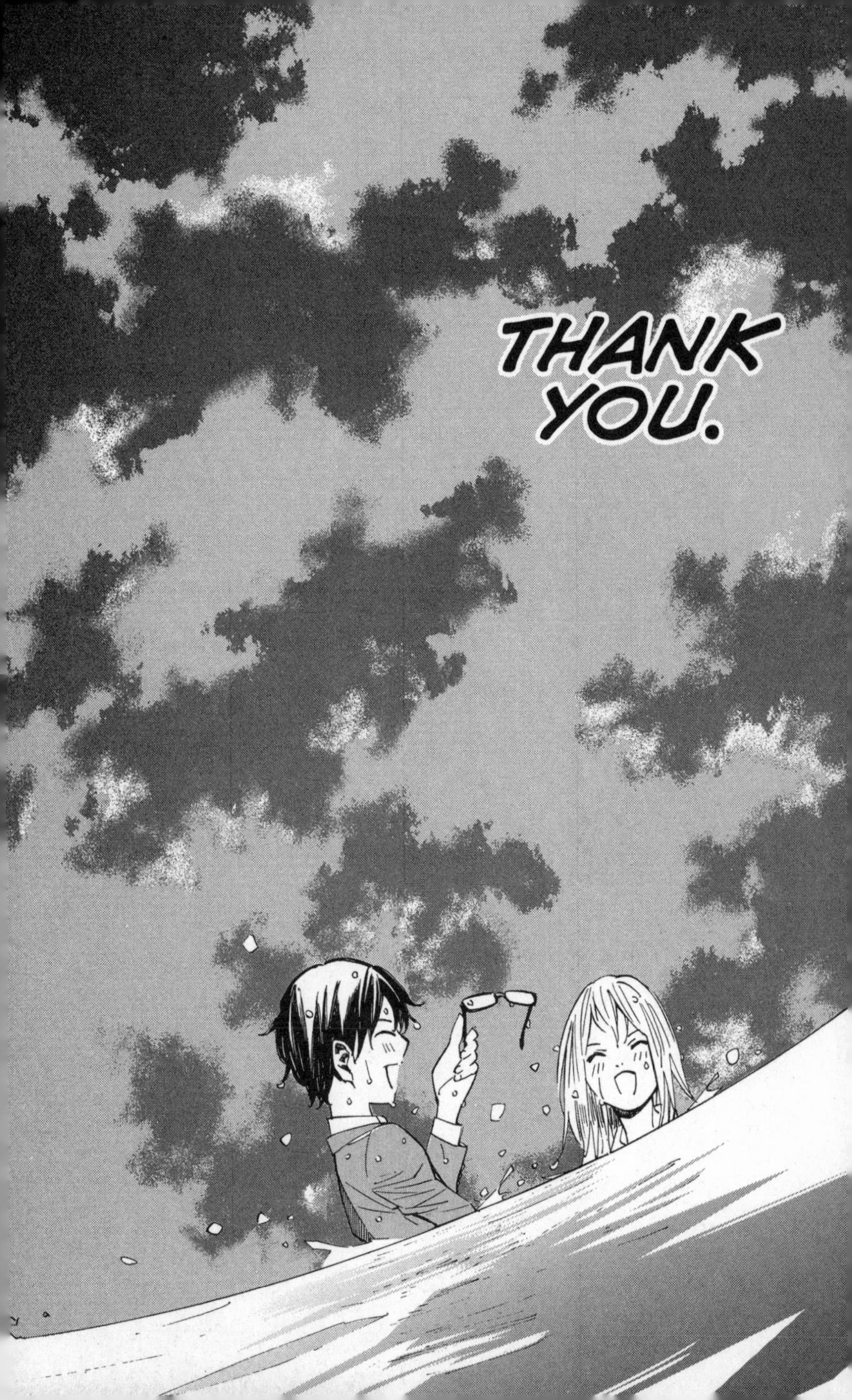
THANK YOU.

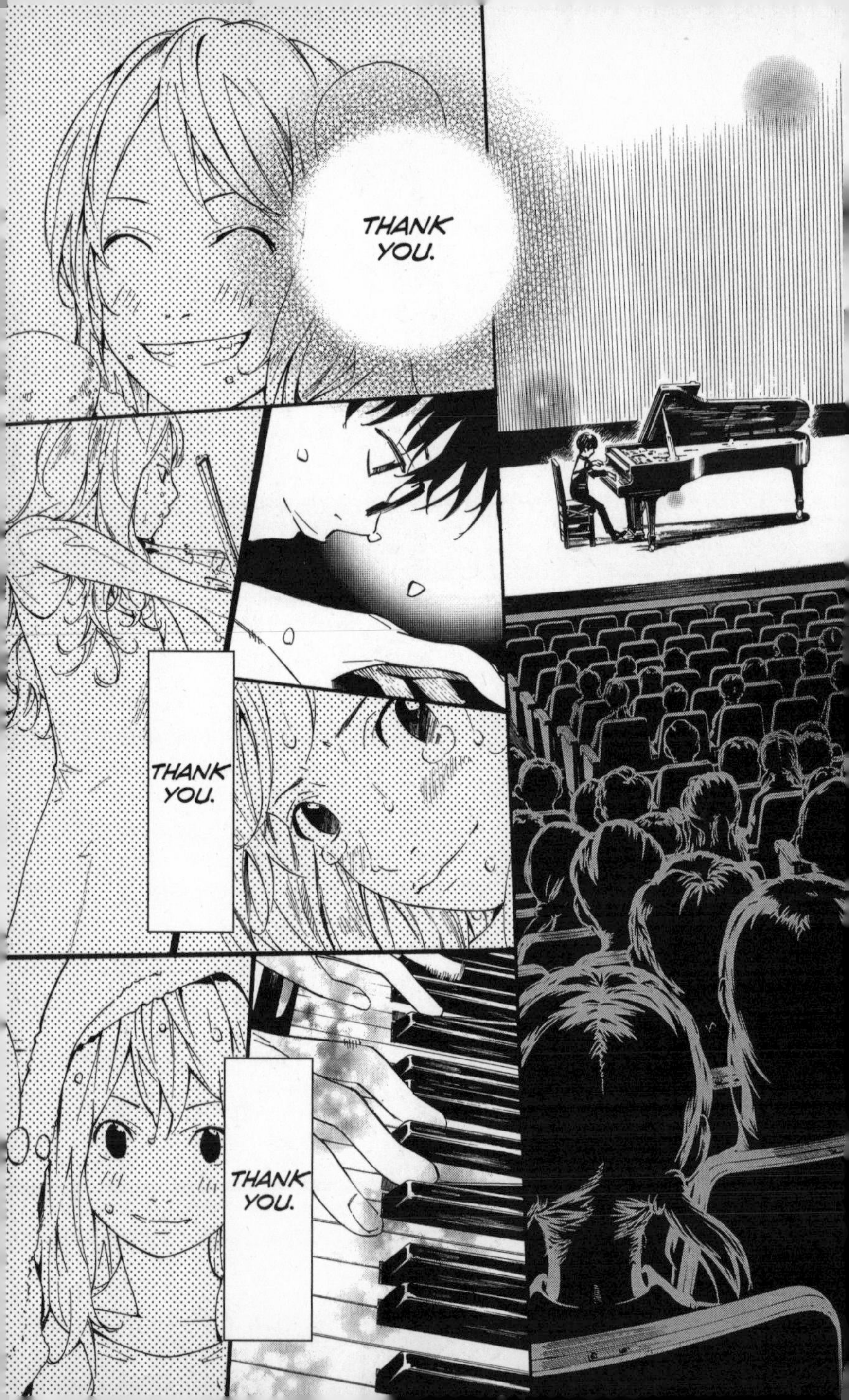
THANK YOU.
THANK YOU.
THANK YOU.

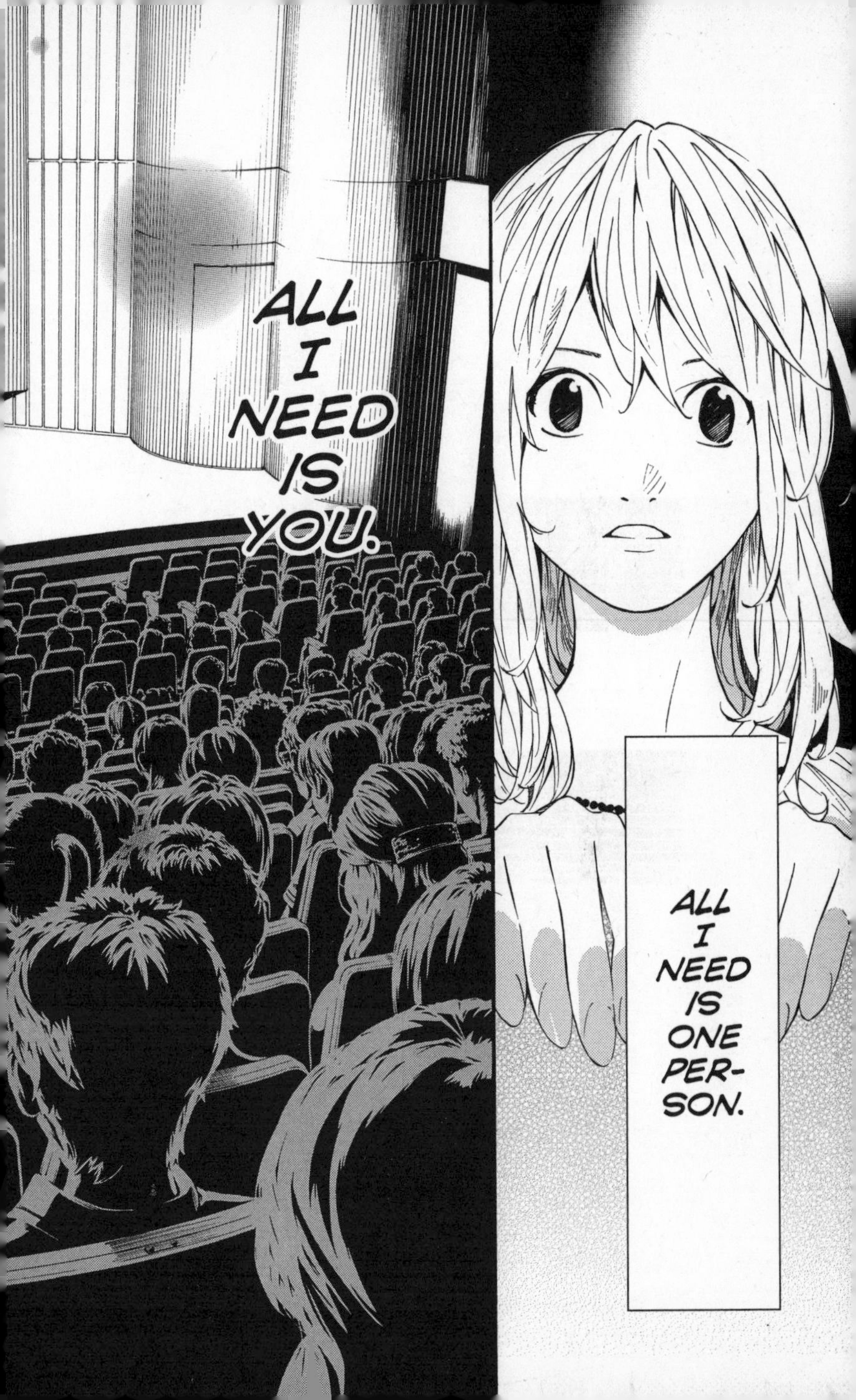
ALL I NEED IS ONE PER-SON.
ALL I NEED IS YOU.

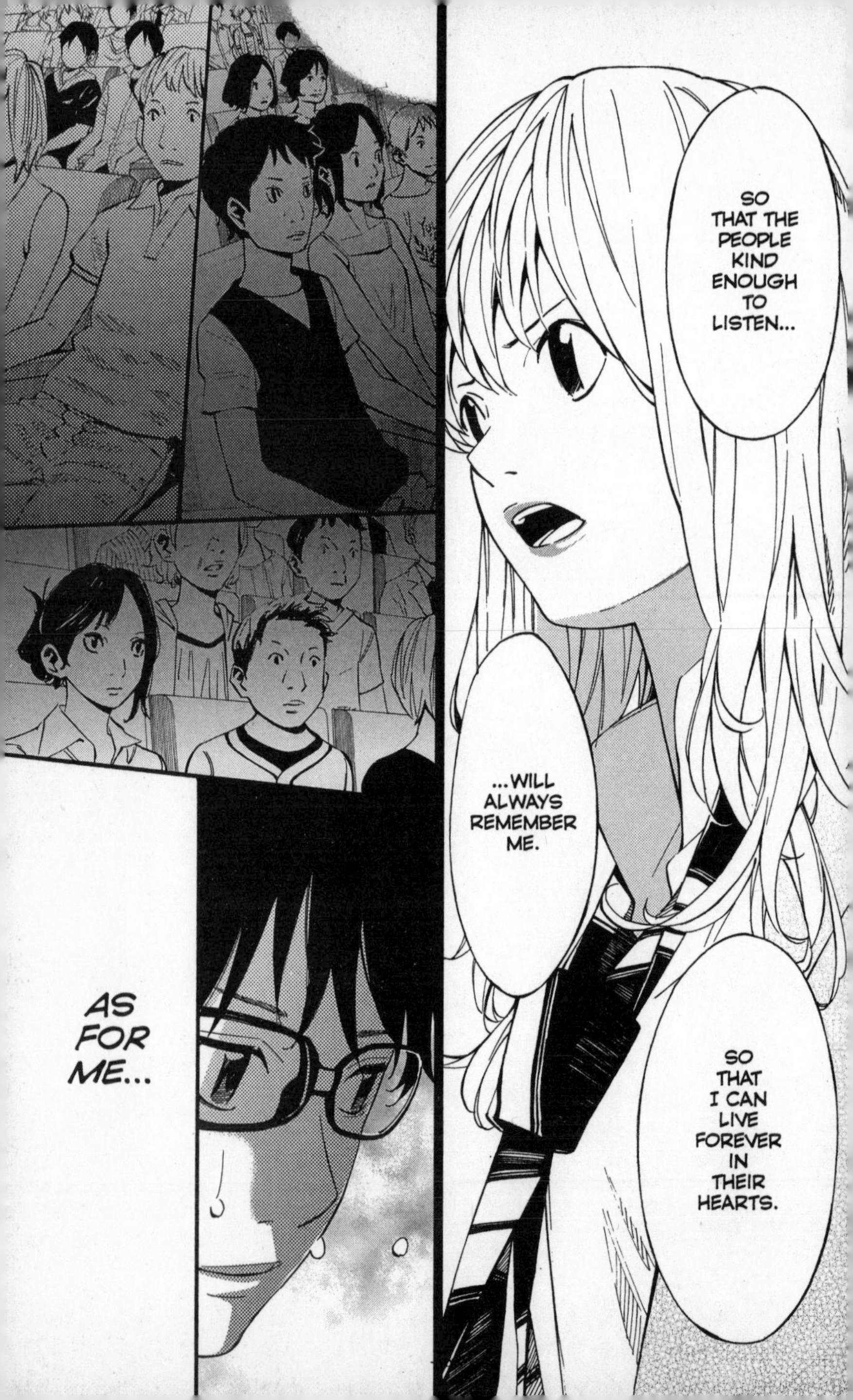
SO THAT THE PEOPLE KIND ENOUGH TO LISTEN...
...WILL ALWAYS REMEMBER ME.
SO THAT I CAN LIVE FOREVER IN THEIR HEARTS.
AS FOR ME...

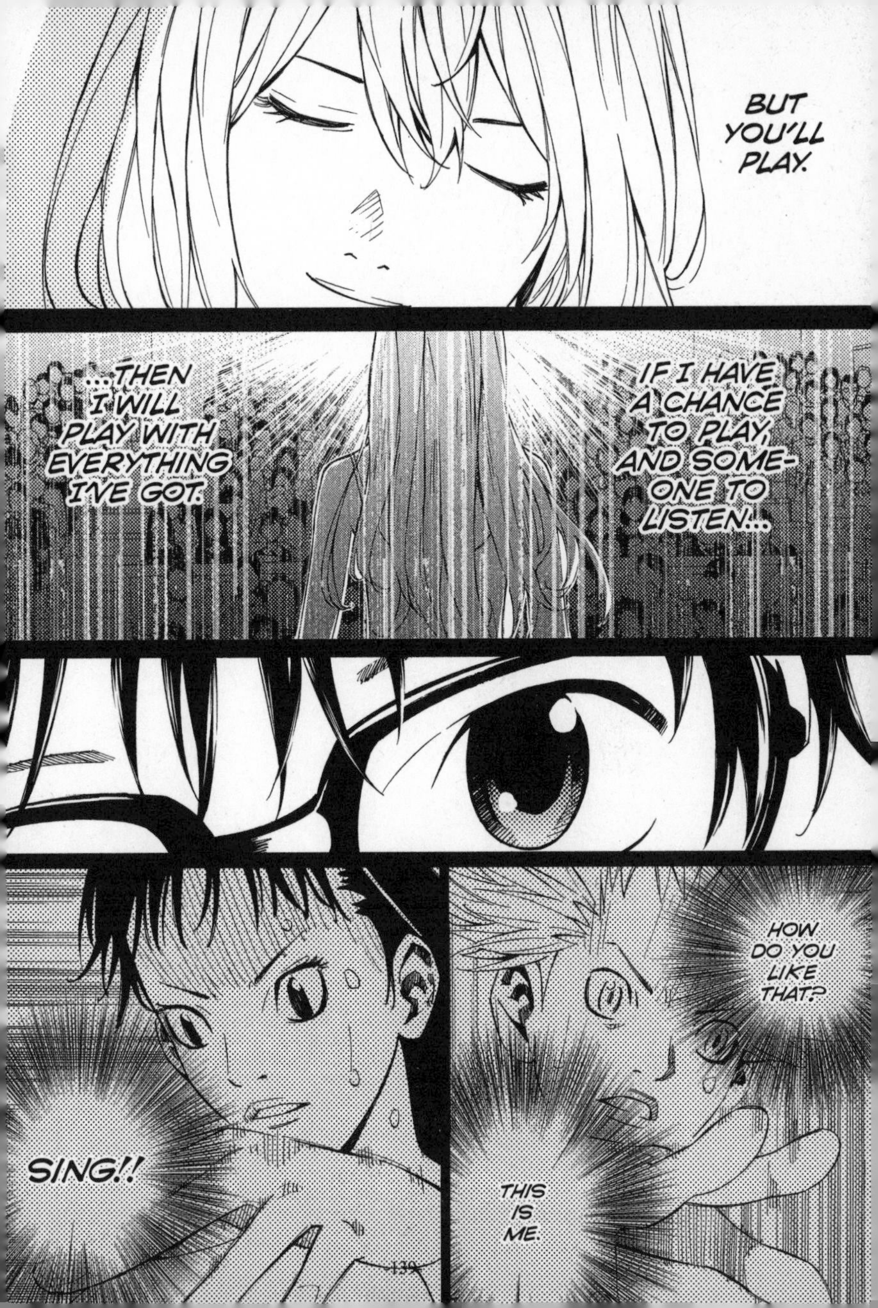
BUT YOU'LL PLAY.
IF I HAVE A CHANCE TO PLAY, AND SOME-ONE TO LISTEN...
...THEN I WILL PLAY WITH EVERYTHING I'VE GOT.
HOW DO YOU LIKE THAT?
THIS IS ME.
SING!!

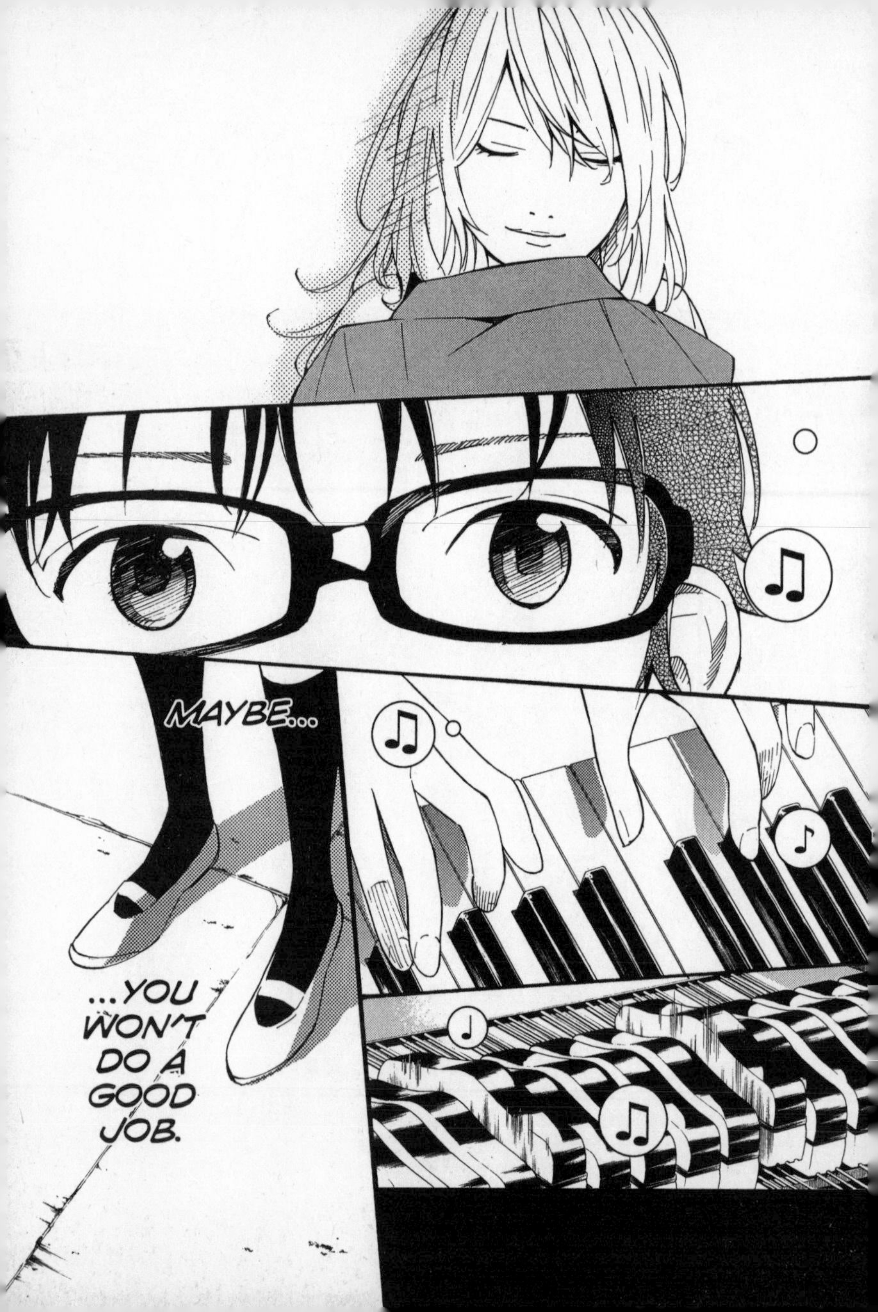

MAYBE...
...YOU WON'T DO A GOOD JOB.

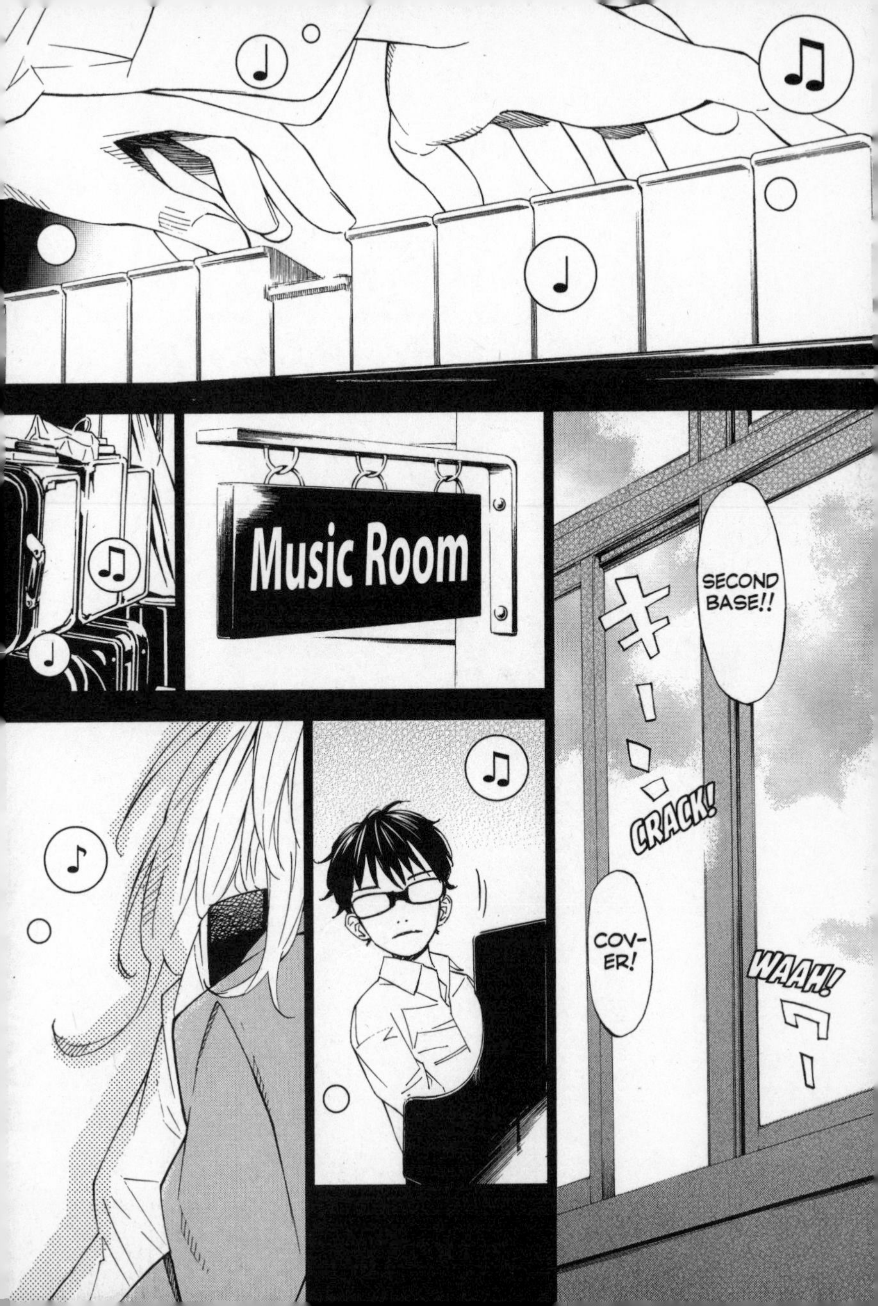

Music Room
SECOND BASE!!
キー
CRACK!
COV-ER!
WAAH!

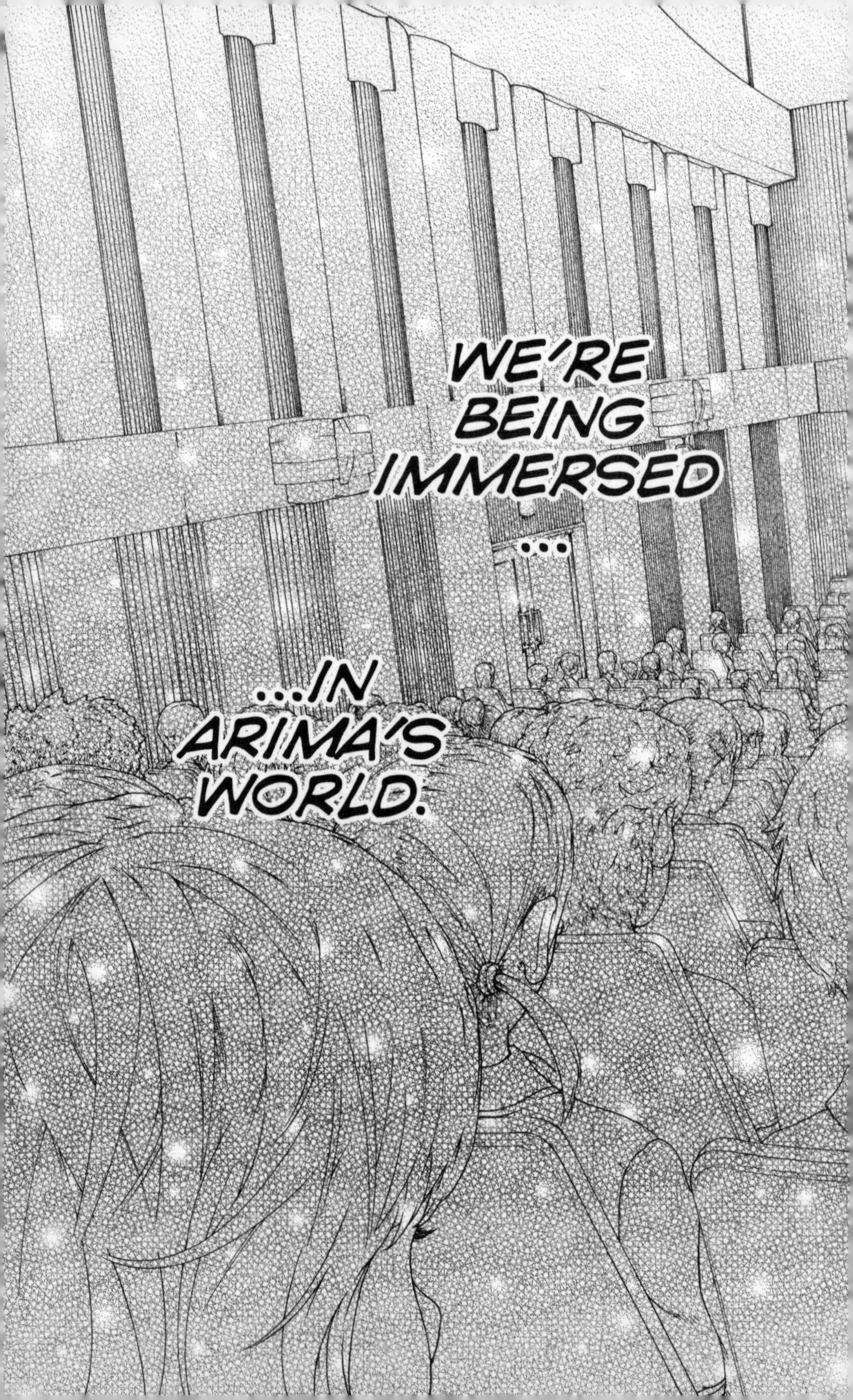
WE'RE BEING IMMERSED...
...IN ARIMA'S WORLD.

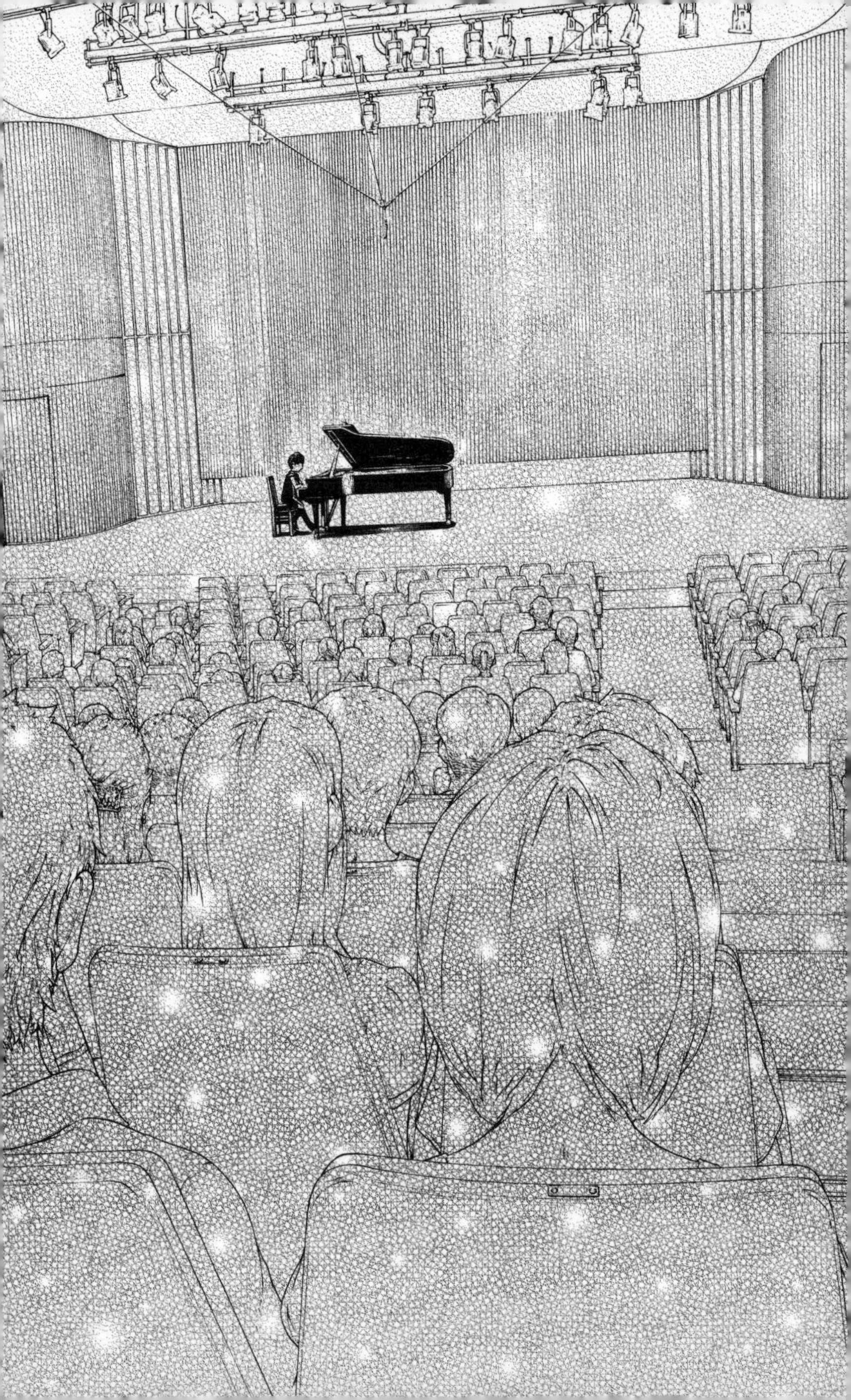

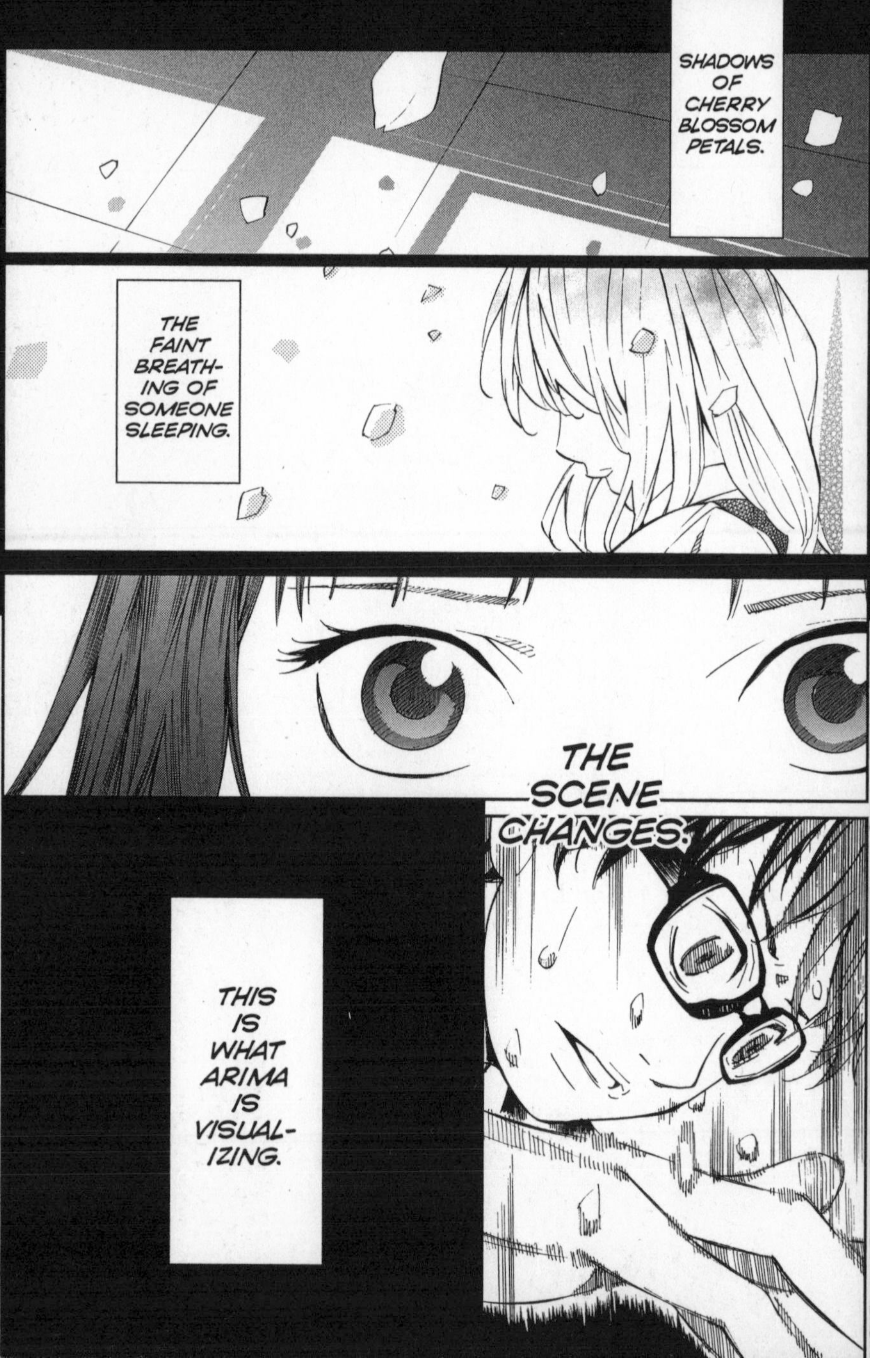
SHADOWS OF CHERRY BLOSSOM PETALS.
THE FAINT BREATH-ING OF SOMEONE SLEEPING.
THE SCENE CHANGES.
THIS IS WHAT ARIMA IS VISUAL-IZING.

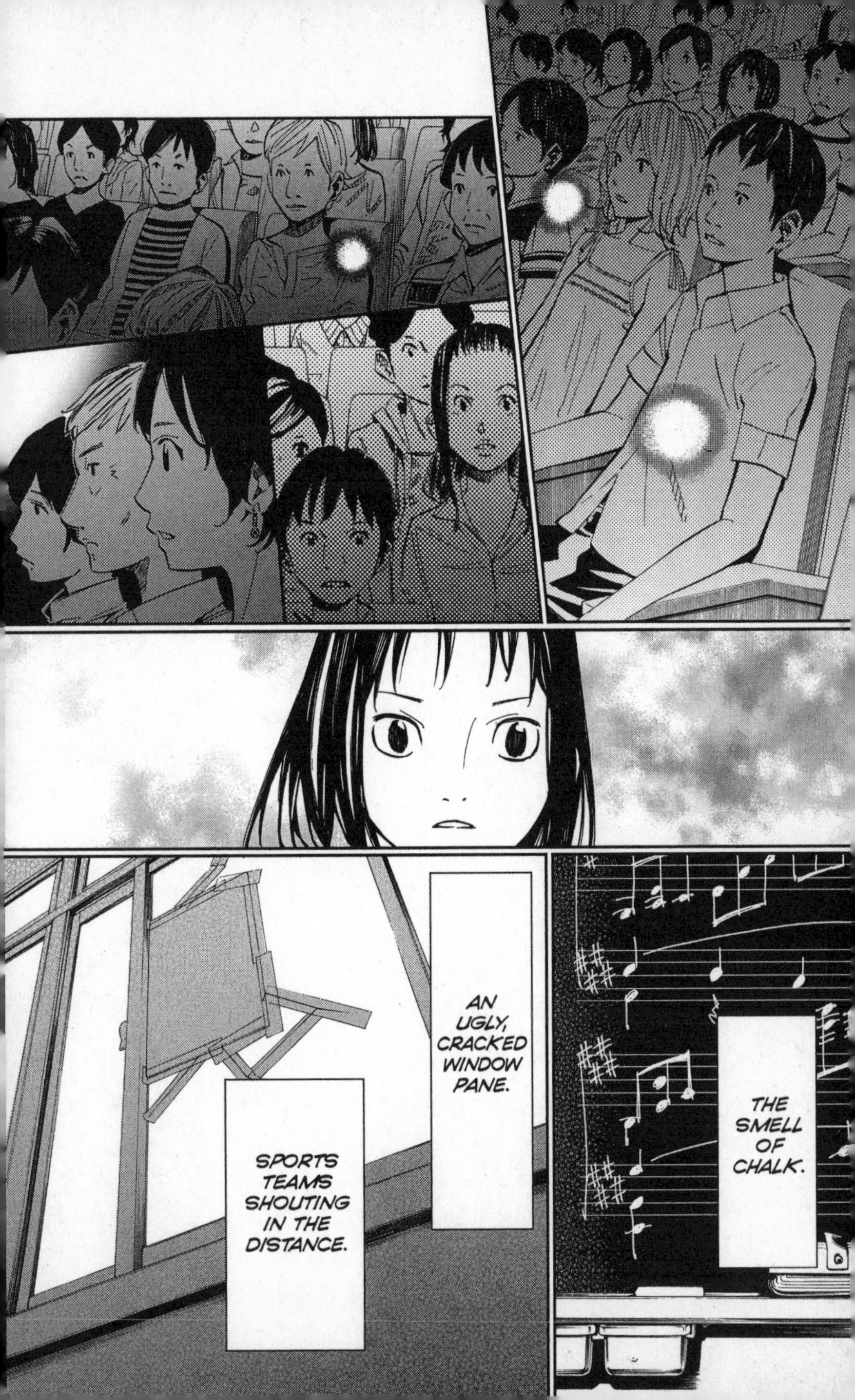
THE SMELL OF CHALK.
AN UGLY, CRACKED WINDOW PANE.
SPORTS TEAMS SHOUTING IN THE DISTANCE.

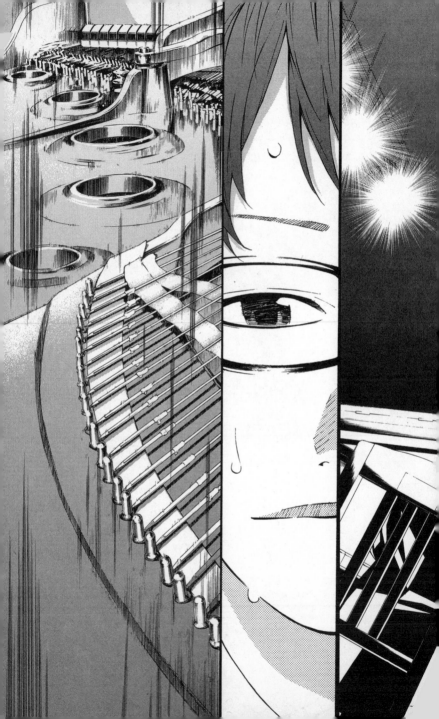

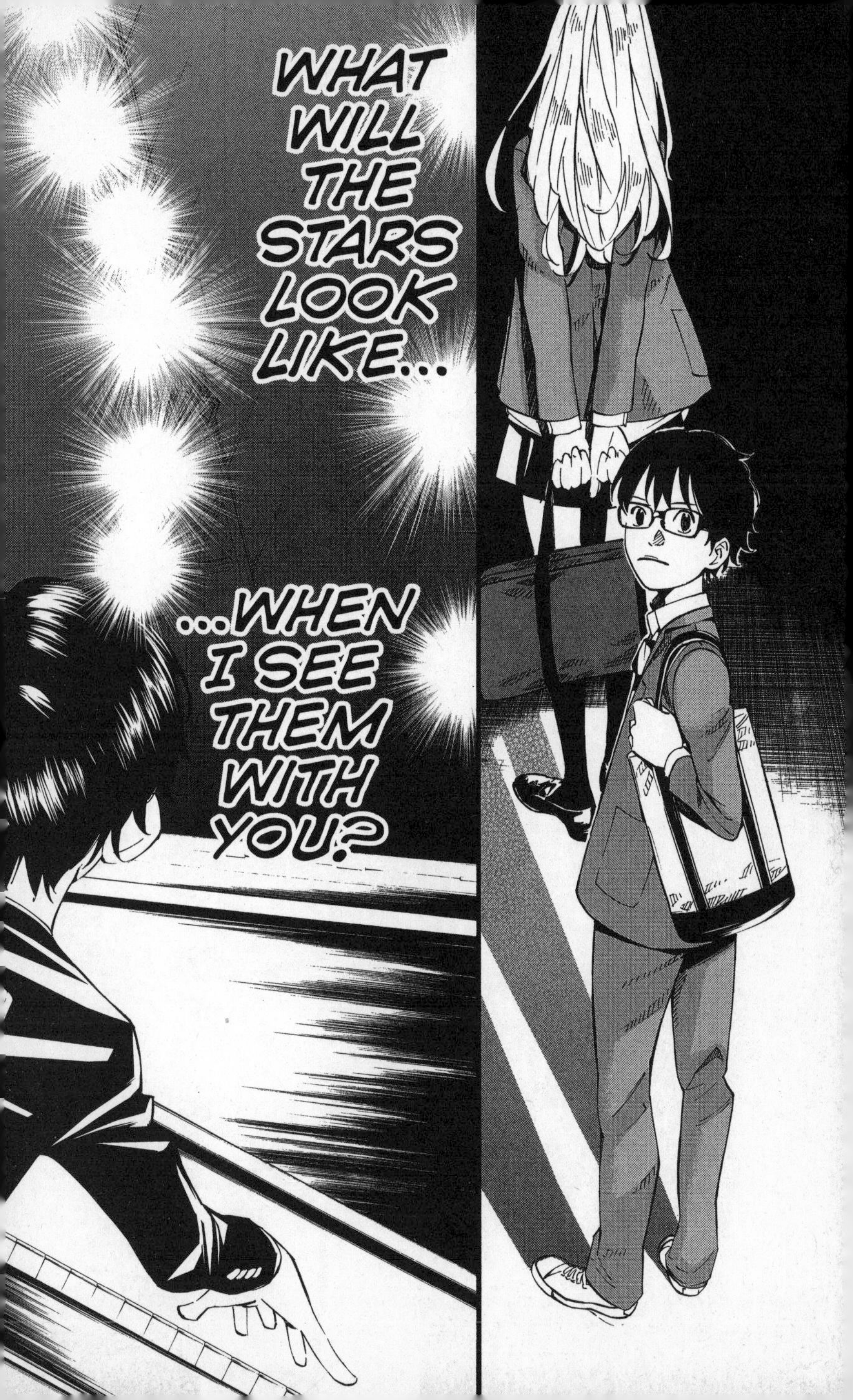
WHAT WILL THE STARS LOOK LIKE...
...WHEN I SEE THEM WITH YOU?

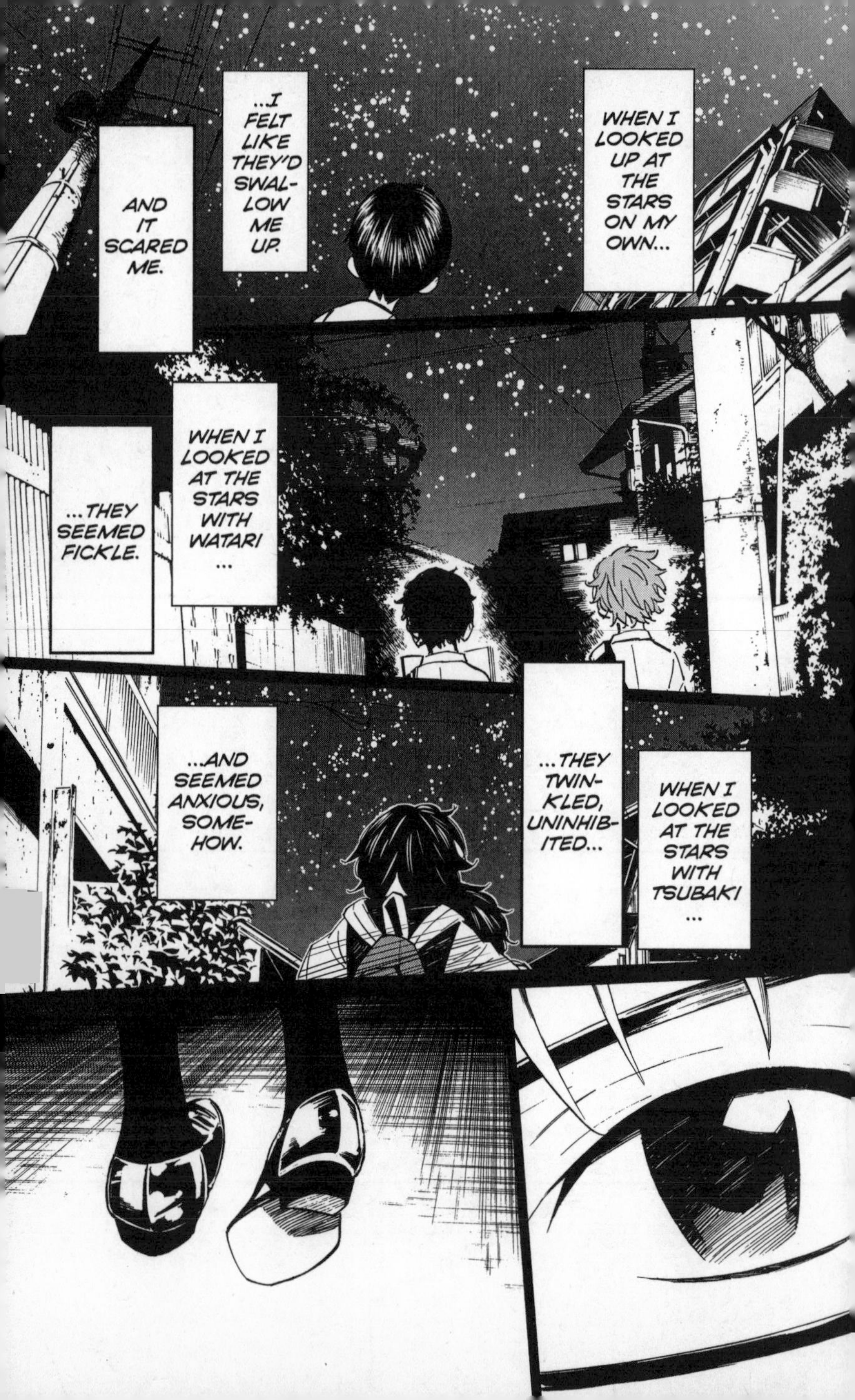
WHEN I LOOKED UP AT THE STARS ON MY OWN...
...I FELT LIKE THEY'D SWALLOW ME UP.
AND IT SCARED ME.
WHEN I LOOKED AT THE STARS WITH WATARI ...
...THEY SEEMED FICKLE.
WHEN I LOOKED AT THE STARS WITH TSUBAKI ...
...THEY TWINKLED, UNINHIBITED...
...AND SEEMED ANXIOUS, SOMEHOW.

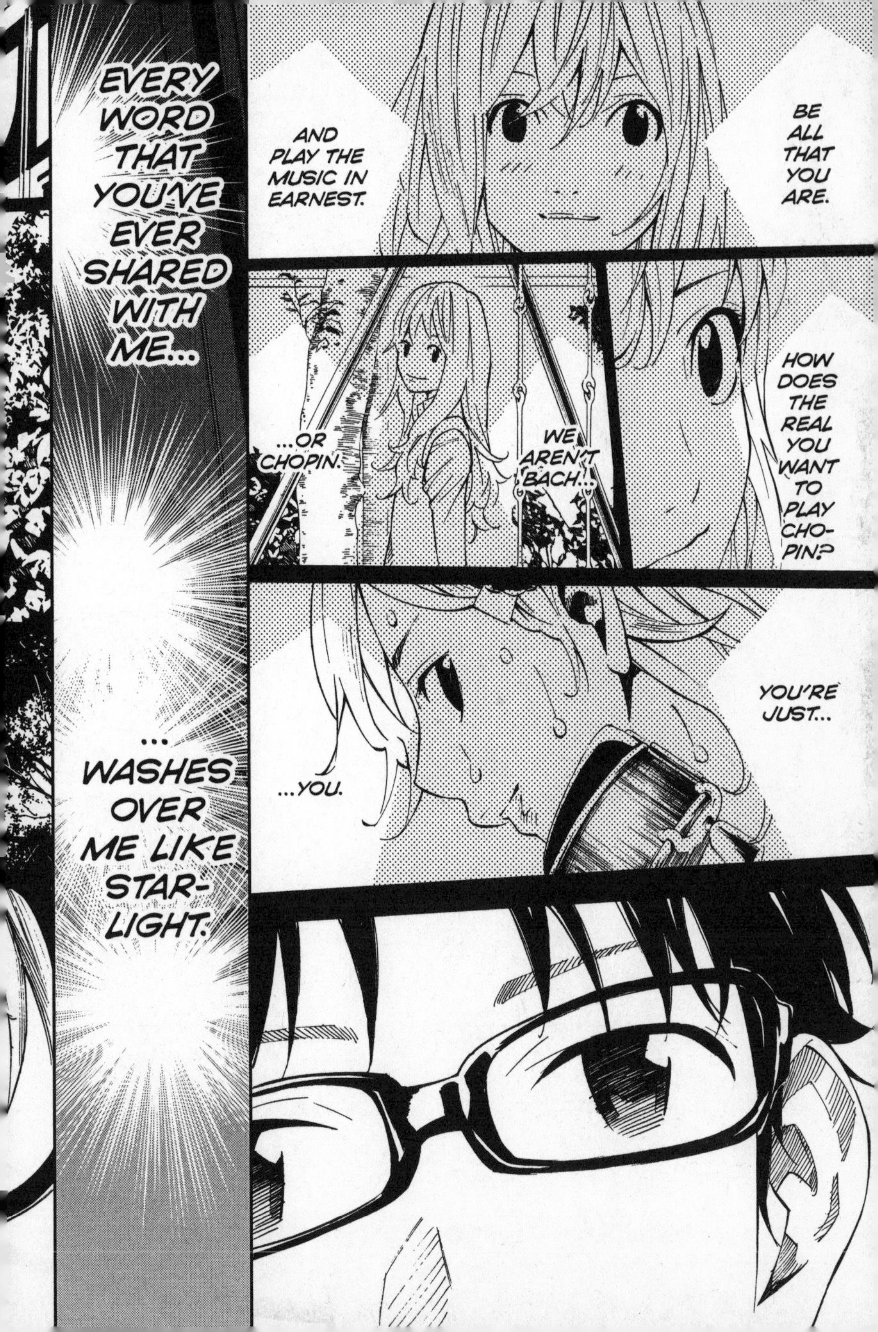
BE ALL THAT YOU ARE.
AND PLAY THE MUSIC IN EARNEST.
HOW DOES THE REAL YOU WANT TO PLAY CHOPIN?
WE AREN'T BACH...
...OR CHOPIN.
YOU'RE JUST...
...YOU.
EVERY WORD THAT YOU'VE EVER SHARED WITH ME...
...WASHES OVER ME LIKE STARLIGHT.

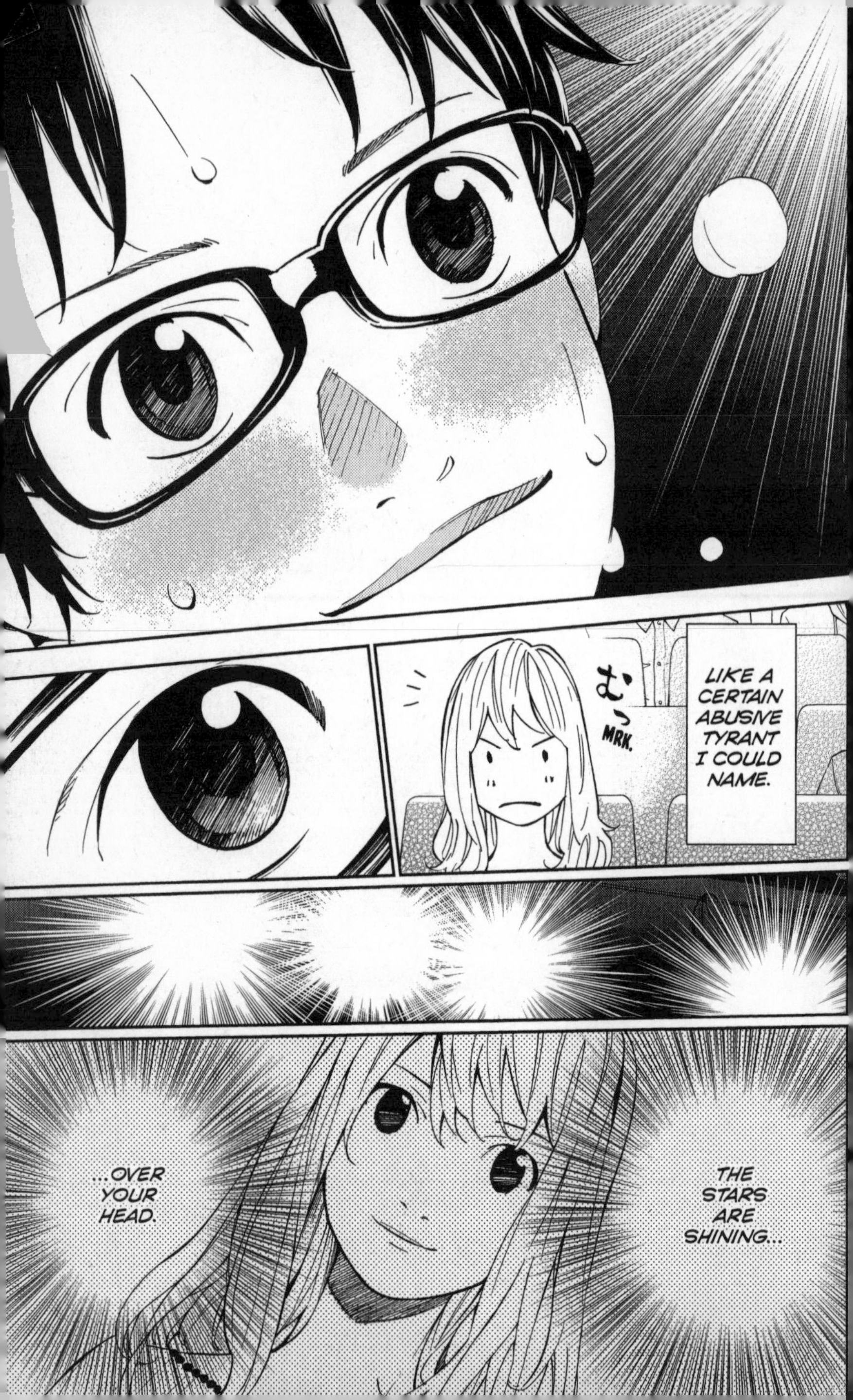
LIKE A CERTAIN ABUSIVE TYRANT I COULD NAME.
むっ
MRK.
THE STARS ARE SHINING...
...OVER YOUR HEAD.

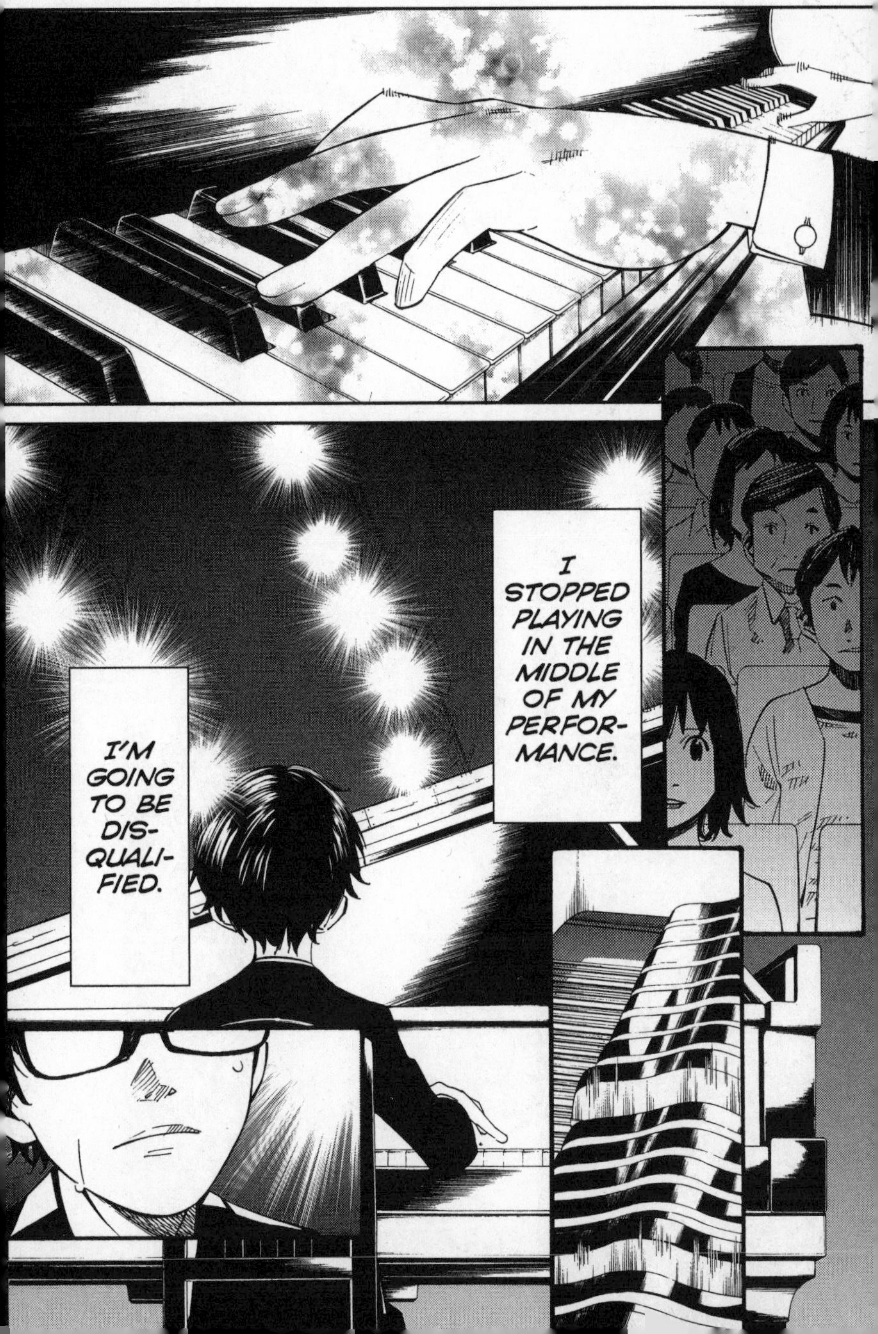
I STOPPED PLAYING IN THE MIDDLE OF MY PERFORMANCE.
I'M GOING TO BE DISQUALIFIED.

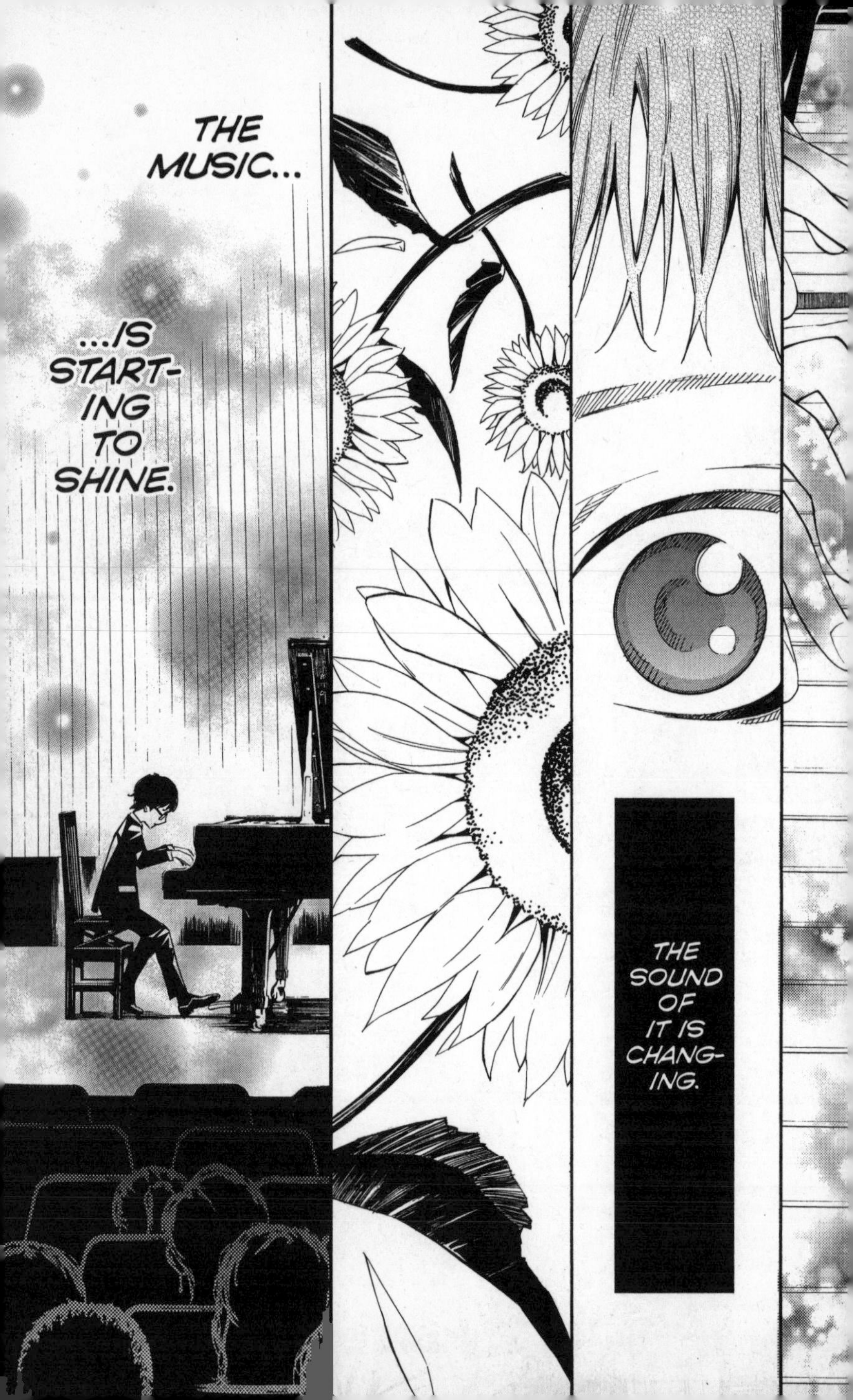
THE SOUND OF IT IS CHANGING.
THE MUSIC...
...IS STARTING TO SHINE.

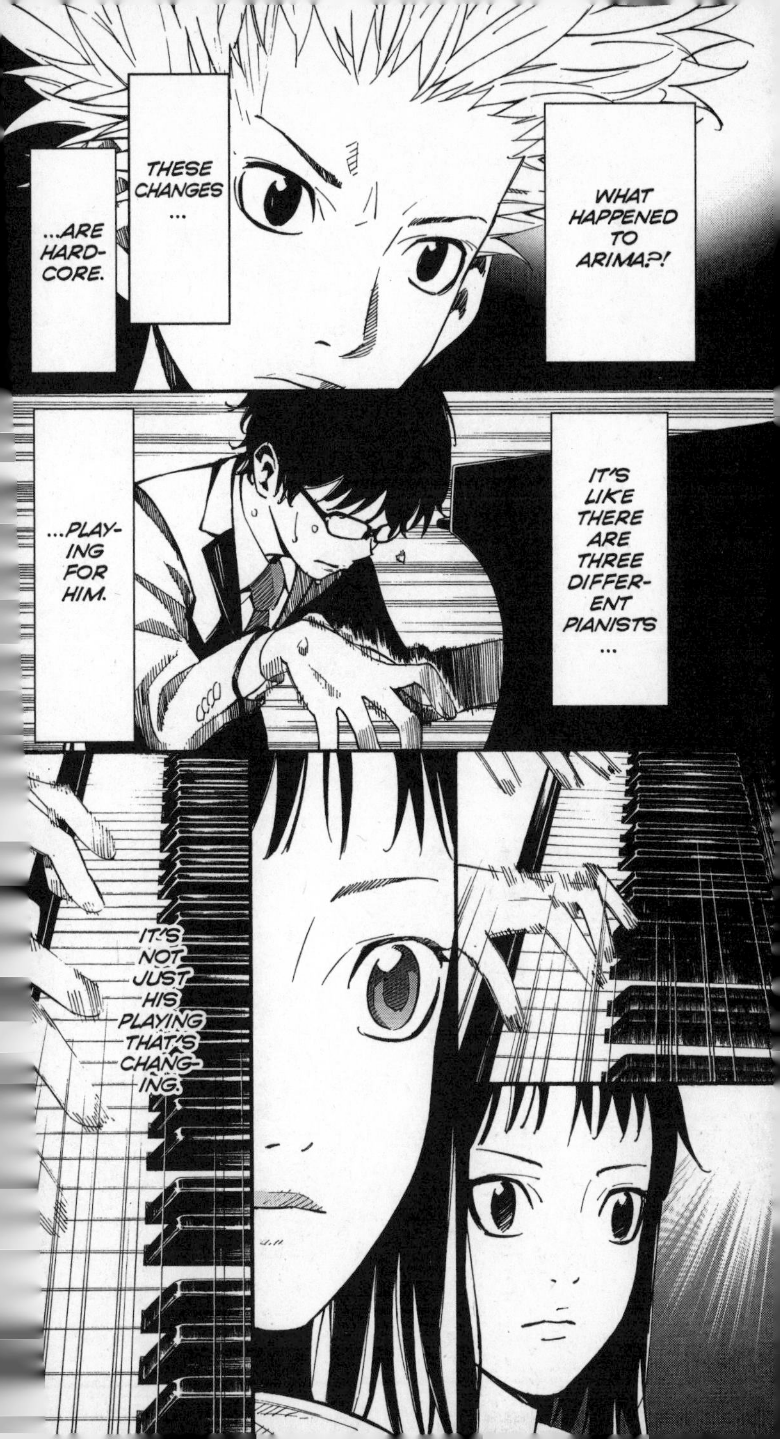
WHAT HAPPENED TO ARIMA?!
THESE CHANGES...
...ARE HARDCORE.
IT'S LIKE THERE ARE THREE DIFFERENT PIANISTS...
...PLAYING FOR HIM.
IT'S NOT JUST HIS PLAYING THAT'S CHANGING.

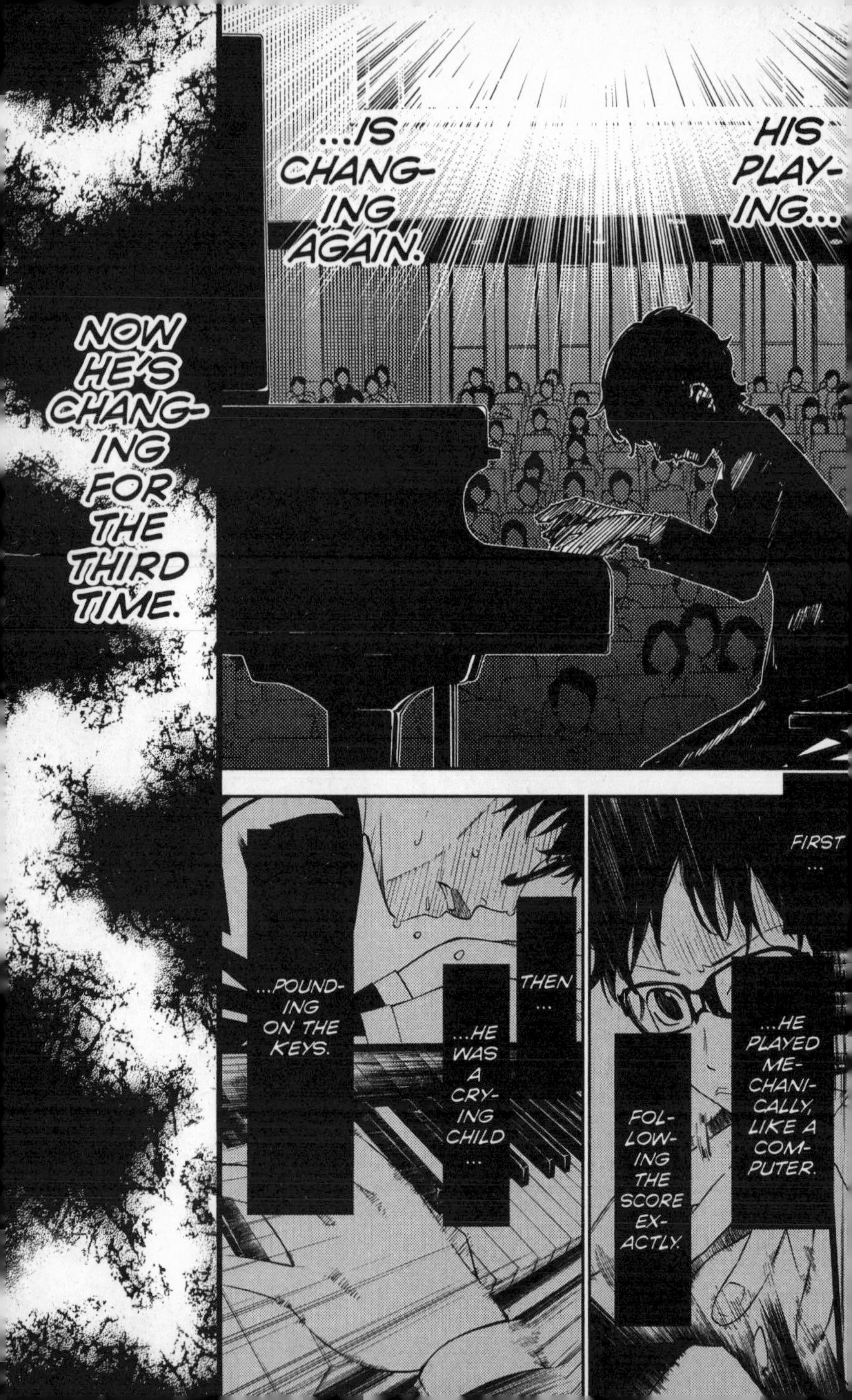
HIS PLAYING...
...IS CHANGING AGAIN.
FIRST...
...HE PLAYED MECHANICALLY, LIKE A COMPUTER.
FOLLOWING THE SCORE EXACTLY.
THEN...
...HE WAS A CRYING CHILD...
...POUNDING ON THE KEYS.
NOW HE'S CHANGING FOR THE THIRD TIME.

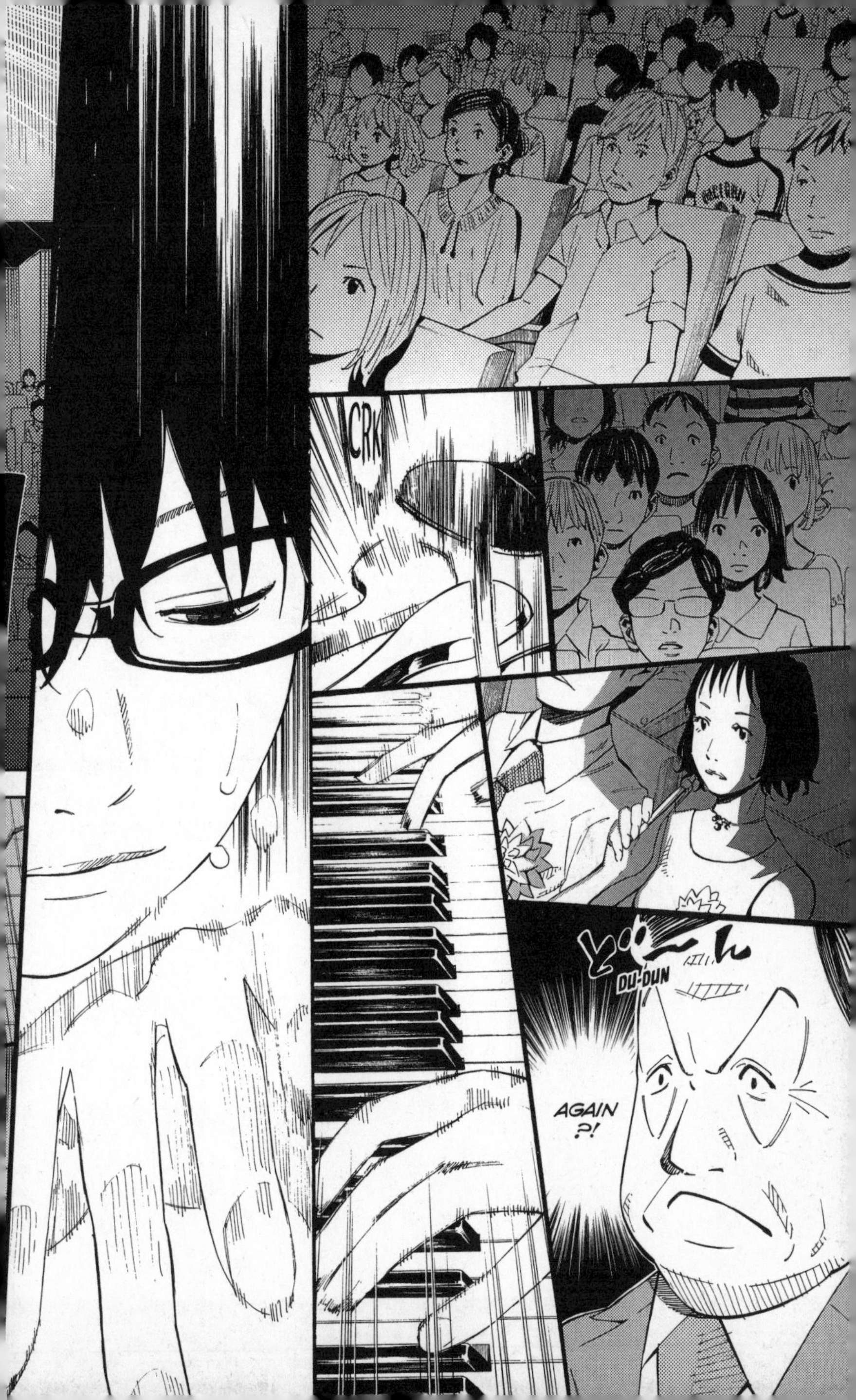
CRK
ど〜ん
DU-DUN
AGAIN ?!

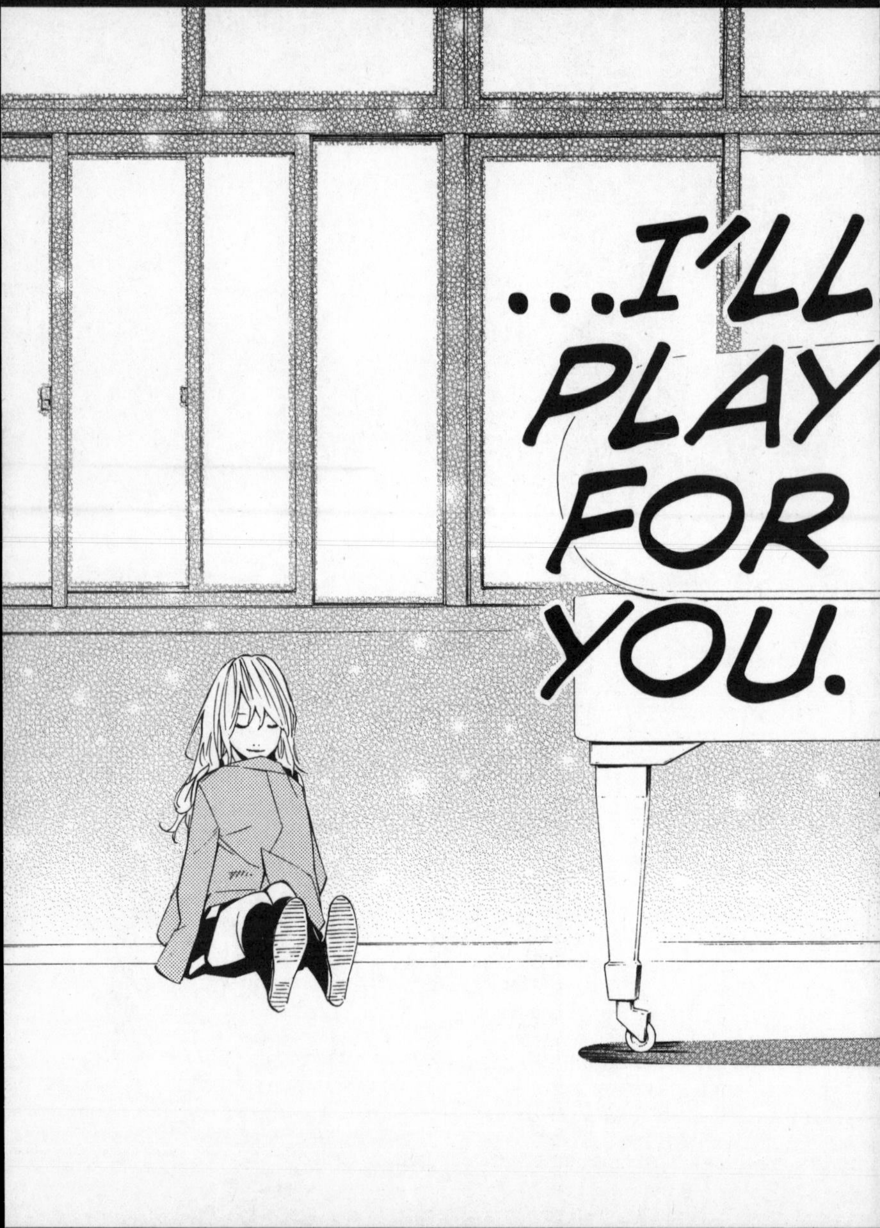
...I'LL PLAY FOR YOU.

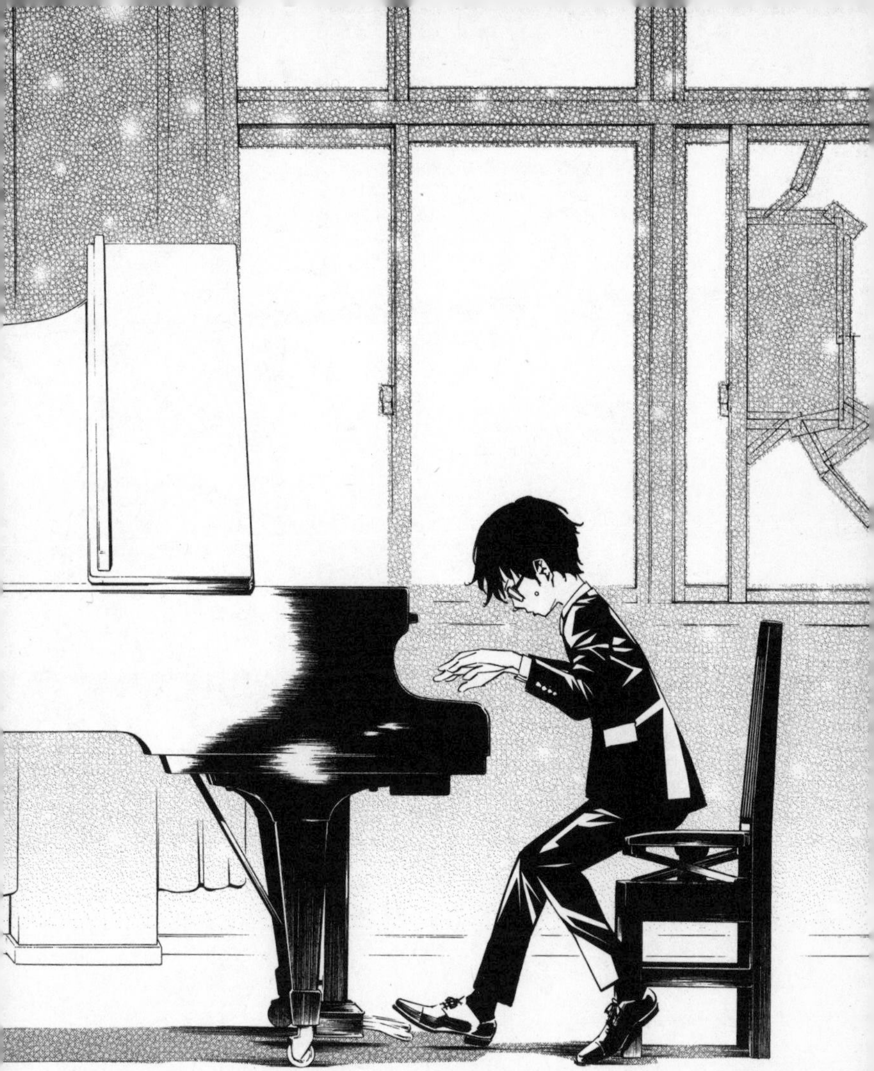

Chapter 18: The Scenery When I'm with You

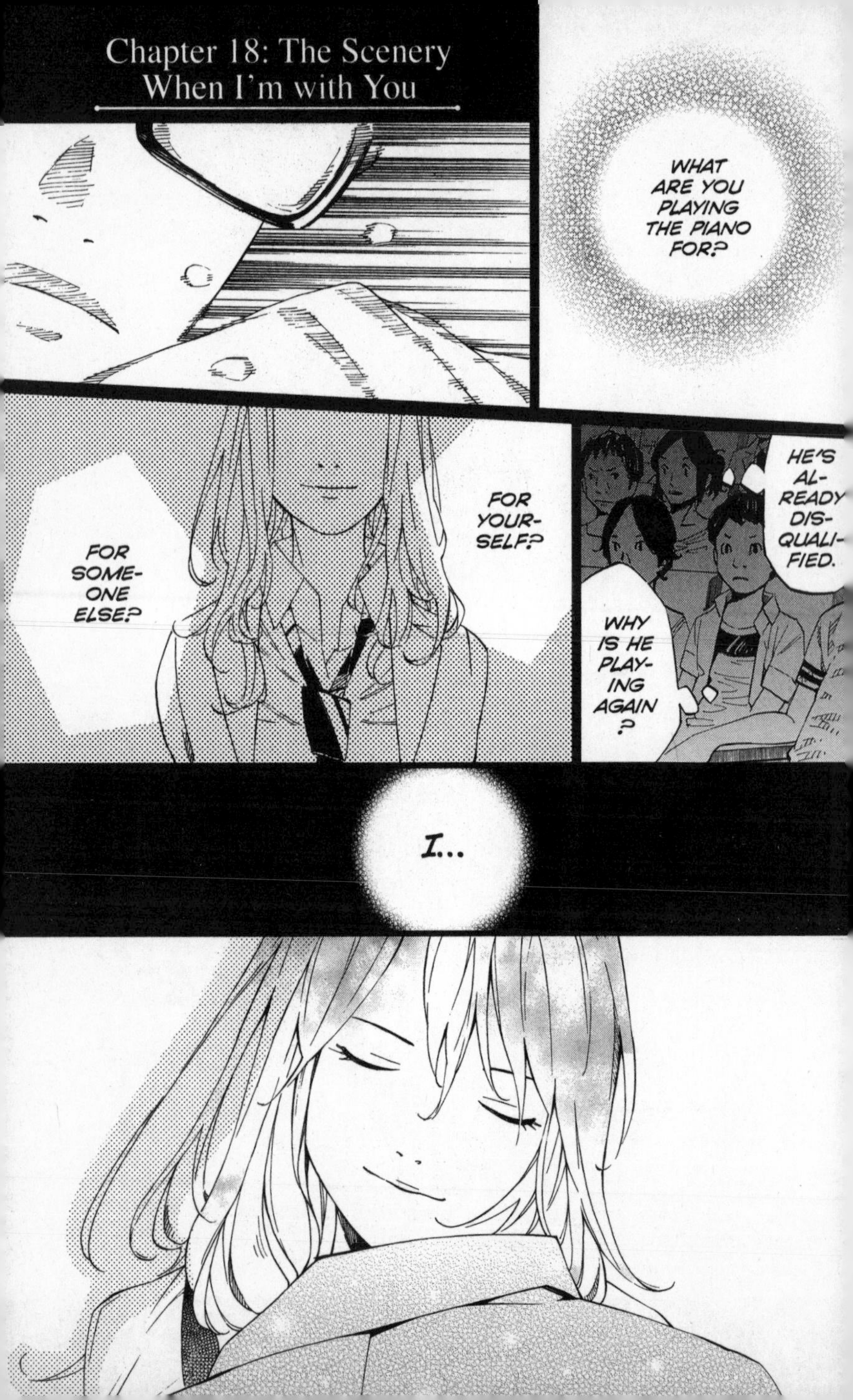
WHAT ARE YOU PLAYING THE PIANO FOR?
HE'S ALREADY DISQUALIFIED.
WHY IS HE PLAYING AGAIN?
FOR YOURSELF?
FOR SOMEONE ELSE?
I...

Your Lie in April

I met the girl under full-bloomed cherry blossoms, and my fate has begun to change.

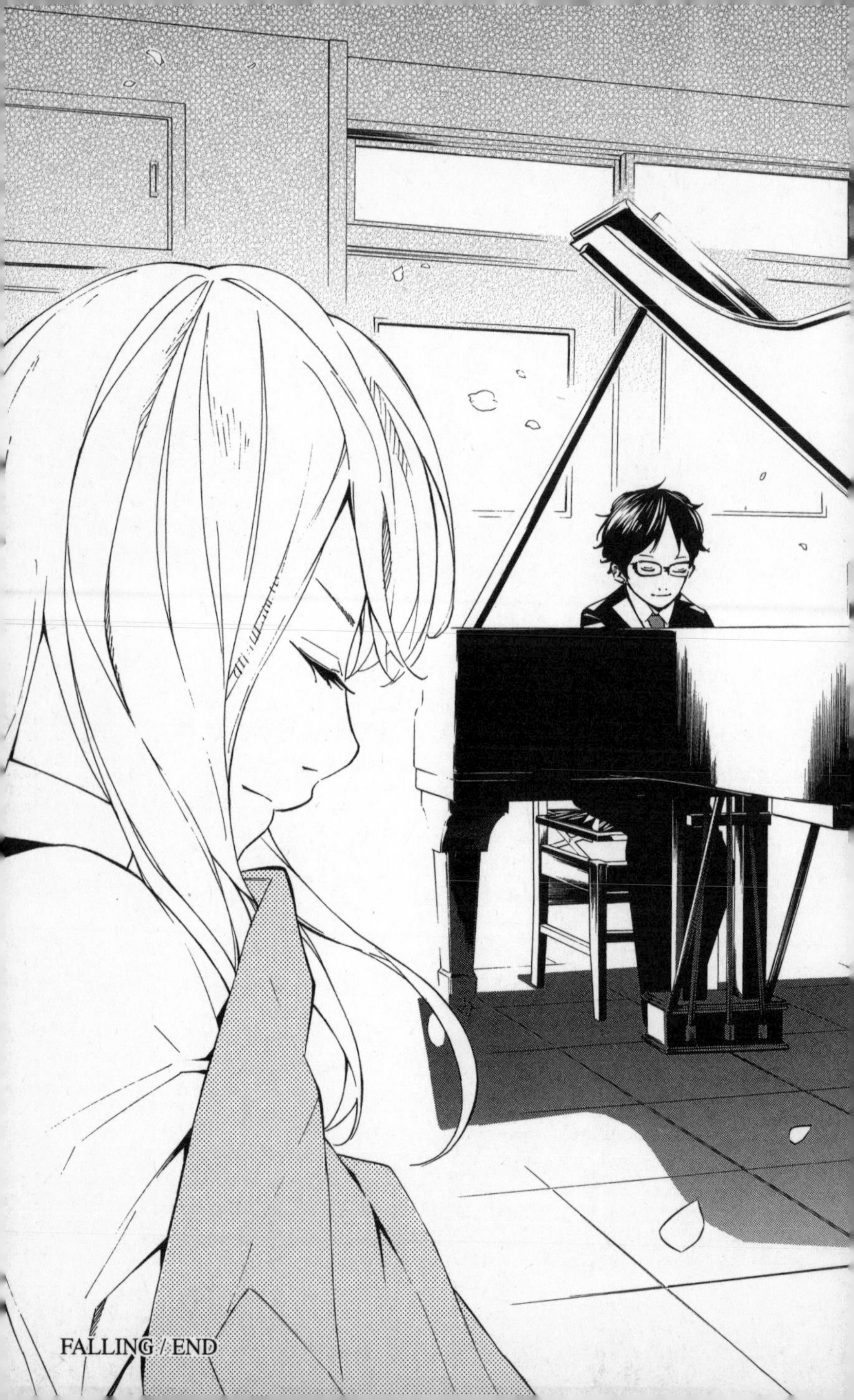
FALLING / END

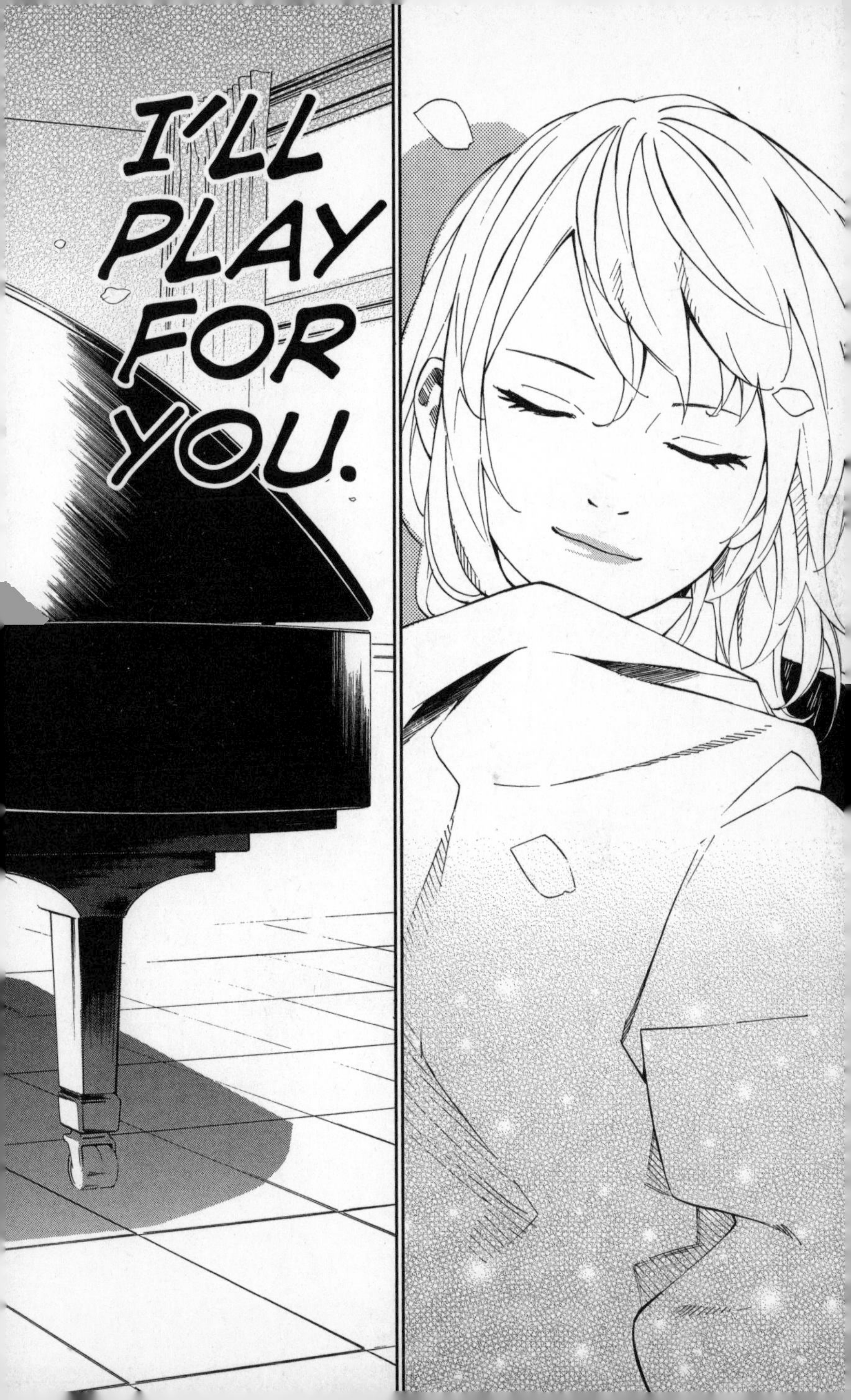
I'LL PLAY FOR YOU.

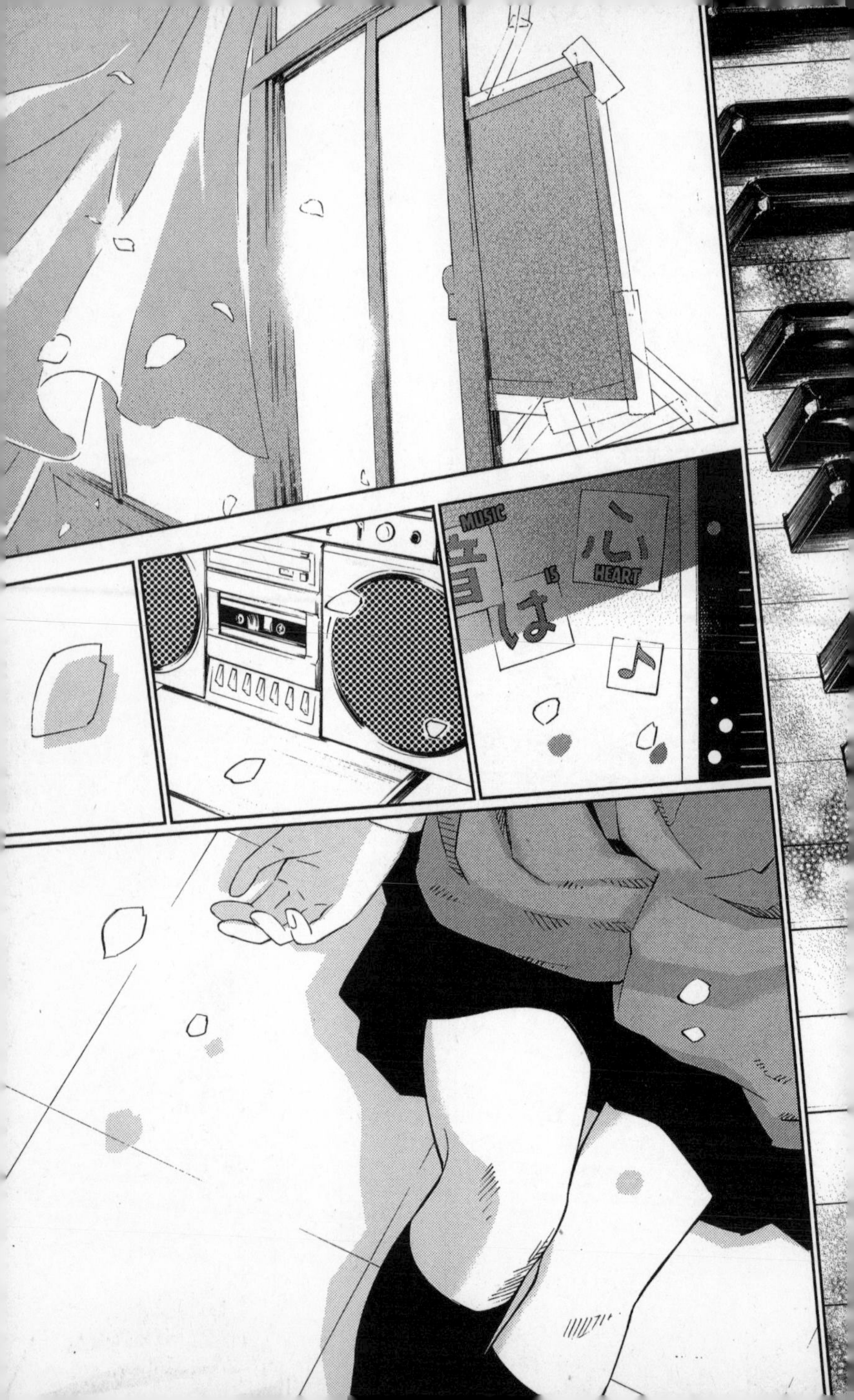
MUSIC
音は
IS
心
HEART
♪

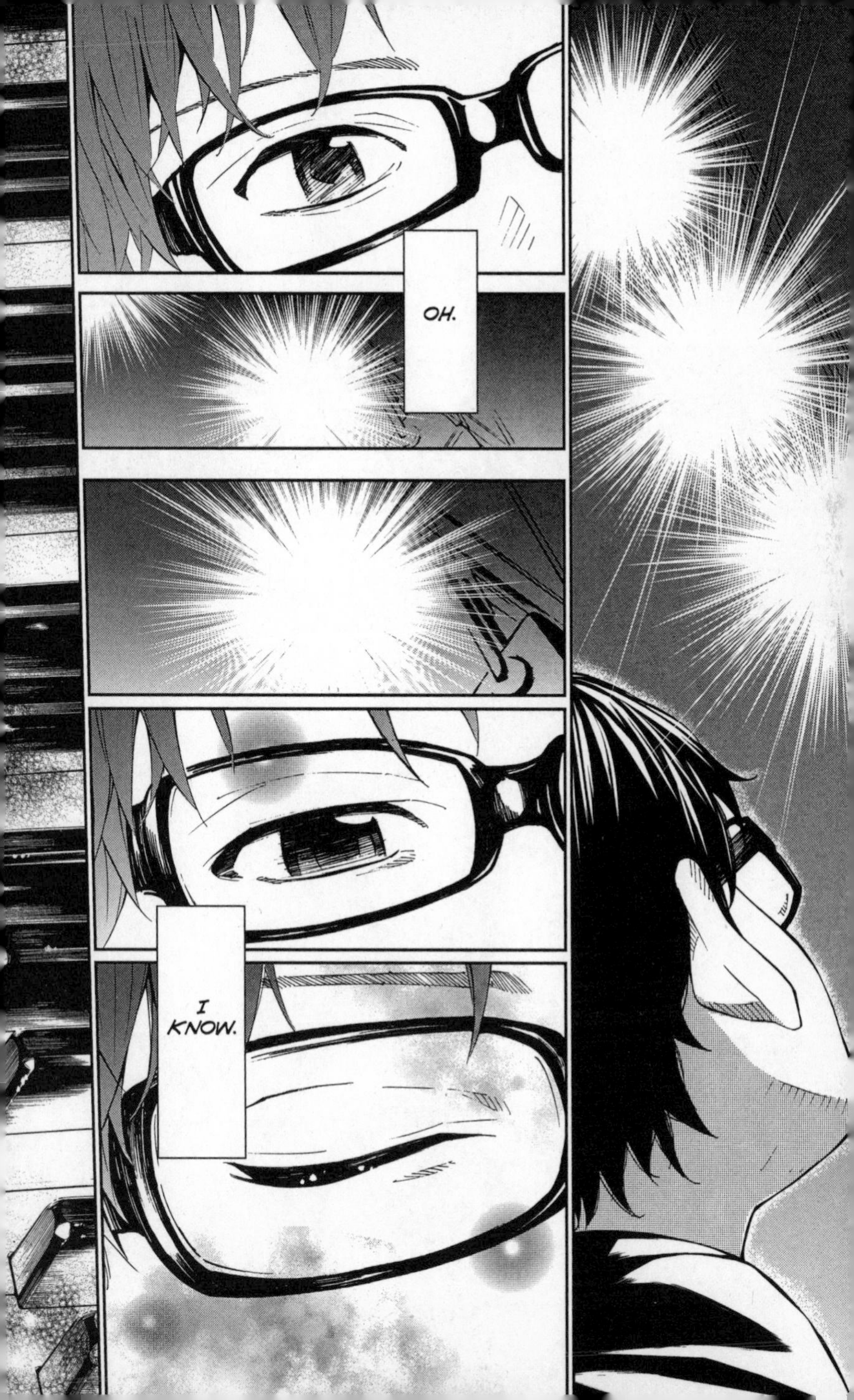
OH.
I KNOW.

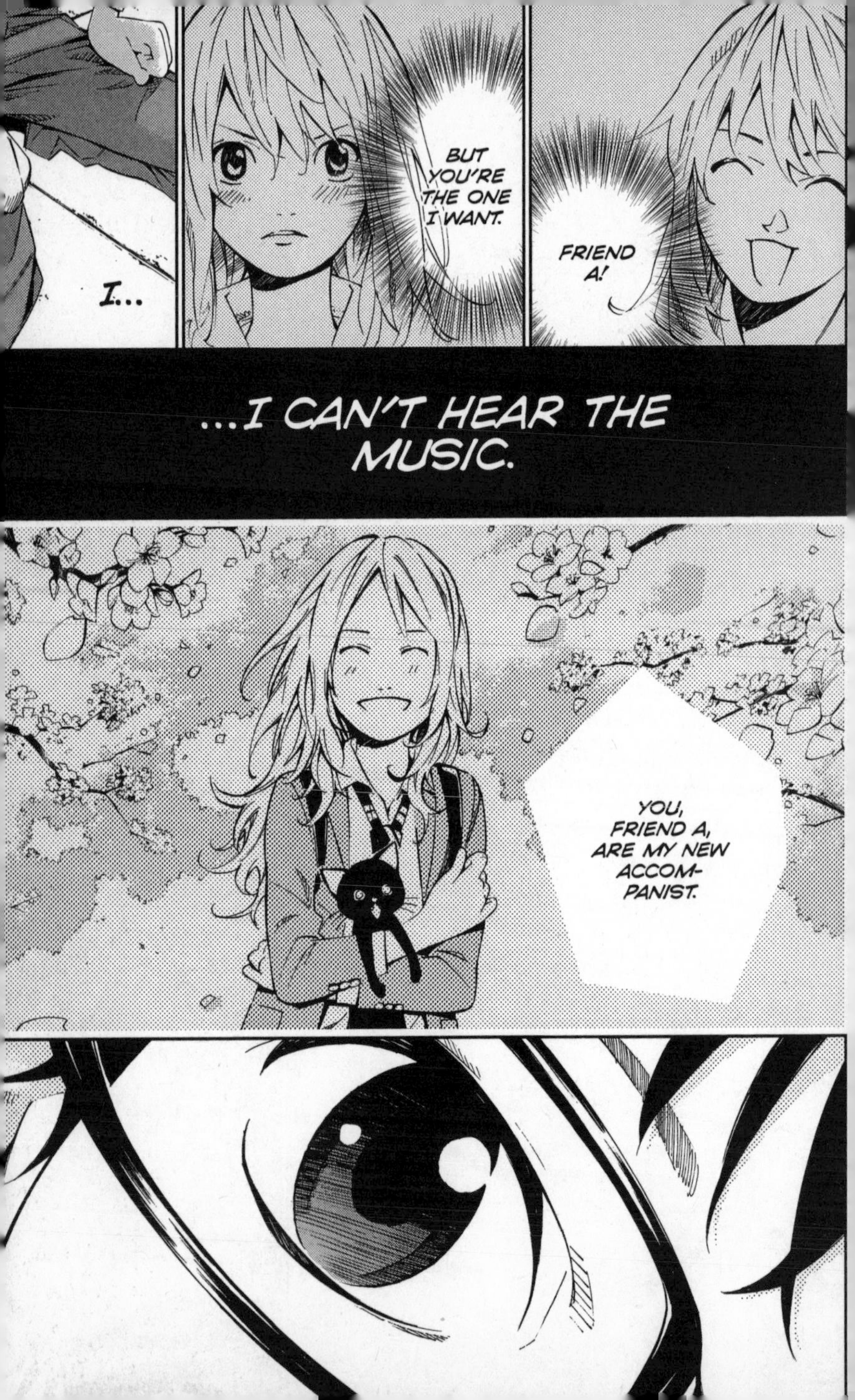
FRIEND A!
BUT YOU'RE THE ONE I WANT.
I...
...I CAN'T HEAR THE MUSIC.
YOU, FRIEND A, ARE MY NEW ACCOM-PANIST.

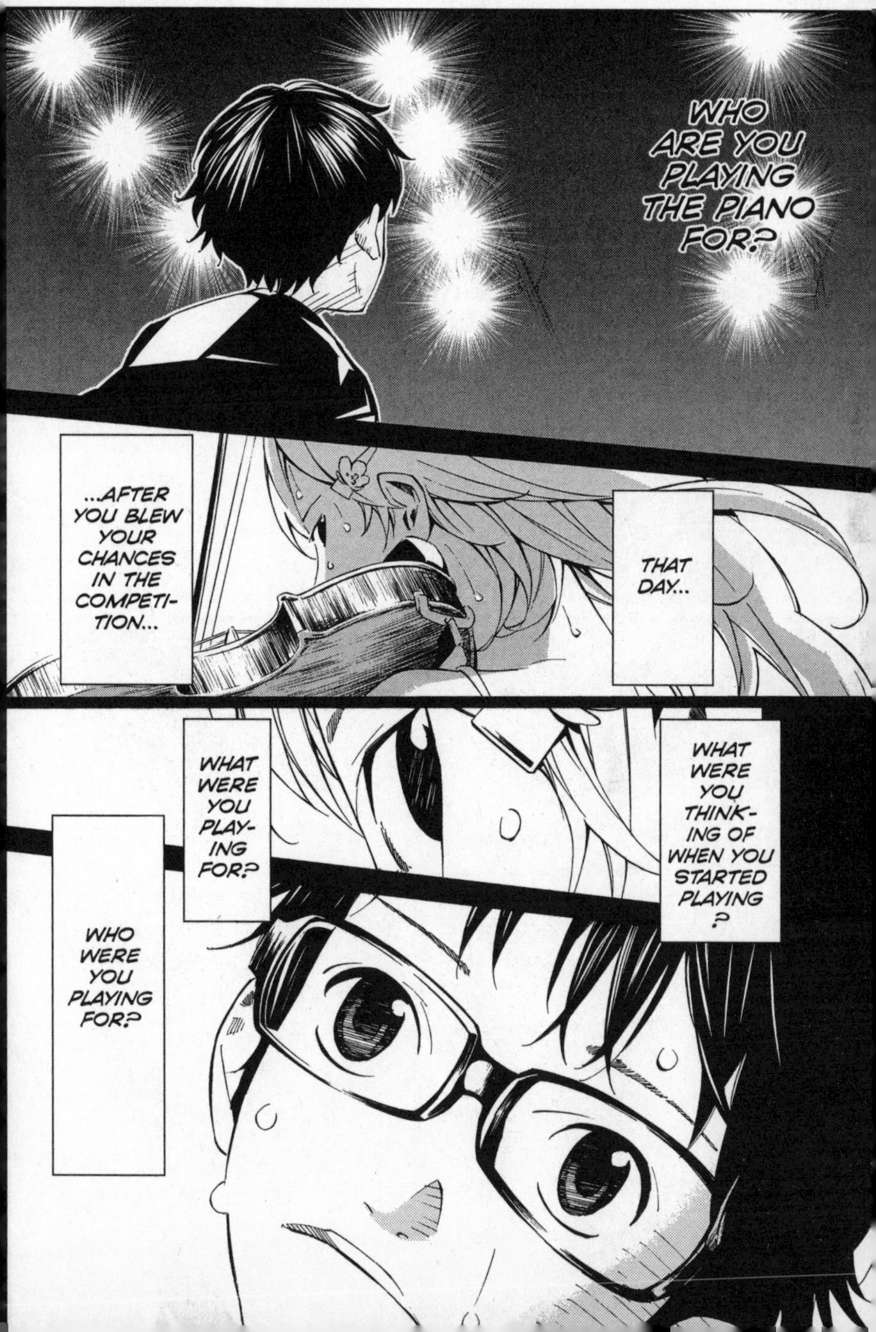
WHO ARE YOU PLAYING THE PIANO FOR?
THAT DAY...
...AFTER YOU BLEW YOUR CHANCES IN THE COMPETITION...
WHAT WERE YOU THINKING OF WHEN YOU STARTED PLAYING?
WHAT WERE YOU PLAYING FOR?
WHO WERE YOU PLAYING FOR?

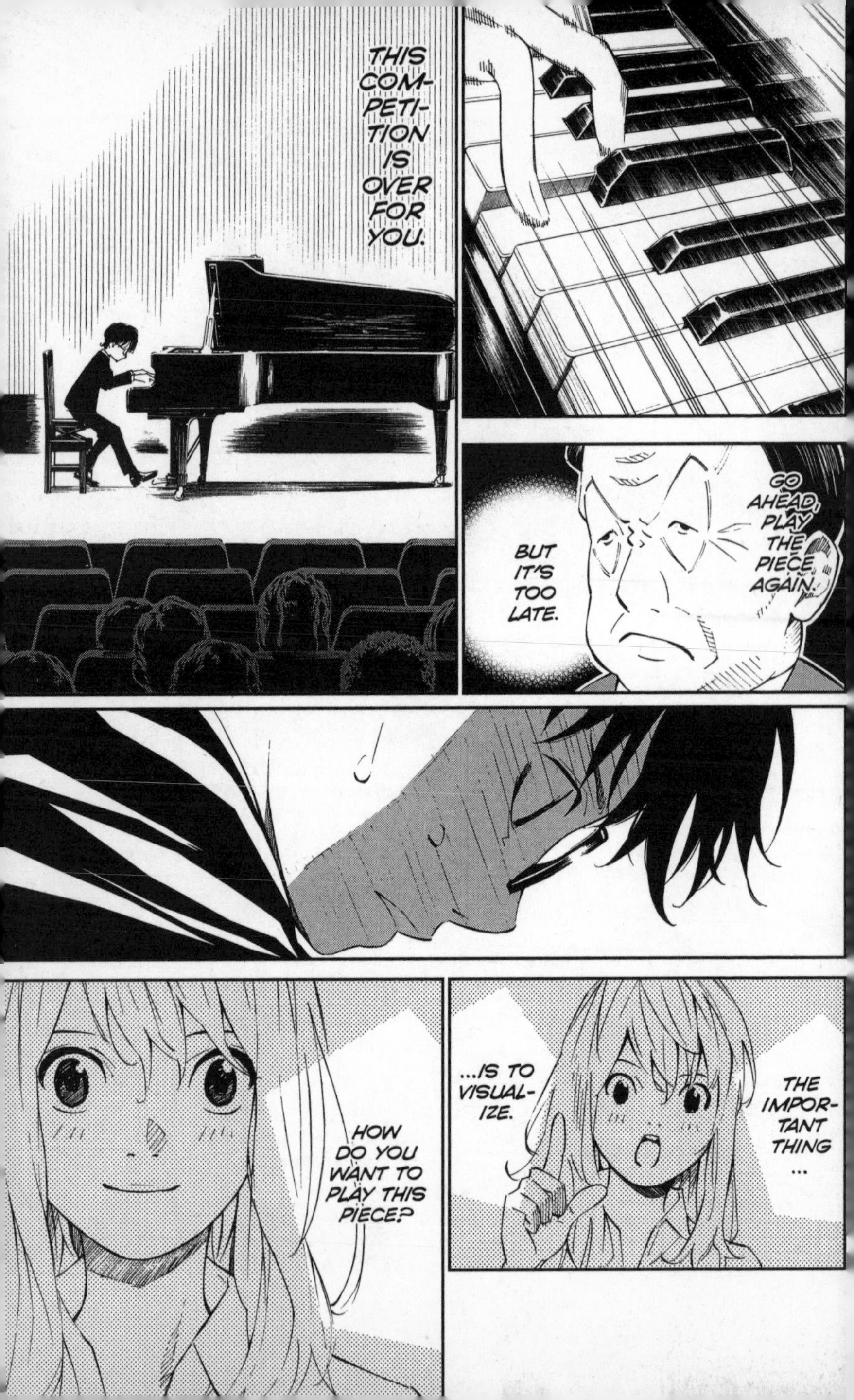
GO AHEAD, PLAY THE PIECE AGAIN.
BUT IT'S TOO LATE.
THIS COMPETITION IS OVER FOR YOU.
THE IMPORTANT THING...
...IS TO VISUALIZE.
HOW DO YOU WANT TO PLAY THIS PIECE?

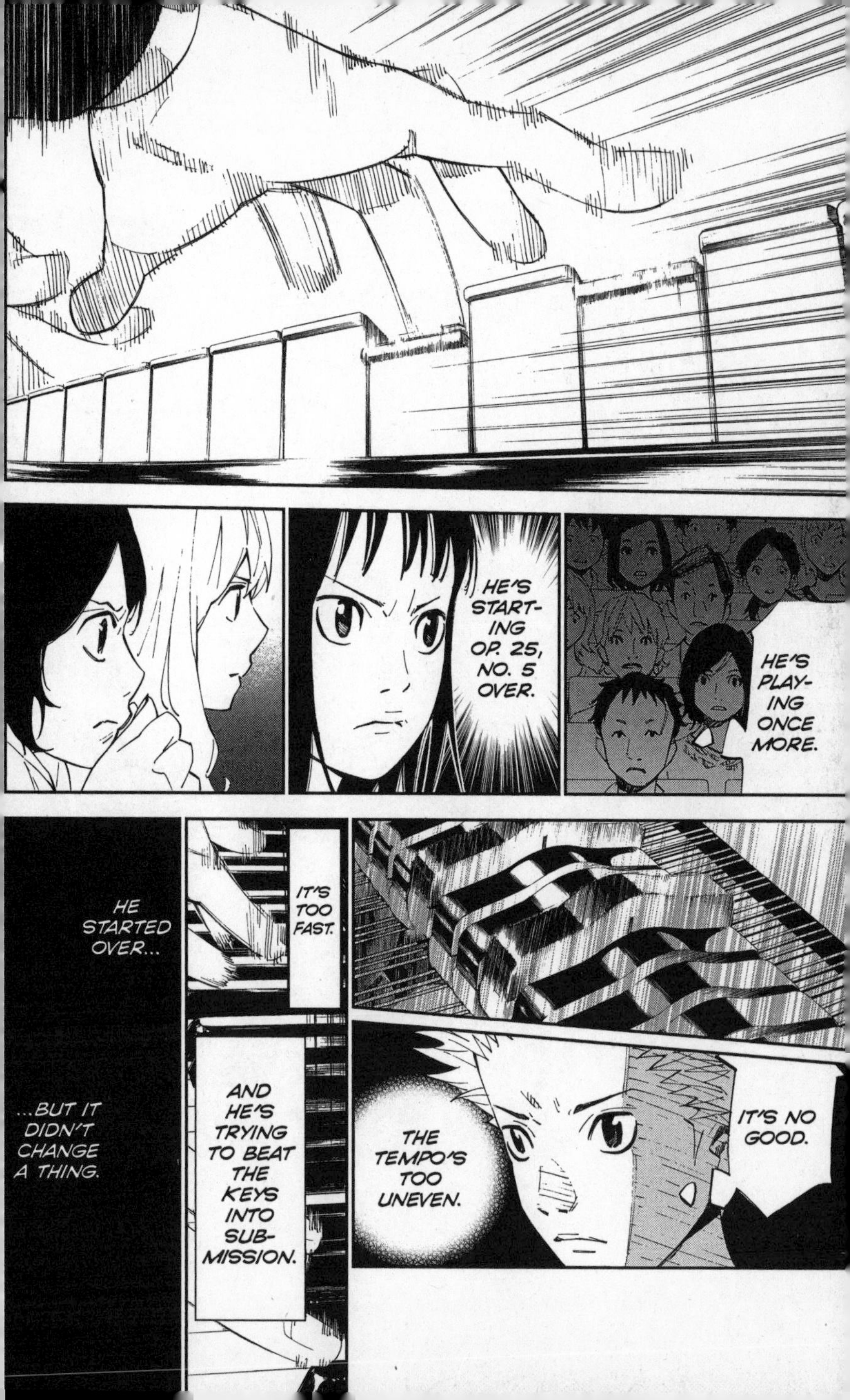
HE'S PLAYING ONCE MORE.
HE'S STARTING OP. 25, NO. 5 OVER.
IT'S NO GOOD.
THE TEMPO'S TOO UNEVEN.
IT'S TOO FAST.
AND HE'S TRYING TO BEAT THE KEYS INTO SUBMISSION.
HE STARTED OVER...
...BUT IT DIDN'T CHANGE A THING.

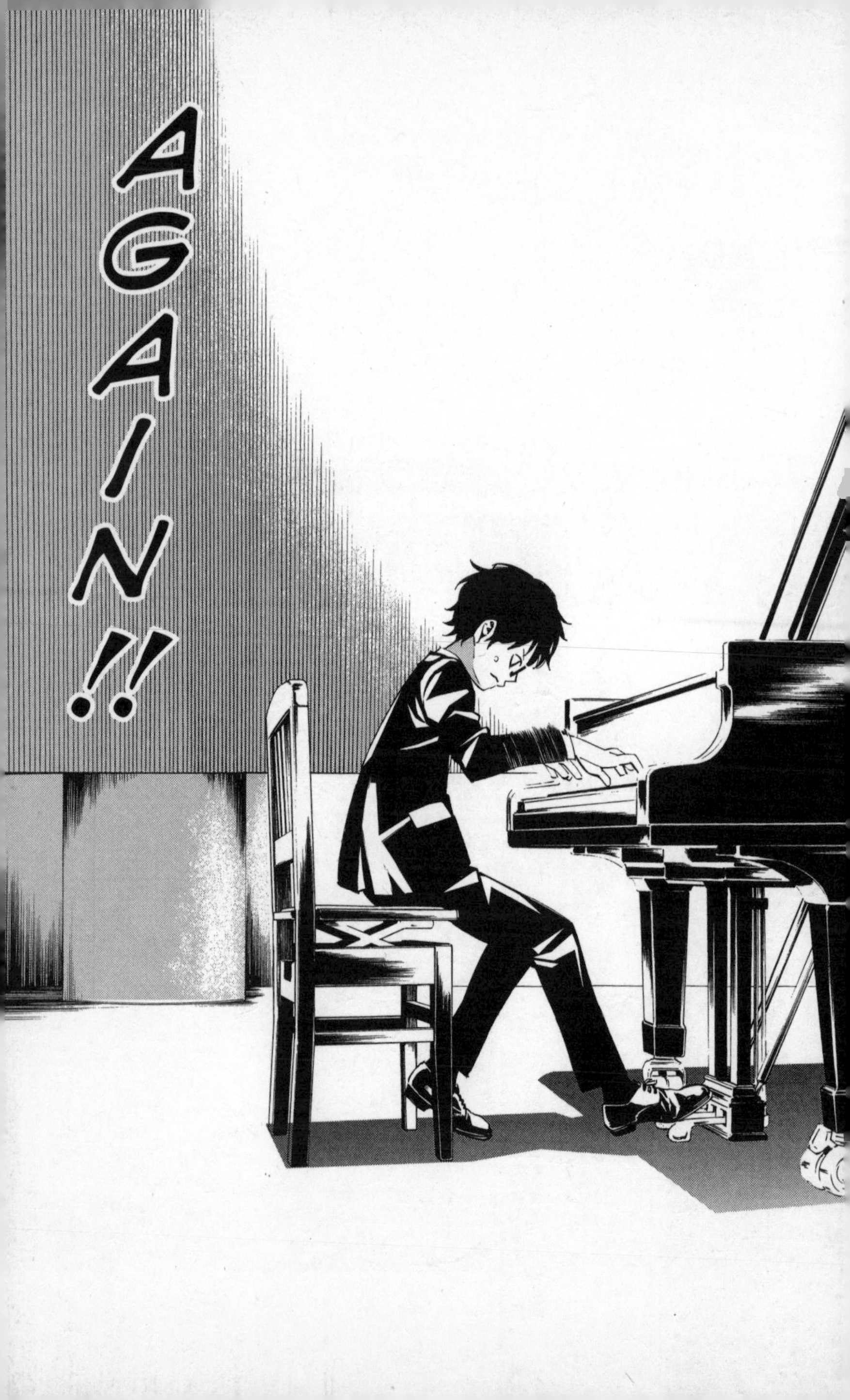
AGAIN!!

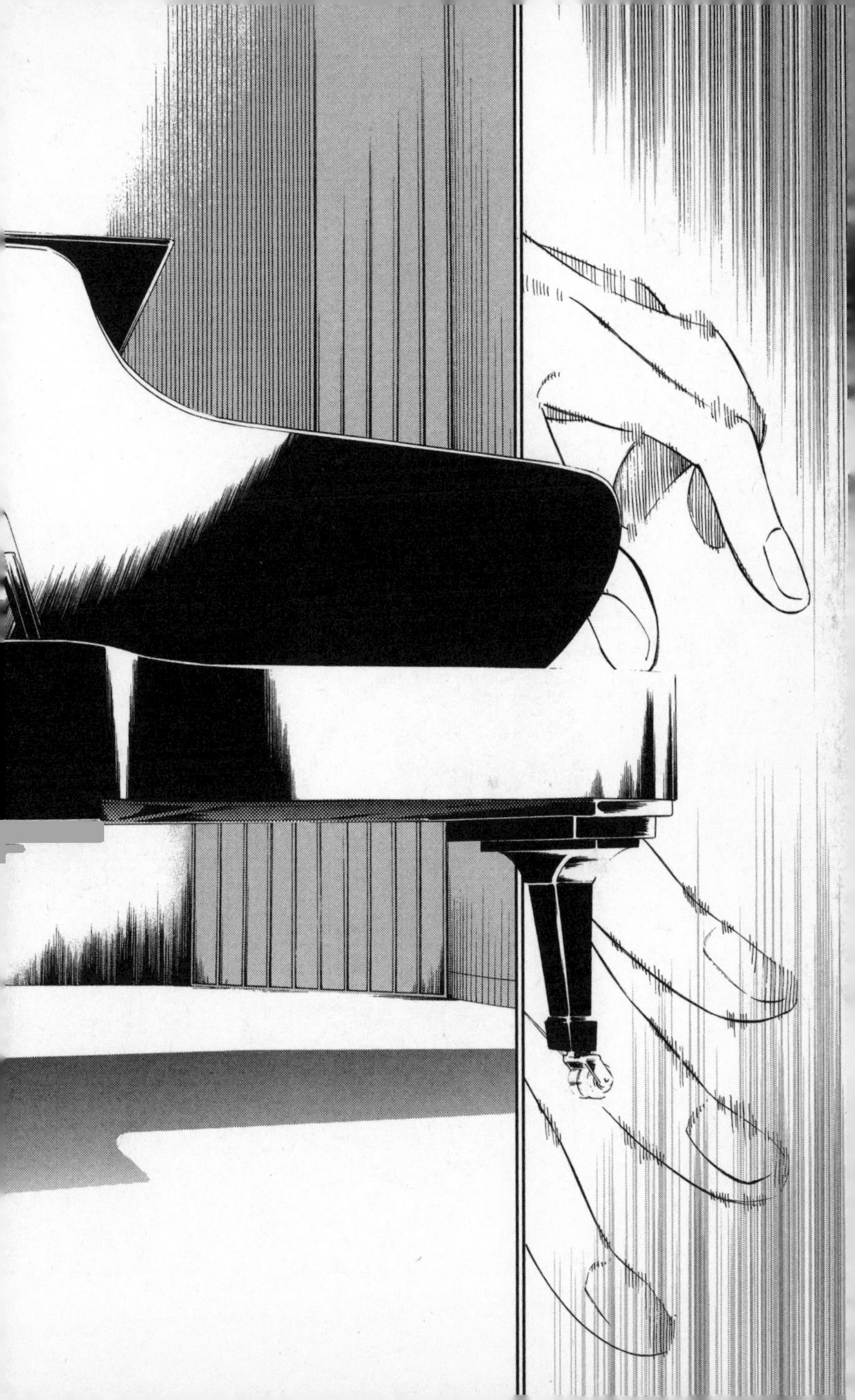

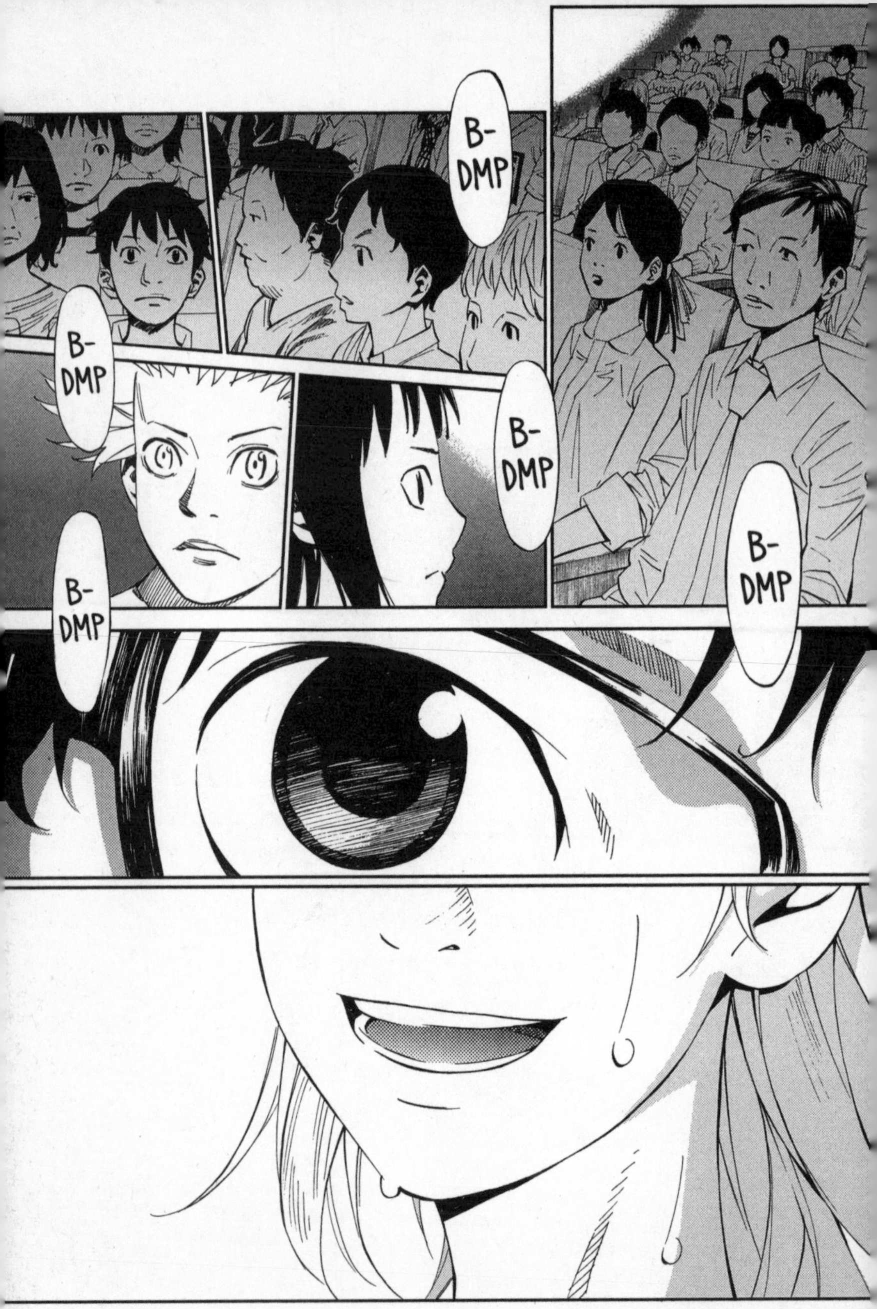
B-DMP
B-DMP
B-DMP
B-DMP
B-DMP

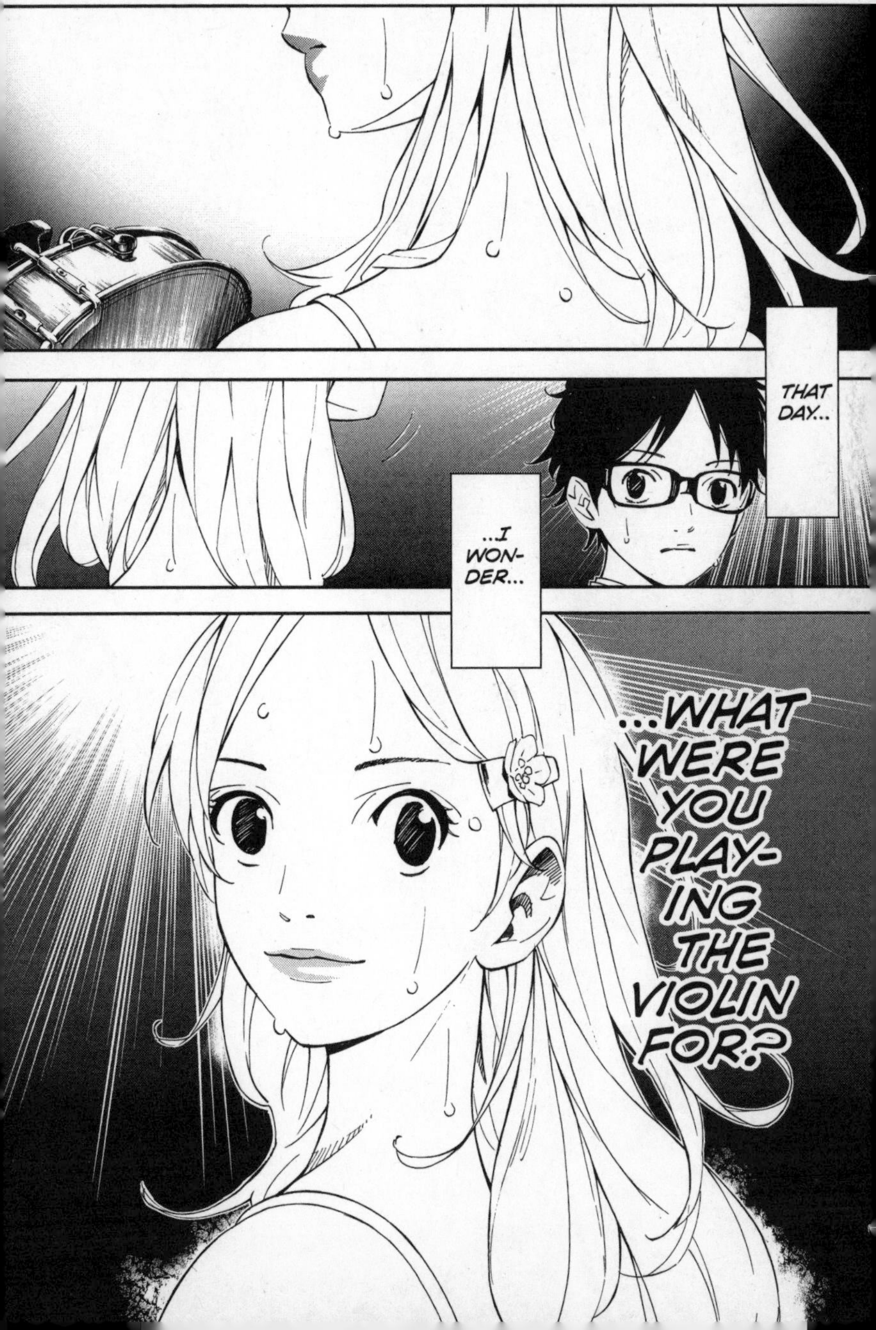
THAT DAY...
...I WON-DER...
...WHAT WERE YOU PLAY-ING THE VIOLIN FOR?

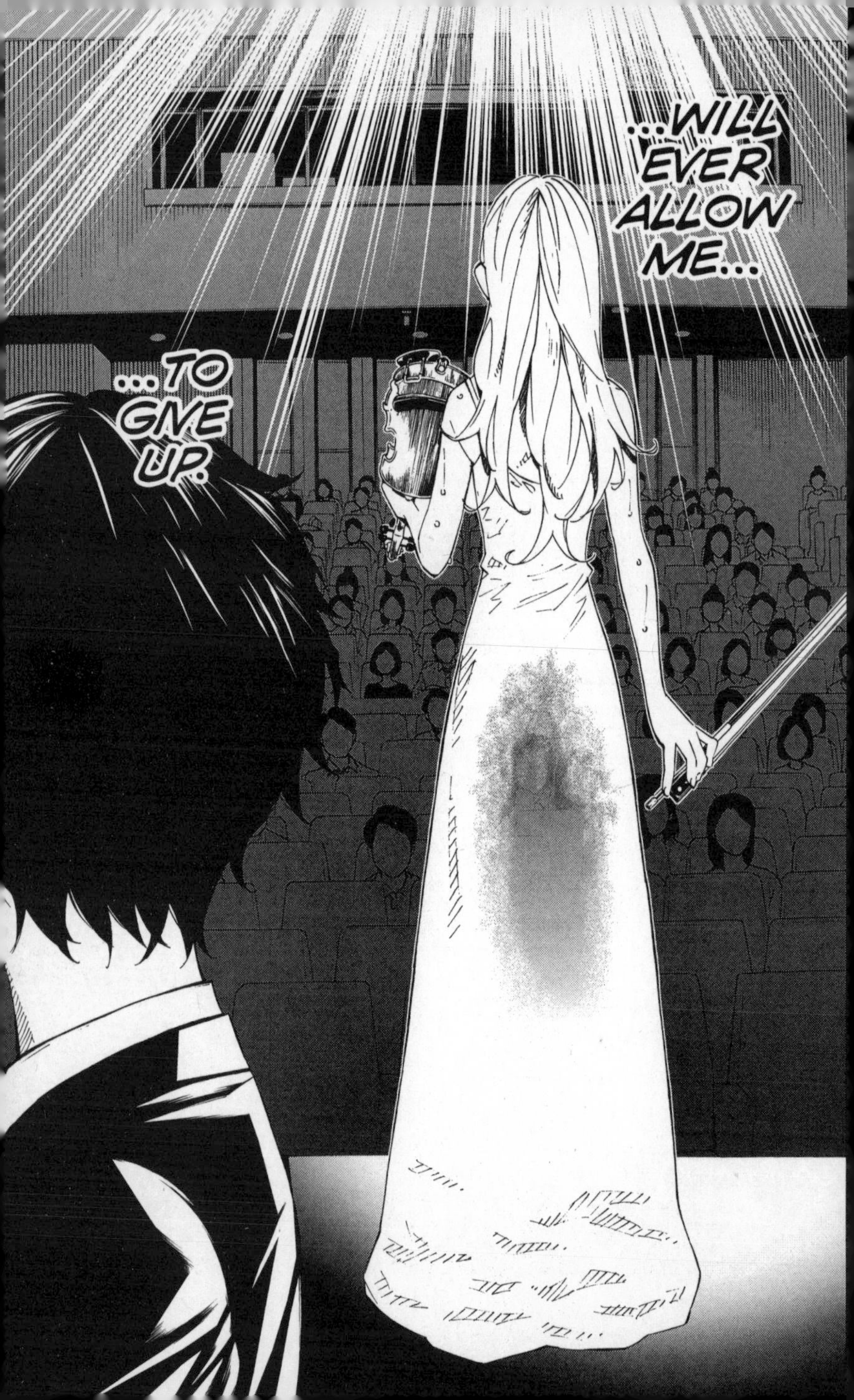
...WILL EVER ALLOW ME...
...TO GIVE UP.

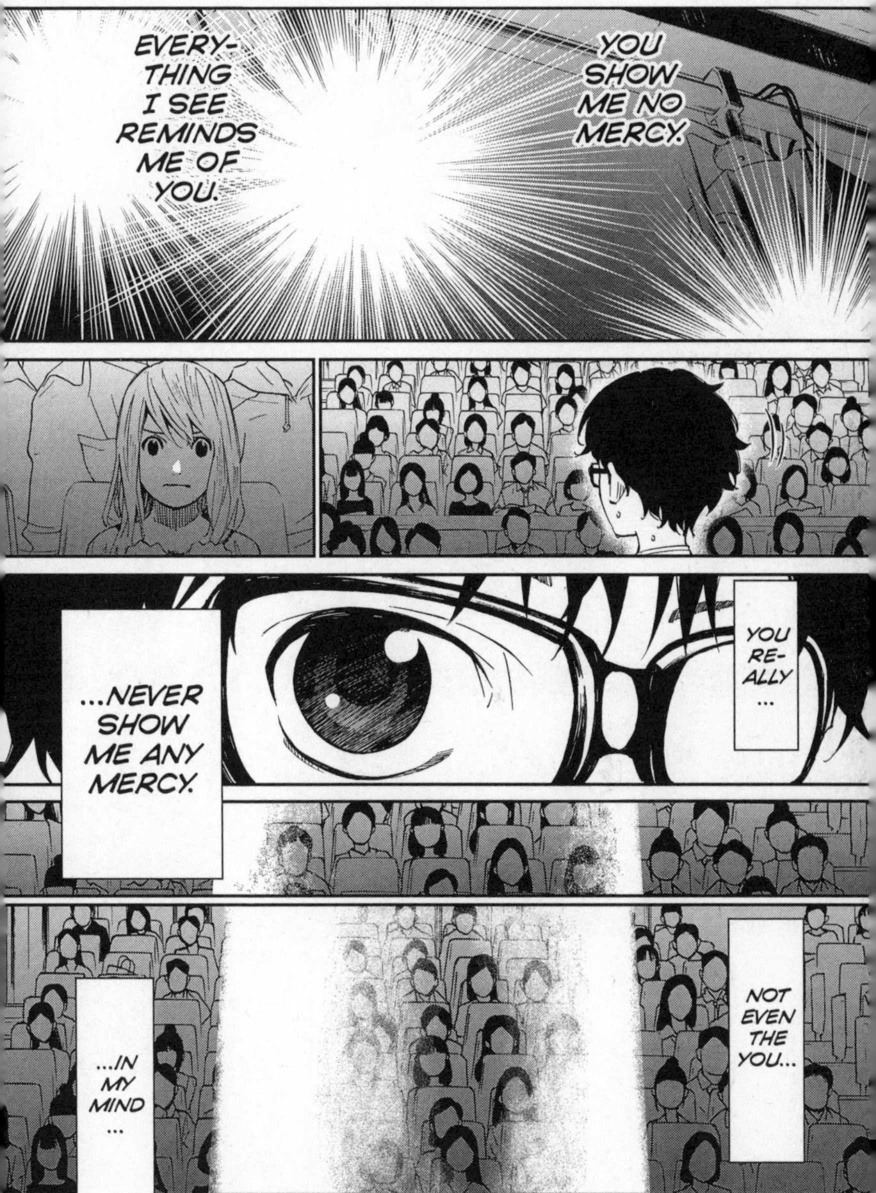
YOU SHOW ME NO MERCY.
EVERY-THING I SEE REMINDS ME OF YOU.
YOU RE-ALLY ...
...NEVER SHOW ME ANY MERCY.
NOT EVEN THE YOU...
...IN MY MIND ...

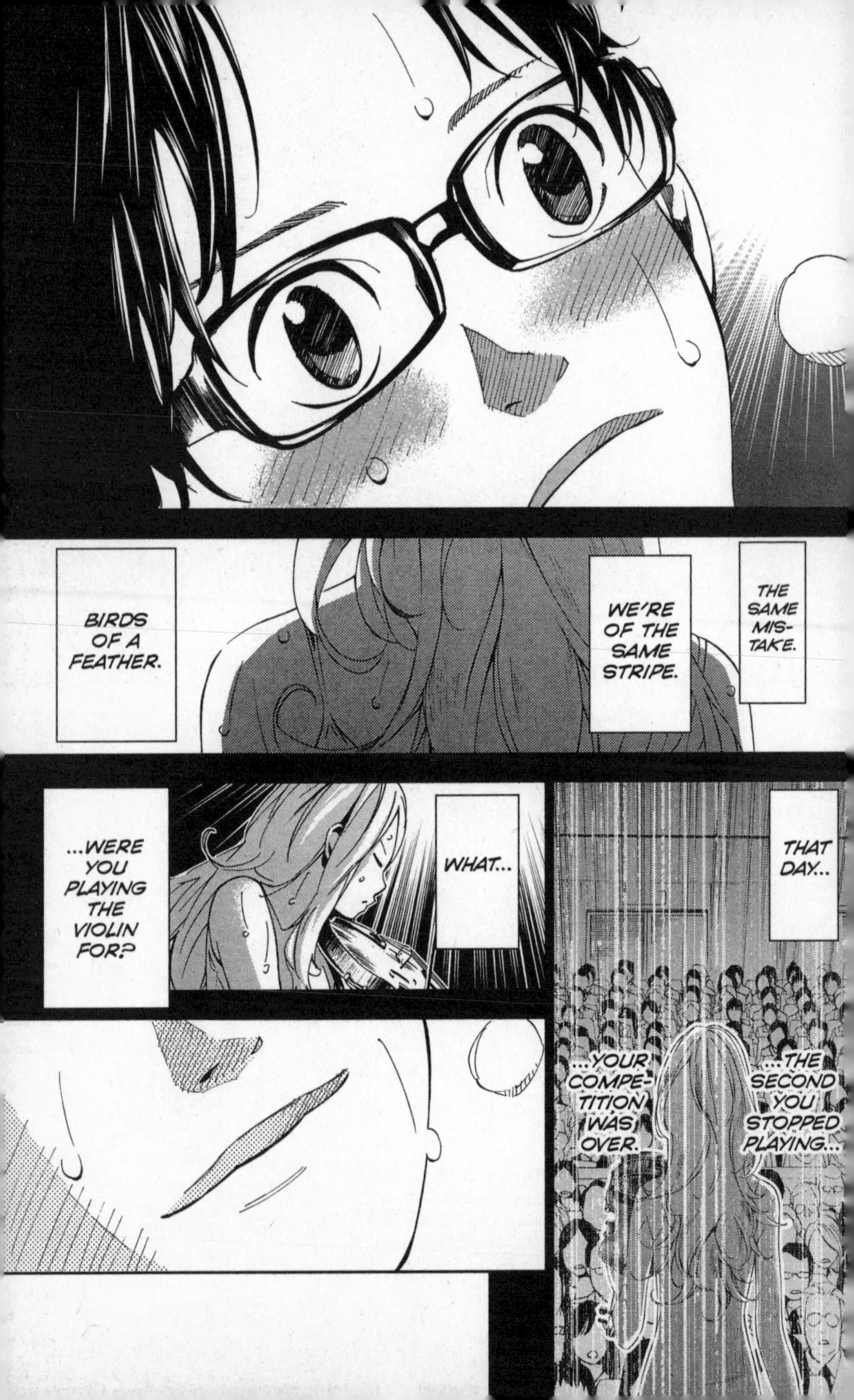
THE SAME MIS-TAKE.
WE'RE OF THE SAME STRIPE.
BIRDS OF A FEATHER.
THAT DAY...
...THE SECOND YOU STOPPED PLAYING...
...YOUR COMPE-TITION WAS OVER.
WHAT...
...WERE YOU PLAYING THE VIOLIN FOR?

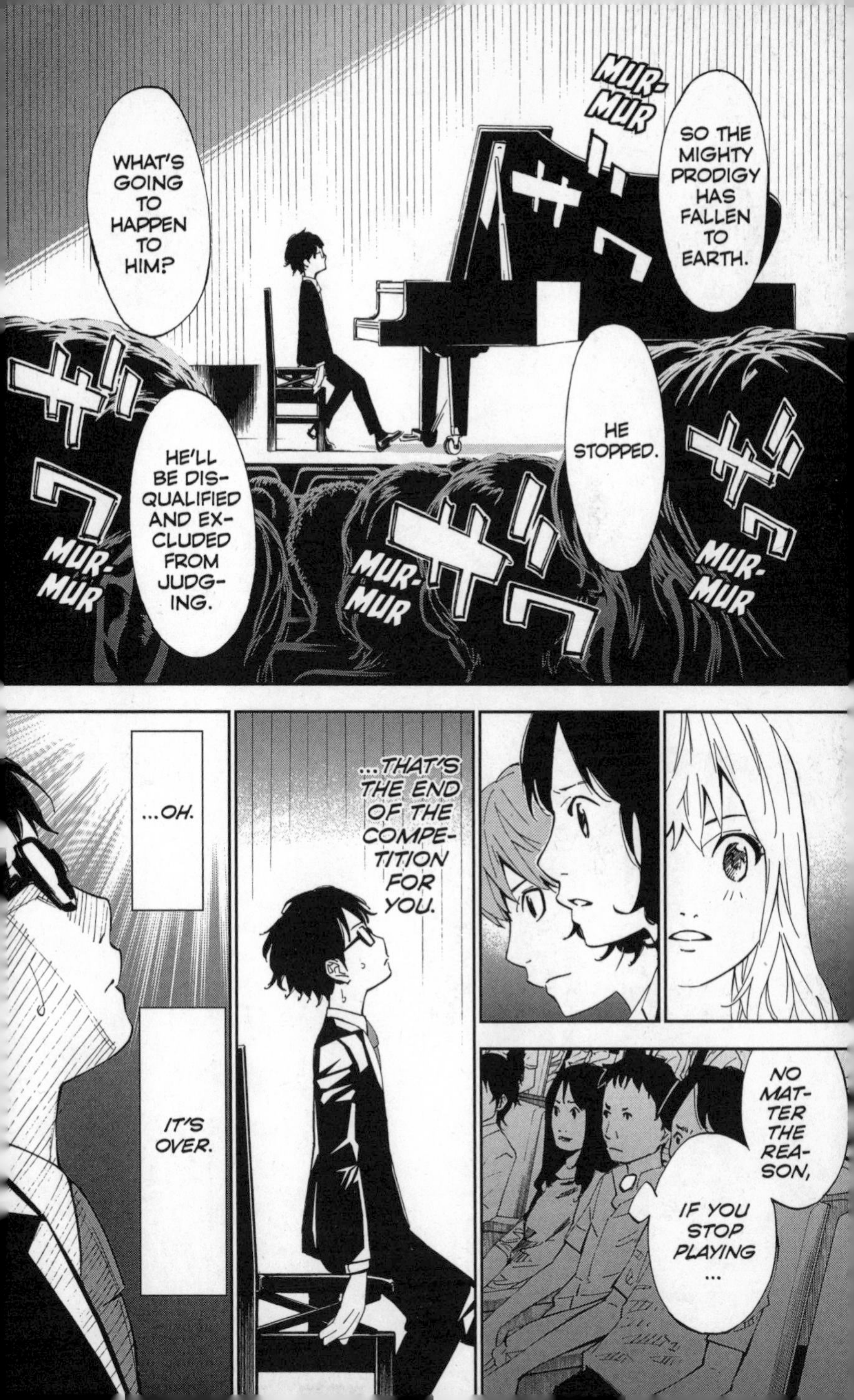
MUR-MUR
SO THE MIGHTY PRODIGY HAS FALLEN TO EARTH.
WHAT'S GOING TO HAPPEN TO HIM?
HE STOPPED.
MUR-MUR
MUR-MUR
HE'LL BE DISQUALIFIED AND EXCLUDED FROM JUDGING.
MUR-MUR
NO MATTER THE REASON,
IF YOU STOP PLAYING ...
...THAT'S THE END OF THE COMPETITION FOR YOU.
...OH.
IT'S OVER.

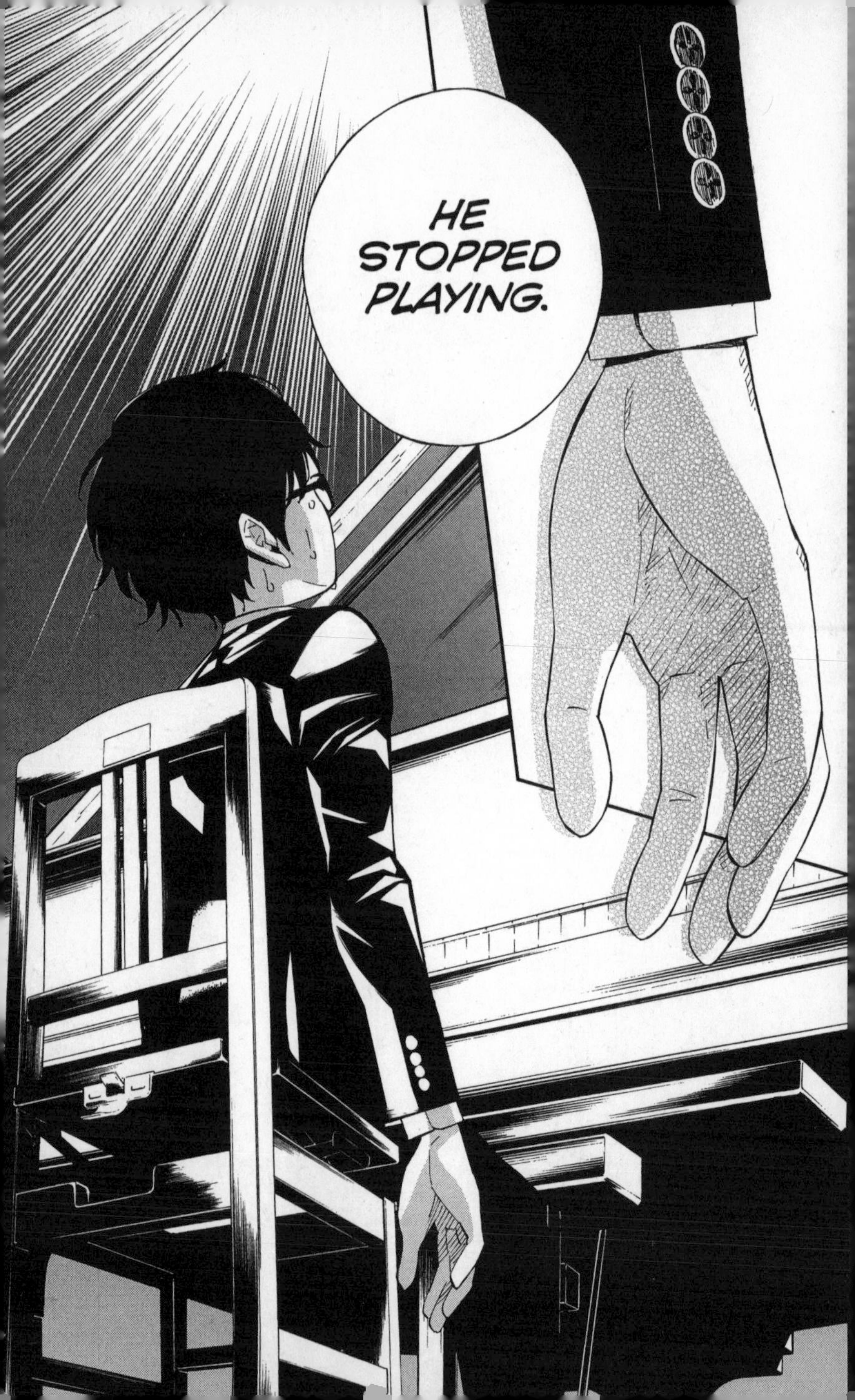
HE STOPPED PLAYING.

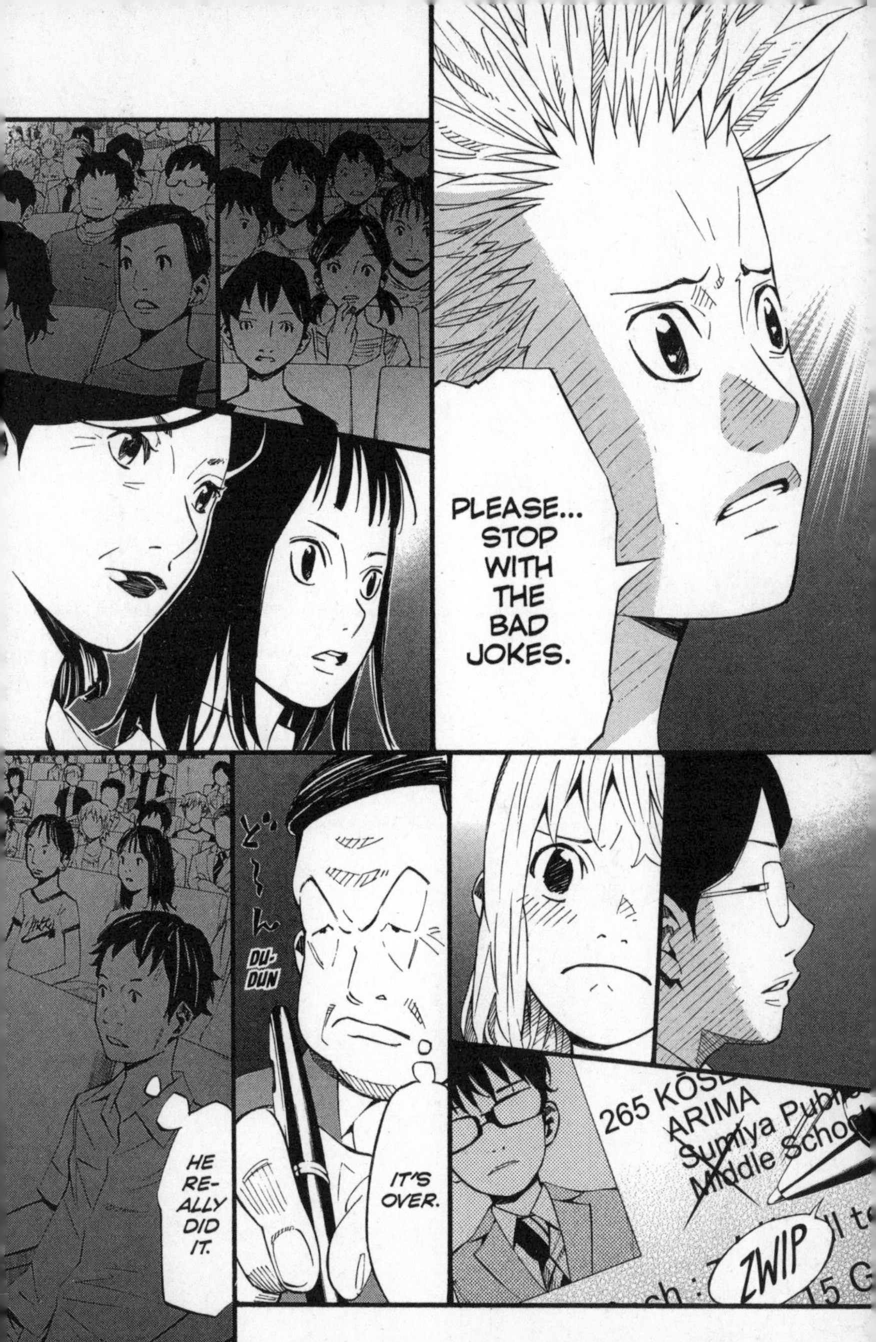
PLEASE... STOP WITH THE BAD JOKES.
265 KŌS
ARIMA
Sumiya Publ
Middle Schoo
ZWIP
どーん
DU-DUN
IT'S OVER.
HE RE-ALLY DID IT.

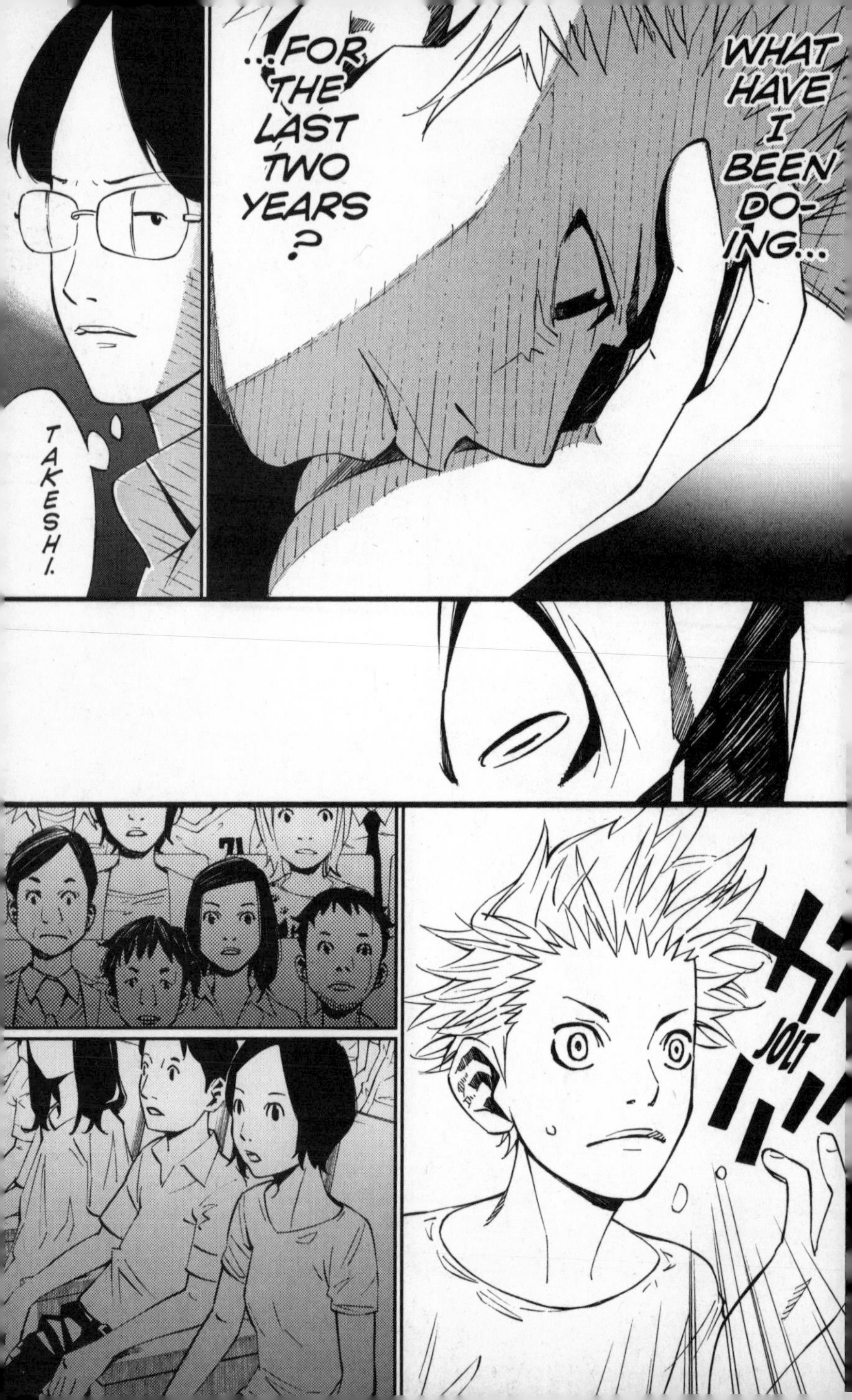
WHAT HAVE I BEEN DOING...
...FOR THE LAST TWO YEARS?
TAKESHI.
JOLT

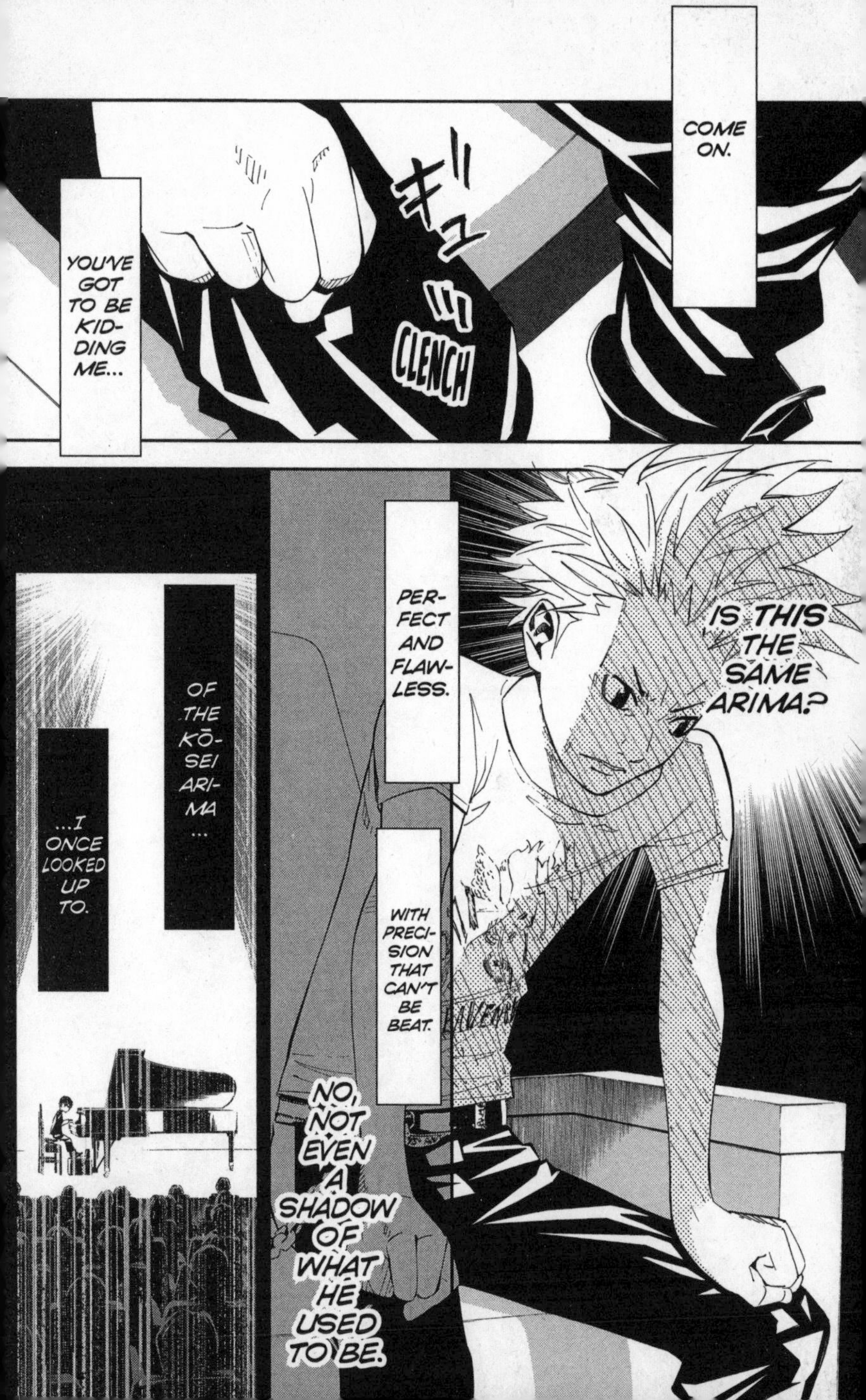
COME ON.
ギュッ
CLENCH
YOU'VE GOT TO BE KID-DING ME...
IS THIS THE SAME ARIMA?
PERFECT AND FLAW-LESS.
WITH PRECISION THAT CAN'T BE BEAT.
NO, NOT EVEN A SHADOW OF WHAT HE USED TO BE.
OF THE KŌSEI ARI-MA...
...I ONCE LOOKED UP TO.

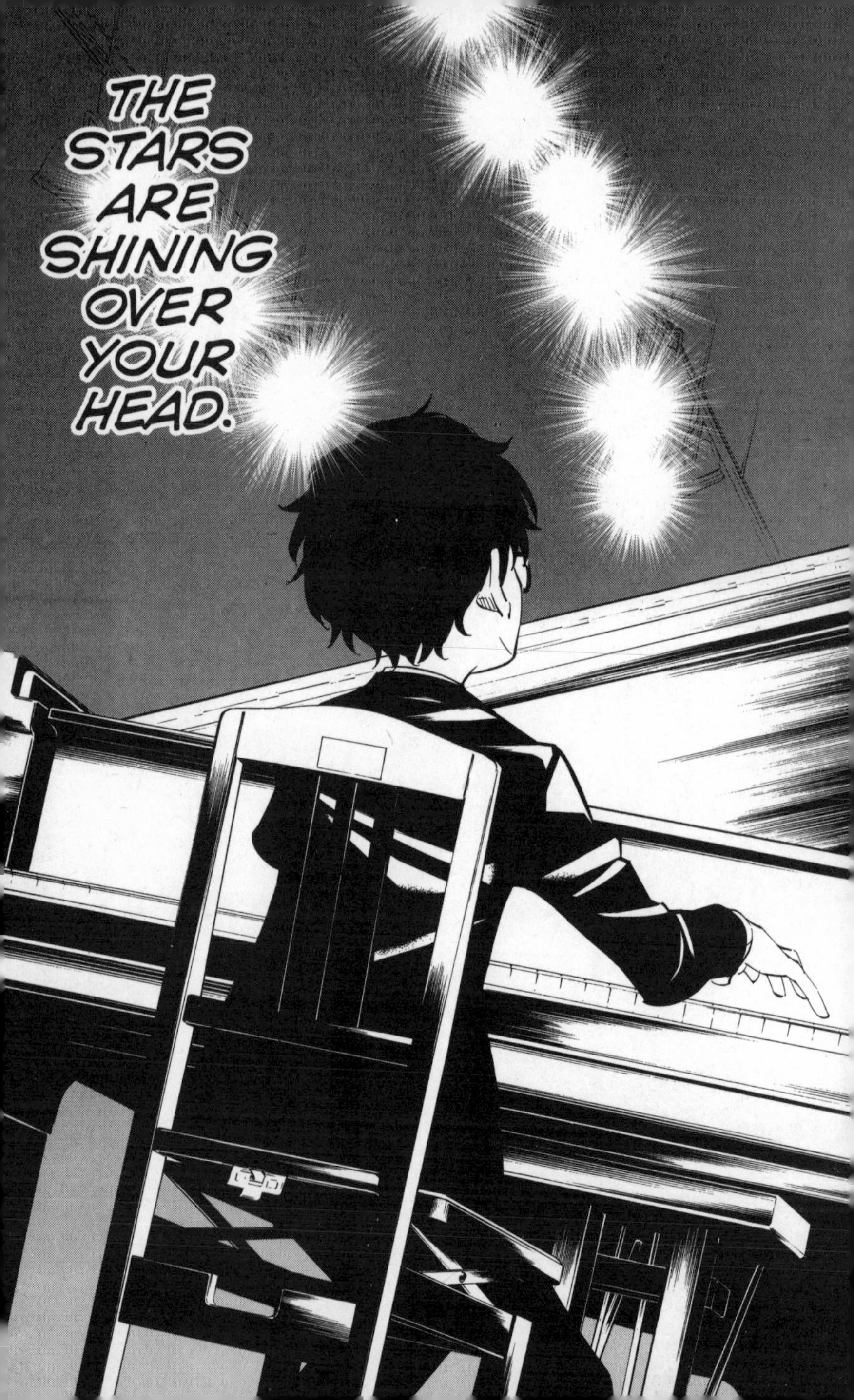
THE STARS ARE SHINING OVER YOUR HEAD.

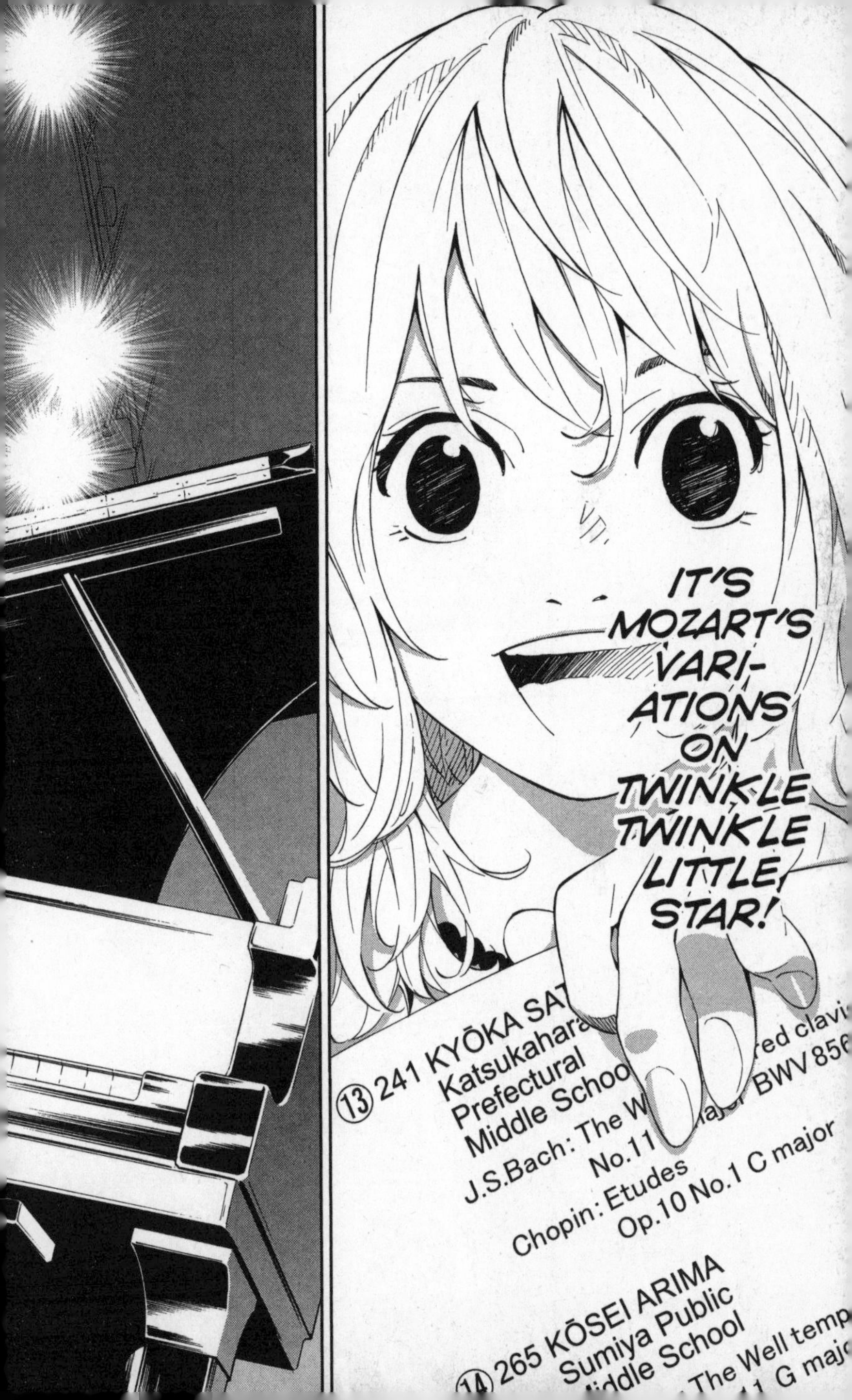
IT'S MOZART'S VARI-ATIONS ON TWINKLE TWINKLE LITTLE STAR!
⑬ 241 KYŌKA SAT
Katsukahara
Prefectural
Middle Schoo
J.S.Bach: The W
red clavi
major BWV 856
No.11
Chopin: Etudes
Op.10 No.1 C major
265 KŌSEI ARIMA
Sumiya Public
iddle School
The Well temp
G majo

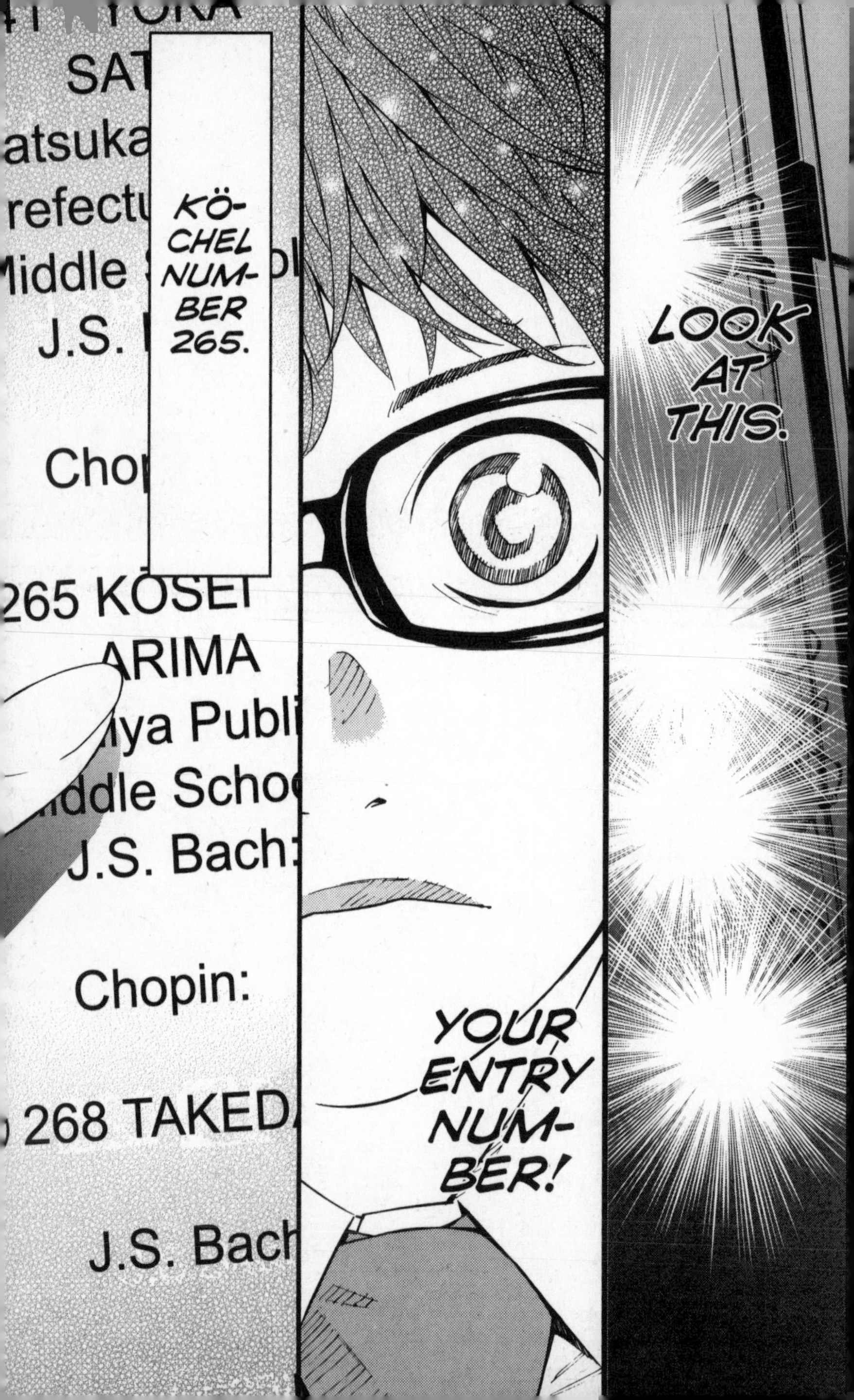
LOOK AT THIS.
YOUR ENTRY NUMBER!
KÖCHEL NUMBER 265.
265 KŌSEI ARIMA
Chopin:
J.S. Bach

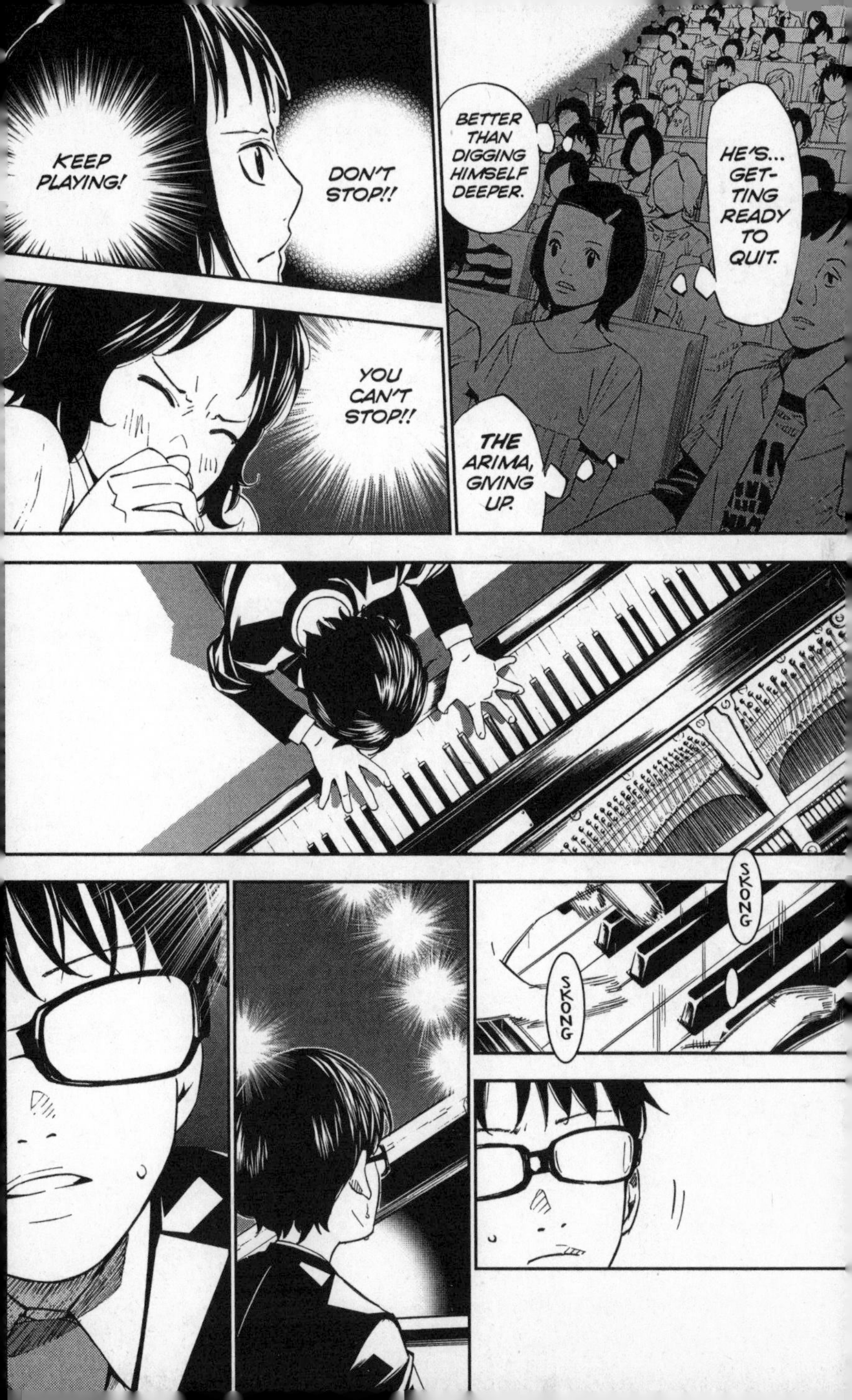
HE'S... GET-TING READY TO QUIT.
BETTER THAN DIGGING HIMSELF DEEPER.
THE ARIMA, GIVING UP.
DON'T STOP!!
KEEP PLAYING!
YOU CAN'T STOP!!
SKONG
SKONG

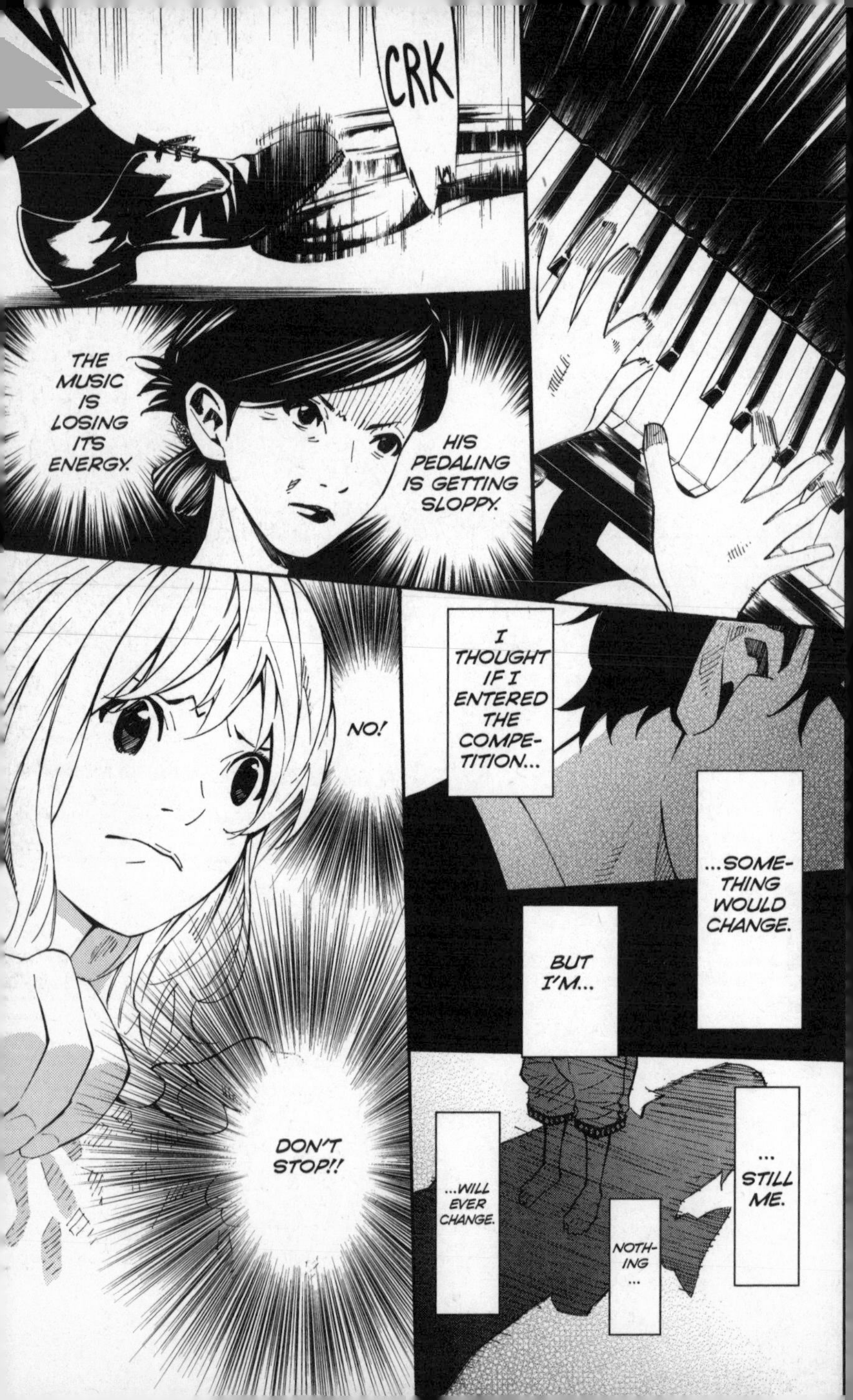
CRK
HIS PEDALING IS GETTING SLOPPY.
THE MUSIC IS LOSING ITS ENERGY.
I THOUGHT IF I ENTERED THE COMPETITION...
...SOMETHING WOULD CHANGE.
BUT I'M...
...STILL ME.
NOTHING...
...WILL EVER CHANGE.
NO!
DON'T STOP!!

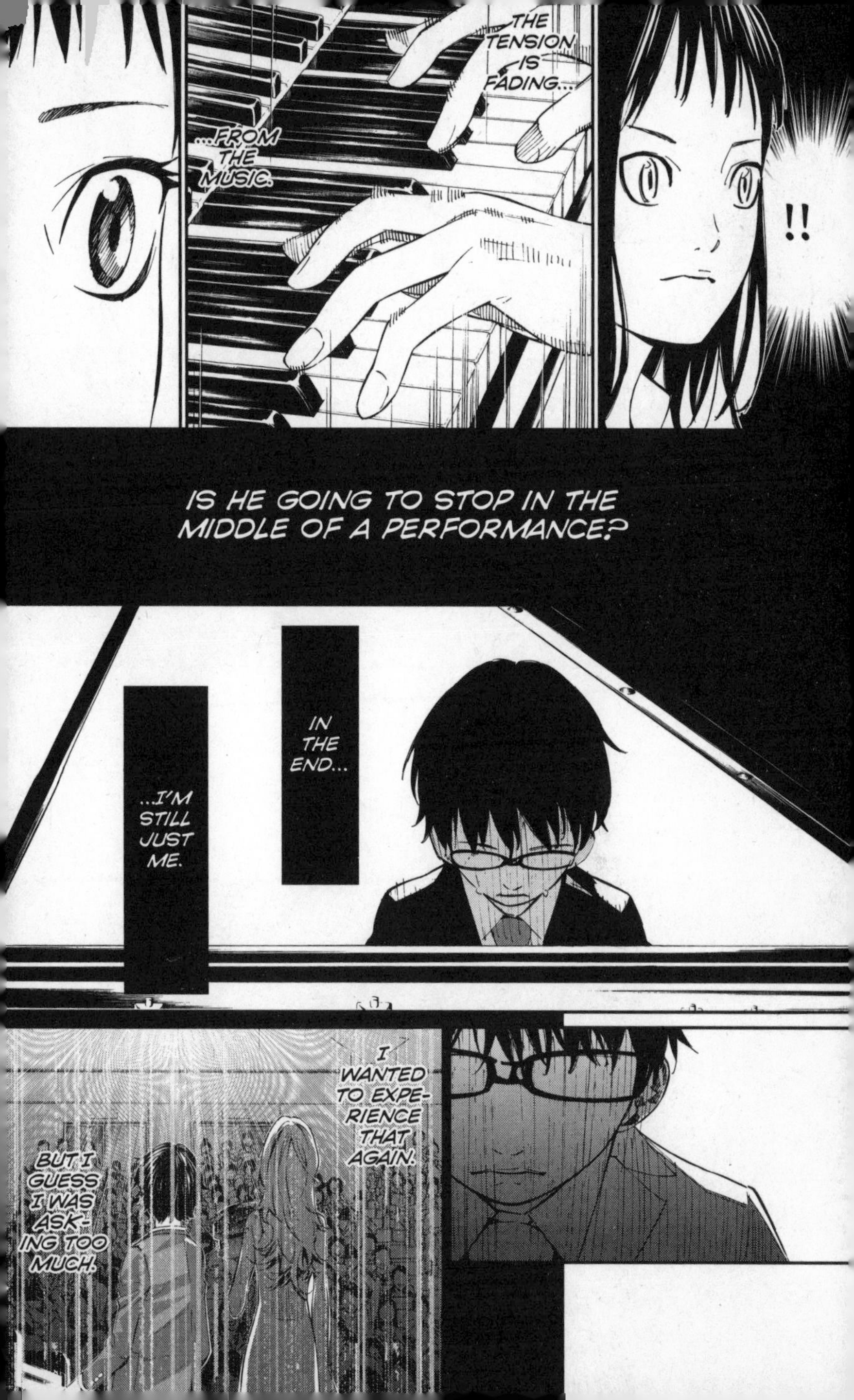
!!
THE TENSION IS FADING...
...FROM THE MUSIC.
IS HE GOING TO STOP IN THE MIDDLE OF A PERFORMANCE?
IN THE END...
...I'M STILL JUST ME.
I WANTED TO EXPE-RIENCE THAT AGAIN.
BUT I GUESS I WAS ASK-ING TOO MUCH.

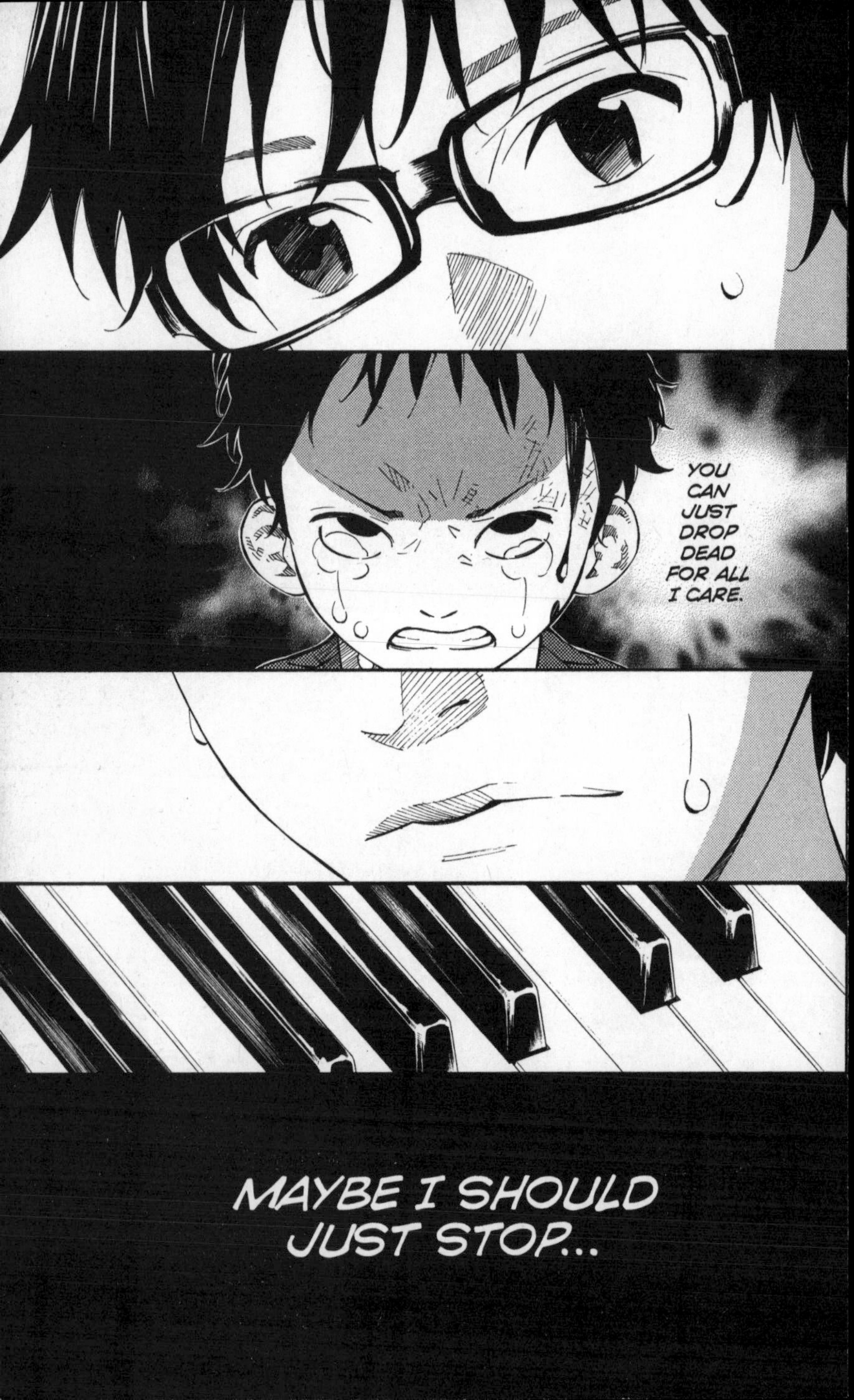
YOU CAN JUST DROP DEAD FOR ALL I CARE.
MAYBE I SHOULD JUST STOP...

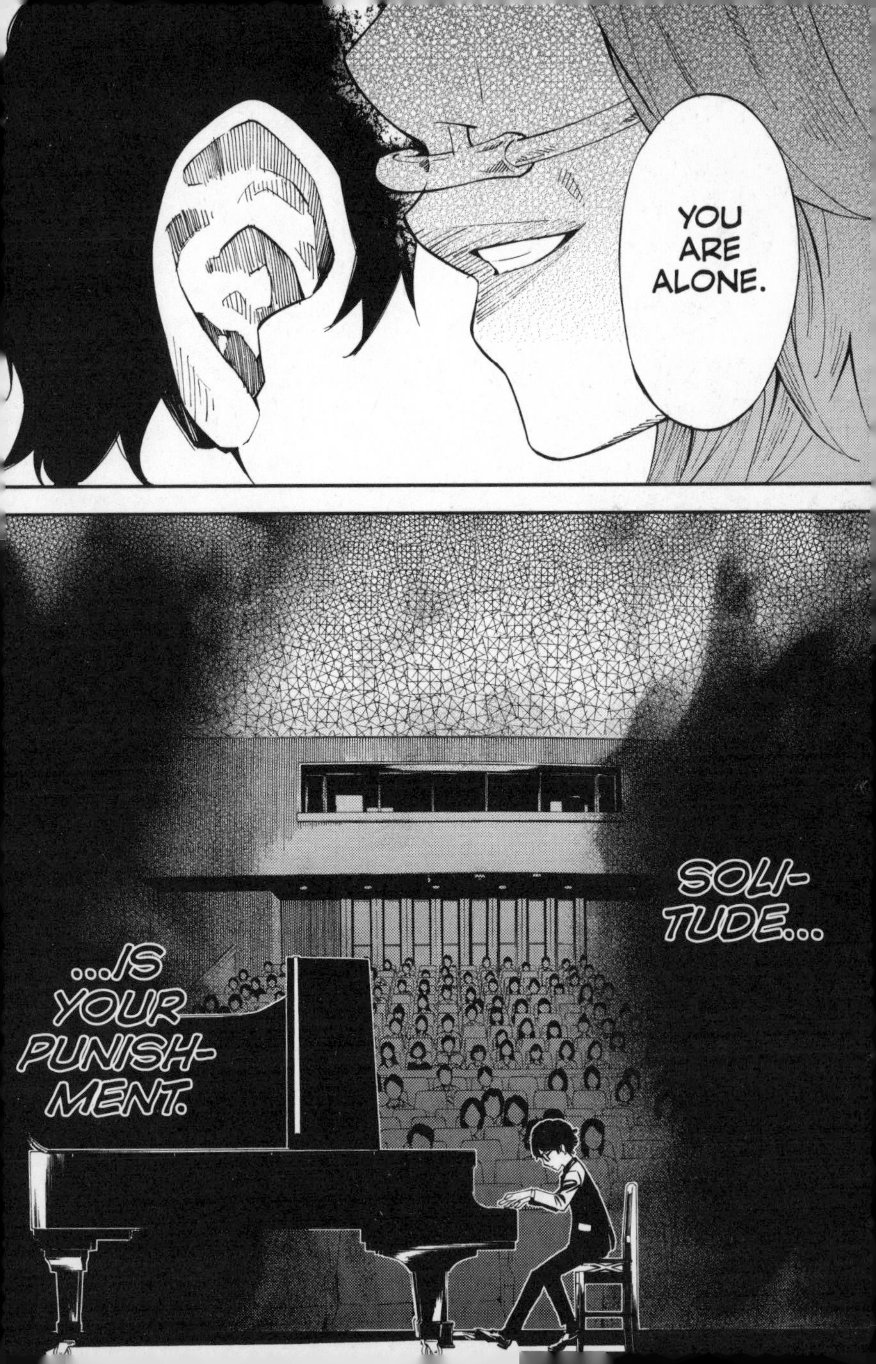
YOU ARE ALONE.
SOLI-TUDE...
...IS YOUR PUNISH-MENT.

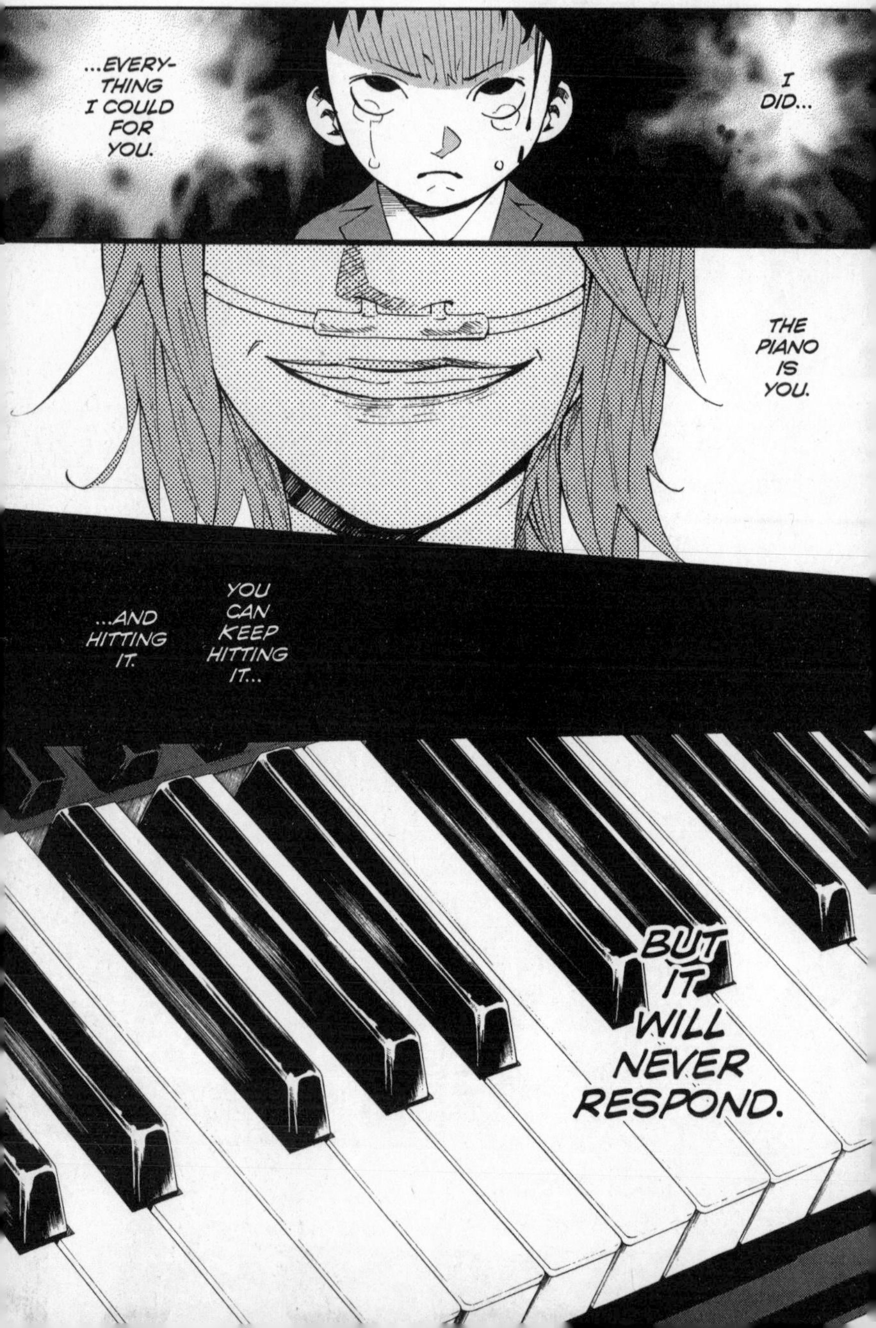
I DID...
...EVERY-THING I COULD FOR YOU.
THE PIANO IS YOU.
YOU CAN KEEP HITTING IT...
...AND HITTING IT.
BUT IT WILL NEVER RESPOND.

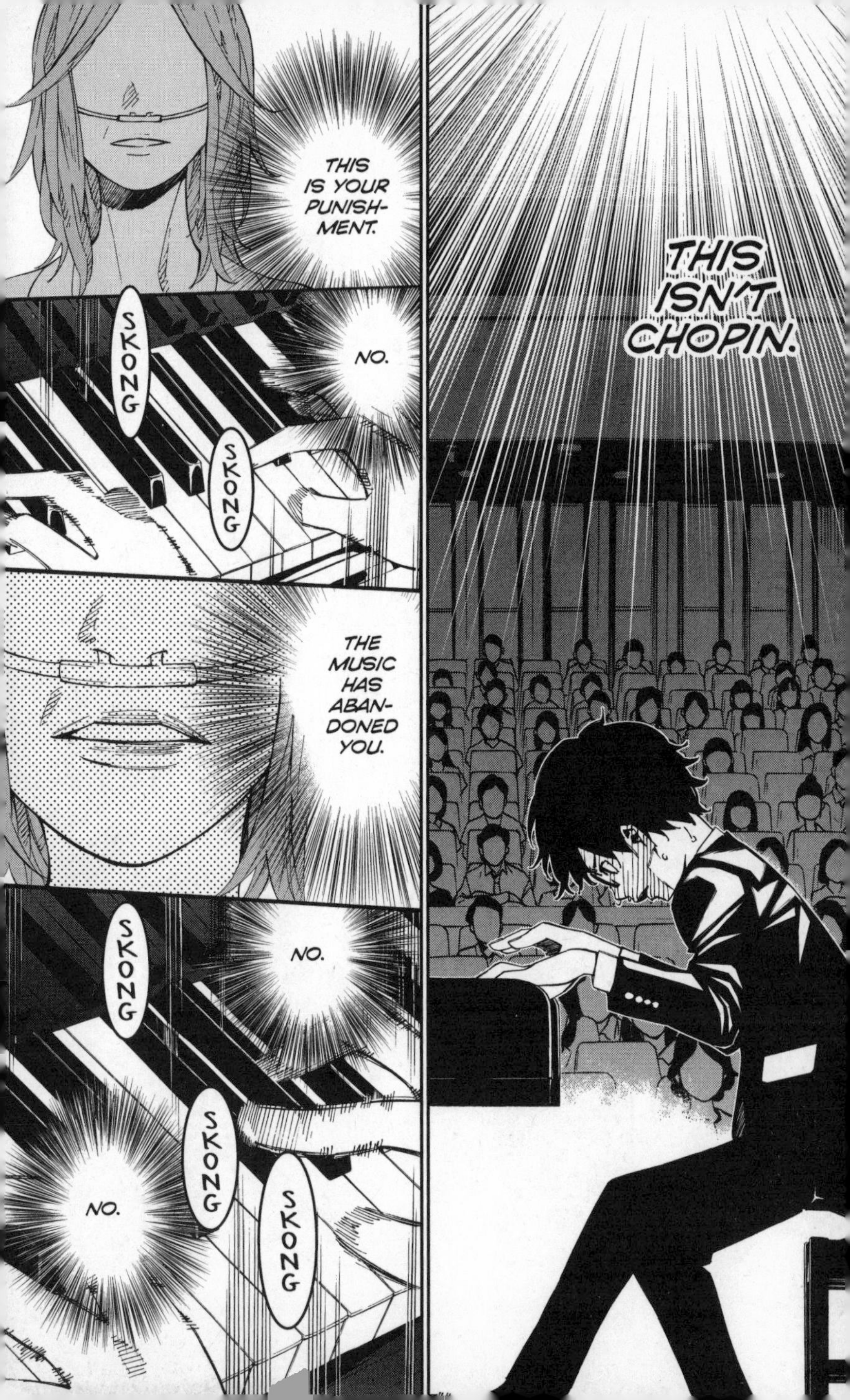
THIS ISN'T CHOPIN.
THIS IS YOUR PUNISHMENT.
NO.
SKONG
SKONG
THE MUSIC HAS ABANDONED YOU.
NO.
SKONG
SKONG
SKONG
NO.

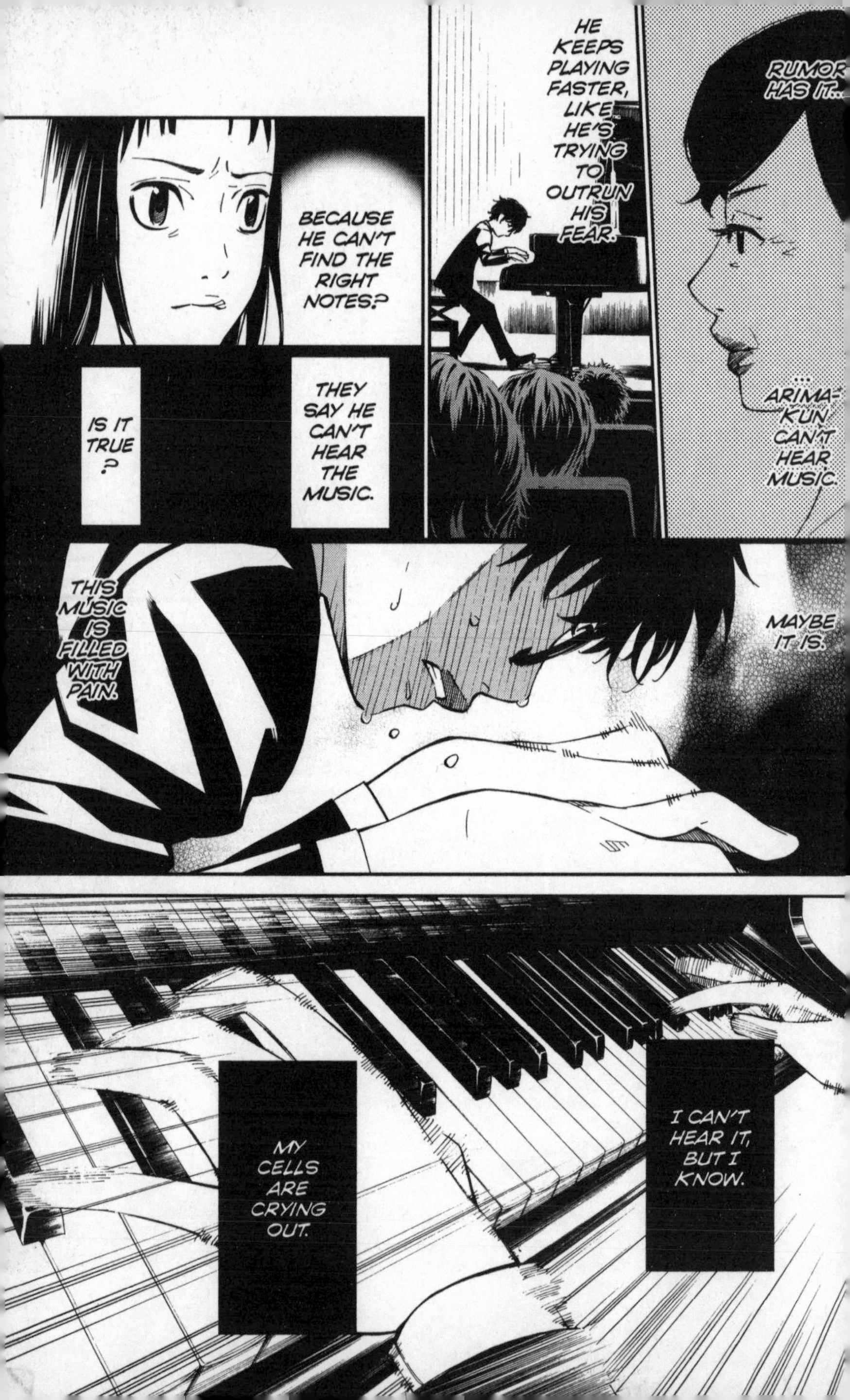
RUMOR HAS IT...
...ARIMA-KUN CAN'T HEAR MUSIC.
HE KEEPS PLAYING FASTER, LIKE HE'S TRYING TO OUTRUN HIS FEAR.
BECAUSE HE CAN'T FIND THE RIGHT NOTES?
THEY SAY HE CAN'T HEAR THE MUSIC.
IS IT TRUE?
MAYBE IT IS.
THIS MUSIC IS FILLED WITH PAIN.
I CAN'T HEAR IT, BUT I KNOW.
MY CELLS ARE CRYING OUT.

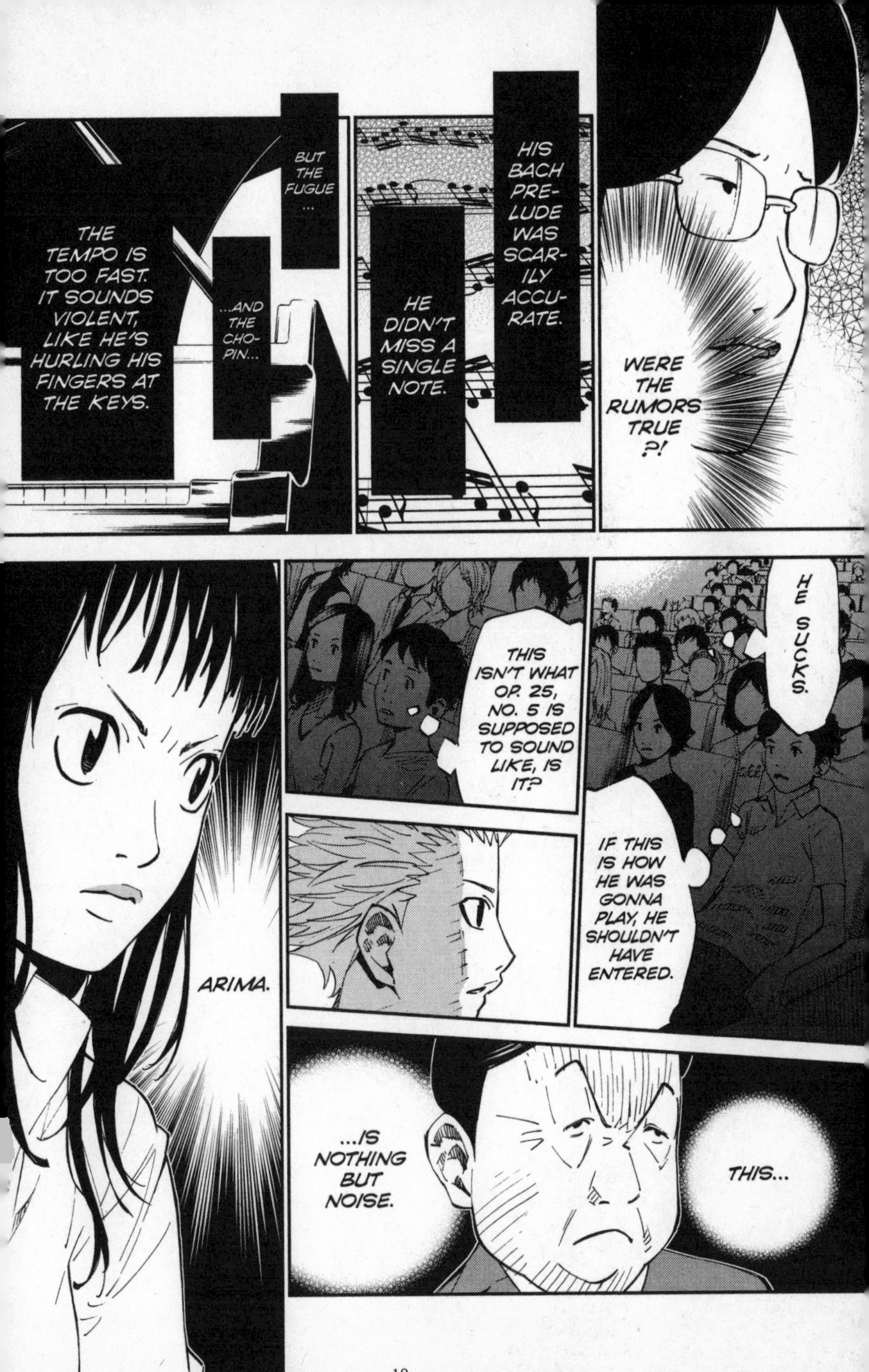
WERE THE RUMORS TRUE ?!
HIS BACH PRELUDE WAS SCARILY ACCURATE.
HE DIDN'T MISS A SINGLE NOTE.
BUT THE FUGUE...
...AND THE CHOPIN...
THE TEMPO IS TOO FAST. IT SOUNDS VIOLENT, LIKE HE'S HURLING HIS FINGERS AT THE KEYS.
HE SUCKS.
IF THIS IS HOW HE WAS GONNA PLAY, HE SHOULDN'T HAVE ENTERED.
THIS ISN'T WHAT OP. 25, NO. 5 IS SUPPOSED TO SOUND LIKE, IS IT?
THIS...
...IS NOTHING BUT NOISE.
ARIMA.

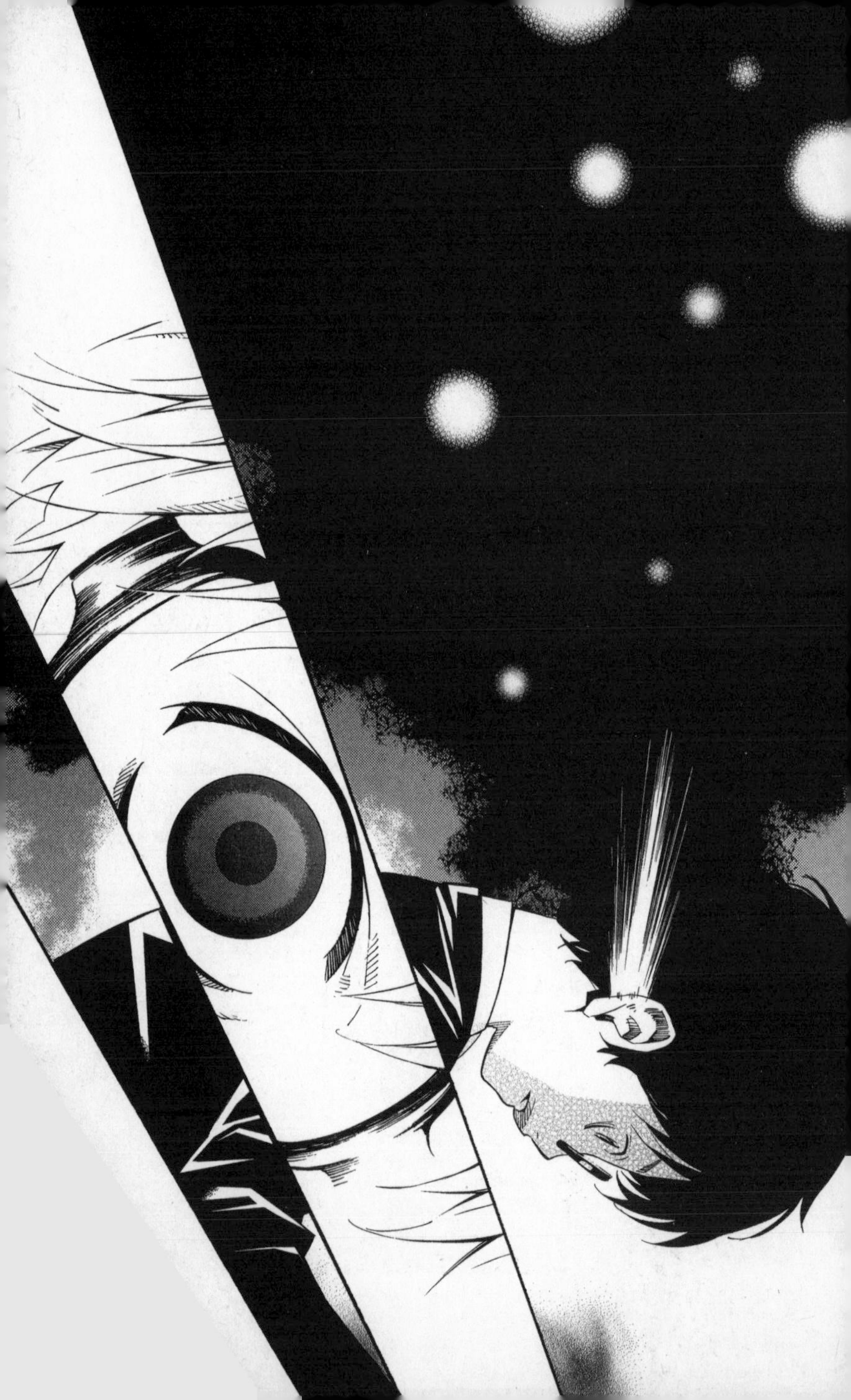

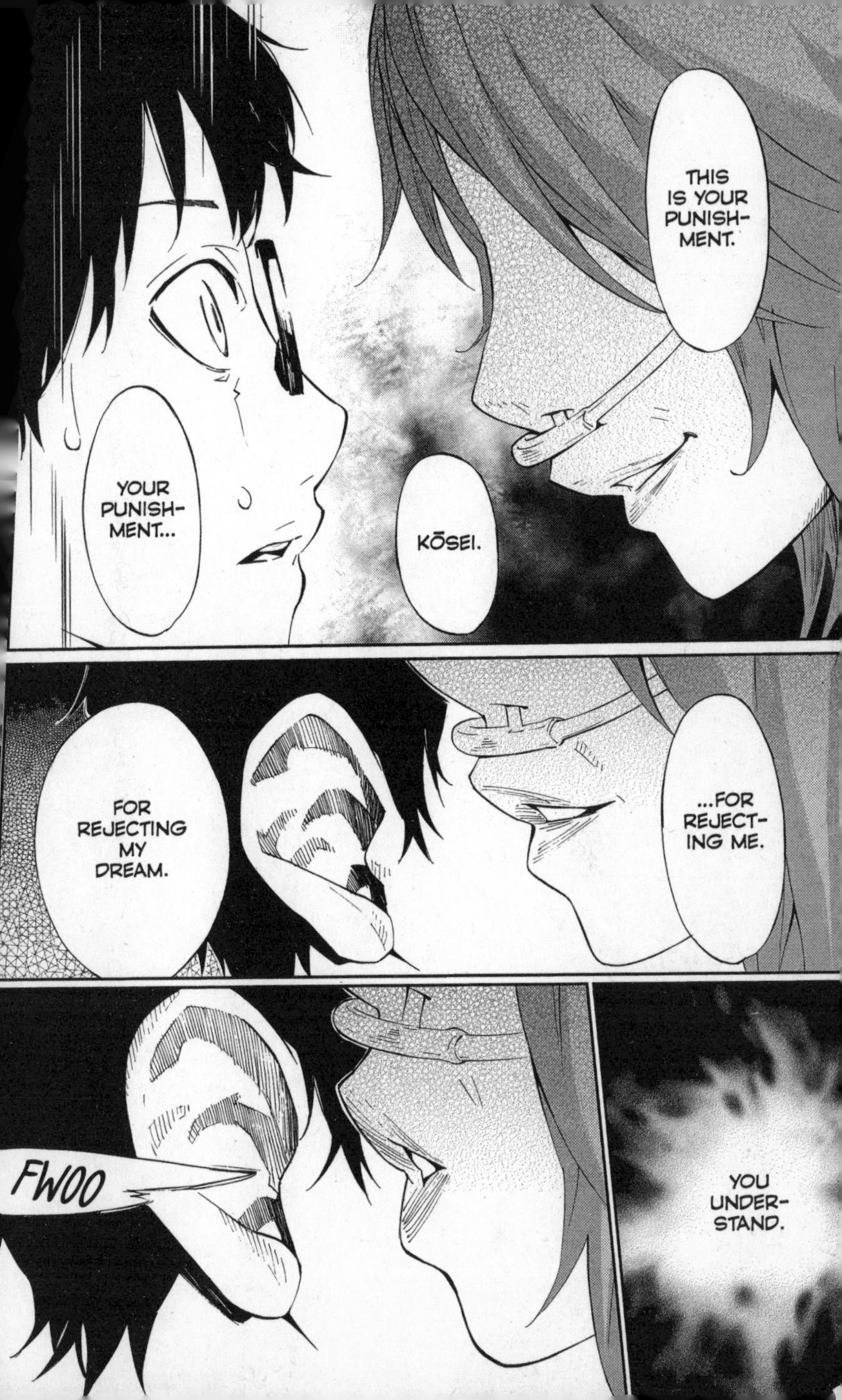
THIS IS YOUR PUNISHMENT.
KŌSEI.
YOUR PUNISHMENT...
...FOR REJECTING ME.
FOR REJECTING MY DREAM.
YOU UNDERSTAND.
FWOO

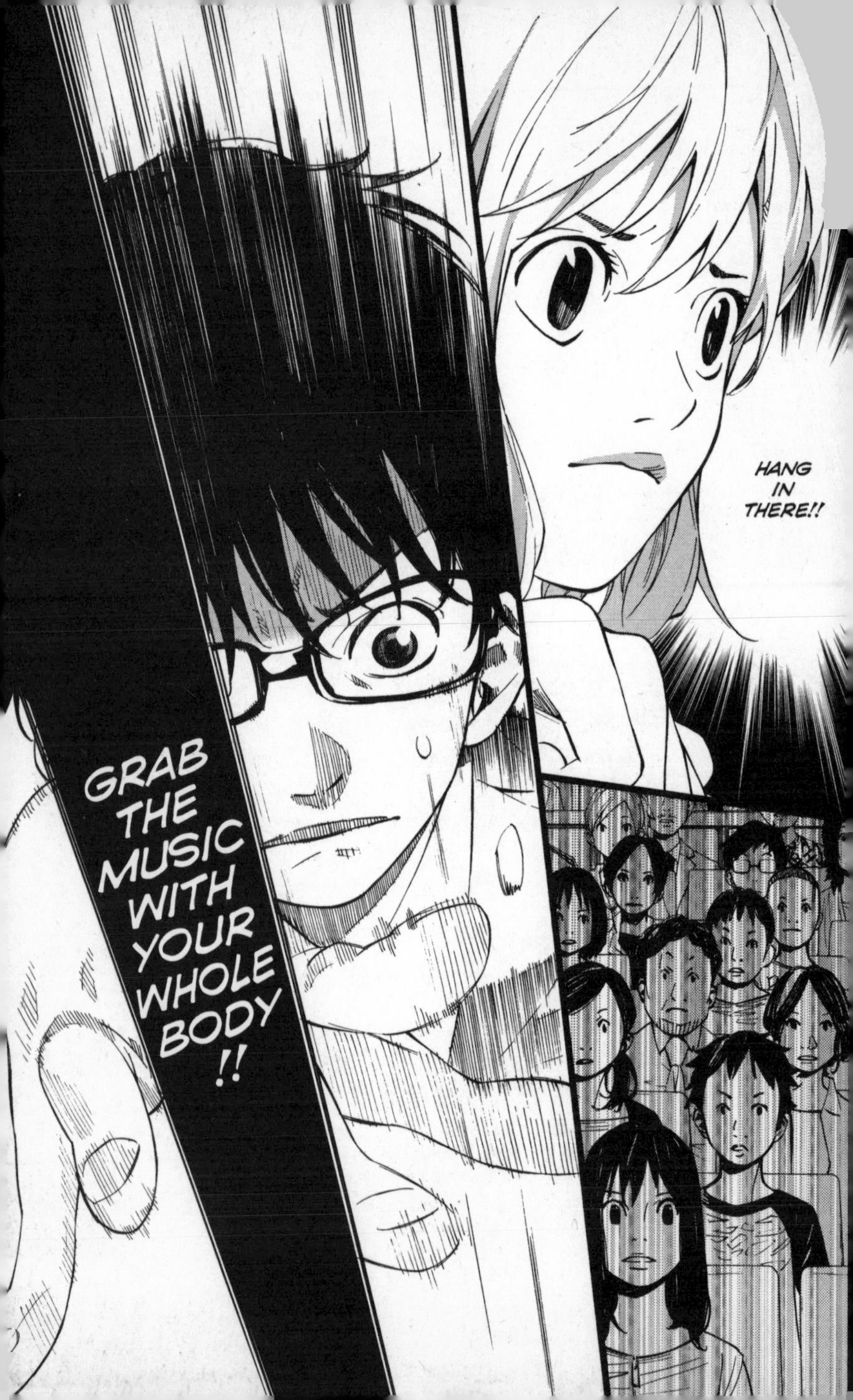
HANG IN THERE!!
GRAB THE MUSIC WITH YOUR WHOLE BODY!!

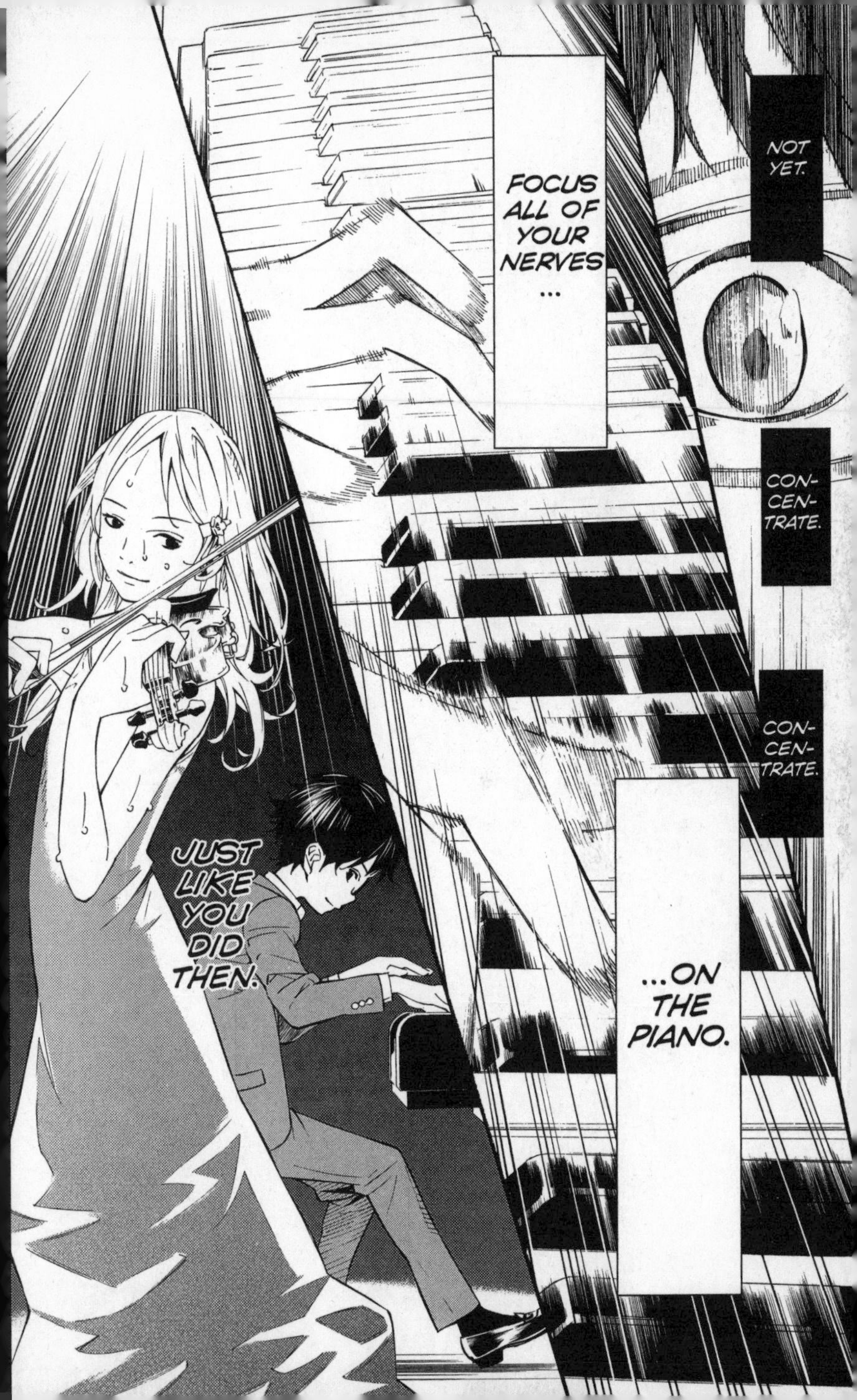
NOT YET.
FOCUS ALL OF YOUR NERVES...
CON-CEN-TRATE.
CON-CEN-TRATE.
...ON THE PIANO.
JUST LIKE YOU DID THEN.

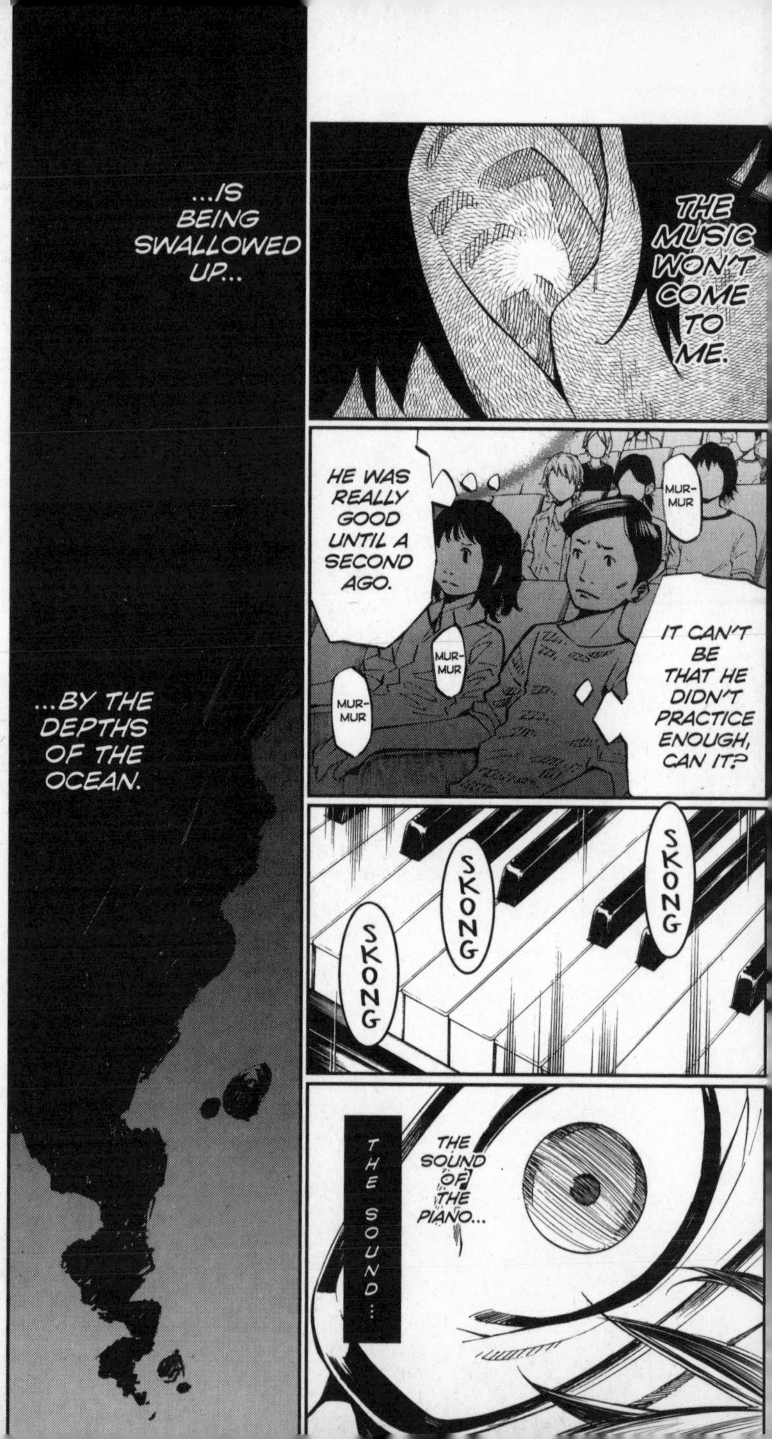
THE MUSIC WON'T COME TO ME.
MUR-MUR
HE WAS REALLY GOOD UNTIL A SECOND AGO.
IT CAN'T BE THAT HE DIDN'T PRACTICE ENOUGH, CAN IT?
MUR-MUR
MUR-MUR
SKONG
SKONG
SKONG
THE SOUND...
THE SOUND OF THE PIANO...
...IS BEING SWALLOWED UP...
...BY THE DEPTHS OF THE OCEAN.

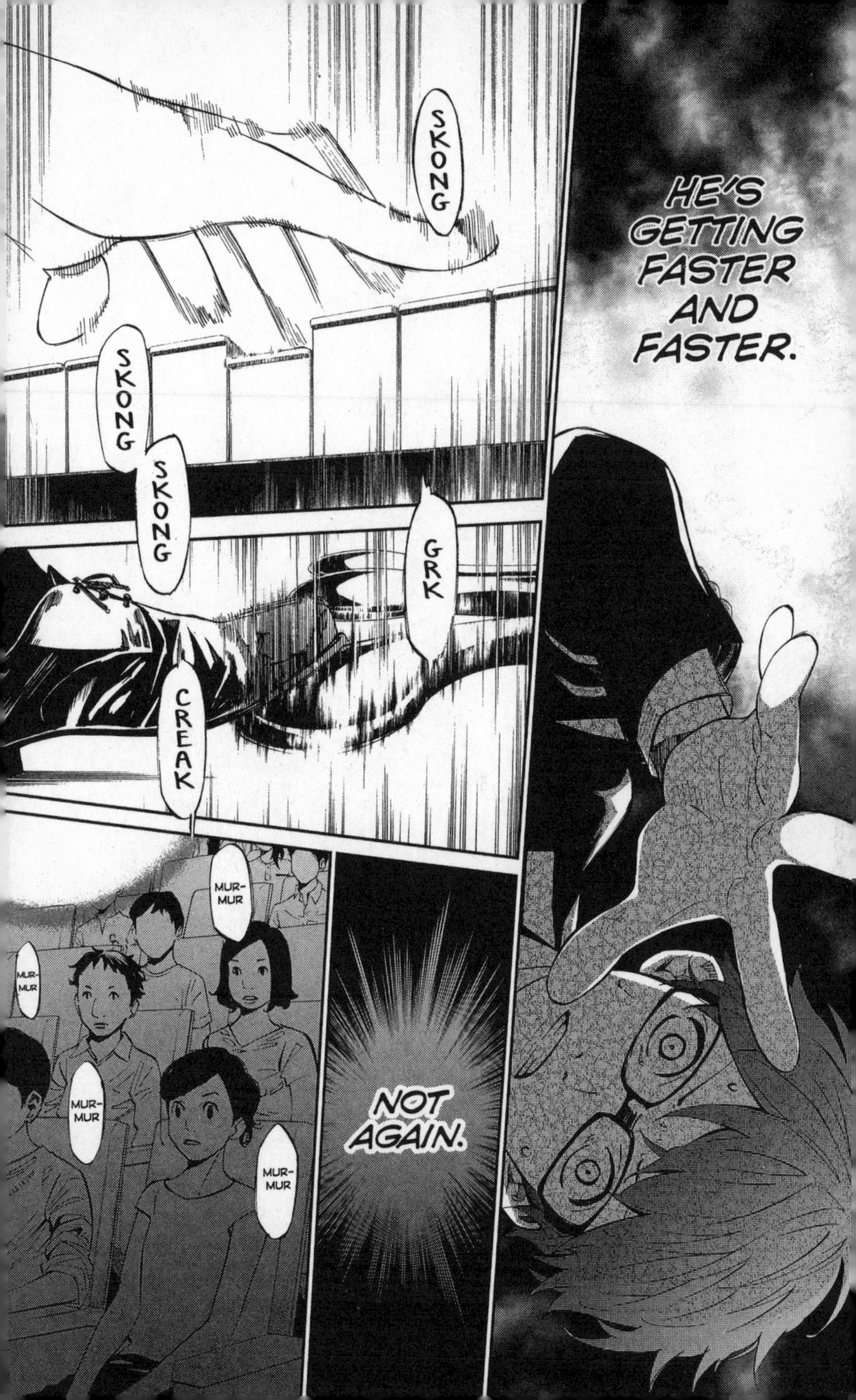
HE'S GETTING FASTER AND FASTER.
SKONG
SKONG
SKONG
GRK
CREAK
NOT AGAIN.
MUR-MUR
MUR-MUR
MUR-MUR
MUR-MUR

CLENCH
IT'S A DIFFERENT PIECE, BUT THE SAME PROBLEM!!
BAM
BAM
ARGH.
IT'S JUST LIKE WHEN HE WAS PLAY-ING FOR KAO-CHAN.
THE SOUND IS ALL UNEVEN.

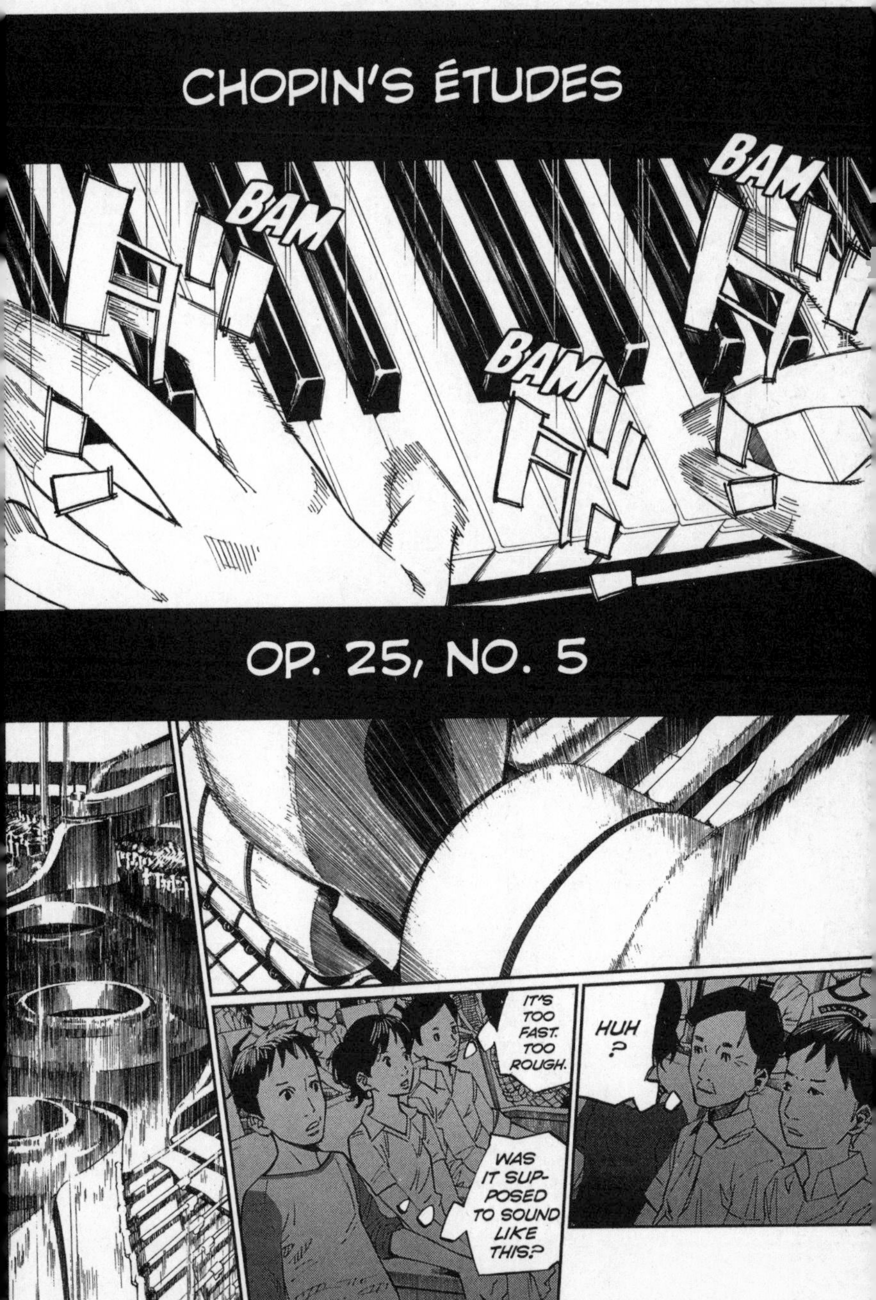
CHOPIN'S ÉTUDES
BAM
BAM
BAM
OP. 25, NO. 5
HUH?
IT'S TOO FAST. TOO ROUGH.
WAS IT SUP-POSED TO SOUND LIKE THIS?

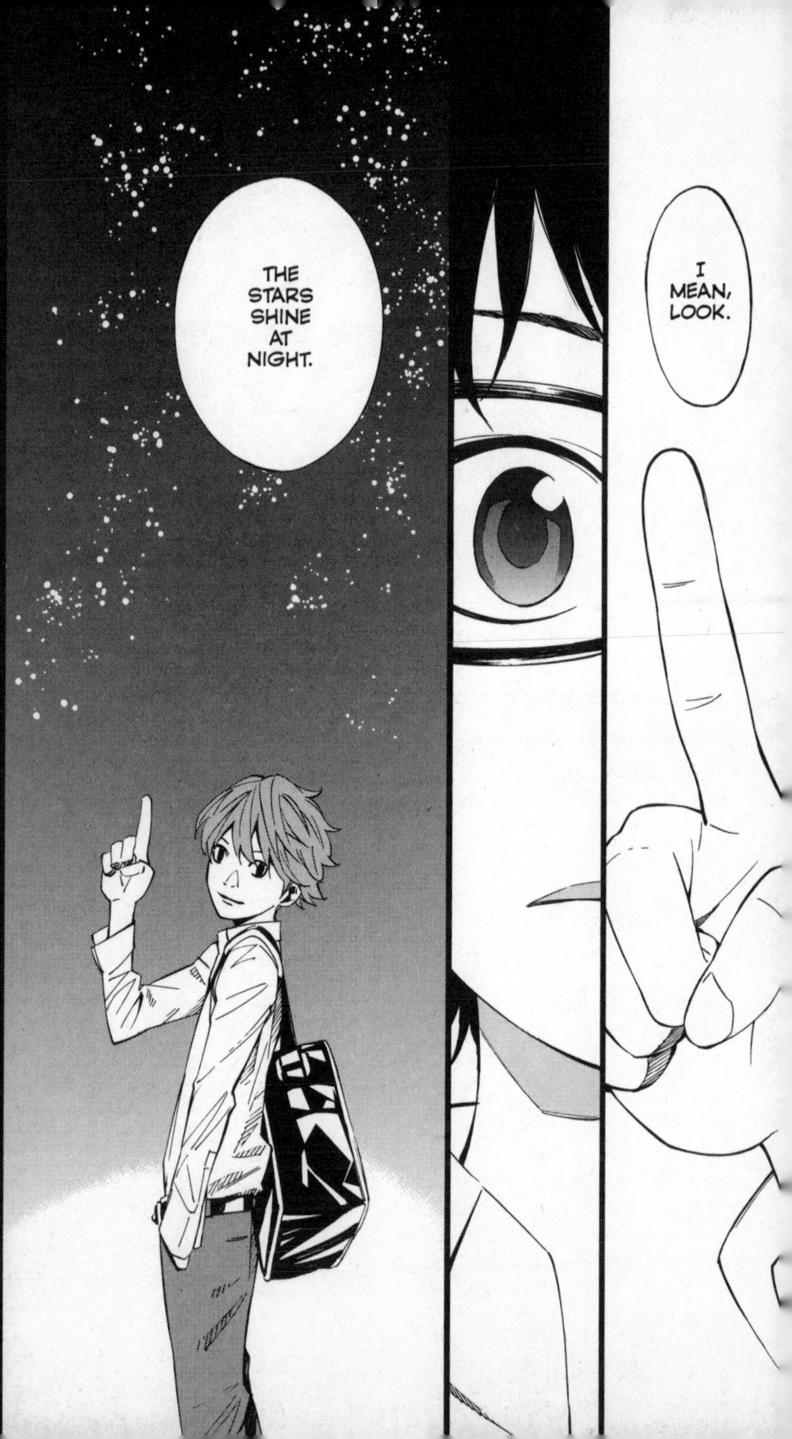
I MEAN, LOOK.
THE STARS SHINE AT NIGHT.

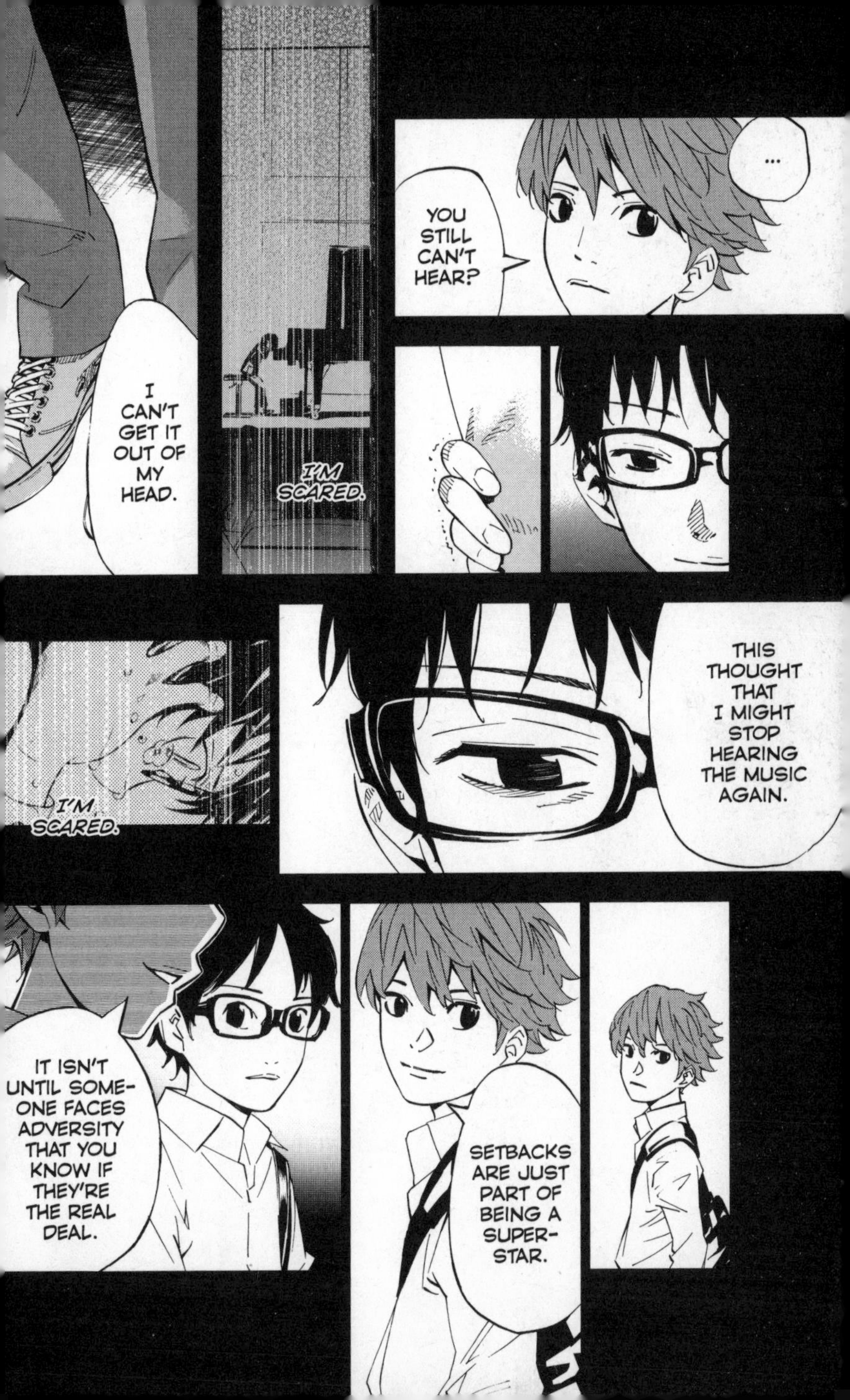
...
YOU STILL CAN'T HEAR?
I'M SCARED.
I CAN'T GET IT OUT OF MY HEAD.
THIS THOUGHT THAT I MIGHT STOP HEARING THE MUSIC AGAIN.
I'M SCARED.
SETBACKS ARE JUST PART OF BEING A SUPER-STAR.
IT ISN'T UNTIL SOME-ONE FACES ADVERSITY THAT YOU KNOW IF THEY'RE THE REAL DEAL.

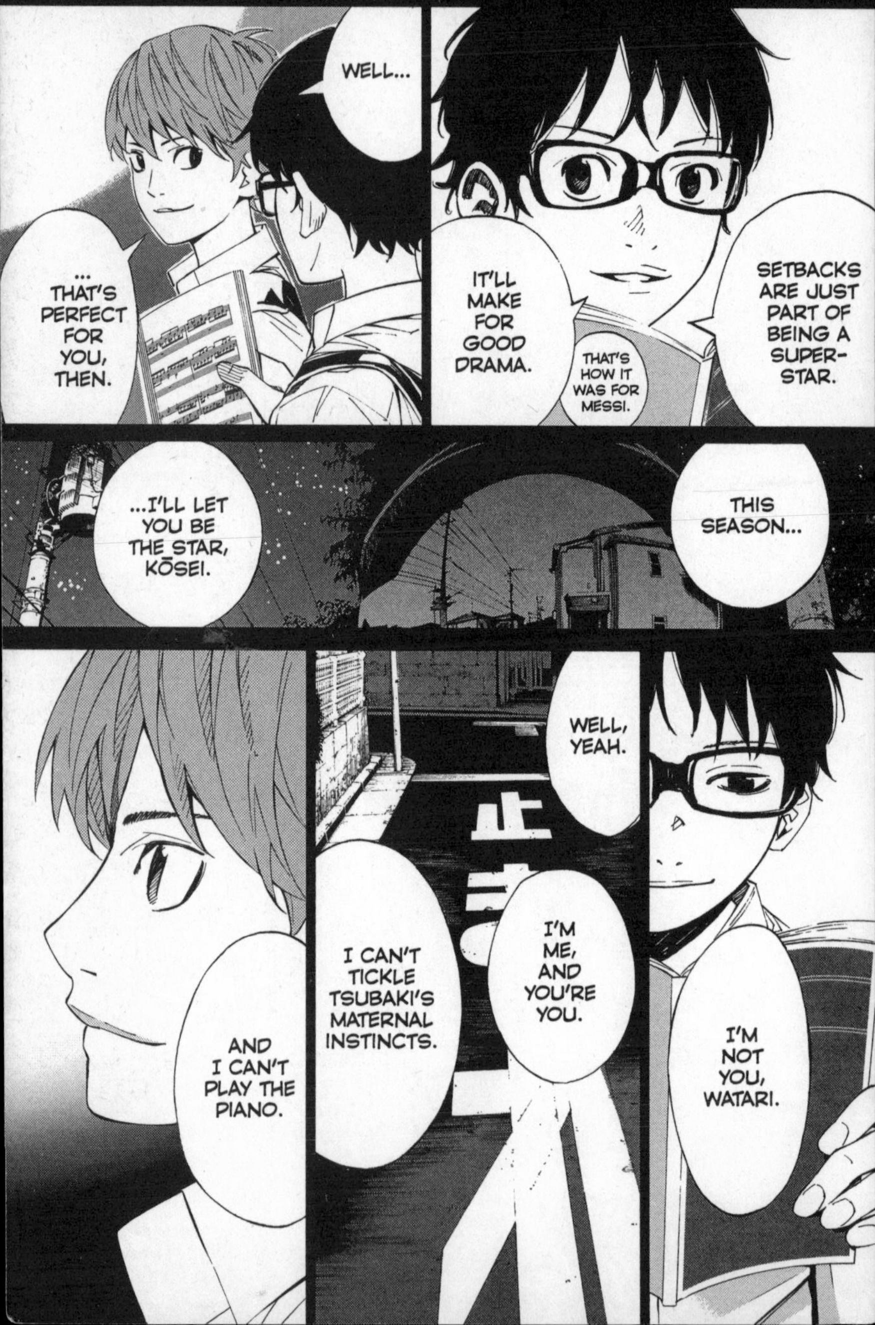
SETBACKS ARE JUST PART OF BEING A SUPER-STAR.
THAT'S HOW IT WAS FOR MESSI.
IT'LL MAKE FOR GOOD DRAMA.
WELL...
... THAT'S PERFECT FOR YOU, THEN.
THIS SEASON...
...I'LL LET YOU BE THE STAR, KŌSEI.
I'M NOT YOU, WATARI.
WELL, YEAH.
I'M ME, AND YOU'RE YOU.
I CAN'T TICKLE TSUBAKI'S MATERNAL INSTINCTS.
AND I CAN'T PLAY THE PIANO.

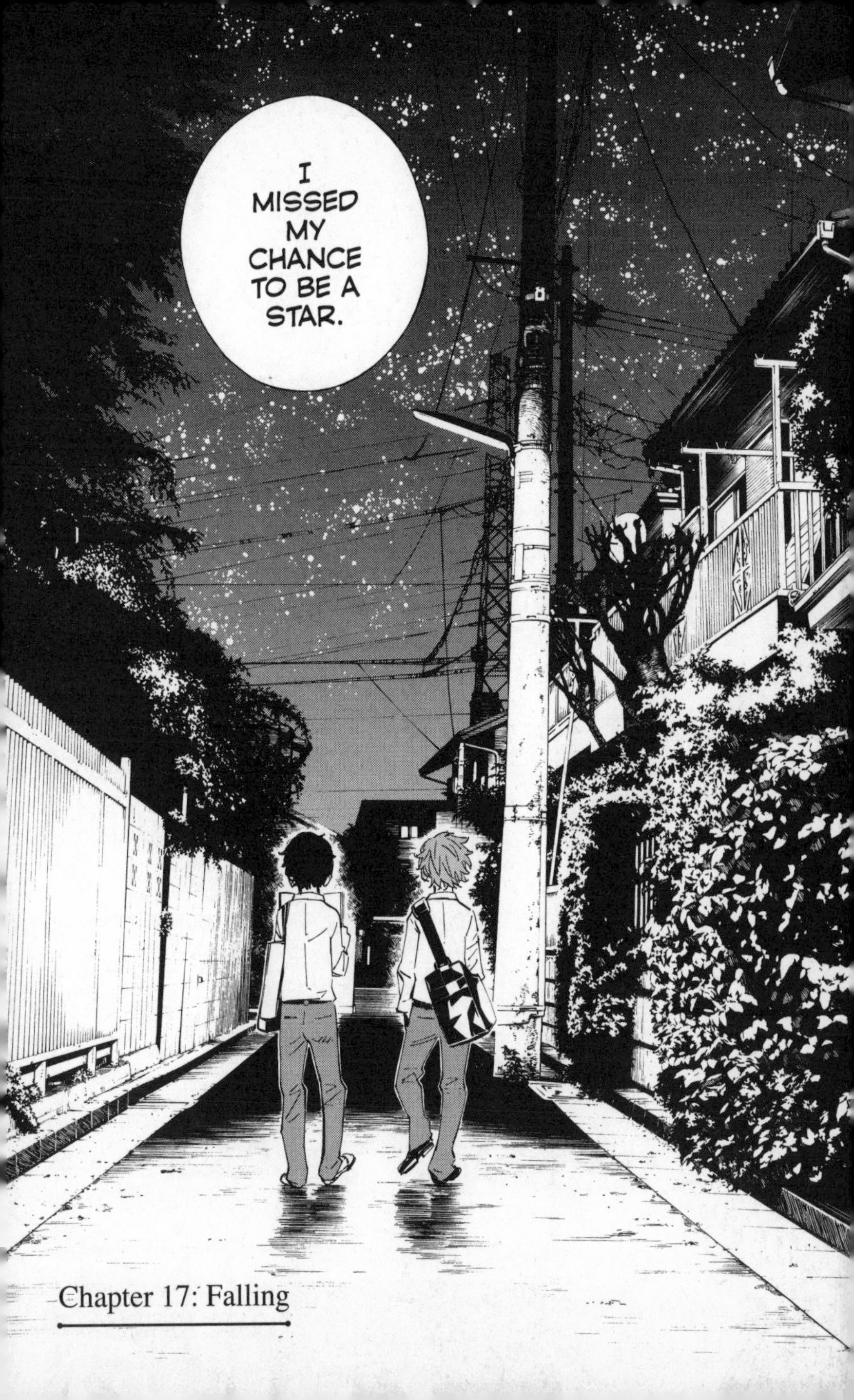
I MISSED MY CHANCE TO BE A STAR.

Chapter 17: Falling

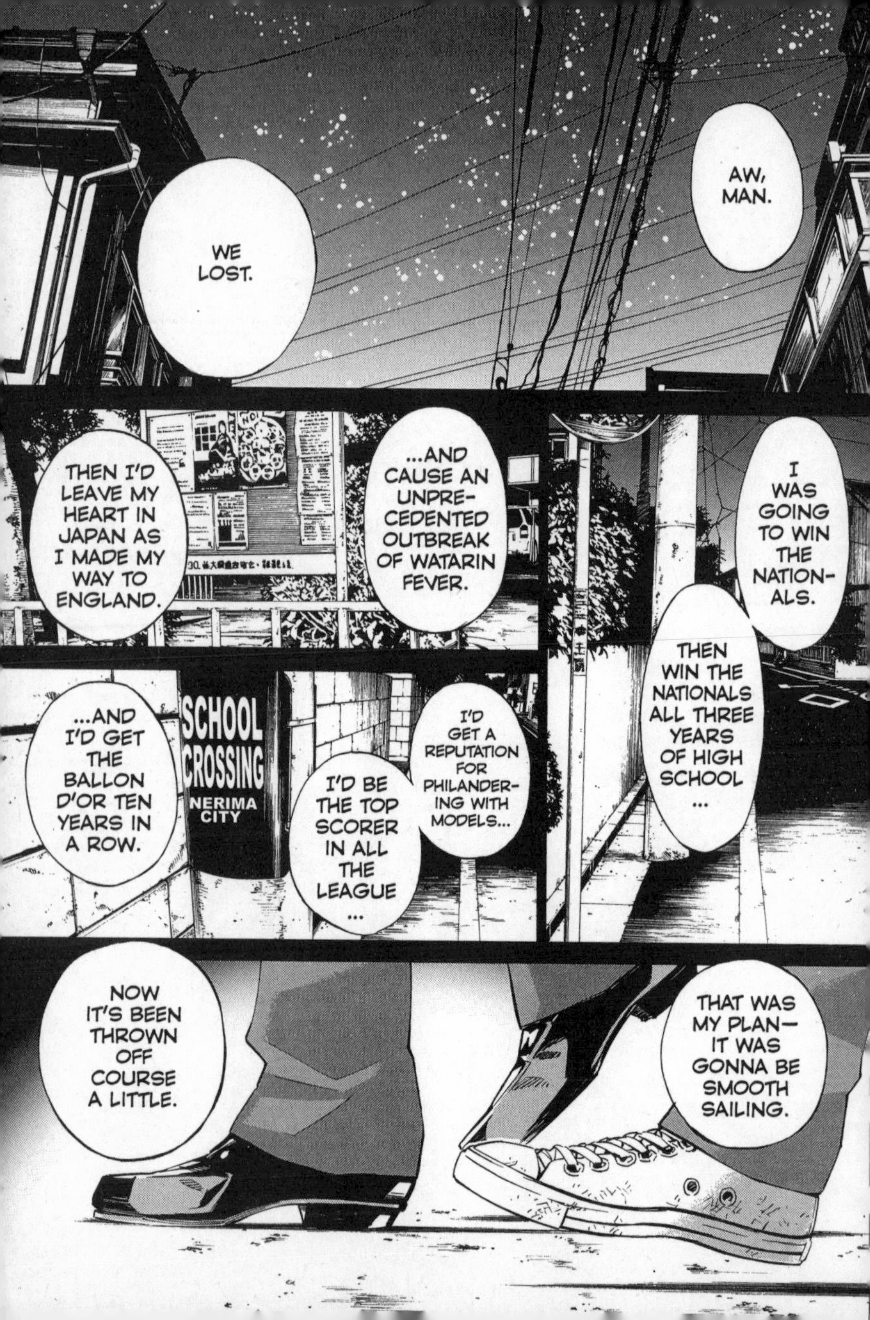
AW, MAN.
WE LOST.
I WAS GOING TO WIN THE NATIONALS.
THEN WIN THE NATIONALS ALL THREE YEARS OF HIGH SCHOOL ...
THEN I'D LEAVE MY HEART IN JAPAN AS I MADE MY WAY TO ENGLAND.
...AND CAUSE AN UNPRECEDENTED OUTBREAK OF WATARIN FEVER.
I'D GET A REPUTATION FOR PHILANDERING WITH MODELS...
I'D BE THE TOP SCORER IN ALL THE LEAGUE ...
SCHOOL CROSSING
NERIMA CITY
...AND I'D GET THE BALLON D'OR TEN YEARS IN A ROW.
THAT WAS MY PLAN— IT WAS GONNA BE SMOOTH SAILING.
NOW IT'S BEEN THROWN OFF COURSE A LITTLE.

contents

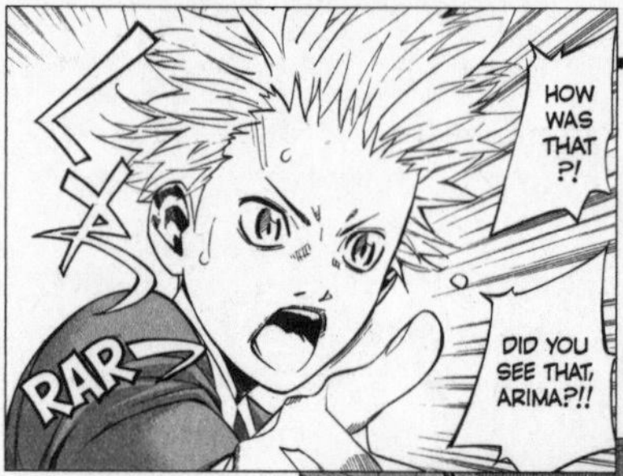
HOW WAS THAT ?!
DID YOU SEE THAT, ARIMA?!!
RAR

❊ Takeshi Aiza

A rival of Kōsei's since they were young boys. He could never beat Kōsei in the past, but now he has grown to a point where he could make a career for himself in Europe.

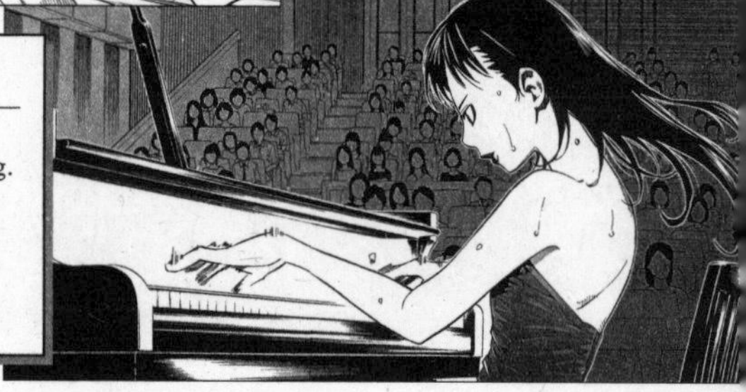

❊ Emi Igawa

Another rival of Kōsei's since they were very young. She had been in a slump since Kōsei vanished from competitions, but she is making a comeback in the Maihō Competition!

Little by little, Kōsei's feelings for music grew within him. Kaori seemed to sense this and told him to participate in the Maihō Music Competition. This was his first competition in three years, and his former rivals, having improved their own skills, awaited him.

Takeshi Aiza, who always aspired to be like Kōsei, entered the competition as the favorite to win. He delivered a masterful performance, and won the audience's acclamation. And Emi Igawa, who found herself in a slump after Kōsei stopped performing, gave a performance overflowing with emotion—the best of her career…

Then, it was finally Kōsei's turn to go on. He played his prelude precisely, without a single mistake. Everyone thought the prodigy had returned, but it wasn't long before the music vanished from the boy's world… His performance is interrupted as he is seized by darkness.

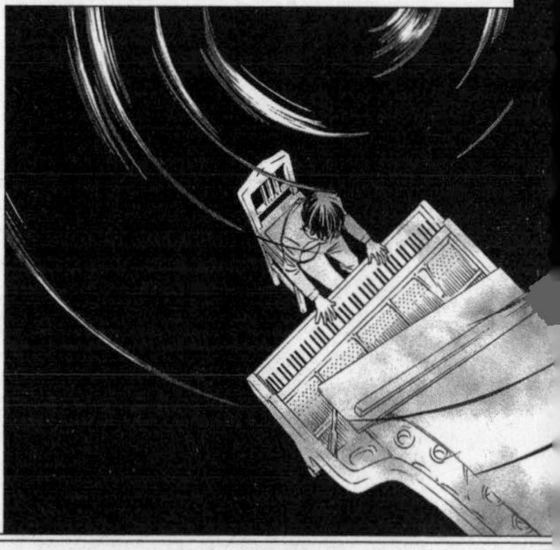